# Lecture Notes in Computer Science    8685

*Commenced Publication in 1973*
Founding and Former Series Editors:
Gerhard Goos, Juris Hartmanis, and Jan van Leeuwen

Evangelos Kanoulas   Mihai Lupu
Paul Clough   Mark Sanderson   Mark Hall
Allan Hanbury   Elaine Toms (Eds.)

# Information Access Evaluation

## Multilinguality, Multimodality, and Interaction

5th International Conference
of the CLEF Initiative, CLEF 2014
Sheffield, UK, September 15-18, 2014
Proceedings

 Springer

Volume Editors

Evangelos Kanoulas
Google Switzerland GmbH, Zurich, Switzerland
E-mail: ekanoulas@gmail.com

Mihai Lupu
Vienna University of Technology, Austria
E-mail: lupu@ifs.tuwien.ac.at

Paul Clough
University of Sheffield, UK
E-mail: p.d.clough@sheffield.ac.uk

Mark Sanderson
RMIT University, Melbourne, VIC, Australia
E-mail: mark.sanderson@rmit.edu.au

Mark Hall
Edge Hill University, Ormskirk, UK
E-mail: hallmark@edgehill.ac.uk

Allan Hanbury
Vienna University of Technology, Austria
E-mail: hanbury@ifs.tuwien.ac.at

Elaine Toms
University of Sheffield, UK
E-mail: e.toms@sheffield.ac.uk

ISSN 0302-9743                          e-ISSN 1611-3349
ISBN 978-3-319-11381-4                   e-ISBN 978-3-319-11382-1
DOI 10.1007/978-3-319-11382-1
Springer Cham Heidelberg New York Dordrecht London

Library of Congress Control Number: 2014947878

LNCS Sublibrary: SL 3 – Information Systems and Application, incl. Internet/Web
and HCI

*Typesetting:* Camera-ready by author, data conversion by Scientific Publishing Services, Chennai, India
Printed on acid-free paper
Springer is part of Springer Science+Business Media (www.springer.com)

# Preface

The Conference and Labs of the Evaluation Forum (CLEF) celebrates its 15th anniversary this year. It was conceived in 2000 as the Cross-Language Evaluation Forum to stimulate research and innovation in multimodal and multilingual information access and retrieval. Over the years, it has actively nurtured and engaged a vibrant, multidisciplinary research community in the study, design, and implementation of evaluation methods that test multiple tasks using diverse data sets in many languages.

For its first 10 years, CLEF conducted a series of experimental labs that were reported annually at workshops held in conjunction with the European Conference on Digital Libraries. In 2010, now a mature and well-respected evaluation forum, it expanded to include a complementary peer-reviewed conference for reporting the evaluation of information access and retrieval systems regardless of data type, format, language, etc. Since then CLEF has continued that format with keynotes, contributed papers, lab sessions, and poster sessions, including reports from other benchmarking initiatives from around the world.

CLEF 2014, hosted by the Information School, University of Sheffield, UK, continued this august formula, but with a difference which demonstrated its maturity – this was the first CLEF to operate under the auspices of a self-organizing body, the CLEF Initiative. This year's theme, Information Access Evaluation meets Multilinguality, Multimodality, and Interaction, reflected the diversity that CLEF now represents.

Three eminent scholars in the field headlined each day of the conference, and perhaps surprisingly, all took a human-centered focus to their talks. Ann Blandford (University College London) put the user at the center of an information seeking and retrieval process which she called an information journey and examined ways in which that user experience process may be evaluated. Susan Dumais (Microsoft Research) re-visited the query, a perennial problem child of information access research, to put the query in its context rather than treating it as an independent unit, in order to address user intent, and to consider how to represent user context to improve search quality. Fabio Ciravegna (The University of Sheffield) discussed the web of interconnectivity extracted from social media messages that requires an understanding of the human context and the need for real-time large scale text and data analysis tools.

In addition 16 peer-reviewed papers included a range of research in information access. Some papers focused on task types such as question answering, finding similar content or passages, finding experts, or author identification. Others were domain specific such as health. The work reported used multiple languages, and multiple types and formats of data. One paper considerd what the 15 years of CLEF have found. Some focused on novel measures, the use of interim data, personalization or the summarization from disparate data sets.

The range across these 16 reports of research represented a broad, diverse body of work in information access.

Eight benchmarking labs reported results of year long activities that culminated in 124 submissions:

- ImageCLEF: offered four types of image retrieval tasks;
- INEX: experimented with interactive book search, social book search and twitter contextualization tasks;
- LifeCLEF: used biological data, including images of plants, audio of bird calls and video of fish, to identify each species;
- NewsReel: developed a real-time system, a living lab, to test news recommendation algorithms;
- PAN: tested software (rather than just the output) for plagiarism detection, author identification and author profiling;
- Question Answering: tested natural language queries from biomedical experts and open domains;
- RepLab: used Twitter data to classify tweets by reputation measures, and to profile authors;
- ShARe/CLEF eHealth: used medical information and data to test support for patients and friends in extracting useful information from medical reports.

The details for each lab are contained in a separate publication, *the Working Notes*, which were distributed at the CLEF 2014 and are available online. An overview paper from each lab is contained in this volume.

The success of CLEF 2014 would not have been possible without the contributions of many people including the emerging CLEF Initiative organization, the Program Committee, the Lab Organizing Committee, the local arrangement group at the University of Sheffield, the reviewers, and the many students and volunteers who contributed along the way. We also thank very much the support we received from our sponsors.

July 2014

Evangelos Kanoulas
Mihai Lupu
Paul Clough
Mark Sanderson
Mark Hall
Allan Hanbury
Elaine Toms

# Organization

## Program Committee

| | |
|---|---|
| Shlomo Argamon | Illinois Institute of Technology, USA |
| Alexandra Balahur | European Commission Joint Research Centre, Italy |
| Paul Clough | University of Sheffield, UK |
| Walter Daelemans | University of Antwerp, Belgium |
| Nicola Ferro | University of Padua, Italy |
| Norbert Fuhr | University of Duisburg-Essen, Germany |
| Mark Hall | Edge Hill University, UK |
| Allan Hanbury | Vienna University of Technology, Austria |
| Sanda Harabagiu | University of Texas at Dallas, USA |
| Antoine Isaac | Europeana & VU University Amsterdam, The Netherlands |
| Alexis Joly | Inria, France |
| Evangelos Kanoulas | Google Inc., Switzerland |
| Birger Larsen | Aalborg University, Denmark |
| Johannes Leveling | Dublin City University, Ireland |
| Mihai Lupu | Vienna University of Technology, Austria |
| Walid Magdy | Qatar Computing Research Institute, Qatar |
| Thomas Mandl | University of Hildesheim, Germany |
| Paul McNamee | Johns Hopkins University, USA |
| Manuel Montes-Y-Gómez | National Institute of Astrophysics, Optics and Electronics, Mexico |
| Henning Müller | University of Applied Sciences and Arts Western Switzerland, Switzerland |
| Jian-Yun Nie | University of Montreal, Canada |
| Roberto Paredes | Polytechnic University of Valencia, Spain |
| Vivien Petras | HU Berlin, Germany |
| Anselmo Peñas | National Distance Education University, Spain |
| Florina Piroi | Vienna University of Technology, Austria |
| Martin Potthast | Bauhaus University Weimar, Germany |
| Alvaro Rodrigo | National Distance Education University, Spain |
| Paolo Rosso | Polytechnic University of Valencia, Spain |
| Tobias Schreck | University of Konstanz, Germany |
| Azadeh Shakery | University of Tehran, Iran |

Efstathios Stamatatos         University of the Aegean, Greece
Benno Stein                   Bauhaus-University Weimar, Germany
Bart Thomee                   Yahoo! Research, USA
Juan-Manuel Torres-Moreno     Laboratoire Informatique d'Avignon, France
Theodora Tsikrika             Centre for Research and Technology-Hellas,
                                Greece
Jose Luis Vicedo              University of Alicante, Spain
Robert Villa                  The University of Sheffield, UK
Christa Womser-Hacker         University of Hildesheim, Germany
David Zellhoefer              BTU Cottbus, Germany

# Keynote Presentations

# Information Interaction Evaluation

Ann Blandford

University College London

**Abstract.** Most evaluations of information access systems put the system at the centre. In this talk, I will present an alternative focus: on the person, who may be actively seeking, or may simply be encountering information as they engage with a variety of information resources. The 'information journey' is a way of framing our understanding of both directed seeking and encountering. This framework was developed based on empirical studies of people interacting with information across a variety of contexts. This perspective emphasises the importance of evaluating the user experience of interacting with systems, and how they support the individual's information journey. The system has to support people's work, as well as being effective and usable. In this talk, I will present the information journey, relating it to models of information retrieval and information seeking. I will then present approaches to evaluating information access systems that start from the premise that every evaluation study has a purpose, that the study design has to be appropriate for that purpose, and that, ultimately, the success of any system depends on how it is used by people engaged in information work in their daily lives.

## Biography

Ann Blandford is Professor of Human-Computer Interaction at UCL and former Director of UCL Interaction Centre. Her first degree is in Maths (from Cambridge) and her PhD in Artificial Intelligence (from the Open University). She started her career in industry, as a software engineer, but soon moved into academia, where she developed a focus on the use and usability of computer systems. She leads research on how people interact with and make sense of information, and how technology can better support people's information needs, with a focus on situated interactions. She has over 200 international, peer-reviewed publications, including a Synthesis Lecture on "Interacting with Information".

# Search and Context

Susan T. Dumais

Microsoft Research

**Abstract.** It is very challenging task for search engines to understand a short query, especially if that query is considered in isolation. Query understanding is much easier if we consider the 'context' in which the query arises, e.g., previous queries, location, and time. Traditionally search engines have returned the same results to everyone who asks the same question. However, using a single ranking for everyone, in every context limits how well a search engine can do. I begin by outlining a framework to characterize the extent to which different people have the same (or different) intents for a query. I then describe several examples of how we represent and use context to improve search quality. Finally I conclude by highlighting some challenges in developing contextually-aware algorithms at web scale including system optimization, transparency, and evaluation.

## Biography

Susan Dumais a Distinguished Scientist at Microsoft and Deputy Managing Director of the Microsoft Research Lab in Redmond. Prior to joining Microsoft Research, she was at Bell Labs and Bellcore, where she worked on Latent Semantic Analysis, techniques for combining search and navigation, and organizational impacts of new technology. Her current research focuses on user modeling and personalization, context and search and temporal dynamics of information. She has worked closely with several Microsoft groups (Bing, Windows Desktop Search, SharePoint, and Office Online Help) on search-related innovations. Susan has published widely in the fields of information science, human-computer interaction and cognitive science, and holds several patents on novel retrieval algorithms and interfaces. Susan is also an adjunct professor in the Information School at the University of Washington. She is Past-Chair of ACM's Special Interest Group in Information Retrieval (SIGIR), and serves on several editorial boards, technical program committees, and government panels. She was elected to the CHI Academy in 2005, an ACM Fellow in 2006, received the SIGIR Gerard Salton Award for Lifetime Achievement in 2009, was elected to the National Academy of Engineering (NAE) in 2011, and received the ACM Athena Lecturer Award in 2014.

# Playing *Where's Wally?* with Social Media

Fabio Ciravegna

The University of Sheffield

**Abstract.** The ubiquitous use of mobile devices and their use for social activities make possible to see events and their development through the eyes and the senses of the participants. In this talk I will discuss my experience in working with emergency services and organisers of very large events involving hundreds of thousands of participants to help identify planned and unplanned situations through social media. This involves analysis of social media messages (Twitter, Facebook, etc.) as part of the tasks of the emergency service control room. Applications range from tackling natural and man-made disasters (floods, earthquakes, large fires, etc.), to overseeing very large events such as City and Music Festivals.

The task requires high focus on the geographic area, understanding of the social context and the event nature, as well as instinct and experience to cope with large crowds and their sometimes erratic behaviour. It is fundamentally a human centred task that requires important support by computers, as long uncomfortable shifts may be involved (sometimes 24/7) and the amount of material to cope with can be huge (millions of messages and pictures to shift through).

From a technical point of view, this support requires real-time large-scale text and data analysis, visual analytics and human computer interaction. In this talk I will discuss the requirements for this support, focussing mostly on the social media analysis part. I will discuss the issues, some of the current technical solutions and a roadmap for future development.

## Biography

Fabio Ciravegna is professor of Language and Knowledge Technologies at the Department of Computer Science at the University of Sheffield. His research field concerns Knowledge and Information Management over large scale, covering 3 main areas: (i) How to capture information over large scale from multiple sources and devices (the Web, the Social Web, distributed organisational archives, mobile devices, etc.), (ii) how to use the captured information (e.g. for knowledge management, business intelligence, customer analysis, management of large scale events, etc.); and (iii) how to communicate the information (to final users, problem owners, etc.). He is the director of the European Project WeSenseIt on citizen observatories of water and principal investigator in the EPSRC project LODIE (Large Scale Information Extraction using Linked Open Data). He has developed with Neil Ireson and Vita Lanfranchi methodologies for event monitoring in social media that have been used to support the emergency services and organisers in several large scale events involving hundreds of thousands of people; among them the Glastonbury Festival (200,000 participants), the Bristol Harbour Festival (250,000), the Tour de France (UK part), the evacuation of 30,000 people from the City of Vicenza and many others. He has co-created two companies: K-Now Ltd who commercialises the social media analysis technology and The Floow Ltd who develops technology currently monitoring hundreds of thousands of drivers for motor insurance via mobile phones.

# Table of Contents

## Evaluation

## Domain-Specific Approaches

# Alternative Search Tasks

# CLEF Lab Overviews

# Making Test Corpora for Question Answering More Representative

Andrew Walker[1], Andrew Starkey[2], Jeff Z. Pan[1], and Advaith Siddharthan[1]

[1] Computing Science, University of Aberdeen, UK
{r05aw0,jeff.z.pan,advaith}@abdn.ac.uk
[2] Engineering, University of Aberdeen, UK
a.starkey@abdn.ac.uk

**Abstract.** Despite two high profile series of challenges devoted to question answering technologies there remains no formal study into the representativeness that question corpora bear to real end-user inputs. We examine the corpora used presently and historically in the TREC and QALD challenges in juxtaposition with two more from natural sources and identify a degree of disjointedness between the two. We analyse these differences in depth before discussing a candidate approach to question corpora generation and provide a juxtaposition on its own representativeness. We conclude that these artificial corpora have good overall coverage of grammatical structures but the distribution is skewed, meaning performance measures may be inaccurate.

## 1 Introduction

Question Answering (QA) technologies were envisioned early on in the artificial intelligence community. At least 15 experimental English language QA systems were described by [13]. Notable early attempts include BASEBALL [11] and LUNAR [17,18]. New technologies and resources often prompt a new wave of QA solutions using them. For example: relational databases [8] with PLANES [16]; the semantic web [2] by [3]; and Wikipedia [15] by [7].

Attempts to evaluate QA technologies are similarly diverse. The long-running Text REtrieval Conferences[1] (TREC) making use of human assessors in conjunction with a nugget pyramid method [12], while the newer Question Answering over Linked Data[2] (QALD) series uses an automated process that compares results with a gold standard.

In both cases, however, the matter of whether or not the questions being posed to the challenge participants actually capture the range and diversity of questions that real users would make of a QA system is not addressed. We explore the distribution of grammatical relationships present in various artificial and natural question corpora in two primary aspects: coverage and representativeness. Coverage is important for QA solution developers to gauge gaps in their

---

[1] http://trec.nist.gov/
[2] http://greententacle.techfak.uni-bielefeld.de/~cunger/qald/

E. Kanoulas et al. (Eds.): CLEF 2014, LNCS 8685, pp. 1–6, 2014.

system's capacity, whereas evaluations are dependent on the representativeness of their corpora for valid comparisons between systems.

## 2   Corpora Sources

To evaluate a QA system for commercial use, it would be preferable to test it on real user questions. That is, questions that have been posed by potential or real end-users rather than system developers or testers. Although artificial questions may be used to capture additional grammatical forms, the most important aspect for a functional QA system is to answer those put by real users.

We collected questions from 4 distinct corpora, 2 artificial and 2 natural:

1. TREC has been running since 1992 and published 2,524 unique questions with which to evaluate text retrieval system submissions. These questions are artificial by the track organisers and often pertain to given contexts not found in the questions themselves. For example, a question "What was her name?" makes sense within a context, but is essentially meaningless alone.
2. The QALD challenges have been running since 2011, publishing 453 unique questions focussed on DBpedia [1,4] and MusicBrainz [14] data. These also are artificial but are always context independent.
3. We extracted 329,510 questions from Yahoo! Answers[3] tagged as English. These are the question titles put by the general public for other members of the public to propose answers to, and so in some cases do not form typical question structures – leaving the details of the question to the post's body.
4. A set of 78 questions put by participants of OWL tutorials to a Pizza ontology. These are considered natural as the participants were not experts and the questions include some grammatical and spelling errors.

## 3   Analysis and Comparison of Question Corpora

We seek to compare the entries of the various corpora in order to discern if the artificial questions currently being used for QA system evaluation are representative of the questions real end-users might pose. If some feature or aspect of natural language questions are over- or under-represented in an evaluation corpus this will cause evaluation measurements to be inaccurate as accounts of a QA system's performance in an end-system.

Rather than manually inspecting the grammatical forms of all 332,565 entries, we ran a statistical analysis comparing the distribution of various grammatical relations found in the corpora. Using the Stanford Parser[4] [10,9] we derived the dependency graph for each question and then, for each corpus $D$, computed frequency vectors for each dependency type $t$, normalised by $tf$-$idf$[5]. We then

---

[3] http://answers.yahoo.com/

[4] Stanford CoreNLP version 1.3.5 trained with the provided English PCFG model

[5] Term frequency - inverse document frequency

$tfidf(t, D) = \log(f(t, D) + 1) \times \log \frac{N}{|\{d \in D : t \in d\}|}$ where $t$ is a dependency type and $D$ is a corpus of questions.

compared the distribution of dependency types across the four corpora in two ways: by calculating pairwise cosine similarity, and by calculating pairwise Pearson correlation between corpora. These comparisons are shown in Table 1.

**Table 1.** Pairwise comparison of dependency type distributions across corpora

| Yahoo! | Pizza | QALD | |
|---|---|---|---|
| 0.7847 | 0.7479 | 0.8593 | TREC |
| | 0.6060 | 0.7428 | Yahoo! |
| | | 0.8373 | Pizza |

| Yahoo! | Pizza | QALD | |
|---|---|---|---|
| −0.1018 | 0.2350 | **0.4942** | TREC |
| | **-0.5492** | −0.2023 | Yahoo! |
| | | **0.5345** | Pizza |

(a) Cosine similarity                     (b) Pearson. **Bold** indicates $p < 0.05$

Of note in Table 1a is the strong similarity of distributions between the two artificial corpora, QALD and TREC, where comparisons with them and the natural corpora show weaker correspondence. The Yahoo! corpus shows relatively low similarity with any other corpus – perhaps due to its heavy reliance on colloquialisms and overwhelming prominence of ungrammatical content. Table 1b emphasises the dissimilarity of Yahoo! to the other sources.

**Table 2.** Dependency relations that are over- and under-represented in artificial corpora. Discussed relations are in **bold**. A * indicates possible over-representation, and a † under-representation.

| relation | trec | pizza | qald | yahoo | relation | trec | pizza | qald | yahoo |
|---|---|---|---|---|---|---|---|---|---|
| det* | 17.63 | 13.66 | 18.19 | 9.36 | appos† | 0.26 | 0.46 | 0.04 | 0.39 |
| prep* | 12.52 | 9.95 | 12.90 | 10.30 | neg† | 0.02 | 0.46 | 0.07 | 0.58 |
| nn* | 10.56 | 3.47 | 12.09 | 7.28 | agent* | 0.37 | 0 | 0.59 | 0.07 |
| aux† | 4.38 | 4.86 | 2.68 | 7.57 | ccomp† | 0.20 | 1.16 | 0.22 | 2.13 |
| dep† | 2.08 | 6.48 | 2.72 | 5.73 | mark† | 0.14 | 0.46 | 0.11 | 1.26 |
| attr* | 5.52 | 0.69 | 2.68 | 1.36 | advcl† | 0.15 | 0.23 | 0.04 | 1.08 |
| conj† | 0.64 | 5.09 | 0.51 | 2.67 | csubj† | 0.01 | 0.23 | 0.18 | 0.24 |
| cop† | 0.63 | 3.24 | 1.18 | 2.15 | predet† | 0.01 | 0.46 | 0 | 0.08 |
| auxpass* | 3.16 | 0.69 | 2.54 | 0.63 | cc† | 0 | 0.23 | 0.07 | 0.13 |
| nsubjpass* | 3.16 | 0.69 | 2.57 | 0.55 | preconj† | 0 | 0.23 | 0 | 0.01 |
| xcomp† | 0.60 | 1.62 | 0.44 | 1.99 | | | | | |

There are some grammatical dependency relations that are interesting in their under-representation within artificial question corpora.

The `predet` relation (predeterminer) is found only twice in TREC and never in QALD, but enjoys greater usage in the Pizza and Yahoo! corpora. This relation is typically found connecting a noun and the word "all", as in "Find all the pizzas with less than 3 toppings".

Similarly, the `preconj` relation (preconjunct) is never found in QALD or TREC, but has limited exposure in both Pizza and Yahoo! corpora. This is a relation "between the head of [a noun-phrase] and a word that appears at the beginning bracketing a conjunction (and puts emphasis on it), such as 'either', 'both', 'neither')", as in "Which pizza has neither vegetables nor seafood?".

The artificial corpora contain many more `attr` relations, which are used to attach the main verb to a leading *wh-* word, suggesting that the corpora authors are relying too heavily on *wh-* formulations.

The `nn` relation (noun compound modifier) sees heavy use in both TREC and QALD but is not similarly represented in the natural Pizza and Yahoo! corpora. This may be due in part to domain dependence, with questions focussed on named entities.

## 4    Constructing Evaluation Corpora

Having established that artificial and natural corpora of natural language questions have discrepancies in grammatical form and variation, we ask how one might compose an evaluation corpus of such questions for a given domain that maintains representativeness of real end-user inputs. We suggest a lexical substitution approach, taking examples from natural question sets and replacing mappable concepts with those from the required domain. This is applied to two scenarios: first, with a case study of QALD seeking to improve its representativeness in Sect. 4.1 and second on building a new corpus from scratch in Sect. 4.2. It is the corpus engineer's responsibility to ensure sensible substitutions.

### 4.1    Extending QALD to Improve Representativeness

For this section we will be using the QALD-3 DBpedia testing corpus, which consists of 100 questions collectively bearing a 0.5952 cosine similarity with the Yahoo! Answers corpus, in terms of *tf-idf* distribution.

We draw entries from Yahoo! at random and calculate the effect its inclusion would have on the cosine similarity score. When a positive effect is found, that entry is examined for suitability. For any with suitable dependency graphs, we apply lexical substitution to render the question appropriate for the target ontology while maintaining the original grammatical structure.

For example, imagine that the question "what is the percentage of men who have visted[*sic*] prostitutes?"[6] was one selected in this manner. We can identify the core concepts of the question and substitute them with concepts and instances from MusicBrainz. In this case we could choose "What is the percentage of artists who have released compilations?", as shown in Fig. 1. Figure 2 shows the growth of similarity score with just a few iterations of this method. This process can be repeated as desired to build a corpus of relevant questions with more representative distributions of grammatical dependencies.

---

[6] Although this entry contains typographic errors, the parser nevertheless gives a usable dependency graph.

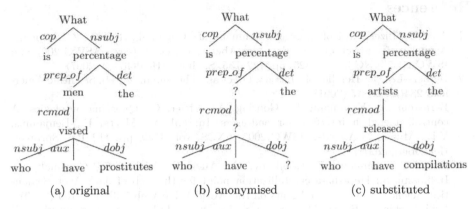

(a) original                    (b) anonymised                   (c) substituted

**Fig. 1.** Lexical substitution within a question by dependency graph [7]

## 4.2  Building a New Evaluation Corpus

The strategy also applies to the construction of entirely new corpora. We would initially choose questions that individually bear the greatest similarity to Yahoo! as a whole and then reiterate with the process as before, for extending an existing corpus.

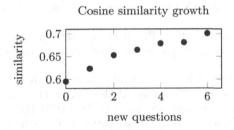

**Fig. 2.** Similarity growth with new questions

## 5  Conclusions and Future Work

Two corpora of artificial English questions demonstrate stronger similarity with each other than either of two corpora of natural English questions. This suggests that results of evaluations of QA systems using these artificial corpora may not be indicative of performance on natural questions. We proposed a methodology for creating natural questions within a domain by performing lexical substitution within samples of natural-provenance questions from other domains.

This study pertains to low-level analysis of English questions and does not address coverage and representativeness of other linguistic features. Although substitutions are tailored to a given context, no effort is made explicit here to emulate the distribution of question topics; this should be the responsibility of the corpus engineer.

---

[7] For conciseness we use the collapsed graphs using "`prep_of`" but this has no bearing on the result.

# References

1. Auer, S., Bizer, C., Kobilarov, G., Lehmann, J., Cyganiak, R., Ives, Z.: DBpedia: A nucleus for a web of open data. In: Aberer, K., et al. (eds.) ASWC 2007 and ISWC 2007. LNCS, vol. 4825, pp. 722–735. Springer, Heidelberg (2007)
2. Berners-Lee, T., Hendler, J., Lassila, O., et al.: The semantic web. Scientific American 284(5), 28–37 (2001)
3. Bernstein, A., Kaufmann, E., Göhring, A., Kiefer, C.: Querying ontologies: A controlled english interface for end-users. In: Gil, Y., Motta, E., Benjamins, V.R., Musen, M.A. (eds.) ISWC 2005. LNCS, vol. 3729, pp. 112–126. Springer, Heidelberg (2005)
4. Bizer, C., Lehmann, J., Kobilarov, G., Auer, S., Becker, C., Cyganiak, R., Hellmann, S.: Dbpedia-a crystallization point for the web of data. Web Semantics: Science, Services and Agents on the World Wide Web 7(3), 154–165 (2009)
5. Brill, E., Lin, J., Banko, M., Dumais, S., Ng, A., et al.: Data-intensive question answering. In: Proceedings of the Tenth Text REtrieval Conference, TREC 2001 (2001)
6. Brin, S., Page, L.: The anatomy of a large-scale hypertextual web search engine. Computer Networks and ISDN Systems 30(1), 107–117 (1998)
7. Buscaldi, D., Rosso, P.: Mining knowledge from wikipedia for the question answering task. In: Proceedings of the International Conference on Language Resources and Evaluation (2006)
8. Codd, E.F.: A relational model of data for large shared data banks. Communications of the ACM 13(6), 377–387 (1970)
9. De Marneffe, M.C.: What's that supposed to mean? Ph.D. thesis, Stanford University (2012)
10. De Marneffe, M.C., MacCartney, B., Manning, C.D.: Generating typed dependency parses from phrase structure parses. In: Proceedings of LREC, vol. 6, pp. 449–454 (2006)
11. Green, Jr., B.F., Wolf, A.K., Chomsky, C., Laughery, K.: Baseball: an automatic question-answerer. Papers Presented at the May 9-11, 1961, western joint IRE-AIEE-ACM Computer Conference, pp. 219–224. ACM (1961)
12. Lin, J., Demner-Fushman, D.: Will pyramids built of nuggets topple over? In: Proceedings of the main Conference on Human Language Technology Conference of the North American Chapter of the Association of Computational Linguistics, pp. 383–390. Association for Computational Linguistics (2006)
13. Simmons, R.F.: Answering english questions by computer: a survey. Commun. ACM 8(1), 53–70 (1965), http://doi.acm.org/10.1145/363707.363732
14. Swartz, A.: Musicbrainz: A semantic web service. IEEE Intelligent Systems 17(1), 76–77 (2002)
15. Wales, J., Sanger, L.: Wikipedia, the free encyclopedia (2001), http://en.wikipedia.org/w/index.php?title=Wikipedia&oldid=551616049 (accessed April 22, 2013)
16. Waltz, D.L.: An english language question answering system for a large relational database. Communications of the ACM 21(7), 526–539 (1978)
17. Woods, W.A.: Progress in natural language understanding: an application to lunar geology. In: Proceedings of the National Computer Conference and Exposition, AFIPS 1973, June 4-8, 1973, pp. 441–450. ACM, New York (1973), http://doi.acm.org/10.1145/1499586.1499695
18. Woods, W.A.: Lunar rocks in natural english: Explorations in natural language question answering. Linguistic Structures Processing 5, 521–569 (1977)

# Towards Automatic Evaluation
# of Health-Related CQA Data

Alexander Beloborodov[1], Pavel Braslavski[1,2], and Marina Driker[3]

[1] Ural Federal University
xander-beloborodov@yandex.ru
[2] Kontur Labs
pbras@yandex.ru
[3] Ural State Medical University
mdriker@yandex.ru

**Abstract.** The paper reports on evaluation of Russian community question answering (CQA) data in health domain. About 1,500 question–answer pairs were manually evaluated by medical professionals, in addition automatic evaluation based on reference disease–medicine pairs was performed. Although the results of the manual and automatic evaluation do not fully match, we find the method still promising and propose several improvements. Automatic processing can be used to dynamically monitor the quality of the CQA content and to compare different data sources. Moreover, the approach can be useful for symptomatic surveillance and health education campaigns.

## 1 Introduction

The web has become an important source of health information for lay-people. In 2012, 59% of the US adults looked online for health information; 45% of them searched for specific disease or medical problem [9]. These figures are lower in Russia, but still substantial and growing: in 2013, 13% of Russian population searched for health-related information online, with the proportion much higher in big cities [1]. Although general search engines remain the primary tool for searching medical information online, there are also other options. One of the popular destinations is community question answering (CQA) sites that allow users to post questions on virtually any subject to other community members, answer questions, rate and comment answers, and gain points and badges. Yahoo!Answers[1] and WikiAnswers[2] are examples of popular CQA platforms. CQA is a good complement to web search that allows for a more detailed description of information need, delivers more social and personalized search experience, suits users with low search engine proficiency, etc. CQA data are large, diverse, and dynamic, but content quality can be the major issue, which is critical in case of medical information.

---

[1] https://answers.yahoo.com/
[2] http://wiki.answers.com/

E. Kanoulas et al. (Eds.): CLEF 2014, LNCS 8685, pp. 7–18, 2014.

There are guidelines for medical websites with editorial content that enable veracity of the information provided online. For example, the Health On the Net Foundation (HON)[3] elaborated HONcode and reviews websites to comply with it. More than 7,300 sites are certified by the HON to date. Obviously, this approach cannot be applied to sites that are fueled with extensive and loosely controlled users' input.

Several approaches aimed at automatic detection of high-quality content in CQA were proposed in the literature (see next section). In contrast to these studies we experiment with an automatic method for quality assessment focused on *health-related* CQA. The idea of the approach is to perform evaluation on a narrowed subset – questions asking for medication for a specific symptom or disease, for example (all examples are originally in Russian):

> **Q:** *Please suggest good [runny nose] drops. need to hold out an important meeting, at least 2 hours without snivel...*
> **A:** *Take [Sanorin] or [Nazol Advance]*

According to different studies [1,9,7,21] this type of information need is among the most common ones. We hypothesize that this type of questions is exemplary enough to reflect the overall quality of CQA health-related content. The approach can be used for comparison of different CQA services in the health domain or longitudinal observation of a CQA subcategory, rather than as a technique to evaluate individual items.

In our experiment we used health-related questions and answers from the Russian CQA platform Otvety@Mail.Ru[4] (*otvety* means *answers* in Russian). First, we compiled a list of unambiguous medicine designations from a comprehensive registry of drugs. Second, we composed a list of 13 diseases and symptoms, mined corresponding reference drugs from an online resource and performed manual post-processing of the obtained table. Automatic evaluation is straightforward: we count correct and incorrect 'disease-in-question – drug-in-answer' occurrences. This approach is motivated by analysis of disease–drug pair frequencies in our previous study [5]. In parallel we carried out manual evaluation of about 1,500 question–answer pairs. Juxtaposition of both manual and automatic evaluation showed low consistency rate. This can be partly due to discrepant manual evaluation that was quasi crowd-sourced. Another possible reason is that the automatic approach is too shallow and simplistic. Nevertheless we find the method still promising and propose several improvements.

The paper is organized as follows. Next section surveys literature on detection of high-quality content in CQA and analysis of health-related content in social media. Section 3 describes data used in the study: a general list of drugs, a list of 13 diseases with their reference drugs, and Otvety@Mail.Ru dataset. Section 4 describes manual and automatic evaluation results and comparison of both. Section 5 discusses the obtained results. Section 6 defines directions for future research and concludes.

---

[3] https://www.hon.ch/

[4] http://otvety.mail.ru/

## 2    Related Work

Our work is related to prior research in detection of high-quality content in CQA and analysis of social media in health domain.

*Content Quality in CQA.* There are several methods aimed at automatic evaluation of CQA data described in the literature. There are slight variations in the notion of a good question or answer. E.g. studies distinguish between asker's [4,18] and 'external' perception of answer quality [3]. Some of the studies consider answers quality only [2,18], some look into questions[10,15,14], the other examine questions and answers simultaneously [3]. Authors classify questions into 'information-seeking' vs. conversational, or entertaining ones [10,15]. Some approaches seek to evaluate content quality on-the-fly, right upon question or answer arrival; the other work with archival data, i.e. containing users' ratings and comments, usage statistics, etc. The methods described in the literature employ machine learning techniques and a wide range of features. The features may include: 1) text features grasping text grammaticality, spelling, visual neatness, readability, etc., 2) user features such as user rating, activity, badges, expertise in the topic, interactions with other users, and 3) content popularity reflected in click statistics. None of the features are domain-specific, and methods can be applied presumably to any subject area. However, authors point out that different CQA categories vary in user interaction patterns, vocabulary, etc. Studies devoted to analysis of questions posted on Stackoverflow[5] (a CQA platform on software programming) take into account domain specifics and make use of dedicated dictionaries [13,8].

*Health Information in Social Media.* It has been shown that Twitter data have a great potential for public health, e.g. for symptomatic surveillance, analyzing symptoms and medication usage, behavioral risk factors, geographic localization of disease outbreaks, etc.[12,17]. In our previous study [5] we applied a similar set of tools to CQA content in health domain and hypothesized that the approach can be used for content quality evaluation. Bhattacharya et al.[6] analyzed health beliefs of the type *smoking causes death* or *tea tree oil treats infection* expressed on Twitter. The way the data were gathered and processed is similar to our approach. Wong et al.[20] proposed an experimental dialog system that uses Yahoo!Answers data for guided conversations on health-related subjects. However, quality issue of CQA data is not addressed in the study.

Dedicated studies on CQA content quality in health domain are relatively few and rely mostly on manual processing. Zhang's study [21] described linguistic features, users' motivations and question types, as well as temporal, emotional and cognitive aspects of a sample of about 270 questions in *Health* category of Yahoo!Answers. Oh et al.[16] outlined a draft of a quality evaluation experiment of health-related content of Yahoo!Answers. The plan features multi-faceted answers judgment by representatives of three groups – questioners, health reference librarians, and nurses; preliminary results for 10 questions are quoted.

---

[5] http://stackoverflow.com/

Kim et al.[11] semi-automatically assessed around 5,400 questions and answers on H1N1 influenza strain posted on Yahoo!Answers. The authors identified major subtopics in H1N1 questions, types of resources askers and answerers referred to, and medical concepts mentioned in the data.

## 3   Resources and Data

### 3.1   Disease and Medicine Dictionaries

The starting point for the formation of the 'disease – medicine' table was data gathered from the Registry of Medicine. The reference book (and its online counterpart[6]) combines comprehensive information on drugs and International Classification of Diseases (ICD)[7] codes.

For the experiment, we selected 13 frequent symptoms/diseases: *allergy/ urticaria, rhinitis, tonsillitis, gastritis, diarrhea, influenza-like illness (ILI), candidiasis, herpes, heartburn, stomatitis, hemorrhoids, dysbiosis,* and *otitis*. In the context of our study it is particularly important that these diseases are often self-treated without consulting a doctor; complementary medicine is often used to treat these symptoms.

ICD is too detailed for our purposes, so we merged groups of diseases with similar symptoms (and corresponding lists of drugs). For example, influenza-like illness (ILI) group is combined of three ICD codes:

> *J06. Acute upper respiratory infections of multiple and unspecified sites;*
> *J10. Influenza due to other identified influenza virus;*
> *J11. Influenza, virus not identified.*

We also provided each disease with its synonyms, including vernacular names – e.g. *runny nose* has nine name variants.

General medicine names were taken from the State Register of Approved Drugs[8] and converted to a list of unambiguous one-word names, toward this end were removed 1) pharmaceutical form designations such as *drops, cream, solution, tablets,* etc.; 2) modifiers of medicine names (e.g. *Aspirin Cardio, 1000 Aspirin, Aspirin York, Aspirin Express → Aspirin*); 3) names consisting of common words. As a result, of 11,926 unique entries in the initial list we came up to the list of 4,120 drugs.

In addition, we manually processed the list of drugs corresponding to the 13 selected diseases. We excluded 1) dietary supplements, multivitamin and mineral complexes with a wide range of indications – selected symptoms are not specific for them; 2) baby nutrition products; 3) psychotropic drugs; 4) drugs with expired registration, as well as drugs that are not currently used in clinical practice because of their low efficiency or high toxicity; 5) drugs with missing formula (only trade names are presented in the registry). Table 1 shows statistics of 'disease – drug' table (a drug may correspond to several diseases).

---

[6] http://rlsnet.ru

[7] http://www.who.int/classifications/icd/en/

[8] http://grls.rosminzdrav.ru/

**Table 1.** Number of unique drug names for each of 13 diseases

| Disease or symptom | # of drugs |
|---|---|
| ILI | 294 |
| rhinitis | 260 |
| tonsillitis | 167 |
| diarrhea | 155 |
| otitis | 149 |
| allergy/urticaria | 118 |
| gastritis | 106 |
| stomatitis | 90 |
| candidiasis | 84 |
| herpes | 64 |
| hemorrhoids | 57 |
| dysbiosis | 53 |
| heartburn | 46 |

## 3.2   Otvety@Mail.Ru

Otvety@Mail.Ru is a Russian counterpart of Yahoo!Answers with similar rules and incentives. The site was launched in 2006 and has accumulated almost 80 million questions and more than 400 million answers by August 2012[9]. Otvety@Mail.Ru has two-level directory with about 30 top-level categories, including *Health and Beauty*, and about 200 subcategories. The users have to assign their questions to a second-level category using drop-down lists.

The initial data set contained 128,370 questions and corresponding answers from four second-level categories: *Diseases and Medicines; Doctors, Clinics, and Insurance; Doctors' answers; and Kids' Health* in the timespan from 1 April 2011 to 31 March 2012. Tables 2 and 3 summarize main characteristics of the corpus used in the experiment. Additional details about Q&A topics and users' demographics can be found in our earlier paper [5].

**Table 2.** Otvety@Mail.Ru Health corpus statistics

| | |
|---|---|
| Number of questions | 128,370 |
| Average number of answers per question | 5 |
| Average question length (words) | 10.1 |
| Average answer length (words) | 21.6 |
| Questions mentioning one of the 13 diseases | 7,147 |
| ...of which with answers mentioning a drug | 4,054 |

---

[9] http://otvet.mail.ru/news/#hbd2012 – accessed July 2013.

**Table 3.** Most frequent diseases and drugs

| Top-5 diseases | |
|---|---|
| rhinitis | 1,606 |
| allergy/urticaria | 1,182 |
| tonsillitis | 802 |
| ILI | 730 |
| candidiasis | 494 |
| **Top-5 medicines** | |
| iodine | 3,291 |
| activated carbon | 2,526 |
| hydrogen peroxide | 2,057 |
| aspirin | 1,873 |
| analgin | 1,531 |
| **Top-5 disease-medicine pairs** | |
| herpes–aciclovir | 274 |
| allergy/urticaria–suprastin | 196 |
| candidiasis–flucostat | 157 |
| herpes–zovirax | 132 |
| diarrhea–activated carbon | 131 |

## 4    Experiment

### 4.1    Data Preparation

As mentioned above, our goal was to automatically evaluate question–answer pairs, where the question is of type "What should one take in case of $X$?" or "How to treat $X$?" ($X$ is a disease or symptom from a predefined list). We indexed Otvety@Mail.Ru data by 13 diseases and their variants (see section 3.1), as well as by all medicines. Medicine and disease names are often misspelled; to improve the retrieval quality we implemented a fuzzy matching algorithm with learned edit distance that captures misspelled mentions of both diseases and medicines.

We sampled randomly about 1,000 questions with their corresponding answers according to a straightforward template '*disease in question – medicine in answer*'. Manual investigation showed that for questions with at least one answer containing medicine mention, only 53% belong to the sought type. When we additionally require that at least one answer contains *two or more medicine mentions*, this rate increases to 79%. We opted for this simple criterion with satisfactory precision for data selection, although it can deliver false positives of the kind:

> **Q:** *I have got a [coldsore] on my lip. Should I go to school?*
> **A:** *Haha... 90% of the population have herpes and go to school and work. You should buy [Kagocel] and [Aciclovir] at the pharmacy. Get well )*

For manual evaluation we selected 255 questions with at least one answer containing two or more medicine mentions (from 1,000 sampled previously), which resulted in 977 question-answer pairs. Additionally, we randomly sampled 500 question-answer pairs as a complement to the questions of the particular type.

## 4.2  Manual Evaluation

We sent an invitation to participate in the evaluation of health-related community questions and answers to selected staff members of the Ural State Medical University. Seven assessors took part in the evaluation (including one of the authors – MD), all holding a university degree in medicine. The evaluation was conducted using an online tool, no personal meetings and instruction took place. Before the start of the evaluation assessors were exposed an instruction and several examples. Assessors could pause evaluation any time and return to it at a convenient time; there was also no 'minimum assignment' – assessors could determine the comfortable volume of labeling by themselves, which resulted in an uneven distribution of answers labelled by individual assessors (406 : 267 : 197 : 102 : 58 : 50 : 11). Evaluation queue was generated randomly, so that the answers to the same question did not appear straightly one after another. Assessors were presented a question-answer pair that they could evaluate on a three-grade scale: 0 – low quality (potentially harmful), 1 – potentially useful answer, 2 – high-quality answer. The left-hand side of table 4 summarizes the results of manual evaluation, including randomly sampled question–answer pairs (i.e. not of the type 'how to treat a particular disease or symptom').

Inter-assessor agreement calculated on 100 double-judged items is quite low: raters' labels coincide only in 21% of cases, Cohen's $\kappa$ is 0.51 (calculated taking into account distances between labels).

## 4.3  Automatic Matching

Automatic processing of question–answer pairs is straightforward: we count 'correct' and 'incorrect' disease-in-question—drug-in-answer pairs; when multiple drug mentions occur in answer, the final score (0 or 1) is calculated based on majority voting (e.g. two 'correct' mentions out of three result in 1). Right-hand side of table 4 shows automatically obtained scores for manually labeled data; the rightmost column reports the proportion of matching scores (manual scores are binarized as follows: $0 \rightarrow 0$; $1, 2 \rightarrow 1$). Table 5 shows automatic scores for the whole subset of question–answer pairs matching the pattern 'questions with at least one answer with 1+ drug mentions'; figure 1 depicts the distribution of the values over the year.

**Table 4.** Manual and automatic evaluation results

| Disease | # | Manual labels (M) 0 | | Manual labels (M) 1 | | Manual labels (M) 2 | | Automatic scores (A) 0 | | Automatic scores (A) 1 | | M&A matches | |
|---|---|---|---|---|---|---|---|---|---|---|---|---|---|
| rhinitis | 182 | 68 | 0.37 | 70 | 0.38 | 44 | 0.24 | 60 | 0.33 | 122 | 0.67 | 112 | 0.62 |
| allergy/urticaria | 149 | 81 | 0.54 | 39 | 0.26 | 29 | 0.19 | 24 | 0.16 | 125 | 0.84 | 56 | 0.38 |
| candidiasis | 148 | 48 | 0.32 | 66 | 0.45 | 34 | 0.23 | 18 | 0.12 | 130 | 0.88 | 96 | 0.65 |
| herpes | 136 | 49 | 0.36 | 57 | 0.42 | 30 | 0.22 | 15 | 0.11 | 121 | 0.89 | 88 | 0.65 |
| tonsillitis | 107 | 23 | 0.21 | 50 | 0.47 | 34 | 0.32 | 15 | 0.14 | 92 | 0.86 | 79 | 0.74 |
| diarrhea | 70 | 27 | 0.39 | 28 | 0.40 | 15 | 0.21 | 7 | 0.10 | 63 | 0.90 | 44 | 0.63 |
| heartburn | 53 | 17 | 0.32 | 20 | 0.38 | 16 | 0.30 | 5 | 0.09 | 48 | 0.91 | 33 | 0.62 |
| stomatitis | 48 | 18 | 0.38 | 24 | 0.50 | 6 | 0.13 | 7 | 0.15 | 41 | 0.85 | 31 | 0.65 |
| dysbiosis | 28 | 16 | 0.57 | 6 | 0.21 | 6 | 0.21 | 2 | 0.07 | 26 | 0.93 | 14 | 0.50 |
| ILI | 24 | 7 | 0.29 | 11 | 0.46 | 6 | 0.25 | 2 | 0.08 | 22 | 0.92 | 17 | 0.71 |
| otitis | 13 | 3 | 0.23 | 4 | 0.31 | 6 | 0.46 | 5 | 0.38 | 8 | 0.62 | 9 | 0.69 |
| gastritis | 12 | 5 | 0.42 | 4 | 0.33 | 3 | 0.25 | 3 | 0.25 | 9 | 0.75 | 6 | 0.50 |
| hemorrhoids | 7 | 2 | 0.29 | 3 | 0.43 | 2 | 0.29 | 3 | 0.43 | 4 | 0.57 | 4 | 0.57 |
| **Total** | **977** | **364** | **0.37** | **382** | **0.39** | **231** | **0.24** | **166** | **0.17** | **811** | **0.83** | **589** | **0.60** |
| Random sample | 500 | 207 | 0.41 | 199 | 0.4 | 94 | 0.19 | | | | | | |

# 5  Discussion

## 5.1  Quality of Manual Assessment

After completion of the manual assessment, we reviewed the results and made certain that many labels appear inconsistent. We had a post-assessment phone interviews with most active assessors. It turned out that doctors were skeptical about the web as a source of reliable and trustworthy medical information in general. In addition, doctors perceive online media as a competitor in some sense – many patients come to doctor's appointment with a diagnosis self-established upon consulting the web. Additionally, doctors tend to rate answers containing *'consult your doctor'* advice higher.

Doctors can hardly disengage from a concrete clinical case, they assume more than is given in the question and may have an individual opinion on the effectiveness and applicability of a specific drug. In general, they tend to underrate answers following the principle *primum non nocere*. At the same time, contrary cases may occur: doctors put a non-zero score to an answer that is apparently not correct but *'will not hurt'*.

Thus, our hypothesis that we can perform a online quasi crowd-sourced evaluation with minimal investment into instructions and training of assessors is not justified. Medicine and Health is a too specific area and medical professionals are too unique to be 'averaged'. A solid preparatory work is needed even in case of a simple task like ours.

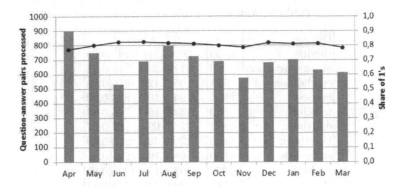

**Fig. 1.** The total number of processed question–answer pairs (bars) and the ratio of 1's (line) by month

## 5.2  Inconsistency of Automatic vs. Manual Labels

We were able to identify several typical cases when automatic assessment did not match manual labeling.

*Diagnosis shift.* The questioner describes their conditions and assumes a diagnosis; the answerer disputes it and suggests treating another illness, for example:

> **Q:** *I have a strange allergy!!! small blisters all over my body, very itchy! help!*
> **A:** *<..>If the spots break out in the area where you scratched, then you have a skin infection. <..>*

*Sentiment of drug mentions.* A medicine's mention does not necessarily mean recommendation. Spam and advertising of drugs (often belonging to alternative medicine) presented in the data are often accompanied by criticism of traditionally used drugs. Users can doubt usefulness of a drug or even warn against taking the drug, for example:

> **Q:** *How can I get rid of herpes?*
> **A:** *Aciclovir does not help me at all.*

> **Q:** *What would help my kid at [diarrhea]? (2 and a half years) A week ago took a course of antibiotics treatment*
> **A:** *<..> don't you get enough chemistry during your disease? Whatever "natural" all [Linex], [Hilak] forte, etc. are – they are produced chemically from inorganic products.*

*Multiple drugs in answer.* Binary score calculated using simple majority voting does not reflect answer quality well. Users often suggest several drugs that they believe will solve the problem comprehensively. For example, in case of herpes

**Table 5.** Automatic evaluation results

| Disease | # | 0 | | 1 | |
|---|---|---|---|---|---|
| rhinitis | 1,653 | 509 | 0.31 | 1,144 | 0.69 |
| allergy/urticaria | 926 | 211 | 0.23 | 715 | 0.77 |
| candidiasis | 771 | 95 | 0.12 | 676 | 0.88 |
| herpes | 920 | 94 | 0.10 | 826 | 0.90 |
| tonsillitis | 889 | 143 | 0.16 | 746 | 0.84 |
| diarrhea | 841 | 74 | 0.09 | 767 | 0.91 |
| heartburn | 440 | 130 | 0.30 | 310 | 0.70 |
| stomatitis | 359 | 68 | 0.19 | 291 | 0.81 |
| dysbiosis | 420 | 63 | 0.15 | 357 | 0.85 |
| ILI | 513 | 88 | 0.17 | 425 | 0.83 |
| otitis | 147 | 45 | 0.31 | 102 | 0.69 |
| gastritis | 269 | 76 | 0.28 | 193 | 0.72 |
| hemorrhoids | 137 | 22 | 0.16 | 115 | 0.84 |
| **Total:** | **8,285** | **1,618** | **0.2** | **6,667** | **0.8** |

– antiherpes cream and immunomodulators; in case of otitis – antibiotics along probiotics to fight dysbiosis as a possible side-effect of antibiotic treatment.

## 5.3   Analysis of User Opinions

Analysis of the answers shows that users tend to advise 'traditional remedies', criticizing the unnaturalness, high prices, and side effects of modern drugs. 'Old good' activated carbon and medical herbs (salvia, calendula, chamomile, etc.) are recommended as a remedy against almost every disease. Widely advertised immunomodulators developed and produced in Russia such as *kagocel* or *arbidol* are very popular in answers; although many medical professionals are skeptical about them, since there are no studies proving their effectiveness in terms of evidence-based medicine. There are also strong misconceptions about the applicability of certain drugs. For example, the advice to apply *corvalol* (barbiturate-based sedative) to herpetic blisters is quite frequent.

## 6   Conclusion

In the course of experiment, about 1,500 question–answer pairs were manually evaluated by medical professionals, which makes this study one of the largest on the subject. Evaluation data are freely available for research purposes[10]. Distribution of assessors' labels on the selected type of questions is very similar to the distribution on the randomly sampled question–answer pairs. Thus, we can assume that the selected type of questions is exemplary for the whole dataset in

---

[10] http://kansas.ru/cqa/data2/

terms of content quality. However, manual assessment results have low consistency, and we will address the issue in our future work.

In addition, automatic evaluation based on reference disease–medicine correspondence was performed. Automatic scores for the selected set of diseases are quite stable over time and do not depend on the volume of the processed data. To the best of our knowledge, the described experiment is the first attempt to automate the evaluation of community questions and answers in health-related domain. Although the results of the manual and automatic evaluations do not fully match, we find the method still promising. We see several directions that can potentially improve the automatic method:

- combination of the proposed domain-specific approach with the general approaches to CQA content evaluation described in the literature;
- application of sentiment analysis methods to detect polarity of drug mentions in answers (i.e. positive/neutral/negative);
- finer-grained selection of content items to be automatically assessed (e.g. classification of sentences into describing diseases vs. describing drugs similarly to [19]).

We will investigate the potential of the method to compare the quality of several datasets of questions and answers in health domain.

Besides the immediate task of automatic estimation of CQA content quality the proposed approach and its modifications can be applied to symptomatic surveillance, survey of drug usage, identifying common misconceptions in lay people thus guiding health education campaigns.

**Acknowledgements.** This work is partially supported by the Russian Foundation for Basic Research, project #14-07-00589 "Data Analysis and User Modelling in Narrow-Domain Social Media". We also thank assessors who volunteered for the evaluation and Mail.Ru for granting us access to the data.

# References

1. Internet kak istochnik informazii o zdorov'e, medizine i lekarstvennykh preparatakh (Internet as a source of information about health, medicine, and medication). Synovate Comcon Healthcare (April 2014), http://www.comcon-2.ru/download.asp?544
2. Adamic, L.A., Zhang, J., Bakshy, E., Ackerman, M.S.: Knowledge sharing and yahoo answers: Everyone knows something. In: Proceedings of WWW 2008, pp. 665–674 (2008)
3. Agichtein, E., Castillo, C., Donato, D., Gionis, A., Mishne, G.: Finding high-quality content in social media. In: Proceedings of WSDM 2008, pp. 183–194 (2008)
4. Agichtein, E., Liu, Y., Bian, J.: Modeling information-seeker satisfaction in community question answering. ACM Trans. Knowl. Discov. Data 3(2), 10:1–10:27 (2009)

5. Beloborodov, A., Kuznetsov, A., Braslavski, P.: Characterizing health-related community question answering. In: Serdyukov, P., Braslavski, P., Kuznetsov, S.O., Kamps, J., Rüger, S., Agichtein, E., Segalovich, I., Yilmaz, E. (eds.) ECIR 2013. LNCS, vol. 7814, pp. 680–683. Springer, Heidelberg (2013)
6. Bhattacharya, S., Tran, H., Srinivasan, P.: Discovering health beliefs in twitter. In: AAAI Fall Symposium on Information Retrieval and Knowledge Discovery in Biomedical Text (2012)
7. Cartright, M.A., White, R.W., Horvitz, E.: Intentions and attention in exploratory health search. In: Proceedings of SIGIR 2011, pp. 65–74 (2011)
8. Correa, D., Sureka, A.: Fit or unfit: Analysis and prediction of 'closed questions' on stack overflow. In: Proceedings of COSN 2013, pp. 201–212 (2013)
9. Fox, S., Duggan, M.: Health online 2013 (January 2013),
   http://www.pewinternet.org/2013/01/15/health-online-2013/
10. Harper, F.M., Moy, D., Konstan, J.A.: Facts or friends?: Distinguishing informational and conversational questions in social q&a sites. In: Proceedings of CHI 2009, pp. 759–768 (2009)
11. Kim, S., Pinkerton, T., Ganesh, N.: Assessment of h1n1 questions and answers posted on the web. American Journal of Infection Control 40(3), 211–217 (2012)
12. Lampos, V., De Bie, T., Cristianini, N.: Flu Detector - Tracking Epidemics on Twitter. In: Balcázar, J.L., Bonchi, F., Gionis, A., Sebag, M. (eds.) ECML PKDD 2010, Part III. LNCS, vol. 6323, pp. 599–602. Springer, Heidelberg (2010)
13. Lezina, G., Kuznezov, A., Braslavski, P.: Learning to predict closed questions on stack overflow. In: Proceedings of Kazan Federal University (in press, 2014)
14. Li, B., Jin, T., Lyu, M.R., King, I., Mak, B.: Analyzing and predicting question quality in community question answering services. In: Proceedings of WWW 2012 (Companion volume), pp. 775–782 (2012)
15. Mendes Rodrigues, E., Milic-Frayling, N.: Socializing or knowledge sharing?: Characterizing social intent in community question answering. In: Proceedings of CIKM 2009, pp. 1127–1136 (2009)
16. Oh, S., Worrall, A., Yi, Y.J.: Quality evaluation of health answers in yahoo! answers: A comparison between experts and users. In: Proceedings of the American Society for Information Science and Technology, vol. 48, pp. 1–3 (2011)
17. Paul, M., Dredze, M.: You are what you tweet: Analyzing twitter for public health. In: Proceedings of ICWSM 2011 (2011)
18. Shah, C., Pomerantz, J.: Evaluating and predicting answer quality in community qa. In: Proceedings of SIGIR 2010, pp. 411–418 (2010)
19. Sondhi, P., Gupta, M., Zhai, C., Hockenmaier, J.: Shallow information extraction from medical forum data. In: Proceedinhs of COLING 2010 (Posters), pp. 1158–1166 (August 2010)
20. Wong, W., Thangarajah, J., Padgham, L.: Health conversational system based on contextual matching of community-driven question-answer pairs. In: Proceedings of CIKM 2011, pp. 2577–2580 (2011)
21. Zhang, Y.: Contextualizing consumer health information searching: An analysis of questions in a social q&a community. In: Proceedings of IHI 2010, pp. 210–219 (2010)

# Rethinking How to Extend Average Precision to Graded Relevance

Marco Ferrante[1], Nicola Ferro[2], and Maria Maistro[2]

[1] Dept. of Mathematics, University of Padua, Italy
ferrante@math.unipd.it
[2] Dept. of Information Engineering, University of Padua, Italy
{ferro,maistro}@dei.unipd.it

**Abstract.** We present two new measures of retrieval effectiveness, inspired by *Graded Average Precision (GAP)*, which extends *Average Precision (AP)* to graded relevance judgements. Starting from the random choice of a user, we define *Extended Graded Average Precision (xGAP)* and *Expected Graded Average Precision (eGAP)*, which are more accurate than GAP in the case of a small number of highly relevant documents with high probability to be considered relevant by the users. The proposed measures are then evaluated on TREC 10, TREC 14, and TREC 21 collections showing that they actually grasp a different angle from GAP and that they are robust when it comes to incomplete judgments and shallow pools.

## 1 Introduction

*Average Precision (AP)* [2] is a simple and popular binary measure of retrieval effectiveness, which has been longly studied and discussed. Robertson et al. [9] proposed *Graded Average Precision (GAP)*, an extension of AP to graded relevance together with a probabilistic interpretation of it, which allows for different emphasis on different relevance grades according to user preferences.

When it comes to graded relevance judgements, the need to develop systems able to better rank highly relevant documents arises but it also poses challenges for their evaluation. Indeed, unstable results may come up due to the relatively few highly relevant documents [10] and this may become further complicated when you consider also a user model as the one of GAP, where varying importance can be attributed to highly relevant documents according to the user view point.

In this paper we propose two extensions to GAP, called *Extended Graded Average Precision (xGAP)* and *Expected Graded Average Precision (eGAP)*, which reformulate the probabilistic model behind GAP putting even more emphasis on the user and which are able to better cope with the case when the user attributes high importance to few highly relevant documents. The experimental evaluation, in terms of correlation analysis and robustness to incomplete judgments, confirms that xGAP and eGAP take a different angle from GAP when it comes to users attributing high importance to few highly relevant documents

E. Kanoulas et al. (Eds.): CLEF 2014, LNCS 8685, pp. 19–30, 2014.

and that they are robust to incomplete judgments and shallow pools, thus not requiring costly assessments. Moreover, the evaluation provides also some more insights on GAP itself, not present in its original study [9].

The paper is organized as follows: Section 2 considers the general problem of passing from binary to multi-graded relevance; Section 3 briefly recalls the GAP measure and outlines some of its possible biases; Section 4 and Section 5 introduce, respectively, the xGAP and the eGAP metrics, outlining the difference with GAP; Section 6 conducts a thorough experimental evaluation of the proposed measures; finally Section 7 draws some conclusions and provides an outlook for future work.

## 2    Mapping Binary Measures into Multi-graded Ones

Given a ranked list of $N$ documents for a given topic, we will denote by $r[j]$ the relevance of the document at the rank $j$. The relevance will be an integer belonging to $S(c) = \{0, \dots, c\}$, where 0 denotes a not relevant document and the higher the integer the higher the relevance. A measure of retrieval effectiveness will be defined *binary* if $c = 1$ and *multi-graded* if $c > 1$.

The basic binary measures of retrieval effectiveness, recall and precision, can be defined as follows $Rec[n] = \frac{\sum_{i=1}^{n} r[i]}{RB}$ and $Prec[n] = \frac{\sum_{i=1}^{n} r[i]}{n}$, where $n \leq N$ is the rank and $RB$, the recall base, is the total number of relevant documents for the given topic. As a consequence, AP can be defined as follows

$$AP = \frac{1}{RB} \sum_{n=1}^{N} r[n]Prec[n] = Rec[N] \; \frac{1}{\sum_{n=1}^{N} r[n]} \sum_{n=1}^{N} r[n]Prec[n] \; . \qquad (1)$$

The last expression highlights how AP can be derived as the product of the recall and the arithmetic mean of the precision at each relevant retrieved document.

When you have to apply these binary measures in a multi-graded context, the typical approach is to map the multi-graded judgments into binary ones according to a fixed threshold $k \geq 1$ in the grade scale and then compute the binary measure according to its definition. This approach actually leads to a family of measures depending on the threshold used to map the multi-graded relevance scale into the binary one. For example, [10] studies the effect of setting this threshold at different levels in the grade scale.

We now show how the above mentioned approach can be directly embedded into evaluation measures, further highlighting that it gives raise to a whole family of measures. Indeed, instead of mapping the judgements to binary ones and then apply a binary measures, you can make a binary measure parametric on the mapping threshold and obtain a different version of it for each threshold. Following [9], we assume that any user owns a binary vision (relevant/not-relevant document), but at a different level of relevance, which is the mapping threshold $k$. Indeed, if for a given topic we denote by $R(k)$ the total number of documents with relevance $k$, their recall base is $RB(k) = R(k) + R(k+1) + \dots + R(c)$. Note that $k \to RB(k)$ is a integer-valued, non negative and non increasing function and it is useful define $\tau := \max\{k : RB(k) > 0\}$.

There, a user with threshold $k$ defines recall as $Rec[n](k) = \frac{\sum_{i=1}^{n} r[i](k)}{RB(k)}$ if $k \leq \tau$ and 0 otherwise, precision as $Prec[n](k) = \frac{\sum_{i=1}^{n} r[i](k)}{n}$ and AP as

$$AP(k) = \frac{1}{RB(k)} \sum_{n=1}^{N} r[n](k) Prec[n](k) = \frac{1}{RB(k)} \sum_{n=1}^{N} \frac{1}{n} \left[ \sum_{m=1}^{n} \delta_{m,n}(k) \right] \qquad (2)$$

for $k \leq \tau$ and zero otherwise, where $r[n](k) = 1$ if $r[n] \geq k$, zero otherwise, and

$$\delta_{m,n}(k) = \begin{cases} 1 & \text{if } r[m] \geq k, r[n] \geq k \\ 0 & \text{otherwise} . \end{cases} \qquad (3)$$

As discussed above, this user's oriented vision leads to a family of measures, depending on the threshold $k$ chosen by each user. In order to obtain a single measure of retrieval effectiveness (and not a family), [9] assumes that the users, and so their thresholds in the grade scale, are distributed in the total population according to a given probability distribution. This opens the way to two alternative approaches to define a multi-graded measures based on user thresholds:

1. To define a new multi-graded measure whose internals are based on some expected quantities dependent on user's thresholds;
2. To evaluate the expectation of a binary measure at different user's thresholds.

GAP is defined following the first approach and in the next section we will argue that it presents some bias when few relevant documents are the only one considered relevant by a user.

To overcome this problem, we provide two solutions corresponding to the two alternative approaches above: in Section 4 we follow the first approach and introduce xGAP which defines a new multi-graded measure from scratch adopting a philosophy similar to GAP; in Section 5 we follow the second approach and introduce eGAP, which provides a new multi-graded extension of AP by taking the expectation of (2).

# 3   Graded Average Precision

Let $\Omega$ be the sample space of all the possible users and assume that a user fixes a threshold $k$ strictly positive in $S(c)$ with probability $g_k$. This can be formalized defining the threshold of a user by a random variable $K$ from $\Omega$ into $S(c)$ with distribution $(g_0, g_1, \ldots, g_c)$, where $g_0 = 0$. Using this notation, in [9] they evaluate the expected precision with respect to $g$ of each relevant document in the ranked list, then sum up all these expected values and normalise the result dividing by its maximum. Their computation leads to the following definition:

$$GAP = \frac{\sum_{n=1}^{N} \frac{1}{n} \sum_{m=1}^{n} \Delta_{m,n}}{\sum_{k=1}^{c} R(k) \sum_{j=1}^{k} g_j}, \qquad (4)$$

where $\Delta_{m,n} = \sum_{h=1}^{\min\{r[m], r[n]\}} g_h$ with the convention that $\sum_{h=1}^{0} = 0$. If $\nu = \min\{i : g_i \neq 0\}$, the previous formula is well defined just for $\nu \leq \tau$. Indeed, if

$\nu > \tau$, none of the relevant documents is considered relevant by any user almost surely and for this reason we will define $GAP = 0$ in this case. Furthermore, it is easy to prove that $\mathbb{E}[RB(K)] = \sum_{k=1}^{c} RB(k)g_k = \sum_{k=1}^{c} R(k)\sum_{j=1}^{k} g_j$, and so

$$GAP = \frac{1}{\mathbb{E}[RB(K)]} \sum_{n=1}^{N} \mathbb{E}[r[n](K)Prec[n](K)].$$

GAP can thus be obtained substituting the expected values of the graded precision and the graded recall base in (1). Note that this is quite different from taking $\mathbb{E}[AP(K)]$, where $AP(K)$ is the composition of $K$ with (2), since $RB(K)$ and $Prec[n](K)$ are not independent and, even if they were, Jensen's inequality ensures that $\mathbb{E}[1/X] < 1/\mathbb{E}[X]$ for any non trivial positive random variable $X$. This confirms that, to introduce a multi-graded measures, GAP adopts the first of the two approaches outlined in the previous section and not the second one.

[9] also defines GAP as the expectation of the following three steps random experiment: (i) select a document that is considered relevant by a user (accordingly to the user model described above) at random and let the rank of this document be $n$; (ii) select a document at or above rank $n$, at random and let the rank of that document be $m$; (iii) output 1 if the document at rank $m$ is also considered relevant by the user.

In the first step, to avoid problems for the possible absence of highly relevant documents, [9] defines the slightly artificial probability to select at random the document at rank $n$ as $\frac{\sum_{j=1}^{r[n]} g_j}{\sum_{i=1}^{c} R(i)\sum_{j=1}^{i} g_j}$. This choice leads to issues exactly in these corner cases. Indeed, consider the case where $c = 2$, $R(1) = 10$ and $R(2) = 1$. If the probabilities $g_1$ and $g_2$ are both $1/2$, we get that the probability to select one of the 10 documents of relevance 1 is equal to $1/12$, while the probability to select the only document with relevance 2 is $1/6$, that appears a reasonable set of values. However, if we increase the probability $g_2$ up to $9/10$, i.e. the unique relevant document for nine users over ten will be that of relevance 2, we get that the probability to select "at random" this document is just equal to $1/2$.

An additional bias in the definition of GAP can be observed in the following case. Let again $c = 2$ and assume that a run presents the first $n$ documents of relevance 1 and then a unique document of relevance 2, followed possibly by additional non relevant documents. It is easy to prove, that for $n$ that goes to infinity, the value of GAP tends to 1, independently from the values of $g_1$ and $g_2$. This means that, even when $g_2$ is close to 1 and the user is interested just in that highly relevant document appearing at the end of a (infinitely) long ranking, GAP will evaluate the system as approaching the performance of the ideal one instead of a very bad one.

## 4    Extended Graded Average Precision (xGAP)

To overcame the previous possible biases, we propose to define an extended version of GAP by reconsidering the "user" role in the previous three steps random experiment . So, to evaluate the probability to select at step 1 at random the document $d_n$ at rank $n$, we will assume to choose first at random a user and then to select at random among the documents considered relevant by this user. This new interpretation leads to the probability to select the document $d_n$ equal to $\sum_{k=1}^{r[n]} \frac{1}{RB(k)} g_k$ where we take into account the different size of any relevance class (recall that $\sum_{k=1}^{0} = 0$). Note that, assuming again that $R(1) = 10$ and $R(2) = 1$, for $g_1 = g_2 = 1/2$ we get here that we choose at random any of the relevance 1 documents with probability $1/22$ and the only relevance 2 document with probability $12/22$, but when $g_2 = 9/10$, the probability to select the document of relevance 2 is now $100/110$.

Following the same computation in [9] for the steps 2 and 3, we again obtain that the probability that the document $d_m$ at rank $m \leq n$ is relevant when $d_n$ is relevant, is equal to $\frac{1}{n} \frac{\sum_{m=1}^{n} \Delta_{m,n}}{\sum_{k=1}^{r[n]} g_k}$ Collecting all the previous results and changing the order of the summation we define the *Extended Graded Average Precision (xGAP)* as:

$$xGAP = \sum_{n=1}^{N} \frac{1}{n} \left[ \frac{\sum_{k=1}^{r[n]} \frac{g_k}{RB(k)}}{\sum_{k=1}^{r[n]} g_k} \left( \sum_{m=1}^{n} \Delta_{m,n} \right) \right] \tag{5}$$

when $\nu \leq \tau$ and 0 otherwise. Note that, in the case of a run with an increasing number of documents with relevance 1, followed by only one document with relevance 2, the value of xGAP as $n$ tends to infinity converges to $1 - g_2^2$, a much more reasonable value.

## 5   Expected Graded Average Precision (eGAP)

Let us now apply the second approach to define a multi-graded extension of AP. Take the function (2), compose this with the random variable $K$ that defines the relevance threshold of any user and take the expectation of this composed random variable. We will obtain the following new measure that we call *Expected Graded Average Precision (eGAP)*

$$eGAP = \mathbb{E}[AP(K)] = \sum_{n=1}^{N} \frac{1}{n} \left[ \sum_{k=1}^{\tau} \frac{g_k}{RB(k)} \left( \sum_{m=1}^{n} \delta_{m,n}(k) \right) \right] \tag{6}$$

Note that eGAP can be also thought as an approximation of the mean areas under the Precision-Recall curves at any threshold $k$.

eGAP itself can be obtained as the expectation of a random experiment. The main issue will be again how to realise the random selection of a relevant document, that we will interpret here as "select at random a user, s/he fixes a threshold and select, at random, one document relevant for this user". This approach can be expressed as a four steps random experiment, whose expectation will provide an alternative definition of eGAP: (i) select at random a user and let $k$ be his/her relevance threshold; (ii) select at random a document relevant to this user. Let its rank be $n$, if in the ranked list, or $\infty$ otherwise; (iii) in the first case, select a document at or above rank $n$ and let its rank be $m$; otherwise let the rank of this second document be $\infty$ as well; (iv) output 1 if the document at rank $m$, is also considered relevant by the user.

This differs from the random experiment used for defining GAP, because the first two steps, that we already implicitly used to derive xGAP, replace the single request to select at random a relevant document for the user. Moreover, in the fourth step the user who still considers relevant the document at rank $m$ is the same user of the first step, something that was unclear in the definition in [9].

Let us now make explicit the random experiment: for simplicity, let us assume that all relevant documents are in the ranked list, so we have not to pay attention to the case of an $\infty$ rank. The first step corresponds to define the random variable $K$ as above which takes values in $S(c)$. The second step consists in choosing a second random variable $X$, whose law conditioned by $\{K = k\}$ will be uniform on $\mathcal{R}(k) = \{j \in \{1, \ldots, N\} : r[j] \geq k\}$. In the third step we define a random variable $Y$ thanks to its conditional law given that $X = n$ and $K = k$, with $Y|X = n, K = k$ uniformly distributed on the set $\{1, 2, \ldots, n\}$. The last step means to define the Binomial random variable $Z = 1_A$, where $A = \{$the document at rank $Y$ is considered relevant by the user$\}$. "Taking the expectation" of this random experiment means evaluate $\mathbb{E}[Z]$. This can be done using the smoothing property of the conditional expectation (see e.g [8], Chapter 10) and we obtain

$$\mathbb{E}[Z] = \sum_{k=1}^{c} \Big[ \sum_{n=1}^{+\infty} \mathbb{P}[r[Y] \geq K | X = n, K = k] \, \mathbb{P}[X = n | K = k] \, g_k \Big] \tag{7}$$

As before, $\mathbb{P}[X = n | K = k] = \frac{1}{RB(k)} \, 1_{\{r[n] \geq k\}} \, g_k$ if $k \leq \tau$ and 0 otherwise, while

$$\mathbb{P}[r[Y] \geq K | X = n, K = k] = \frac{1}{n} \cdot \big| \{i \in \{1, \ldots, n\} : r[i] \geq k\} \big| = \frac{1}{n} \sum_{m=1}^{n} \delta_{m,n}(k)$$

with $\delta_{m,n}(k)$ defined in (3). Changing the order of the summation in (7), we obtain:

$$\mathbb{E}[Z] = \sum_{n=1}^{N} \frac{1}{n} \Big[ \sum_{k=1}^{\tau} \frac{g_k}{RB(k)} \Big( \sum_{m=1}^{n} \delta_{m,n}(k) \Big) \Big]$$

which is exactly eGAP. As for xGAP the way to choose a relevant document at the first step fix the bias in the definition of GAP when few highly relevant documents are present in a topic, but most of the users considers only these as relevant. Moreover, going back to the example of a run with an increasing number $n$ of low-relevance documents followed by a unique highly relevant one, as $n$ approaches $\infty$ the value of eGAP converges to $1 - g_2 = g_1$ which is again a reasonable limit value for this very special situation.

## 6    Evaluation

**Experimental Setup.** We compare our proposed measures eGAP and xGAP to GAP [9] and AP [2], which are the main focus of the paper. We also consider

**Table 1.** Main features of the adopted data sets

| Feature | TREC 10 | TREC 14 | TREC 21 |
|---|---|---|---|
| Track | Web | Robust | Web |
| Corpus | WT10g | AQUAINT | ClueWeb09 |
| # Documents | 1.7M | 1.0M | 1040.0M |
| # Topics (few highly rel/key) | 50 (17) | 50 (6) | 50 (10 / 7) |
| # Runs (above 1Q in terms of MAP) | 95 (71) | 74 (55) | 27 (20) |
| Run Length | 1,000 | 1,000 | 10,000 |
| Relevance Degrees | 3 | 3 | 4 |
| Pool Depth | 100 | 55 | 25 and 30 |
| Minimum # Relevant | 2 | 9 | 6 |
| Average # Relevant | 67.26 | 131.22 | 70.46 |
| Maximum # Relevant | 372 | 376 | 253 |

other measures of interest: *Normalized Discounted Cumulated Gain (nDCG)* [5], *Rank-Biased Precision (RBP)* [7], and, *Binary Preference (bpref)* [1].

We investigate the following aspects: (1) the correlation among measures using Kendall's tau [6,10]; (2) the robustness of the measures to incomplete judgements according to the stratified random sampling method [1].

We used the following data sets: TREC 10, 2001, Web Track [4]; TREC 14, 2005 Robust Tack [11]; and, TREC 21, 2012, Web Track [3], whose features are summarized in Table 1. For binary measures, we adopted a "lenient" mapping, i.e. every document above not relevant is considered as binary relevant. To prevent poorly performing systems from affecting the experiments, we considered only the runs above the first (lower) quartile as measured by MAP.

We explored two distinct cases: (a) considering all the topics in the collection; (b) considering only the topics for which $R(1) \geq 10 \cdot R(k), k = 2, 3$ and $R(k) \neq 0$, i.e. when there are few highly relevant/key documents with respect to the relevant ones and the bias of GAP, addressed by xGAP and eGAP, is more pronounced.

The full source code of the software used to conduct the experiments is available for download[1] in order to ease comparison and verification of the results.

**Correlation Analysis.** Table 2 reports the correlations among measures for the TREC 10 and TREC 14 collections while Table 3 reports those for the TREC 21 collection. Correlations greater than 0.9 should be considered equivalent and those "less than 0.8 generally reflect noticeable changes in rankings" [10]. GAP, xGAP, and eGAP share the same values of $g_1$ and $g_2$ (and $g_3$ in the case of TREC 21). For each measure, the n-ple $\tau_{\text{all\_topics}}/\tau_{\text{fewHRel\_topics}}$, (and also $\tau_{\text{fewKey\_topics}}$ in the case of TREC 21) is reported: the first value indicates the correlation computed considering all the topics; the second value indicates the correlation computed only on those topics with few highly relevant documents ($R(1) \geq 10 \cdot R(2)$)); and, in the case of TREC 21, the third value indicates the correlation computed only on those topics with few key documents ($R(1) \geq 10 \cdot R(3)$).

The correlation among GAP, xGAP, and eGAP is always 1 when only one $g_i = 1.00$ and the others are zero, as a consequence of the fact that in these cases,

---

[1] http://matters.dei.unipd.it/

**Table 2.** Kendall's correlation analysis for TREC 10 and TREC 14

| $(g_1, g_2)$ | TREC 10, 2001, Web | | | | | TREC 14, 2005, Robust | | | | |
|---|---|---|---|---|---|---|---|---|---|---|
| **(0.0, 1.0)** | **GAP** | **AP** | **nDCG** | **RBP** | **bpref** | **GAP** | **AP** | **nDCG** | **RBP** | **bpref** |
| GAP | 1.00/1.00 | 0.69/0.42 | 0.67/0.44 | 0.67/0.61 | 0.68/0.42 | 1.00/1.00 | 0.78/0.26 | 0.73/0.26 | 0.66/0.18 | 0.78/0.23 |
| xGAP | 1.00/1.00 | 0.69/0.42 | 0.67/0.44 | 0.67/0.61 | 0.68/0.42 | 1.00/1.00 | 0.78/0.26 | 0.73/0.26 | 0.66/0.18 | 0.78/0.23 |
| eGAP | 1.00/1.00 | 0.69/0.42 | 0.67/0.44 | 0.67/0.61 | 0.68/0.42 | 1.00/1.00 | 0.78/0.26 | 0.73/0.26 | 0.66/0.18 | 0.78/0.23 |
| **(0.1, 0.9)** | **GAP** | **AP** | **nDCG** | **RBP** | **bpref** | **GAP** | **AP** | **nDCG** | **RBP** | **bpref** |
| GAP | 1.00/1.00 | 0.84/0.80 | 0.75/0.74 | 0.64/0.67 | 0.80/0.76 | 1.00/1.00 | 0.94/0.92 | 0.84/0.76 | 0.63/0.37 | 0.79/0.74 |
| xGAP | 0.86/0.67 | 0.73/0.48 | 0.71/0.51 | 0.69/0.66 | 0.73/0.49 | 0.86/0.61 | 0.83/0.55 | 0.77/0.51 | 0.66/0.27 | 0.79/0.48 |
| eGAP | 0.85/0.64 | 0.72/0.45 | 0.70/0.47 | 0.68/0.64 | 0.72/0.45 | 0.85/0.54 | 0.82/0.49 | 0.76/0.47 | 0.67/0.27 | 0.79/0.43 |
| **(0.2, 0.8)** | **GAP** | **AP** | **nDCG** | **RBP** | **bpref** | **GAP** | **AP** | **nDCG** | **RBP** | **bpref** |
| GAP | 1.00/1.00 | 0.89/0.89 | 0.77/0.76 | 0.63/0.64 | 0.83/0.81 | 1.00/1.00 | 0.97/0.96 | 0.85/0.75 | 0.62/0.38 | 0.78/0.74 |
| xGAP | 0.84/0.64 | 0.76/0.54 | 0.73/0.56 | 0.68/0.68 | 0.75/0.54 | 0.88/0.68 | 0.86/0.65 | 0.79/0.58 | 0.67/0.29 | 0.80/0.55 |
| eGAP | 0.84/0.60 | 0.75/0.49 | 0.72/0.51 | 0.68/0.67 | 0.74/0.50 | 0.86/0.61 | 0.84/0.59 | 0.78/0.54 | 0.66/0.26 | 0.79/0.48 |
| **(0.3, 0.7)** | **GAP** | **AP** | **nDCG** | **RBP** | **bpref** | **GAP** | **AP** | **nDCG** | **RBP** | **bpref** |
| GAP | 1.00/1.00 | 0.92/0.93 | 0.78/0.77 | 0.63/0.63 | 0.84/0.82 | 1.00/1.00 | 0.98/0.98 | 0.85/0.75 | 0.62/0.38 | 0.79/0.75 |
| xGAP | 0.86/0.68 | 0.80/0.61 | 0.77/0.63 | 0.68/0.70 | 0.79/0.60 | 0.90/0.74 | 0.89/0.72 | 0.82/0.63 | 0.66/0.32 | 0.81/0.61 |
| eGAP | 0.84/0.61 | 0.78/0.54 | 0.74/0.54 | 0.68/0.69 | 0.76/0.54 | 0.89/0.68 | 0.87/0.67 | 0.81/0.60 | 0.66/0.29 | 0.80/0.53 |
| **(0.4, 0.6)** | **GAP** | **AP** | **nDCG** | **RBP** | **bpref** | **GAP** | **AP** | **nDCG** | **RBP** | **bpref** |
| GAP | 1.00/1.00 | 0.94/0.95 | 0.79/0.78 | 0.63/0.62 | 0.85/0.82 | 1.00/1.00 | 0.98/0.99 | 0.85/0.76 | 0.62/0.38 | 0.78/0.74 |
| xGAP | 0.88/0.71 | 0.83/0.66 | 0.78/0.67 | 0.68/0.70 | 0.81/0.65 | 0.93/0.80 | 0.92/0.78 | 0.83/0.69 | 0.65/0.34 | 0.80/0.66 |
| eGAP | 0.86/0.65 | 0.81/0.61 | 0.76/0.59 | 0.68/0.71 | 0.79/0.60 | 0.91/0.76 | 0.90/0.75 | 0.83/0.65 | 0.67/0.32 | 0.81/0.59 |
| **(0.5, 0.5)** | **GAP** | **AP** | **nDCG** | **RBP** | **bpref** | **GAP** | **AP** | **nDCG** | **RBP** | **bpref** |
| GAP | 1.00/1.00 | 0.95/0.97 | 0.79/0.78 | 0.62/0.61 | 0.85/0.83 | 1.00/1.00 | 0.99/0.99 | 0.85/0.76 | 0.61/0.39 | 0.78/0.74 |
| xGAP | 0.90/0.76 | 0.86/0.73 | 0.79/0.72 | 0.67/0.69 | 0.82/0.71 | 0.94/0.84 | 0.93/0.83 | 0.84/0.72 | 0.64/0.35 | 0.80/0.70 |
| eGAP | 0.88/0.70 | 0.84/0.67 | 0.77/0.64 | 0.67/0.70 | 0.81/0.65 | 0.92/0.81 | 0.92/0.81 | 0.84/0.69 | 0.65/0.35 | 0.81/0.64 |
| **(0.6, 0.4)** | **GAP** | **AP** | **nDCG** | **RBP** | **bpref** | **GAP** | **AP** | **nDCG** | **RBP** | **bpref** |
| GAP | 1.00/1.00 | 0.96/0.98 | 0.79/0.77 | 0.62/0.61 | 0.84/0.82 | 1.00/1.00 | 0.99/0.99 | 0.85/0.76 | 0.61/0.39 | 0.77/0.74 |
| xGAP | 0.92/0.83 | 0.89/0.80 | 0.80/0.76 | 0.65/0.66 | 0.83/0.76 | 0.96/0.87 | 0.95/0.86 | 0.85/0.73 | 0.64/0.35 | 0.79/0.73 |
| eGAP | 0.91/0.77 | 0.88/0.74 | 0.79/0.70 | 0.66/0.69 | 0.83/0.71 | 0.94/0.87 | 0.94/0.86 | 0.86/0.73 | 0.65/0.38 | 0.80/0.69 |
| **(0.7, 0.3)** | **GAP** | **AP** | **nDCG** | **RBP** | **bpref** | **GAP** | **AP** | **nDCG** | **RBP** | **bpref** |
| GAP | 1.00/1.00 | 0.97/0.99 | 0.79/0.77 | 0.61/0.60 | 0.85/0.82 | 1.00/1.00 | 1.00/1.00 | 0.86/0.76 | 0.61/0.39 | 0.77/0.74 |
| xGAP | 0.94/0.86 | 0.92/0.85 | 0.80/0.77 | 0.65/0.66 | 0.85/0.79 | 0.97/0.91 | 0.97/0.90 | 0.85/0.75 | 0.62/0.36 | 0.78/0.74 |
| eGAP | 0.93/0.83 | 0.90/0.82 | 0.80/0.74 | 0.65/0.67 | 0.83/0.77 | 0.97/0.90 | 0.97/0.90 | 0.86/0.76 | 0.63/0.38 | 0.79/0.71 |
| **(0.8, 0.2)** | **GAP** | **AP** | **nDCG** | **RBP** | **bpref** | **GAP** | **AP** | **nDCG** | **RBP** | **bpref** |
| GAP | 1.00/1.00 | 0.98/0.99 | 0.79/0.77 | 0.61/0.60 | 0.85/0.82 | 1.00/1.00 | 1.00/1.00 | 0.85/0.76 | 0.61/0.39 | 0.77/0.74 |
| xGAP | 0.95/0.91 | 0.94/0.90 | 0.81/0.78 | 0.64/0.63 | 0.85/0.81 | 0.98/0.94 | 0.99/0.93 | 0.86/0.75 | 0.62/0.37 | 0.78/0.74 |
| eGAP | 0.94/0.90 | 0.93/0.89 | 0.79/0.76 | 0.64/0.65 | 0.84/0.80 | 0.98/0.95 | 0.98/0.95 | 0.86/0.77 | 0.62/0.39 | 0.78/0.73 |
| **(0.9, 0.1)** | **GAP** | **AP** | **nDCG** | **RBP** | **bpref** | **GAP** | **AP** | **nDCG** | **RBP** | **bpref** |
| GAP | 1.00/1.00 | 0.99/1.00 | 0.79/0.77 | 0.61/0.60 | 0.85/0.82 | 1.00/1.00 | 1.00/1.00 | 0.86/0.76 | 0.61/0.39 | 0.77/0.74 |
| xGAP | 0.97/0.95 | 0.96/0.94 | 0.80/0.78 | 0.63/0.62 | 0.86/0.82 | 0.99/0.97 | 0.99/0.97 | 0.86/0.76 | 0.61/0.38 | 0.77/0.75 |
| eGAP | 0.97/0.95 | 0.96/0.95 | 0.79/0.77 | 0.63/0.62 | 0.85/0.82 | 1.00/0.98 | 1.00/0.98 | 0.86/0.77 | 0.61/0.39 | 0.77/0.74 |
| **(1.0, 0.0)** | **GAP** | **AP** | **nDCG** | **RBP** | **bpref** | **GAP** | **AP** | **nDCG** | **RBP** | **bpref** |
| GAP | 1.00/1.00 | 1.00/1.00 | 0.79/0.77 | 0.60/0.60 | 0.85/0.82 | 1.00/1.00 | 1.00/1.00 | 0.86/0.76 | 0.61/0.39 | 0.77/0.74 |
| xGAP | 1.00/1.00 | 1.00/1.00 | 0.79/0.77 | 0.60/0.60 | 0.85/0.82 | 1.00/1.00 | 1.00/1.00 | 0.86/0.76 | 0.61/0.39 | 0.77/0.74 |
| eGAP | 1.00/1.00 | 1.00/1.00 | 0.79/0.77 | 0.60/0.60 | 0.85/0.82 | 1.00/1.00 | 1.00/1.00 | 0.86/0.76 | 0.61/0.39 | 0.77/0.74 |

all the three measures conflate to the same value. Moreover, the correlation with AP is always 1 when $g_1 = 1.00$ and the others are zero, since this corresponds exactly to the "lenient" strategy for mapping to binary relevance, when all these measures are equal, confirming that GAP, xGAP, and eGAP actually extend AP to graded relevance.

As a general behaviour, you can note that as $g_1$ increases from zero towards one (and thus the other $g_i$ decrease correspondingly) the correlation between AP, xGAP, and eGAP increases. This is a consequence of the fact that increasing $g_1$ moves measures more and more toward the "lenient" mapping to binary relevance adopted for computing AP. For example, in TREC 10, moving from $(g_1, g_2) = (0.1, 0.9)$ and to $(g_1, g_2) = (0.3, 0.7)$ increases the correlations $\tau_{AP,xGAP} = 0.73$ and $\tau_{AP,eGAP} = 0.72$ to $\tau_{AP,xGAP} = 0.80$ and $\tau_{AP,eGAP} = 0.78$; similarly, in TREC 21, moving from $(g_1, g_2, g_3) = (0.2, 0.2, 0.6)$ to $(g_1, g_2, g_3) = (0.4, 0.2, 0.4)$ increases the correlations $\tau_{AP,xGAP} = 0.62$ and $\tau_{AP,eGAP} = 0.61$ to $\tau_{AP,xGAP} = 0.83$ and $\tau_{AP,eGAP} = 0.82$. In a similar fashion, as $g_1$ increases, also the correlation between GAP xGAP and eGAP increases, as an effect of the flattening towards a "lenient" mapping to binary relevance.

**Table 3.** Kendall's tau correlation analysis for TREC 21

| $(g_1, g_2, g_3)$ | TREC 21, 2012, Web | | | | |
|---|---|---|---|---|---|
| **(0.0, 0.0, 1.0)** | **GAP** | **AP** | **nDCG** | **RBP** | **bpref** |
| **GAP** | 1.00/1.00/1.00 | 0.41/0.49/-0.15 | 0.25/0.36/-0.12 | 0.58/0.57/-0.39 | 0.26/0.02/-0.18 |
| **xGAP** | 1.00/1.00/1.00 | 0.41/0.49/-0.15 | 0.25/0.36/-0.12 | 0.58/0.57/-0.39 | 0.26/0.02/-0.18 |
| **eGAP** | 1.00/1.00/1.00 | 0.41/0.49/-0.15 | 0.25/0.36/-0.12 | 0.58/0.57/-0.39 | 0.26/0.02/-0.18 |
| **(0.0, 0.2, 0.8)** | **GAP** | **AP** | **nDCG** | **RBP** | **bpref** |
| **GAP** | 1.00/1.00/1.00 | 0.49/0.53/0.13 | 0.19/0.35/0.09 | 0.81/0.59/-0.03 | 0.34/0.06/-0.09 |
| **xGAP** | 0.68/0.99/0.54 | 0.44/0.54/-0.04 | 0.22/0.36/-0.05 | 0.63/0.57/-0.26 | 0.27/0.06/-0.24 |
| **eGAP** | 0.65/0.99/0.51 | 0.44/0.54/-0.05 | 0.23/0.36/-0.02 | 0.61/0.58/-0.25 | 0.28/0.07/-0.23 |
| **(0.0, 0.4, 0.6)** | **GAP** | **AP** | **nDCG** | **RBP** | **bpref** |
| **GAP** | 1.00/1.00/1.00 | 0.52/0.52/0.15 | 0.14/0.34/0.12 | 0.82/0.61/-0.07 | 0.34/0.04/-0.07 |
| **xGAP** | 0.79/0.99/0.67 | 0.53/0.53/-0.01 | 0.28/0.35/0.00 | 0.78/0.60/-0.23 | 0.36/0.06/-0.19 |
| **eGAP** | 0.77/0.98/0.75 | 0.51/0.54/0.02 | 0.28/0.36/0.01 | 0.76/0.59/-0.22 | 0.35/0.06/-0.18 |
| **(0.0, 0.6, 0.4)** | **GAP** | **AP** | **nDCG** | **RBP** | **bpref** |
| **GAP** | 1.00/1.00/1.00 | 0.51/0.48/0.15 | 0.13/0.31/0.12 | 0.81/0.58/-0.07 | 0.33/0.01/-0.07 |
| **xGAP** | 0.89/0.98/0.74 | 0.51/0.51/0.03 | 0.20/0.33/0.00 | 0.83/0.58/-0.21 | 0.34/0.03/-0.17 |
| **eGAP** | 0.85/0.96/0.79 | 0.47/0.53/0.06 | 0.20/0.35/0.03 | 0.85/0.58/-0.20 | 0.31/0.05/-0.16 |
| **(0.0, 0.8, 0.2)** | **GAP** | **AP** | **nDCG** | **RBP** | **bpref** |
| **GAP** | 1.00/1.00/1.00 | 0.52/0.46/0.14 | 0.13/0.28/0.13 | 0.81/0.52/-0.04 | 0.33/-0.01/-0.06 |
| **xGAP** | 0.98/0.97/0.85 | 0.54/0.45/0.07 | 0.15/0.27/0.04 | 0.83/0.53/-0.15 | 0.33/-0.02/-0.13 |
| **eGAP** | 0.97/0.96/0.89 | 0.52/0.44/0.09 | 0.14/0.26/0.08 | 0.82/0.54/-0.13 | 0.32/-0.03/-0.11 |
| **(0.0, 1.0, 0.0)** | **GAP** | **AP** | **nDCG** | **RBP** | **bpref** |
| **GAP** | 1.00/1.00/1.00 | 0.49/0.48/0.15 | 0.11/0.28/0.14 | 0.79/0.52/-0.05 | 0.31/-0.01/-0.05 |
| **xGAP** | 1.00/1.00/1.00 | 0.49/0.48/0.15 | 0.11/0.28/0.14 | 0.79/0.52/-0.05 | 0.31/-0.01/-0.05 |
| **eGAP** | 1.00/1.00/1.00 | 0.49/0.48/0.15 | 0.11/0.28/0.14 | 0.79/0.52/-0.05 | 0.31/-0.01/-0.05 |
| **(0.2, 0.0, 0.8)** | **GAP** | **AP** | **nDCG** | **RBP** | **bpref** |
| **GAP** | 1.00/1.00/1.00 | 0.96/0.89/0.98 | 0.59/0.63/0.80 | 0.41/0.57/0.61 | 0.75/0.36/0.69 |
| **xGAP** | 0.60/0.79/0.28 | 0.58/0.71/0.28 | 0.37/0.53/0.27 | 0.64/0.59/-0.02 | 0.43/0.15/0.08 |
| **eGAP** | 0.59/0.73/0.23 | 0.57/0.66/0.23 | 0.37/0.46/0.22 | 0.63/0.61/-0.05 | 0.40/0.08/0.03 |
| **(0.2, 0.2, 0.6)** | **GAP** | **AP** | **nDCG** | **RBP** | **bpref** |
| **GAP** | 1.00/1.00/1.00 | 0.94/0.89/0.94 | 0.57/0.61/0.74 | 0.43/0.59/0.67 | 0.73/0.34/0.63 |
| **xGAP** | 0.64/0.79/0.27 | 0.62/0.72/0.34 | 0.38/0.54/0.33 | 0.68/0.58/0.05 | 0.45/0.16/0.14 |
| **eGAP** | 0.63/0.75/0.24 | 0.61/0.67/0.31 | 0.35/0.47/0.29 | 0.71/0.62/-0.02 | 0.44/0.11/0.11 |
| **(0.2, 0.4, 0.4)** | **GAP** | **AP** | **nDCG** | **RBP** | **bpref** |
| **GAP** | 1.00/1.00/1.00 | 0.91/0.87/0.93 | 0.54/0.61/0.75 | 0.46/0.61/0.66 | 0.69/0.29/0.62 |
| **xGAP** | 0.68/0.83/0.34 | 0.61/0.73/0.40 | 0.31/0.55/0.35 | 0.72/0.59/0.10 | 0.44/0.17/0.18 |
| **eGAP** | 0.72/0.78/0.22 | 0.64/0.65/0.27 | 0.29/0.47/0.24 | 0.73/0.62/-0.03 | 0.47/0.16/0.05 |
| **(0.2, 0.6, 0.2)** | **GAP** | **AP** | **nDCG** | **RBP** | **bpref** |
| **GAP** | 1.00/1.00/1.00 | 0.90/0.87/0.92 | 0.51/0.61/0.76 | 0.49/0.61/0.65 | 0.69/0.29/0.63 |
| **xGAP** | 0.66/0.87/0.33 | 0.56/0.77/0.37 | 0.23/0.59/0.34 | 0.77/0.55/0.11 | 0.37/0.21/0.17 |
| **eGAP** | 0.73/0.77/0.32 | 0.63/0.65/0.38 | 0.26/0.47/0.33 | 0.74/0.57/0.07 | 0.44/0.16/0.16 |
| **(0.2, 0.8, 0.0)** | **GAP** | **AP** | **nDCG** | **RBP** | **bpref** |
| **GAP** | 1.00/1.00/1.00 | 0.89/0.86/0.95 | 0.51/0.60/0.79 | 0.49/0.60/0.62 | 0.68/0.28/0.66 |
| **xGAP** | 0.72/0.84/0.35 | 0.61/0.71/0.36 | 0.22/0.53/0.33 | 0.78/0.51/0.09 | 0.40/0.15/0.16 |
| **eGAP** | 0.73/0.69/0.34 | 0.62/0.58/0.35 | 0.23/0.38/0.32 | 0.77/0.51/0.11 | 0.41/0.08/0.15 |
| **(0.4, 0.0, 0.6)** | **GAP** | **AP** | **nDCG** | **RBP** | **bpref** |
| **GAP** | 1.00/1.00/1.00 | 0.97/0.93/0.99 | 0.60/0.64/0.79 | 0.40/0.56/0.62 | 0.76/0.37/0.68 |
| **xGAP** | 0.79/0.87/0.59 | 0.78/0.82/0.60 | 0.58/0.64/0.55 | 0.46/0.54/0.27 | 0.63/0.26/0.38 |
| **eGAP** | 0.80/0.82/0.46 | 0.79/0.77/0.47 | 0.53/0.57/0.42 | 0.53/0.61/0.17 | 0.62/0.19/0.27 |
| **(0.4, 0.2, 0.4)** | **GAP** | **AP** | **nDCG** | **RBP** | **bpref** |
| **GAP** | 1.00/1.00/1.00 | 0.97/0.94/0.96 | 0.60/0.63/0.76 | 0.40/0.57/0.65 | 0.76/0.36/0.65 |
| **xGAP** | 0.82/0.88/0.56 | 0.83/0.82/0.61 | 0.53/0.64/0.55 | 0.52/0.54/0.27 | 0.66/0.26/0.39 |
| **eGAP** | 0.81/0.85/0.52 | 0.82/0.79/0.56 | 0.47/0.59/0.50 | 0.57/0.60/0.24 | 0.65/0.21/0.36 |
| **(0.4, 0.4, 0.2)** | **GAP** | **AP** | **nDCG** | **RBP** | **bpref** |
| **GAP** | 1.00/1.00/1.00 | 0.97/0.93/0.96 | 0.58/0.63/0.76 | 0.42/0.58/0.65 | 0.76/0.35/0.65 |
| **xGAP** | 0.81/0.89/0.58 | 0.80/0.83/0.62 | 0.47/0.65/0.55 | 0.55/0.53/0.32 | 0.61/0.27/0.38 |
| **eGAP** | 0.81/0.87/0.61 | 0.78/0.80/0.65 | 0.41/0.60/0.56 | 0.61/0.58/0.31 | 0.59/0.22/0.43 |
| **(0.4, 0.6, 0.0)** | **GAP** | **AP** | **nDCG** | **RBP** | **bpref** |
| **GAP** | 1.00/1.00/1.00 | 0.97/0.93/0.96 | 0.58/0.62/0.76 | 0.42/0.58/0.65 | 0.76/0.35/0.65 |
| **xGAP** | 0.76/0.89/0.63 | 0.73/0.82/0.65 | 0.34/0.62/0.58 | 0.66/0.54/0.33 | 0.52/0.24/0.41 |
| **eGAP** | 0.81/0.82/0.54 | 0.78/0.77/0.56 | 0.39/0.55/0.48 | 0.61/0.55/0.29 | 0.57/0.17/0.36 |
| **(0.6, 0.0, 0.4)** | **GAP** | **AP** | **nDCG** | **RBP** | **bpref** |
| **GAP** | 1.00/1.00/1.00 | 0.97/0.97/1.00 | 0.60/0.62/0.80 | 0.40/0.56/0.61 | 0.76/0.37/0.69 |
| **xGAP** | 0.87/0.94/0.81 | 0.88/0.91/0.81 | 0.60/0.66/0.76 | 0.44/0.56/0.44 | 0.74/0.35/0.59 |
| **eGAP** | 0.89/0.92/0.82 | 0.91/0.88/0.82 | 0.56/0.62/0.75 | 0.48/0.60/0.45 | 0.74/0.31/0.62 |
| **(0.6, 0.2, 0.2)** | **GAP** | **AP** | **nDCG** | **RBP** | **bpref** |
| **GAP** | 1.00/1.00/1.00 | 0.98/0.96/0.98 | 0.59/0.61/0.78 | 0.41/0.57/0.63 | 0.77/0.36/0.67 |
| **xGAP** | 0.89/0.88/0.82 | 0.89/0.86/0.84 | 0.55/0.68/0.79 | 0.47/0.54/0.45 | 0.71/0.31/0.62 |
| **eGAP** | 0.91/0.91/0.84 | 0.91/0.86/0.86 | 0.56/0.60/0.77 | 0.48/0.62/0.47 | 0.74/0.28/0.64 |
| **(0.6, 0.4, 0.0)** | **GAP** | **AP** | **nDCG** | **RBP** | **bpref** |
| **GAP** | 1.00/1.00/1.00 | 0.98/0.96/0.97 | 0.59/0.61/0.77 | 0.41/0.57/0.65 | 0.77/0.36/0.66 |
| **xGAP** | 0.91/0.88/0.80 | 0.91/0.86/0.83 | 0.52/0.65/0.74 | 0.48/0.54/0.48 | 0.69/0.28/0.59 |
| **eGAP** | 0.89/0.87/0.79 | 0.87/0.85/0.80 | 0.48/0.59/0.68 | 0.52/0.61/0.47 | 0.66/0.25/0.58 |
| **(0.8, 0.0, 0.2)** | **GAP** | **AP** | **nDCG** | **RBP** | **bpref** |
| **GAP** | 1.00/1.00/1.00 | 0.99/0.99/1.00 | 0.60/0.60/0.80 | 0.40/0.56/0.61 | 0.78/0.37/0.69 |
| **xGAP** | 0.97/0.94/0.93 | 0.96/0.93/0.93 | 0.61/0.66/0.83 | 0.41/0.54/0.54 | 0.79/0.35/0.66 |
| **eGAP** | 0.98/0.93/0.96 | 0.97/0.92/0.96 | 0.62/0.63/0.82 | 0.42/0.59/0.56 | 0.80/0.34/0.69 |
| **(0.8, 0.2, 0.0)** | **GAP** | **AP** | **nDCG** | **RBP** | **bpref** |
| **GAP** | 1.00/1.00/1.00 | 0.99/0.98/0.99 | 0.60/0.60/0.79 | 0.40/0.56/0.62 | 0.78/0.35/0.68 |
| **xGAP** | 0.97/0.91/0.94 | 0.96/0.91/0.95 | 0.57/0.64/0.81 | 0.43/0.56/0.56 | 0.75/0.33/0.66 |
| **eGAP** | 0.95/0.91/0.96 | 0.94/0.91/0.97 | 0.55/0.58/0.81 | 0.45/0.62/0.60 | 0.73/0.28/0.68 |
| **(1.0, 0.0, 0.0)** | **GAP** | **AP** | **nDCG** | **RBP** | **bpref** |
| **GAP** | 1.00/1.00/1.00 | 1.00/1.00/1.00 | 0.61/0.59/0.80 | 0.41/0.57/0.61 | 0.79/0.36/0.69 |
| **xGAP** | 1.00/1.00/1.00 | 1.00/1.00/1.00 | 0.61/0.59/0.80 | 0.41/0.57/0.61 | 0.79/0.36/0.69 |
| **eGAP** | 1.00/1.00/1.00 | 1.00/1.00/1.00 | 0.61/0.59/0.80 | 0.41/0.57/0.61 | 0.79/0.36/0.69 |

The biases introduced in GAP and discussed in Section 3 become evident by looking at the correlation between GAP and AP. As soon as some weight is provided on $g_1$, the correlation between GAP and AP suddenly becomes quite high, even if it should not, since a low $g_1$ corresponds to a "hard" mapping strategy to binary relevance (all but highly relevant/key documents are considered not relevant) which is the opposite from the "lenient" one adopted for computing AP. For example, with $(g_1, g_2) = (0.1, 0.9)$ we have $\tau_{AP,GAP} = 0.84$ in TREC 10 and $\tau_{AP,GAP} = 0.94$ in TREC 14, which are already extremely high; while with $(g_1, g_2, g_3) = (0.2, 0.2, 0.6)$ we have $\tau_{AP,GAP} = 0.94$ in TREC 21. This indicates that GAP tends to overestimate the weight of $g_1$ and to saturate the ranking. On the other hand, for the same parameters, we have $\tau_{AP,xGAP} = 0.73$ and $\tau_{AP,eGAP} = 0.72$ in TREC 10, $\tau_{AP,xGAP} = 0.83$ and $\tau_{AP,eGAP} = 0.82$ in TREC 14, and $\tau_{AP,xGAP} = 0.62$ and $\tau_{AP,eGAP} = 0.61$ in TREC 21, which indicate how the weights $g_i$ assigned by the user are more correctly taken into account.

This effect is even more exacerbated when you consider the topics with few highly relevant / key documents. For example, with $(g_1, g_2) = (0.1, 0.9)$, in TREC 10 the correlation $\tau_{AP,GAP} = 0.84$ on all topics is quite similar to the correlation $\tau_{AP,GAP} = 0.80$ on topics with few highly relevant documents, indicating a lack of sensitivity of GAP to this important case and its flattening on AP. On the other hand, the correlations for xGAP and eGAP fall from $\tau_{AP,xGAP} = 0.73$ and $\tau_{AP,eGAP} = 0.72$ to $\tau_{AP,xGAP} = 0.48$ and $\tau_{AP,eGAP} = 0.45$, indicating that they treat the case when the user attributes more weight ($g_2$ high) to the few high relevant documents quite differently from AP, which flattens out everything with a "lenient" mapping to binary relevance. Similar behaviors can be observed also in the case of TREC 14 and TREC 21.

The correlation with nDCG, the only other graded measure, increases as the value of $g_1$ increases, i.e. the more you move away from an "hard" strategy for mapping to binary relevance. Moreover, in the case of topics with few highly relevant / key documents and with a low $g_1$, the correlation between GAP and nDCG is always higher than the one between xGAP/eGAP and nDCG, indicating that both GAP and nDCG are less sensitive to this case.

**Robustness to Incomplete Judgments.** The *stratified random sampling* of the pools allows us to investigate the behavior of the measures as relevance judgment sets become less complete following the methodology presented in [1], which is here adapted to the case of multi-graded relevance.

The plots in Figure 1 and 2 show the Kendall's tau correlations between the system rankings produced using progressively down-sampled pools from 100% (complete pool) to 5%. Each line shows the behavior of a measure; the flatter (and closer to 1.0) the line, the more robust the measure. In fact, a flat line indicates that the measure continues to rank systems in the same relative order with different levels of relevance judgments incompleteness. In this respect, nDCG and bpref exhibit the best behaviour.

As an example of the main case of interest in the paper ($g_1$ low), when all the topics are considered (Figure 1, on the left), xGAP and eGAP behave similarly to GAP for TREC 10 and 14, even if they improve for quite shallow pools (10%

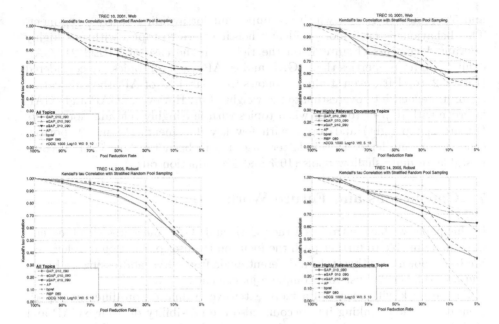

**Fig. 1.** Kendall's rank correlation at pool reduction rates on TREC 10 (top row) and TREC 14 (bottom row) for all topics (left) and topics with few highly relevant documents (right). GAP, xGAP, and eGAP with $(g_1, g_2) = (0.1, 0.9)$.

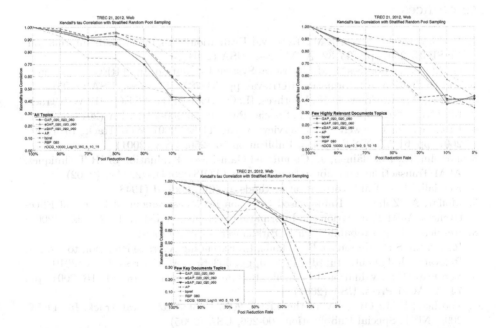

**Fig. 2.** Kendall's rank correlation at pool reduction rates on TREC 21 for all topics (top left), topics with few highly relevant documents (top right), and topics with few key documents (bottom center). GAP, xGAP, and eGAP with $(g_1, g_2, g_3) = (0.2, 0.2, 0.6)$.

and 5% reduction rates), which are important for avoiding costly assessment. This behaviour is even more evident when it comes to topics with few highly relevant documents (Figure 1, on the right). In the case of TREC 21, GAP exhibits better properties than xGAP and eGAP when all topics are considered (Figure 2, top left), even it almost follows the behaviour of AP, thus indicating again its tendence to overestimate the weight of $g_1$. However, xGAP and eGAP improve with respect to GAP when topics with few highly relevant documents (Figure 2, top right) and topics with few key documents (Figure 2, bottom center) are considered; in this latter case, it can be noted how GAP become unstable for quite shallow pools (10% and 5% reduction rates).

## 7  Conclusions and Future Work

In this paper we have introduced the xGAP and eGAP measures which extend GAP and are able to further push the focus on the user perception of relevance. We have shown how they take a different angle from GAP addressing its biases and how they are robust to incomplete judgements.

Future work will consist of a more extensive evaluation on different experimental collections, taking into account also the possibility of using xGAP and eGAP as objective metric for learning to rank algorithms, as well as exploring their discriminative power.

## References

1. Buckley, C., Voorhees, E.M.: Retrieval Evaluation with Incomplete Information. In: SIGIR 2007, pp. 25–32. ACM Press, USA (2004)
2. Buckley, C., Voorhees, E.M.: Retrieval System Evaluation. In: TREC. Experiment and Evaluation in Information Retrieval, pp. 53–78. MIT Press, USA (2005)
3. Clarke, C.L.A., Craswell, N., Voorhees, H.: Overview of the TREC 2012 Web Track. In: TREC 2012, pp. 1–8. NIST, Special Publication 500-298, USA (2013)
4. Hawking, D., Craswell, N.: Overview of the TREC-2001 Web Track. In TREC 2001, pp. 61–67. NIST, Special Publication 500-250, USA (2001)
5. Järvelin, K., Kekäläinen, J.: Cumulated Gain-Based Evaluation of IR Techniques. ACM Transactions on Information Systems (TOIS) 20(4), 422–446 (2002)
6. Kendall, M.G.: Rank correlation methods. Griffin, Oxford (1948)
7. Moffat, A., Zobel, J.: Rank-biased Precision for Measurement of Retrieval Effectiveness. ACM Transactions on Information Systems (TOIS) 27(1), 2:1–2:27 (2008)
8. Resnick, S.I.: A Probability Path. Birkhäuser, Boston (2005)
9. Robertson, S.E., Kanoulas, E., Yilmaz, E.: Extending Average Precision to Graded Relevance Judgments. In: SIGIR 2010, pp. 603–610. ACM Press, USA (2010)
10. Voorhees, E.: Evaluation by Highly Relevant Documents. In: SIGIR 2001, pp. 74–82. ACM Press, USA (2001)
11. Voorhees, E.M.: Overview of the TREC 2005 Robust Retrieval Track. In: TREC 2005. NIST, Special Pubblication 500-266, USA (2005)

# CLEF 15<sup>th</sup> Birthday:
# What Can We Learn From Ad Hoc Retrieval?

Nicola Ferro and Gianmaria Silvello

University of Padua, Italy
{ferro,silvello}@dei.unipd.it

**Abstract.** This paper reports the outcomes of a longitudinal study on the CLEF Ad Hoc track in order to assess its impact on the effectiveness of monolingual, bilingual and multilingual information access and retrieval systems. Monolingual retrieval shows a positive trend, even if the performance increase is not always steady from year to year; bilingual retrieval has demonstrated higher improvements in recent years, probably due to the better linguistic resources now available; and, multilingual retrieval exhibits constant improvement and performances comparable to bilingual (and, sometimes, even monolingual) ones.

## 1 Motivations and Approach

Experimental evaluation has been a key driver for research and innovation in the information retrieval field since its inception. Large-scale evaluation campaigns such as Text REtrieval Conference (TREC)[1], Conference and Labs of Evaluation Forum (CLEF)[2], NII Testbeds and Community for Information access Research (NTCIR)[3], and Forum for Information Retrieval Evaluation (FIRE)[4] are known to act as catalysts for research by offering carefully designed evaluation tasks for different domains and use cases and, over the years, to have provided both qualitative and quantitative evidence about which algorithms, techniques and approaches are most effective. In addition, the evaluation campaigns have played a key role in the development of researcher and developer communities with multidisciplinary competences as well as in the development of linguistic resources and information retrieval systems.

As a consequence, some attempts have been made to determine their impact. For example, in 2010 an assessment of the economic impact of TREC pointed out that "for every $1 that NIST and its partners invested in TREC, at least $3.35 to $5.07 in benefits accrued to IR researchers. The internal rate of return (IRR) was estimated to be over 250% for extrapolated benefits and over 130% for unextrapolated benefits" [11, p. ES-9]. The bibliometric impact and its effect on scientific production and literature has been studied both for TRECVid [17] and CLEF [18,19], showing how influential evaluation campaigns are.

---

[1] http://trec.nist.gov/
[2] http://www.clef-initiative.eu/
[3] http://research.nii.ac.jp/ntcir/
[4] http://www.isical.ac.in/~fire/

E. Kanoulas et al. (Eds.): CLEF 2014, LNCS 8685, pp. 31–43, 2014.

However, in the literature there have been few systematic longitudinal studies about the impact of evaluation campaigns on the overall effectiveness of Information Retrieval (IR) systems. One of the most relevant works compared the performances of eight versions of the SMART system on eight different TREC ad-hoc tasks (i.e. TREC-1 to TREC-8) and showed that the performances of the SMART system has doubled in eight years [5]. On the other hand, these results "are only conclusive for the SMART system itself" [20] and this experiment is not easy to reproduce in the CLEF context because we would need to use different versions of one or more systems – e.g. a monolingual, a bilingual and a multilingual system – and to test them on many collections for a great number of tasks. Furthermore, today's systems increasingly rely on-line linguistic resources (e.g. MT systems, Wikipedia, on-line dictionaries) which continuously change over time, thus preventing comparable longitudinal studies even when using the same systems.

Therefore, the goal of this paper is to carry out a longitudinal study on the Ad-Hoc track of CLEF in order to understand its impact on monolingual, bilingual, and multilingual retrieval.

To this end, we adopt the score standardization methodology proposed in [20] which allows us to carry out inter-collection comparison between systems by limiting the effect of collections (i.e. corpora of documents, topics and relevance judgments) and by making system scores interpretable in themselves. Standardization directly adjusts topic scores by the observed mean score and standard deviation for that topic in a sample of the systems. Let us say that topic $t$ has mean $\mu_t = \bar{M}_{*t}$ and standard deviation $\sigma_t = sd(\bar{M}_{*t})$ for a given measure over a sample of systems and that system $s$ receives a score $m_{st}$ for that topic. Then, the standardized score $m'_{st}$ (i.e. the *z-score* of $m_{st}$) is:

$$m'_{st} = \frac{m_{st} - \mu_t}{\sigma_t} \tag{1.1}$$

The z-score is directly informative in a way the unstandardized score is not: "one can tell directly from a runs score whether the system has performed well for the topic" [20]. Given that standardized scores are centered around zero and unbounded, whereas the majority of IR measures are in the interval $[0, 1]$, we map z-scores in this range by adopting the cumulative density function of the standard normal distribution; this also has the effect of reducing the influence of outlier data points:

$$F_X(m') = \int_{-\infty}^{m'} \frac{1}{\sqrt{2\pi}} e^{-x^2/2} dx \tag{1.2}$$

For this study we apply standardization to Average Precision (AP) calculated for all the runs submitted to the ad-hoc tracks of CLEF (i.e. monolingual, bilingual and multilingual tasks from 2000 to 2007) and to The European Library (TEL) tracks (i.e. monolingual and bilingual tasks from 2008 to 2009). In order to use reliable standardization factors we do not consider the tasks for which less than 9 valid runs have been submitted; we consider a run as valid if it retrieves documents for each topic of the collection. In the following we indicate with sMAP the mean of the standardized AP.

All the CLEF results that we analysed in this paper are available through the Distributed Information Retrieval Evaluation Campaign Tool (DIRECT) system[5] [2]; the software library (i.e. MATTERS) used for calculating measure standardization as well as for analysing the performances of the systems is publicly available at the URL: http://matters.dei.unipd.it/.

The paper is organized as follows: Section 2 introduces the research questions we are investigating and provides a very short summary of the main findings for each of them; Section 3 reports the outcomes of our analyses and detailed answers to the research questions; finally, Section 4 outlines possible future directions for continuing these kinds of studies.

## 2    Research Questions

In this section we summarize the four research questions we tackle in this paper by reporting a brief insight of our findings.

**RQ1. Do performances of monolingual systems increase over the years? Are more recent systems better than older ones?**

From the analysis of sMAP across monolingual tasks we can see an improvement of performances, even if it is not always steady from year to year. The best systems are rarely the most recent ones; this may be due to a tendency towards tuning well performing systems relying on established techniques in the early years of a task while focusing on understanding and experimenting new techniques and methodologies in later years. In general, the assumption for which the life of a task is summarized by increase in system performances, plateau and termination oversimplifies reality: researchers and developers an not just incrementally adding new pieces on existing algorithms, rather they often explore completely new ways or add new components to the systems, causing a temporary drop in performances. Thus, we do not have a steady increase but rather a general positive trend.

**RQ2. Do performances of bilingual systems increase over the years and what is the impact of source languages?**

System performances in bilingual tasks show a growing trend across the years although it is not always steady and it depends on the number of submitted runs as well as on the number of newcomers. The best systems for bilingual tasks are often the more recent ones showing the importance of advanced linguistic resources that become available and improved over the years. Source languages have a high impact on the performances of a given target language, showing that some combinations are better performing than others – e.g. Spanish to Portuguese has a higher median sMAP than German to Portuguese.

---

[5] http://direct.dei.unipd.it/

**RQ3. Do performances of multilingual systems increase over the years?**

Multilingual systems show a steady growing trend of performances over the years despite the variations in target and source languages from task to task.

**RQ4. Do monolingual systems have better performances than bilingual and multilingual systems?**

Systems which operate on monolingual tasks prove to be more performing than bilingual ones in most cases, even if the difference between top monolingual and top bilingual systems reduces year after year and sometimes the ratio is even inverted. In some cases, multilingual systems turn out to have higher performances than bilingual ones and the top multilingual system has the highest sMAP of all the systems which participated in CLEF tasks from 2000 to 2009: the work done for dealing with the complexity of multilingual tasks pays off in terms of overall performances of the multilingual systems.

## 3   Experimental Analysis

**RQ1. Do performances of monolingual systems increase over the years? Are more recent systems better than older ones?**

With regard to monolingual tasks, there is no clear trend showing a steady improvement of sMAP over the years – see Figure 1 and Table 1. Figure 1 reports the median sMAP for all the monolingual tasks of CLEF for which more than nine valid runs were submitted; we can see that a more evident improvement over the years is shown by the languages introduced in 2004 [6] and 2005 [7]: Bulgarian, Hungarian and Portuguese – see Figure 2 where the median for Portuguese and Hungarian of the last year is higher than in the first year of the tasks. We can see that both for Portuguese and Hungarian the distribution of scores spreads out overs the years as far as the number of submitted runs and newcomers increase; on the other hand, the best system for Hungarian participated in the last year this task was performed (2007), whereas the best system for Portuguese participated in the first year of the task (2004) and it was outperformed afterwards.

The same trend is clear for French and German in the TEL tasks showing that monolingual retrieval in these languages over bibliographical records improved from 2008 [1] to 2009 [8] – see also Table 1. Note that for the TEL monolingual tasks the median increased over the years, whereas the best system participated, for both the languages, in the first year of the task. Furthermore, both for French and German, the best system for the ad-hoc tasks outperforms the best system for the TEL ones (i.e. 0.8309 versus 0.7388 for German and 0.8257 versus 0.7242 for French).

By contrast, examining the median sMAP of the monolingual tasks from 2000 to 2009 shows several examples of languages for which performances decrease – e.g. Dutch, Spanish and Italian. A closer analysis shows that for these languages the number of research groups along with the number of newcomers participating

**Table 1.** Statistics of the CLEF bilingual tasks started in 2000 or 2001

| Task | Year | Groups(new) | Runs | Best sMAP | Median sMAP |
|---|---|---|---|---|---|
| AH Bili DE | 2002 | 6(-) | 13 | .6674 (-) | .5340 (-) |
| TEL Bili DE | 2008 | 6(4) | 17 | .6268 (-6,08%) | .4599 (-13.88%) |
| | 2009 | 6(3) | 26 | **.7179** (14.53%) | .4731 (+2.87%) |
| AH Bili EN | 2000 | 10(-) | 26 | .7463 (-) | .5196 (-) |
| | 2001 | 19(15) | 55 | .7725 (+3.51%) | .5618 (+8.12%) |
| | 2002 | 5(3) | 16 | .6983 (-9.60%) | .4524 (-19.47%) |
| | 2003 | 3(3) | 15 | .6980 (-0.04%) | .4074 (-9.95%) |
| | 2004 | 4(4) | 11 | .5895 (-15.54%) | .5251 (+28.89%) |
| | 2005 | 8(8) | 31 | **.7845** (+33.08%) | **.5667** (+7.92%) |
| | 2006 | 5(4) | 32 | .7559 (-3.64%) | .4808 (-15.16%) |
| | 2007 | 10(9) | 67 | .7746 (+2.47%) | .4835 (0.56%) |
| TEL Bili EN | 2008 | 8(7) | 24 | .7611 (-1,74%) | .5382 (+11.31%) |
| | 2009 | 10(7) | 43 | .7808 (2.59%) | .4719 (-12.32%) |
| AH Bili ES | 2002 | 7(-) | 16 | **.6805** (-) | .4969 (-) |
| | 2003 | 9(7) | 15 | .6737 (-1.01%) | **.5394** (+8.55%) |
| AH Bili FR | 2002 | 7(-) | 14 | .6708 (-) | .5647 (-) |
| | 2004 | 7(5) | 24 | .6015 (-10.33%) | .5211 (-7.72%) |
| | 2005 | 9(8) | 31 | **.7250** (+20.53%) | **.5703** (+9.44%) |
| | 2006 | 4(3) | 12 | .6273 (-13.47%) | .4886 (-14.33%) |
| TEL Bili FR | 2008 | 5(5) | 15 | .6358 (+1,35%) | .4422 (-9.50%) |
| | 2009 | 6(4) | 23 | .7151 (+12.47%) | .4355 (-1.52%) |
| AH Bili IT | 2002 | 6(-) | 13 | .5916 (-) | .5306 (-) |
| | 2003 | 8(5) | 21 | **.7119** (+20.34%) | **.5309** (+0.05%) |
| AH Bili PT | 2004 | 4(-) | 15 | .6721 (-) | .4278 (-) |
| | 2005 | 8(5) | 24 | **.7289** (+7.71%) | **.5020** (+17.34%) |
| | 2006 | 6(4) | 22 | .6539 (-9.67%) | .4804 (-4.30%) |
| AH Bili RU | 2003 | 2(-) | 9 | **.6894** (-) | .4810 (-) |
| | 2004 | 8(7) | 26 | .6336 (-8.09%) | **.5203** (+8.17%) |

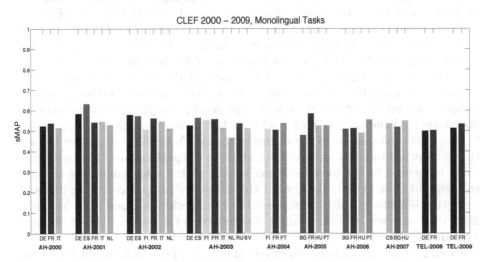

**Fig. 1.** Median sMAP of the CLEF monolingual tasks 2000-2009

in the tasks as well as the number of submitted runs increased over the years by introducing a high degree of variability in the performances.

The analysis of best sMAP tells us something different from the analysis of median sMAP. As an example, for the Dutch language, while the median decreases every year, the best sMAP increases showing an advancement of retrieval methods applied to this language. Also for the Italian task we can observe an improvement of best sMAP over the years given that the top systems show a

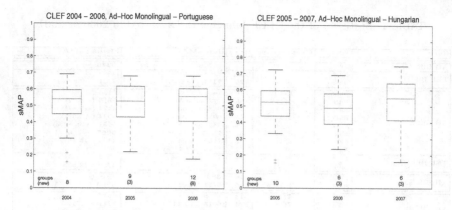

**Fig. 2.** Monolingual Portuguese and Hungarian Tasks Performance Breakdown

big improvement from 2000 to 2001 and then a plateau until 2003. Indeed, the best system (i.e. University of Neuchâtel [12]) in 2001 has a sMAP only 1.51% higher than the sMAP of the best system in 2002 (i.e. the PROSIT system [3] of Fondazione Ugo Bordoni) showing that the big improvement from 2000 (i.e. +22.13%) is due to a consistent advancement of retrieval techniques applied to the Italian language. In 2003 there was a 7.79% drop in sMAP for the best system with respect to the previous year; in 2003 the best system is still the one of Fondazione Ugo Bordoni, but with some differences from the system used in 2002 [4]: in 2002 they used the full enhanced PROSIT system with $B_E L2$ weighting schema, bigrams and coordination level matching, furthermore they focused only on the title of the queries and used a simple form of stemmer; in 2003 they used the same weighting schema, but focused on title plus description fields of the topics and used the Porter stemmer. From this analysis we can see that a more advanced stemmer did not improve the performances that also seem to be influenced by the topic fields considered; on the other hand, it is relevant to highlight that in 2003 the goal of this research group was to test different weighting schema in order to establish the best performing one [4], whereas in 2002 their aim was to test a fully enhanced retrieval system. This could also explain the drop in the median sMAP in 2003 with respect to 2002; in 2003 research groups that participated in previous years (i.e. ~70%) might have been more interested in testing new techniques and retrieval settings rather than tuning already well performing systems for achieving slightly better performances. In general, this could explain why best performances are rarely achieved in the last year of a task, but one or two years before its termination; similar examples are the French and Spanish monolingual tasks.

This hypothesis is also corroborated by the best performances analysis, where we can see how in the first years of a task research groups dedicated much effort to tuning and enhancing good systems already tested in previous campaigns. The top system of all CLEF monolingual tasks is the Berkeley one [9] (i.e. 0.8309 sMAP) which participated in the German task in 2000, closely followed by the

**Table 2.** Statistics of the CLEF monolingual tasks started in 2000 or 2001

| Task | Year | Groups(new) | Runs | Best sMAP | Median sMAP |
|------|------|-------------|------|-----------|-------------|
| AH Mono ES | 2001 | 10(-) | 22 | .7402 (-) | **.6321** (-) |
| | 2002 | 13(5) | 28 | **.8065** (+8.22%) | .5723 (-9.46%) |
| | 2003 | 16(8) | 38 | .7016 (-14.95%) | .5630 (-1.62) |
| AH Mono DE | 2000 | 11(-) | 13 | **.8309** (-) | .5235 (-) |
| | 2001 | 12(9) | 24 | .6857 (-17.47%) | **.5839** (+11.53%) |
| | 2002 | 12(5) | 20 | .6888 (+0.45%) | .5780 (-1.01%) |
| | 2003 | 13(7) | 29 | .7330 (+6.42%) | .5254 (-9.10%) |
| TEL Mono DE | 2008 | 10(7) | 27 | .7388 (+0.79%) | .4985 (-5.11%) |
| | 2009 | 9(4) | 34 | .6493 (-12.11%) | .5123 (+2.76%) |
| AH Mono FR | 2000 | 9(-) | 10 | .6952 (-) | .5370 (-) |
| | 2001 | 9(6) | 15 | .6908 (-0.63%) | .5412 (+0.78%) |
| | 2002 | 12(7) | 16 | **.8257** (+19.53%) | .5609 (+3.64%) |
| | 2003 | 16(9) | 35 | .6758 (-18.15%) | .5565 (-0.78%) |
| | 2004 | 13(4) | 38 | .6777 (+0.28%) | .5034 (-9.54%) |
| | 2005 | 12(7) | 38 | .7176 (+5.89%) | **.5833** (+15.87%) |
| | 2006 | 8(5) | 27 | .6992 (-2.56%) | .5120 (-12.22%) |
| TEL Mono FR | 2008 | 9(8) | 15 | .7242 (+3.58%) | .5018 (-1.99%) |
| | 2009 | 9(5) | 23 | .6838 (-5.58%) | .5334 (+6.30%) |
| AH Mono IT | 2000 | 9(-) | 10 | .6114 (-) | .5150 (-) |
| | 2001 | 8(5) | 14 | **.7467** (+22.13%) | **.5461** (+6.04%) |
| | 2002 | 14(7) | 25 | .7354 (-1.51%) | **.5461** (-) |
| | 2003 | 13(4) | 27 | .6796 (-7.59%) | .5142 (-5.84%) |
| AH Mono NL | 2001 | 9(-) | 18 | .6844 (-) | **.5296** (-) |
| | 2002 | 11(4) | 19 | .7128 (+4.15%) | .5118 (-3.36%) |
| | 2003 | 11(4) | 32 | **.7231** (+1.45%) | .4657 (-10.53) |

University of Neuchâtel system [13] (i.e. 0.8257 sMAP), which participated in the French task in 2002. The Berkeley system participated in several cross-lingual retrieval tasks in previous TREC campaigns; queries were manually formulated and expanded and the searcher spent about 10 to 25 minutes per topic [9]. We can see that this research group spent much time tuning an already good system by employing tested retrieval techniques enhanced with substantial manual intervention. Similarly, the Neuchâtel system is a careful improvement of techniques and methodologies introduced and tested in previous CLEF campaigns [13].

**RQ2. Do performances of bilingual systems increase over the years and what is the impact of source languages?**

For bilingual tasks we have to consider both the target language (i.e. the language of the corpus) and the source languages (i.e. the languages of the topics). In Figure 3 we show the median sMAP of the CLEF bilingual tasks divided by target language and on each bar we report the sources. As we can see, it is not always possible to identify a steady improvement of performances for a given target language over the years.

In Table 1 we report more detailed statistics about the bilingual tasks where we can see, unlike for the monolingual tasks, that the higher median sMAP as well as the best sMAP are achieved in the last years of each task. This is an indicator of the improvement of language resources – e.g. dictionaries, external resources like Wikipedia and the use of semantic rather than syntactic resources –

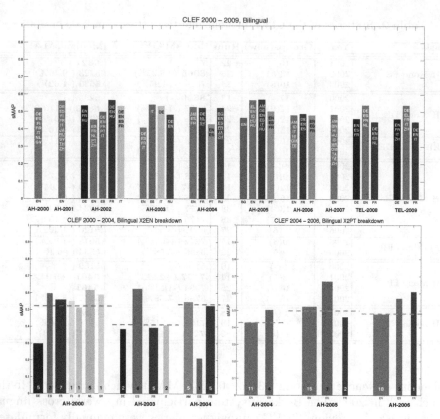

**Fig. 3.** Median sMAP of the CLEF bilingual tasks 2000-2009

that could be exploited by the bilingual systems. For instance, the best bilingual system for the "X2FR" task (i.e. University of Neuchâtel system [15], 0.7250 sMAP) exploited "seven different machine translation systems, three bilingual dictionaries" [15] and ten freely available translation tools; the best bilingual system in the TEL "X2DE" task (i.e. Chemnitz University of Technology [10], 0.7179 sMAP) exploited three out-the-box retrieval systems (i.e. Lucene, Lemur and Terrier) and the high quality of the Google translation service contributed substantially to achieving the final result [10].

The fluctuation of performances within the same task is due to the significant turnover of research groups and, more importantly, to the different source languages employed each year. In the lower part of Figure 3, we can see a performance breakdown for the "X2EN" and the "X2PT" tasks where we report the median sMAP achieved by the systems working on English and Portuguese target languages divided by the source language employed; inside each single bar we report the number of runs submitted for that source language and the thickness of each bar is weighted by this number. For "X2EN" we report data for the tasks carried out in 2000, 2003, and 2004; we can see that in 2003 the

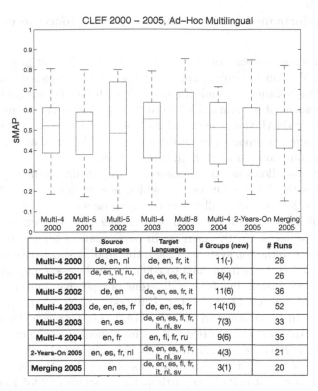

CLEF 2000 – 2005, Ad–Hoc Multilingual

|  | Source Languages | Target Languages | # Groups (new) | # Runs |
|---|---|---|---|---|
| **Multi-4 2000** | de, en, nl | de, en, fr, it | 11(-) | 26 |
| **Multi-5 2001** | de, en, nl, ru, zh | de, en, es, fr, it | 8(4) | 26 |
| **Multi-5 2002** | de, en | de, en, es, fr, it | 11(6) | 36 |
| **Multi-4 2003** | de, en, es, fr | de, en, es, fr | 14(10) | 52 |
| **Multi-8 2003** | en, es | de, en, es, fi, fr, it, nl, sv | 7(3) | 33 |
| **Multi-4 2004** | en, fr | en, fi, fr, ru | 9(6) | 35 |
| **2-Years-On 2005** | en, es, fr, nl | de, en, es, fi, fr, it, nl, sv | 4(3) | 21 |
| **Merging 2005** | en | de, en, es, fi, fr, it, nl, sv | 3(1) | 20 |

**Fig. 4.** sMAP scores distribution for all the CLEF multilingual tasks

median sMAP dropped with respect to 2000 and then it recovered in 2004. In 2003, only 3 groups (all newcomers) participated by submitting fewer runs than in 2000; in 2004 the median sMAP recovered, even if there were still fewer groups (only 4 and all newcomers) than in 2000 and even fewer runs than in 2003. The main influence on performances came from the source languages used. In 2000, more than 50% of the runs used French, Spanish, Italian and Dutch languages and their performances were fairly good; the most difficult source language was German. In 2003 performances of runs using Spanish as source language further improved, but they dropped for French and Italian and showed little improvement for German. In 2004 the higher global sMAP is due to the improvement of French runs, the removal of German as source language and the introduction of Amharic for which very good runs were submitted even if this language was initiated that very year. For the "X2PT" task, we can see that global sMAP depends on the English source language for which there are more runs every year and that always performs worse than Spanish. This analysis shows that Spanish to Portuguese was always performed better than English to Portuguese; this could be due to the morphology of languages, given that Spanish and Portuguese are closer to each other than English and Portuguese; we cannot say much about French to Portuguese because there are a small number of available runs.

## RQ3. Do performances of multilingual systems increase over the years?

In Figure 4 we show the boxplot of sMAP for each CLEF multilingual task from 2000 to 2005. We can identify a growing trend of performances especially for top systems. For instance, for multilingual task with four languages we can see a major improvement of median sMAP from 2002 to 2003 even if the top system of 2003 has lower sMAP than the one of 2002; at the same time, the multilingual task with 8 languages reports the lowest median sMAP and, at the same time, the best performing system of all multilingual tasks.

Standardization allows us to reconsider an important result reported in [7] while discussing the 2-Years-On task in which new systems (i.e. 2005 systems) operated on the 2003 multi-8 collection; the purpose was to compare the performances of 2003 systems with the 2005 ones on the same collection[6]. Di Nunzio et alii in [7] reported a 15.89% increase in performances for the top system of 2005 with respect to the top system of 2003; this finding showed an improvement of multilingual IR systems from 2003 to 2005. Nevertheless, analysing sMAP we draw a similar conclusion, but from a different perspective; indeed, the top system in 2003 achieved 0.8513 sMAP (i.e. University of Neuchâtel [14]), whereas the top system in 2005 achieved 0.8476 sMAP (i.e. Carnegie Mellon University [16]), reporting a 0.44% decrease in performances. On the other hand, the median sMAP in 2003 was 0.4277 and in 2005 it was 0.5117 thus reporting an overall increase of 16.41%; this result is even stronger than the findings reported in [7], since it shows that half of the participating systems in 2005 improved with respect to 2003 ones.

## RQ4. Do monolingual systems have better performances than bilingual and multilingual systems?

In Figure 5 we report the median sMAP and the best sMAP of the monolingual tasks compared to the bilingual tasks for the same target language. We can see that in most cases the median sMAP of the monolingual tasks overcome the median sMAP of the corresponding bilingual task with the exception of French in 2002 and 2004 and Italian in 2003. On the other hand, the best sMAP ratio between monolingual and bilingual tasks reports another viewpoint where the gap between top monolingual and top bilingual systems is progressively reduced across the years and in several cases the trend is inverted with bilingual systems performing better than monolingual ones.

In Table 3 we report aggregate statistics where we calculated the median, best and mean sMAP for all the systems which participated in the monolingual, bilingual and multilingual tasks.

We can see that bilingual and multilingual systems have a similar median and mean sMAP even though they are slightly higher for the multilingual and

---

[6] Note that the multi-8 collection had 60 topics, whereas in 2005 a subset of 40 topics was actually used by the systems; the 20 remaining were employed for training purposes [7].

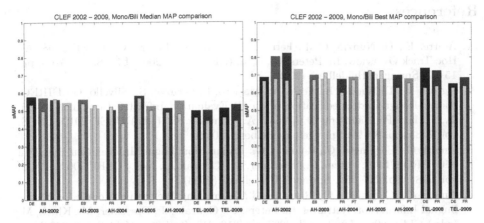

**Fig. 5.** Mono/Bili Median and Best sMAP comparison. The thick bars indicate monolingual tasks and thin bars bilingual tasks.

**Table 3.** Aggregate sMAP of mono, bili and multilingual CLEF ad-hoc and TEL tasks from 2000 to 2009

| sMAP | Monolingual | Bilingual | Multilingual |
|------|-------------|-----------|--------------|
| Best | .8309 | .7845 | **.8513** |
| Median | **.5344** | .5165 | .5173 |
| Mean | **.5054** | .4898 | .4914 |

both are exceeded by the monolingual systems. It is interesting to note that the best system is the multilingual one that has a sMAP 8.52% higher than the top bilingual and 2.46% higher than the top monolingual system.

## 4   Future Works

This study opens up diverse analysis possibilities and as future works we plan to investigate several further aspects regarding the cross-lingual evaluation activities carried out by CLEF; we will: (i) apply standardization to other largely-adopted IR measures – e.g. Precision at 10, RPrec, Rank-Biased Precision, bpref – with the aim of analysing system performances from different perspectives; (ii) aggregate and analyse the systems on the basis of adopted retrieval techniques to better understand their impact on overall performances across the years; and (iii) extend the analysis of bilingual and multilingual systems grouping them on a source and target language basis thus getting more insights into the role of language morphology and linguistic resources in cross-lingual IR.

# References

1. Agirre, E., Di Nunzio, G.M., Ferro, N., Mandl, T., Peters, C.: CLEF 2008: Ad Hoc Track Overview. In: Peters, C., et al. (eds.) CLEF 2008. LNCS, vol. 5706, pp. 15–37. Springer, Heidelberg (2009)
2. Agosti, M., Di Buccio, E., Ferro, N., Masiero, I., Peruzzo, S., Silvello, G.: DIREC-Tions: Design and Specification of an IR Evaluation Infrastructure. In: Catarci, T., Forner, P., Hiemstra, D., Peñas, A., Santucci, G. (eds.) CLEF 2012. LNCS, vol. 7488, pp. 88–99. Springer, Heidelberg (2012)
3. Amati, G., Carpineto, C., Romano, G.: Italian Monolingual Information Retrieval with PROSIT. In: Peters, C., Braschler, M., Gonzalo, J. (eds.) CLEF 2002. LNCS, vol. 2785, pp. 257–264. Springer, Heidelberg (2003)
4. Amati, G., Carpineto, C., Romano, G.: Comparing Weighting Models for Mono-lingual Information Retrieval. In: Peters, C., Gonzalo, J., Braschler, M., Kluck, M. (eds.) CLEF 2003. LNCS, vol. 3237, pp. 310–318. Springer, Heidelberg (2004)
5. Buckley, C.: The SMART project at TREC. In: TREC — Experiment and Evalu-ation in Information Retrieval, pp. 301—320. MIT Press (2005)
6. Braschler, M., Di Nunzio, G.M., Ferro, N., Peters, C.: CLEF 2004: Ad Hoc Track Overview and Results Analysis. In: Peters, C., Clough, P., Gonzalo, J., Jones, G.J.F., Kluck, M., Magnini, B. (eds.) CLEF 2004. LNCS, vol. 3491, pp. 10–26. Springer, Heidelberg (2005)
7. Di Nunzio, G.M., Ferro, N., Jones, G.J.F., Peters, C.: CLEF 2005: Ad Hoc Track Overview. In: Peters, C., et al. (eds.) CLEF 2005. LNCS, vol. 4022, pp. 11–36. Springer, Heidelberg (2006)
8. Ferro, N., Peters, C.: CLEF 2009 Ad Hoc Track Overview: TEL and Persian Tasks. In: Peters, C., Di Nunzio, G.M., Kurimo, M., Mandl, T., Mostefa, D., Peñas, A., Roda, G. (eds.) CLEF 2009. LNCS, vol. 6241, pp. 13–35. Springer, Heidelberg (2010)
9. Gey, F.C., Jiang, H., Petras, V., Chen, A.: Cross-Language Retrieval for the CLEF Collections - Comparing Multiple Methods of Retrieval. In: Peters, C. (ed.) CLEF 2000. LNCS, vol. 2069, pp. 116–128. Springer, Heidelberg (2001)
10. Kürsten, J.: Chemnitz at CLEF 2009 Ad-Hoc TEL Task: Combining Different Re-trieval Models and Addressing the Multilinguality. In: CLEF 2009 Working Notes, on-line
11. Rowe, B.R., Wood, D.W., Link, A.L., Simoni, D.A.: Economic Impact Assessment of NIST's Text REtrieval Conference (TREC) Program. RTI International, USA (2010)
12. Savoy, J.: Report on CLEF-2001 Experiments: Effective Combined Query-Translation Approach. In: Peters, C., Braschler, M., Gonzalo, J., Kluck, M. (eds.) CLEF 2001. LNCS, vol. 2406, pp. 27–43. Springer, Heidelberg (2002)
13. Savoy, J.: Report on CLEF 2002 Experiments: Combining Multiple Sources of Evidence. In: Peters, C., Braschler, M., Gonzalo, J. (eds.) CLEF 2002. LNCS, vol. 2785, pp. 66–90. Springer, Heidelberg (2003)
14. Savoy, J.: Report on CLEF-2003 Multilingual Tracks. In: Peters, C., Gonzalo, J., Braschler, M., Kluck, M. (eds.) CLEF 2003. LNCS, vol. 3237, pp. 64–73. Springer, Heidelberg (2004)
15. Savoy, J., Berger, P.-Y.: Monolingual, Bilingual, and GIRT Information Retrieval at CLEF-2005. In: Peters, C., et al. (eds.) CLEF 2005. LNCS, vol. 4022, pp. 131–140. Springer, Heidelberg (2006)

16. Si, L., Callan, J.: CLEF 2005: Multilingual Retrieval by Combining Multiple Multilingual Ranked Lists. In: Peters, C., et al. (eds.) CLEF 2005. LNCS, vol. 4022, pp. 121–130. Springer, Heidelberg (2006)
17. Thornley, C.V., Johnson, A.C., Smeaton, A.F., Lee, H.: The Scholarly Impact of TRECVid (2003–2009). JASIST 62(4), 613–627 (2011)
18. Tsikrika, T., de Herrera, A.G.S., Müller, H.: Assessing the Scholarly Impact of ImageCLEF. In: Forner, P., Gonzalo, J., Kekäläinen, J., Lalmas, M., de Rijke, M. (eds.) CLEF 2011. LNCS, vol. 6941, pp. 95–106. Springer, Heidelberg (2011)
19. Tsikrika, T., Larsen, B., Müller, H., Endrullis, S., Rahm, E.: The Scholarly Impact of CLEF (2000–2009). In: Forner, P., Müller, H., Paredes, R., Rosso, P., Stein, B. (eds.) CLEF 2013. LNCS, vol. 8138, pp. 1–12. Springer, Heidelberg (2013)
20. Webber, W., Moffat, A., Zobel, J.: Score standardization for inter-collection comparison of retrieval systems. In: SIGIR 2008, pp. 51–58. ACM Press (2008)

# An Information Retrieval Ontology for Information Retrieval Nanopublications*

Aldo Lipani, Florina Piroi, Linda Andersson, and Allan Hanbury

Institute of Software Technology and Interactive Systems (ISIS),
Vienna University of Technology, Austria
{surname}@ifs.tuwien.ac.at

**Abstract.** Retrieval experiments produce plenty of data, like various experiment settings and experimental results, that are usually not all included in the published articles. Even if they are mentioned, they are not easily machine-readable. We propose the use of IR nanopublications to describe in a formal language such information. Furthermore, to support the unambiguous description of IR domain aspects, we present a preliminary IR ontology. The use of the IR nanopublications will facilitate the assessment and comparison of IR systems and enhance the degree of reproducibility and reliability of IR research progress.

## 1 Motivation

An important part of information retrieval research consists of running retrieval experiments, beginning with choosing test collections, selecting indexing algorithms, tuning parameters, evaluating outcomes and concluding with publishing summaries of the results in conference or journal articles. A research article, however, "is not the scholarship itself, it is merely advertising of the scholarship. The actual scholarship is the complete software development environment and the complete [data] set of instructions which generated the figures" [3]. Making available the necessary components to reproduce IR research results is beneficial for the IR community, most of all to the authors of the published research [6].

The map of availability solutions for IR experiments has currently an island-like geography. Tools like EvaluatIR[1] or Direct[2] concentrate on IR system comparison by examining their outputs in retrieval experiments. Details about the IR systems are not available through these tools and experiments cannot be cited *per se*. The same can be said about the music IR domain where experiments and comparisons of algorithm results are available since 2005[3] or about the myExperiment community dedicated to sharing scientific workflows and packets of research objects, like data and/or algorithms[4].

---

* This research was partly funded by the Austrian Science Fund (FWF) project number P25905-N23 (ADmIRE).

[1] http://evaluatir.org
[2] http://direct.dei.unipd.it/
[3] http://www.music-ir.org/mirex/wiki/MIREX_HOME
[4] http://www.myexperiment.org/

E. Kanoulas et al. (Eds.): CLEF 2014, LNCS 8685, pp. 44–49, 2014.

In life-sciences, where high throughput experiments are not uncommon, the need to publish supplemental information to research articles has led to the development of nanopublications. Nanopublications offer the possibility to publish statements about data and experiments, together with references that establish the authorship and provenance of the statements in a machine-readable format.

The content of a nanopublication is expressed using ontologies which ensure a common understanding on the published statements/assertions. In information retrieval research, ontologies are mostly used to improve the retrieval accuracy in some given domain [10,4]. We present, here, the outline of an IR ontology that can be used in creating nanopublications on statements about IR.

We advocate, thus, the publication of supplemental material for IR publications, in form of IR nanopublications, with the ultimate goal that such publications will make the assessment of research progress on any given IR topic quick and reliable, and significantly improve the reproducibility of IR research results.

We underline that this is preliminary work to present the concept, with changes to our proposed IR ontology and IR nanopublications being expected.

## 2   Ontology Description

The IR domain is affected by a lack of formality caused, not least, by how research results are published. For example, important information is omitted for the sake of brevity, or because it is considered implicit in the publication's context; or new names for well-known concepts are introduced, making them ambiguous [13, Chapter 1]. It is, therefore, difficult to reconcile results published over longer periods of time. We believe that the design of an IR domain specific ontology is a natural solution to this issue.

With the ontology we describe here[5] we aim at a formal representation of the concepts in the IR domain, establishing a common discourse ground for the publication of (meta-)data that forms the basis of research articles. The IR domain ontology we propose consists of a vocabulary of concepts specific to the IR domain and the relationships between them. With it we want to model the evaluation activities taking place in this domain. This is in line with what a domain ontology should contribute to the respective domain [7].

Our methodology to establish the ontology is a mix of top down and bottom up approaches. First, manually parse a number of publications—more than 50—from the NTCIR, CLEF, and TREC series of publications, as well as by now classic teaching books (e.g. [11]), in order to identify taxonomy categories. Second, on a collection of documents (e.g. the almost 5,000 CLEF publications we have access to) compute the noun phrase termhood (e.g. C-value [5]). And third, manually go through the top terms in the termhood list to create ontology individuals. We present here the outcome of the first step of our methodology, as steps two and three are work in progress.

---

[5] http://ifs.tuwien.ac.at/~admire/ir_ontology/ir

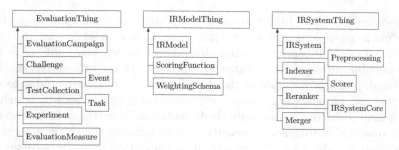

**Fig. 1.** Fragment of the IR taxonomy

The proposed IR ontology, developed using the Protégé framework[6] and the OWL Web Ontology Language, is composed of three sections that represent the following fundamental aspects of the IR research: evaluation, IR models and IR systems. The three main concept categories, are as follows (see also Figure 1):

**EvaluationThing:** models concepts like evaluation measures, experiments and evaluation campaigns with their events and challenges;

**IRModelThing:** models the theoretical concepts of the IR models with their theoretical definitions of scoring functions, weighting schemata, etc.;

**IRSystemThing:** models concepts used in describing concrete IR systems with their constituent parts and components which are usually instances of the theoretical concepts modeled by IRModelThing conceps.

The IRSystemThing section is closely coupled with the IRModelThing and the EvaluationThing sections by concept relationships which, first, make explicit the theoretical foundations of the IR systems modelled by the IRModelThing section, and, second, explicit a system's assessment and presence in evaluation campaign events modelled by the EvaluationThing section.

**Modelling IR Evaluation Activities.** Evaluating IR systems is an important and well-developed aspect of information retrieval research [9,12] which aims at objective measurements of IR algorithms and technique improvements.

EvaluationThing's subclasses define three related concepts: i) **Experiment** models the execution and assessment of a given IR system on an evaluation setup (collection of documents, a set of queries and a set of relevance judgements, measures); ii) **EvaluationCampaign** models a series of evaluation events, such as the TREC, NTCIR, CLEF, FIRE, and ROMIP; and iii) **EvaluationMeasure** models the measures available for the performance evaluation of an IR system (Precision, Recall, MAP, Precision@$n$, etc.).

In addition to these three concepts—modelled as EvaluationThing subclasses—other concepts are present in this category: the TestCollection class, whose elements are TestCollection components (Collection,

---

[6] http://protege.stanford.edu, supported by grant GM10331601 from the National Institute of General Medical Sciences of the United States National Institutes of Health.

Groundtruth, and Topics), experiment components (Run, TestCollection, and Score), to name a few.

An EvaluationCampaign consists of one or more Events (TREC-1, TREC-2, etc.), with each Event one or more Challenges are associated (AdHoc Track, Robust Track, etc.). A Challenge is an area of research focus aiming to solve a particular retrieval problem. A Challenge is part of an Event and to each Challenge one or more TestCollections can be associated. Evaluation measures are used to assess the performance of a given information retrieval system on a test collection. The EvaluationMeasure category models the function and properties of the different measures (parametric, set-based, ranking vs. non-ranking, etc.).

**Modelling the IR Model.** Models of information retrieval form the foundation of IR research, being the result of theoretical and empirical analysis of specific IR problems. It is this kind of analysis that contributes to the definitions of weighting schemata and scoring functions, as well as to their interpretations.

Weighting schemata, like TF-IDF, LM1, RSJ, etc., are in essence a way of representing selected elements in a collection of documents within an index. Scoring functions provide the means to make comparisons between a given topic and the (previously indexed) collection documents.

In our proposed ontology we list many IR models and weighting schemata, connected with scoring functions.

**Modelling the IR System.** In the proposed ontology, the IRSystemThing category models the structure and the particular software components of an IR system. At the same time, the ontology allows us to express the interplay between an Experiment, a TestCollection, and the realization of an IRModelThing via an IRSystemThing. This realization is defined by the relationships between the IRModel subclasses (WeightingSchema, ScoringFunction) and the IRSystem subclasses (Indexer, Scorer, etc.). This design allows us to make explicit IR systems based on more than one IR model.

# 3   Nanopublications in IR

One of the driving ideas behind nanopublications is the need to disseminate information about experiments and experimental data, and, more importantly, do it in a way that can be attributed and cited. In essence, nanopublications are the smallest unit of publication, containing an assertion which is uniquely identified and attributed to an author [1]. A nanopublication should contain two main parts: an *assertion*, which is the scientific statement of the nanopublication, expressed as a triple <subject, predicate, object>, and the *provenance*, which documents how the statement in the assertion was reached. The provenance usually include supporting meta-data (algorithms, data sets, etc.) and attribution meta-data (authors, institutions, etc.).

Besides the main nanopublication parts mentioned above, there are currently no established standards for the format and additional content of the nanopublications. The Concept Web Alliance[7] advocates a Named Graphs/RDF format which allows to later aggregate nanopublications about some research topic [8].

Below is an example nanopublication describing `IR-Experiment-1` produced by `IR-System-1` running on `TestCollection-1`, with a MAP score of 0.24.

```
@prefix  :   <http://www.example.org/nanopub/this-ir-example > .
@prefix np:  <http://www.nanopub.org/nschema# > .
@prefix ir:  <http://ifs.tuwien.ac.at/~admire/ir_ontology/1.0/ir# > .
@prefix pav: <http://purl.org/pav/ > .
@prefix xsd: <http://www.w3.org/2001/XMLSchema# > .

: {
  : a np:Nanopublication ;
    np:hasAssertion  :IR-Experiment-1 ;
    np:hasProvenance  :Provenance ;
    np:hasPublicationInfo  :PublicationInfo .   }

:IR-Experiment-1 {
  :Exp-1 a ir:Experiment ;
         ir:hasExperimentComponent  :Run-file ;
         ir:hasExperimentComponent  :TestCollection-1 ;
         ir:hasScore  :MAP-Exp-1 .

  :Run-file a ir:Run ;
            ir:belongsToIRSystem  :IR-System-1 .

  :TestCollection-1 a ir:TestCollection .
  :IR-System-1 a ir:IRSystem .

  :MAP-Exp-1 a ir:Score ;
             ir:measuredByEvaluationMeasure ir:MeanAveragePrecision ;
             ir:hasValue 0.24 .   }

:Provenance {
  : pav:derivedFrom <http://dx.doi.org/example/doiID > .   }

:PublicationInfo {
  : pav:authoredBy <http://orcid.org/author-orcid-id > .
  : pav:createdOn "2013-10-02T10:47:11+01:00"^^xsd:dateTime .   }
```

In our view, a collection of IR nanopublications can be used in a natural language question and answering system (Q&A). In this application, the IR ontology will be used as an intermediary layer contributing to the natural language understanding module [2]. Such a system will be able to answer requests like: *'Give me all retrieval experiments which used Solr on the* CLEF–IP *collection and have a MAP score higher than 0.2'*.

The purpose of this system is not just to return a list of papers containing these words. When existing, we want to have also the nanopublications containing additional data about the experiments, the IR indexing and weighting components, the tuning parameters, etc., together with authorship and publication information. The 'Solr' and 'CLEF–IP' named entities can be identified with the help of the ontology, and assigned to their parent classes. Using a reasoner, then, we can instantiate vague concepts. In this example, we can reason that Solr uses Lucene as a search engine and infer that experiments where Lucene was used, but Solr is not mentioned, may be of interest. In the same example we would be able to distinguish between the four versions of the CLEF–IP

---

[7] http://www.nbic.nl/about-nbic/affiliated-organizations/cwa/

collection (2009–2012), each closely related to specific tasks, not all using MAP as an evaluation measure.

## 4    Future Work

The IR ontology we presented is in its infancy. Our next steps are to extend and consolidate it, validate it through examples, revisiting design phases as needed.

At this phase issues like ontology completeness and maintenance, (central) locations of IR nanopublications, etc. are not dealt with. We expect that discussion rounds with the IR researcher community, either at conferences or dedicated workshops, will contribute towards a solution commonly agreed on. IR nanopublications will then provide means to make experimental data citable and verifiable, as part of the final steps of the operational chain in IR experimentation.

By encouraging researchers in the IR domain to (nano)publish details about their experimental data we encourage them to contribute to their work being reproducible, giving more weight and credibility to their own research statements.

## References

1. Guidelines for nanopublication, http://nanopub.org/guidelines/working_draft/ (last retrieved: May 2014)
2. Allen, J.: Natural Language Understanding, 2nd edn. Benjamin-Cummings Publishing Co., Inc., Redwood City (1995)
3. Buckheit, J., Donoho, D.L.: Wavelab and Reproducible Research. In: Wavelets and Statistics. Springer, Berlin (1995)
4. Fernàndez, M., Cantador, I., Lòpez, V., Vallet, D., Castells, P., Motta, E.: Semantically enhanced Information Retrieval: An ontology-based approach. J. Web Semant. 9(4), 434–452 (2011)
5. Frantzi, K., Ananiadou, S., Mima, H.: Automatic recognition of multi-word terms: the C-value/NC-value method. Int. J. Digit. Libr. 3(2), 115–130 (2000)
6. Freire, J., Bonnet, P., Shasha, D.: Computational Reproducibility: State-of-the-art, Challenges, and Database Research Opportunities. In: Proceedings of the 2012 ACM SIGMOD International Conference on Management of Data, SIGMOD 2012, pp. 593–596. ACM, New York (2012)
7. Gómez-Pérez, A., Fernandez-Lopez, M., Corcho, O.: Ontological engineering, vol. 139. Springer (2004)
8. Groth, P., Gibson, A., Velterop, J.: The Anatomy of a Nanopublication. Inf. Serv. Use 30(1-2), 51–56 (2010)
9. Harman, D.: Information retrieval evaluation. Synthesis Lectures on Information Concepts, Retrieval, and Services 3(2), 1–119 (2011)
10. Li, Z., Raskin, V., Ramani, K.: Developing Engineering Ontology for Information Retrieval. J. Comput. Inform. Sci. Eng. (2008)
11. Manning, C.D., Raghavan, P., Schütze, H.: Introduction to Information Retrieval. Cambridge University Press, New York (2008)
12. Robertson, S.: On the history of evaluation in IR. J. Inform. Sci. 34(4), 439–456 (2008)
13. Roelleke, T.: Information Retrieval Models: Foundations and Relationships. Synthesis Lectures on Information Concepts, Retrieval, and Services 5(3), 1–163 (2013)

# Supporting More-Like-This Information Needs: Finding Similar Web Content in Different Scenarios

Matthias Hagen and Christiane Glimm

Bauhaus-Universität Weimar, Weimar, Germany
`firstname.lastname@uni-weimar.de`

**Abstract.** We examine more-like-this information needs in different scenarios. A more-like-this information need occurs, when the user sees one interesting document and wants to access other but similar documents. One of our foci is on comparing different strategies to identify related web content. We compare following links (i.e., crawling), automatically generating keyqueries for the seen document (i.e., queries that have the document in the top of their ranks), and search engine operators that automatically display related results. Our experimental study shows that in different scenarios different strategies yield the most promising related results.

One of our use cases is to automatically support people who monitor right-wing content on the web. In this scenario, it turns out that crawling from a given set of seed documents is the best strategy to find related pages with similar content. Querying or the related-operator yield much fewer good results. In case of news portals, however, crawling is a bad idea since hardly any news portal links to other news portals. Instead, a search engine's related operator or querying are better strategies. Finally, for identifying related scientific publications for a given paper, all three strategies yield good results.

## 1 Introduction

The problem considered in this paper appears whenever a user browsing or searching the web finds a document with interesting content for which she wants to identify related pages on the web. Search engines often support such information needs by providing specific operators (e.g., "`related:`" + a URL in the Google interface or the "Related articles"-link in GoogleScholar). However, in a scenario that we discussed with researchers monitoring extreme right-wing content on the web, both these possibilities failed in a pilot study. We thus examine different possibilities for finding related pages on the web with one scenario being the described monitoring. In this case, the classic crawling strategy works very well and besides automatic query formulation should form the heart of a an automatic system that supports the monitoring people.

In our study, we examine three different strategies that can be used to automatically find and suggest related documents from the web. The first idea is to simply use the available technology from search engine side (i.e., the mentioned related operators). As these are probably mainly build on click-through information in case of web pages or citation analysis and click-through information in case of scholarly articles, the search engine side techniques do not work in all scenarios. Hence, we compare the

E. Kanoulas et al. (Eds.): CLEF 2014, LNCS 8685, pp. 50–61, 2014.

available related-operators to classic crawling-like link acquisition and to automatically generated queries. The link following strategy will prove extremely useful in case of connected networks like extreme right-wing web pages. Querying is implemented as a standard technique human users would choose to search the web. To this end, we employ the recent idea of keyqueries. A keyquery for a document is a query that returns the document in the top ranks. Other top ranked documents of that query are probably very related (as they appear for the same query) and thus good candidates to be presented to the user.

In our experimental evaluation, we compare the three strategies (crawling, querying, engine operators) for different realistic scenarios. First, we conduct a study on web pages containing extreme right-wing content. For this scenarios, the search engine operators perform not that well as probably not much click-through information is available and respective queries are probably not the main focus of commercial search engines. Instead, the link crawling works very well since typically extreme right pages are well connected on the web.

In contrast, link crawling does not yield satisfying results in the second part of our study. Namely, for news pages using the search engine related-operator performs best (potentially due to a lot of click-through and content analysis at search engine side). Also queries perform better in this case than crawling. A third scenario evaluates the three strategies on scientific publications. Here link crawling is modeled as following citations and references. Still the search engine related operator and automatic queries perform similarly well. Hence, the three scenarios contrast different use cases for which different strategies have to be applied. For the important case of providing an automatic tool that supports people who monitor extreme right-wing content on the web, traditional crawling-style techniques are the best choice.

The paper is organized as follows. In Section 2 we briefly review related work on finding similar documents. The detailed description of the examined approaches follows in Section 3. Our experimental study with the three different usage scenarios is described in Section 4. Some concluding remarks and an outlook on future work closes the paper in Section 5.

## 2    Related Work

We briefly describe several approaches that aim at finding similar content on the web. Note that we do not address the case of duplicate or near-duplicate detection—and thus also do not review the respective literature here. Rather, the focus of our study is on finding different documents with similar content—the "more like this"-scenario.

Classic approaches to identify content from the web are crawling strategies. Given some seed set of URLs, a crawler tries to identify links in the seeds and fetch the respective documents, then links in the new documents are identified, etc. [2]. We follow a very similar approach but only follow links from one given page (the source of the more-like-this need) and also do not crawl the entire part of the web reachable from that document (cf. Section 3 for more details). Note that for papers, similar ideas are to follow citations to and from a given paper to identify related publications. The SOFIA search tool [7] extracts references from a paper and by weighting author groups and topic words in paper titles, extracts a set of publication that are suggested as related to the source document. Since the prototype of SOFIA search is not available, we implemented a basic similar strategy that "crawls" the references and citations (cf. Section 3 for more details).

For another source of related documents that we exploit, no literature exists. In particular, we are using the Google operator related that for a given URL returns up to about 200 related web pages. It is probably based on click-through information from a search engine and page content analysis. A probably similar approach is described by Lee et al. [9] who identify related news stories by observing queries and clicks in a new search engine. However, concrete details about Google's related-operators are not available online such that we use the system as a "black box." In case of scientific papers, we use the "related articles" and "cited by" functionality offered by GoogleScholar as a replacement of the related operator (cf. Section 3 for more details).

Different studies have proposed to derive queries for a given document and use the queries to retrieve similar documents. Fuhr et al. [5] build a theoretical framework for optimum clustering (OCF) based on not comparing document-term-vectors but vectors of document-query similarities. Based on a set of predefined queries, documents with similar similarities for these queries would be grouped in the same cluster. One way of storing the important queries for a document is the reverted index presented by Pickens at al. [13]. Different to the traditional inverted indexes used in most IR systems that basically store for a given term, which documents contain the term, the reverted index stores for each documents for which queries it is returned (weights would correspond to the document's rank in the result set). Initially planned as a means for query expansion, the reverted index could also be applicable to store the queries used in the OCF. Our idea of assuming relatedness of documents returned for the same query builds up on the OCF proposal. Also a couple of previous query formulation strategies to identify documents with similar content on the web are very related to the ideas in Fuhr et al.'s paper.

For instance, Bendersky and Croft deal with the scenario of text reuse detection on the web [3]. Different to previous approaches that deal with text reuse on small-scale corpora, their focus is on reuse of single sentences on the web (but not on complete documents as input). As web-scale prohibits several previous reuse detection strategies, Bendersky and Croft suggest a querying strategy to identify other documents with occurrences of very similar sentences. They also try to identify which of the found documents was the earliest and to analyze information flow which is not our topic. Even though reused text is one form of similarity, our scenario is much different. Still the developed basic query formulation strategy inspired later work that we will employ.

In our setting it would be desirable to use the given document as a query itself ("query by document"). Yang et al. [15] focus on such a scenario in the context of analyzing blog posts. They also try to derive a keyword query that reflects the document's (blog post's) content. Their approach extracts keyphrases from the document, but formulates only a single query from them—backed up by knowledge from Wikipedia and different sources. In contrast, our query formulation will be based on keyphrases instead of words—which was shown beneficial in later studies. Furthermore, Yang et al.'s approach requires to manually select the number of "good" keywords for each document which is not applicable in a fully automatic system.

A more applicable setting which is also related to ours is Dasdan et al.'s work on finding similar documents by using only a search engine interface [4]. Although Dasdan et al. focus on a search engine coverage problem (resolve whether a search engine's index contains a given document or some variant of it), their approach of finding similar documents using keyword interfaces is very related to our setting. Dasdan et al. propose two querying strategies and experimentally show that their approaches indeed find similar documents. However, a later study by Hagen and Stein [8] showed that other query formulation strategies yield even better results. Similar to the text reuse scenario of Bendersky and Croft, Hagen and Stein try to identify potential source documents from the web for text reuse in a given suspicious document. They show that keyphrases are better components for good automatic queries than single keywords. Their proposed strategy also does not formulate just a single query but a whole collection whose combined results are used in the end. Hagen and Stein show their strategy to be much more effective than previous strategies while also being comparably efficient.

In a later paper, the idea of Hagen and Stein is refined to so-called keyqueries [6]. A keyquery for a given document returns the given document in the top ranks while also retrieving other documents. The query is then viewed as very descriptive for the given document's content (since the document is in the top ranks) and since also the other top ranked documents are retrieved, the query probably also is very descriptive for their content. Following Fuhr et al.'s OCF framework and previous query formulation papers, the keyquery's results in some sense then are the most related documents for the input. We will employ the keyquery technique in our query formulation strategy (cf. Section 3 for more details).

## 3   Approach

In this section, we describe the employed strategies for finding similar content web pages. The classical approach of following links (i.e., crawling) is contrasted by search engine provided related-operators, that we employ as a "black box" due to the lack of publically available information on their inner methods, and an automatic query formulation based on keyqueries (i.e., queries that return a given document in the top of their ranks).

### 3.1   Link Crawling

Following links to crawl documents from the web is a classic building block of modern web search engines [2]. The typical implementation extracts hyperlinks from the main content of found web pages —for main content detection we use the boilerpipe[1] library—and then fetches the respective documents. In case of web pages, we simply employ this basic strategy, but only collect links that point to pages on other domains. We thus differentiate between internal links (same domain) and external links (different domain). The underlying assumption is that probably same-domain pages are rather

---

[1] https://code.google.com/p/boilerpipe/, last accessed may 13, 2014.

similar and that more interesting pages (especially in the right-wing monitoring scenario) are pages from different domains. The found external links are added to a standard crawler frontier (i.e., a queue) that returns unseen links in a FIFO manner. Crawling was stopped when 200 external links where retrieved—due to a limitation of 200 results in case of Google's related-operator (see below).

In case of scientific articles, just extracting web links from the documents is not the best choice. Instead, in this case, links are formed by citations and references. For reference extraction from a given paper, we employ the ParsCit[2] tool and the GoogleScholar search for finding citing papers. Differentiating between internal and external links for papers could be modeled by author overlap. However, as a searcher would probably also be interested in related papers from the same author group we simply crawl all papers.

Note that some implementation issues arise for non-available links, password-protected pages, or for differentiating between internal and external links in case of usage of virtual hosts. However, as these issues are not the focus of this paper, we usually just ignored non-available or password protected links and simply checked the URL-strings in case of doubts about internal or external nature.

### 3.2  Search Engine Related-Operator

As a representative of commercial search engines, we use the Google search. Google provides a related-operator as part of its query language.[3] A query `related:+URL` returns pages that are similar to the given URL. There is no information about the inner method of the operator but it probably is based on clickthrough information (i.e., people with similar queries clicking on differnt URLs) and a bit of page content analysis. In a pilot study with people monitoring extreme right-wing content on the web, we observed that for such content the related-operator often did not bring up any results. This is probably in part also due to the fact that in Germany pages promoting hate speech have to be removed from the index—still not all right-wing content pages actually contain hate speech. The lack of support from Google's related operator for monitoring right-wing content was one of the driving inspirations of the presented study. In contrast to right-wing content, for prominent domains like news portals, the related-operator works very well. This also underpins the assumption that clickthrough is an important signal since big news portals probably are much more prominent web pages that right-wing content; resulting in more available clickthrough. Typically, when the related-operator does provide results, the returned list has a length of about 200 entries. Most of the top entries then also are results for related-queries on each others domains.

As for scientific articles we employ the "Related articles" link from the search engine result page that basically provides the same functionality as the related-operator from the main Google page. In this case, the operator might also be based on clickthrough and content analysis but citations (i.e., linking) probably play the biggest role. In this sense, the GoogleScholar related-operator should produce similar results as link crawling for papers (which basically is following references and citations, see above).

---

[2] `http://aye.comp.nus.edu.sg/parsCit/`, last accessed may 13, 2014.

[3] `http://www.googleguide.com/advanced_operators_reference.html`, last accessed May 13, 2014.

### 3.3  Keyqueries

The keyqueries concept was introduced by Gollub et al. [6]. Basically, a keyquery for a given document $d$ is a query that returns $d$ in the top ranks but also returns other documents besides $d$ and thus is not too specific. The original idea is to represent documents by their keyqueries. In our scenario, we will employ keyqueries to identify related content—namely the other results from the top ranks besides $d$. The underlying assumption is that documents returned in the top ranks for the same queries cover very similar content, similar to the OCF assumption [5].

More formally, given the vocabulary $W_d = \{w_1, w_2, \dots, w_n\}$ of a document $d$, let $\mathcal{Q}_d$ denote the family of search queries that can be formulated from $W_d$ without word repetitions; i.e., $\mathcal{Q}_d$ is the power set of $W_d$, $\mathcal{Q}_d = 2^{W_d}$. Note that no distinction is made with respect to the ordering of the words in a query. If it is clear from the context, we omit the subscripts and just use $W$ and $\mathcal{Q}$ to denote the vocabulary and the potential queries from $d$.

A query $q \in \mathcal{Q}$ is a *keyquery* for $d$ with respect to a reference search engine $S$ iff: (1) $d$ is among the top-$k$ results returned by $S$ on $q$, and (2) no subset $q' \subset q$ returns $d$ in its top-$k$ results when submitted to $S$. The parameter $k$ controls the level of keyquery generality and is usually set to some small integer, such as 10 in our case. Let $\mathcal{Q}^*$ denote the set of keyqueries for $d$.

As in the original paper, we form keyqueries from keyphrases extracted from a document's text via the TextRank algorithm [10]. TextRank basically forms a graph with the words in a text as its vertices and edges between vertices when the words are neighbors in the text (after stopword removal). On the graph, in a PageRank style computation [12], weights for the vertices are computed and after convergence phrases are formed from neighboring heavy weight vertices.

Contrary to Gollub et al.'s original approach [6] that uses the Apriori algorithm [1] to find the family $\mathcal{Q}^*$ of all keyqueries for a given document, we employ a simpler gready search to find a handful of keyqueries from the top 12 keyphrases extracted by TextRank. We first try the first phrase, then add the next phrases as long as the desired document is not in the top $k$ ranks. Whenever the document is in the top ranks, we try to find a keyquery starting with the second phrase etc. From the found keyqueries, we use the top-$k$ documents such that 200 documents are fetched—similar to the Google related operator that always presents about 200 documents when successful. For instance, in case of four found keyqueries, the top-50 documents from each form the final result set. Compared to the exhaustive Aprior search, our gready approach significantly reduces the number of queries submitted.

## 4  Evaluation

Having presented the applied approaches for finding related documents on the web, we develop an empirical evaluation based on the following hypothesis. The first hypothesis was formed in a pilot study with people monitoring extreme right-wing content on the web and also is in line with related research on the web structure of right-wing communities [11].

Hypothesis 1: The link crawling strategy is a good choice for highly connected communities like web pages containing extreme right-wing content. For less connected related pages like different news portals, link crawling is not the best choice.

Hypothesis 2: The related-operator is a good choice for frequently visited web pages like news portals while documents with less traffic and much more specific content are not well-covered.

Hypothesis 3: Keyqueries as an automatic query formulation strategy are a good backup strategy whenever some other technique does not perform well enough.

To test our hypothesis and to again emphasize the use case of monitoring extreme right-wing content, our evaluation corpus consists of four different parts (two for extreme right-wing content, two other). Each part contains documents available on the web for which the three strategies described in the previous sections each are run to identify related content. In a last step, human annotators evaluate the quality of the returned documents with respect to their relatedness to the input corpus document.

The first two parts of the corpus are formed by German weblogs (part 1) and web pages (part 2) with extreme right-wing background. These pages form the use case of people monitoring the web for extreme right-wing content to study for instance information spread or to protect young people from seeing the content. The pages in part 1 of our corpus are mined from public German sources collecting extreme right-wing weblogs from less organized right-wing structures. Part 2 pages are formed by web pages of the German extreme right-wing party NPD (a more organized and publically viewable player). With these two different right-wing page types (weblogs and NPD pages), we want to evaluate two different standard use cases that people monitoring such content on the web have. Typically, they manually find such pages, follow links and submit queries. Our study on the first two parts of our corpus should give a first idea of whether such a behavior can be semi- or fully automated.

To contrast the rather "niche"-style pages in the first two parts of our evaluation corpus, we also include public German and English news portals as a third part. Finally, the fourth part is more research oriented as it aims to examine to what extend the search for related work or similar scientific articles can be automated or at least semi-automatically supported. We thus include scientific articles from the field of information retrieval as the fourth part in our corpus.

Each part of the corpus is formed by 25 documents (100 in total). For each document, each of the described three strategies identifies 200 related documents when possible. Two human annotators subjectively classified a sample of 20 pages for each source document following some rough guidelines as "related" or as "not related." Thus a sample of 20 out of at most 200 results for each of the 100 corpus documents was classified. Note that the sampling favored top retrieved documents from the 200 potential ones (the top-10 were always included); however, lower ranked results did have a small probability of also being sampled for classification.

In case of disagreement among the two annotators, a short discussion was arranged. Whenever the two annotators did not agree even after discussion, the result was labeled as "no consensus." Note that in general this case did not occur too often such that most of the cases have a consensus—the exception being right-wing weblogs that often

**Table 1.** Classification of the link crawling results

| Corpus part | Classification | | | Total |
| --- | --- | --- | --- | --- |
| | related | not related | no consensus | classified |
| Right-wing Blogs | 173 | 70 | 248 | 491 |
| NPD web pages | 289 | 24 | 14 | 327 |
| News portals | 18 | 443 | 39 | 500 |
| Scientific publications | 216 | 140 | 109 | 465 |

probably somewhat try to hide their real "orientation" such that our annotators had a tough task for these cases.

### 4.1 Individual Classification Results

We first show the individual performances of the different strategies before we compare them on the whole corpus and check the validity of our initial hypotheses.

*Link Crawling.* Table 1 contains the classification results for the link crawling strategy. Each line corresponds to a specific part of our evaluation corpus. The classification columns show how many of the retrieved documents were classified as related or not by our assessors. The last column shows the total number of classified results. Two interesting observations are striking.

First, not for all the 100 source documents even 20 related results could be identified by crawling. The lowest number is achieved for NPD web pages. On average, only 13 pages were found by link crawling (remember that we are only interested in external links such that other NPD pages do not count).

Second, for extreme right-wing blogs, our annotators faced a tough task depicted by the many results for which no classification consensus could be reached. Still the ratio of related to not-related pages is very good for right-wing documents. As expected, for news portals, link crawling does not yield many related pages. Again, this is not too surprising as typically different news portals do not link to each other—probably in order not to lose their readers.

*Google Related.* Table 2 contains the classification results for the strategy employing Google's related operator. Interestingly, the related operator does not work at all for

**Table 2.** Classification of the Google related results

| Corpus part | Classification | | | Total |
| --- | --- | --- | --- | --- |
| | related | not related | no consensus | classified |
| Right-wing Blogs | 0 | 0 | 0 | 0 |
| NPD web pages | 237 | 136 | 13 | 386 |
| News portals | 406 | 91 | 3 | 500 |
| Scientific publications | 262 | 138 | 25 | 425 |

**Table 3.** Classification of the keyqueries results

| Corpus part | Classification | | | Total classified |
|---|---|---|---|---|
| | related | not related | no consensus | |
| Right-wing Blogs | 52 | 219 | 37 | 308 |
| NPD web pages | 0 | 0 | 0 | 0 |
| News portals | 0 | 0 | 0 | 0 |
| Scientific publications | 82 | 107 | 71 | 260 |

the extreme right-wing blogs. One reason could be a policy of removing hate speech content from display. Another explanation based on the assumption that the related-operator is based on query click-through information, is that there is not much available in the logs. This might show that not much traffic is lead to such pages via Google—which would be a very good sign in our opinion. One further reason probably also is the volatility of the respective blogs that often change their URLs etc. For the other right-wing corpus documents (the NPD pages) the related-operator does produce acceptable results, however, returning rather many not-related documents—but also here not for all corpus documents at least 20 related ones could be identified.

As for the news portals, the assumed underlying click-through information really shows its power. More than 80% (406 out of 500) of the returned results are relevant.

*Keyqueries.* Table 3 contains the classification results for the keyquery strategy. The most striking observations are the failure to produce keyqueries for NPD pages and news portals. For all the corpus documents in these groups no keyqueries could be computed. The reason was not that Google did not return any results due to some treatment of hate speech removal. Instead, typically, the query containing all the 12 extracted keyphrases still did not return the corpus document in its top 10 results—a sign that the phrases are very generic—or even short combinations of only few keyphrases did only return the single corpus document—a sign that the phrases in combination are too specific. In case of news portals, even short queries typically are very specific as they contain non-related phrases from different news stories shown on the news portals' starting pages. Such queries are very specific and often did not yield any other result. In case of the NPD pages, often also the full query containing all the keyphrases was to generic not showing the particular corpus page in the top 10 results such that no keyquery could be computed from the 12 extracted keyphrases. Adding more phrases in this case might help but would harm the comparability with the results on other classes. As for the right-wing blogs, the results are not really satisfying with a lot of results no related to their respective source document.

The case of scientific publications is the strongest for keyqueries among the four different parts of our evaluation corpus. Still, only about 10 documents were found on average and a little more not-related results were classified. One frequent reason (50 of the 71 cases) for the no-consensus decision in this case were access-restricted portals from which our assessors could not acquire a pdf of the proposed document.

## 4.2   Comparison and Hypotheses' Validity

As can be seen from the classification results each of the three techniques has its individual strengths and weaknesses. The link crawling strategy is the best among the tested techniques for extreme right-wing content with a high ratio of related pages found. This confirms our first hypothesis formed with people monitoring extreme right-wing web content on a daily basis. In such scenarios of tightly connected networks, simply following links that also often dynamically point to moved content is the best choice.

Our second hypothesis that Google related has its strengths on frequently visited pages also is clearly confirmed by comparing the results on the news portals. Here, about 80% of related documents found is way ahead of the other techniques.

Our third hypothesis stating that for cases where the others fail is not really confirmed by our experiments. Still, for scientific publications, the keyquery strategy shows some promising results but for news portals or NPD pages completely fails. Thus, the third hypothesis can only partly be confirmed but for pages with diverse content (as news portals or NPD pages are) the hypothesis is falsified.

In total, our results clearly show that the choice of a strategy for finding related content often heavily depends on the input document. In case of our focus use case of finding related right-wing content and building a semi-automatic tool to assist people who monitor such pages, the classic idea of following links still clearly beats advanced search engine features like the related-operator or automatic query formulation strategies based on keyqueries.

## 4.3   Further Observations: Overlap and Efficiency

We could observe an interesting effect when we compared the overlap of the retrieved related documents for the different techniques in the different parts of our corpus. For each two techniques and each corpus category, the overlap of the found related results was at most 10% (often much lower). This means that the different techniques are somewhat complementary to each other and find different related results. Whenever the results of one technique do not yield enough similar documents another technique can be used as a backup; of course, probably only for corpus categories where it retrieves something related. For instance, for our use case of finding related right-wing content, crawling is the best standalone technique but can be backed up by Google-related for NPD pages or keyqueries for blogs since the retrieved related results of that techniques complement the crawling results very well.

As for runtime, using the search engine built-in operators by far is the fastest approach. Crawling links comes with the timing issues that crawling usually exhibits. This includes politeness—not fetching to often from the same server—and also latency—waiting for server responses. Thus crawling usually is slower than a search engine operator. Automatic query formulation was the slowest approach since even our simple greedy strategy submits about 50–80 queries on average to identify the final keyqueries for a document. With the available interfaces of commercial search engines submitting these queries costs a significant amount of time—submitting too many queries simultaneously or in short time frames may even result in blocking from search engine side.

# 5   Conclusion and Outlook

In this paper, we have examined different strategies of finding related content for a given document on the web. Our primary use case emerged from discussions with people monitoring extreme right-wing content on the web. They would like to have an (semi-)automatic tool that retrieves related pages from the web that they then can examine without the burden of retrieval.

We compared three different approaches. Namely, classic link crawling, using Google's related-operator, and automatic query formulation with the recent keyqueries approach. Our evaluation corpus consists of four different parts aiming at examining the three retrieval strategies on different scenarios. In the two first corpus parts, we focus on extreme right-wing content in the form of weblogs and pages from the German NPD party. The third part consists of popular news portals while the fourth part is formed by scientific publications—a use case of particular interest to ourselves as researchers.

Our experimental study is guided by three main hypotheses. The first hypothesis states that link crawling is a particularly good choice for finding related content in scenarios of tightly connected networks. This hypothesis was formed form observations of the people monitoring extreme right-wing content on the web—an example of a volatile but very connected network.

Our second hypothesis is based on the assumption that Google heavily uses click-through information for its related-operator; it states the Google's related-operator should particularly perform well for frequently visited pages but has lower performance for rather unpopular pages like extreme right-wing content. Also this hypothesis could clearly be confirmed.

Our third hypothesis that automatic keyqueries are a good backup when the other techniques might fail, can only be confirmed for scientific publications. Interestingly, for news portals or NPD pages, the keyqueries technique did not retrieve any results since no keyqueries could be computed. The reason often being too specific or too general queries.

Altogether, our results clearly show that the input document's characteristic is an important signal for choosing the "best" strategy of retrieving related content from the web. In the cases represented in our corpus, different strategies have clear strengths and weaknesses for different document characteristics. Thus, an automatic classification and choice of a good strategy for a given input document is an interesting task in the direction of building an automatic related content finder. The work by Qi and Davison [14] might be a good starting point for classifying the input document. Still, in some cases, like our focus topic of monitoring right-wing content, the keyqueries and Google-related complement the crawled results very well as they find different related results (when they find any).

Interesting directions for future work would be a large-scale study of the observed effects. Our corpus consists of only 100 documents (25 for each of the four scenarios) and only 20 potential results were judged by two assessors whether they are related. A large-scale study should contain hundreds of documents for each scenario probably also including different use cases. We are currently evaluating to what extend such relatedness judgments can be crowdsourced—one ethical issue being the extreme right-wing content for two important parts of our corpus that might not be appropriate for potential assessors.

In order to build a semi-automatic system that supports people monitoring extreme right-wing content, also the recall of the strategies is an important but difficult to estimate issue. So far, the link crawling strategy has the lowest rate of false positives in these cases (while Google-related has the lowest false positive rate for news portals). In order to further reduce the number of false positives presented to the user, machine learning classifiers could be trained for different scenarios that are able to detect the retrieve not-related documents. Research in that direction would probably further smooth the user experience of using the semi-automatic crawling strategy.

# References

1. Agrawal, R., Srikant, R.: Fast algorithms for mining association rules in large databases. In: Proceedings of VLDB 1994, pp. 487–499 (1994)
2. Arasu, A., Cho, J., Garcia-Molina, H., Paepcke, A., Raghavan, S.: Searching the web. ACM Trans. Internet Technol. 1(1), 2–43 (2001)
3. Bendersky, M., Croft, W.B.: Finding text reuse on the web. In: Proceedings of WSDM 2009, pp. 262–271 (2009)
4. Dasdan, A., D'Alberto, P., Kolay, S., Drome, C.: Automatic retrieval of similar content using search engine query interface. In: Proceedings of CIKM 2009, pp. 701–710 (2009)
5. Fuhr, N., Lechtenfeld, M., Stein, B., Gollub, T.: The optimum clustering framework: Implementing the cluster hypothesis. Information Retrieval 15(2), 93–115 (2011)
6. Gollub, T., Hagen, M., Michel, M., Stein, B.: From keywords to keyqueries: Content descriptors for the web. In: Proceedings of SIGIR 2013, pp. 981–984 (2013)
7. Golshan, B., Lappas, T., Terzi, E.: SOFIA search: A tool for automating related-work search. In: Proceedings of SIGMOD 2012, pp. 621–624 (2012)
8. Hagen, M., Stein, B.: Candidate document retrieval for web-scale text reuse detection. In: Grossi, R., Sebastiani, F., Silvestri, F. (eds.) SPIRE 2011. LNCS, vol. 7024, pp. 356–367. Springer, Heidelberg (2011)
9. Lee, Y., Jung, H.Y., Song, W., Lee, J.H.: Mining the blogosphere for top news stories identification. In: Proceedings of SIGIR 2010, pp. 395–402 (2010)
10. Mihalcea, R., Tarau, P.: Textrank: Bringing order into texts. In: Proceedings of EMNLP 2004, pp. 404–411 (2004)
11. O'Callaghan, D., Greene, D., Conway, M., Carthy, J., Cunningham, P.: Uncovering the wider structure of extreme right communities spanning popular online networks. In: Proceedings of WebSci 2013, pp. 276–285 (2013)
12. Page, L., Brin, S., Motwani, R., Winograd, T.: The PageRank citation ranking: Bringing order to the web. Technical Report 1999-66, Stanford InfoLab (1999)
13. Pickens, J., Cooper, M., Golovchinsky, G.: Reverted indexing for feedback and expansion. In: Proceedings of CIKM 2010, pp. 1049–1058 (2010)
14. Qi, X., Davison, B.D.: Web page classification: Features and algorithms. ACM Comput. Surv. 41(2), 12:1–12:31 (2009)
15. Yang, Y., Bansal, N., Dakka, W., Ipeirotis, P., Koudas, N., Papadias, D.: Query by document. In: Proceedings of WSDM 2009, pp. 34–43 (2009)

# SCAN: A Swedish Clinical Abbreviation Normalizer
## Further Development and Adaptation to Radiology

Maria Kvist[1,2] and Sumithra Velupillai[1]

[1] Dept. of Computer and Systems Sciences (DSV)
Stockholm University, Forum 100, SE-164 40 Kista, Sweden
[2] Department of Learning, Informatics, Management and Ethics (LIME)
Karolinska Institutet, Sweden
sumithra@dsv.su.se, maria.kvist@karolinska.se

**Abstract.** Abbreviations pose a challenge for information extraction systems. In clinical text, abbreviations are abundant, as this type of documentation is written under time-pressure. We report work on characterizing abbreviations in Swedish clinical text and the development of SCAN: a Swedish Clinical Abbreviation Normalizer, which is built for the purpose of improving information access systems in the clinical domain. The clinical domain includes several subdomains with differing vocabularies depending on the nature of the specialist work, and adaption of NLP-tools may consequently be necessary. We extend and adapt SCAN, and evaluate on two different clinical subdomains: emergency department (ED) and radiology (X-ray). Overall final results are 85% (ED) and 83% (X-ray) F1-measure on the task of abbreviation identification. We also evaluate coverage of abbreviation expansion candidates in existing lexical resources, and create two new, freely available, lexicons with abbreviations and their possible expansions for the two clinical subdomains.

## 1 Introduction

Access to information is crucial in the clinical domain. In health care, the main form of written communication is in narrative form. Today, most clinical texts are written in Electronic Health Records (EHRs). Accessing information from this type of text requires automated solutions, for instance by Natural Language Processing (NLP) tools.

Clinical text is often written as short telegraphic messages under time-pressure, as memory notes for the healthcare team. Subjects, verbs, and content words are frequently omitted, but the text has a high proportion of technical terms [8]. However, there are more formal parts of the records, such as discharge letters and radiology reports, that are communications to another physician. These parts of the EHR may be written with more complete sentences. Abbreviations and acronyms are frequently used in both the formal and informally written parts of the EHR.

E. Kanoulas et al. (Eds.): CLEF 2014, LNCS 8685, pp. 62–73, 2014.

For information extraction, it is necessary to normalize abbreviations by a multistep procedure of detecting an abbreviation, expanding it to its long form and, when necessary, disambiguate.

## 1.1 Related Work

Abbreviation detection in the clinical domain is associated with special difficulties as many of the normal standards for abbreviation creation are set apart and the full form of the word or expression is rarely present or explained.

**Abbreviations in Clinical Text.** Abbreviations and acronyms in EHRs are often domain specific but can also belong to general language use [13,26]. There are established standard acronyms that can be found in medical terminologies, but often abbreviations are created ad hoc, not following standards, and may be ambiguous. An abbreviation can be used with a number of different meanings depending on context [13,18,14]. For example, the abbreviation RA can represent more than 20 concepts, e.g. renal artery, right atrium, refractory anemia, radioactive, right arm, and rheumatoid arthritis [18]. In the Unified Medical Language System (UMLS[1]), 33% of abbreviations had multiple meanings [13]. Furthermore, a certain word or expression can be shortened in several different ways, some of which mimic ordinary words [13]. These meanings can depend on specialty or profession [14].

Clinical texts differ between specialties, as the vocabulary reflects the nature of diagnoses, examinations and the type of work performed, as well as the temperament of the speciality. Hence, an NLP-tool developed in one subdomain may drop in performance when applied on text from another subdomain. The clinical text in radiology reports has been characterized and differences between this sublanguage, the language in physicians' daily notes and general Swedish have been studied [11,22]. Text from the clinical domain contained more abbreviations than general Swedish, both clinical subdomains contained around 8% abbreviations. Moreover, other higher-level language aspects pose challenges for adapting NLP-tools for the clinical domain, e.g. 63% of all sentences in Swedish radiology reports lack a main predicate (verb) [22].

It has been noted that abbreviations are more common for frequently used expressions and multiword expressions, and it has been found that 14% of diagnostic expressions in Swedish clinical text are abbreviated [21]. Some attempts have been made to capture the full form of words and pair with their abbreviations with distributional semantics in Swedish clinical texts [9,23].

**Terminological Resources.** Although there exist terminologies like the UMLS for English, that also covers medical and clinical abbreviations, there are currently no terminologies or lexicons that have full coverage of clinical abbreviations found in clinical notes, and their possible expansions [24]. Similarly

---

[1] http://www.nlm.nih.gov/research/umls/

for Swedish, there is one comprehensive lexicon of medical abbreviations and acronyms [4], as well as scattered online resources - but no resources that handle a majority of the abbreviation variants that could be found in clinical notes.

**Abbreviation Normalizing Tools.** For English, several tools for clinical NLP, including abbreviation handling, have been developed, such as MetaMap [1,2], MedLee [7], and cTakes [20]. However, a study by Wu et al. [24] showed that these systems did not perform well on the abbreviation detection and expansion tasks when applied to new data. Moreover, results from a recent shared task on abbreviation normalization [15,16] for English clinical text showed that automatic mapping of abbreviations to concept identifiers is not trivial. Hence, this is still a challenging task for improved information extraction and access in the clinical domain. Furthermore, most previous work is done for English. To our knowledge, no tools exist for Swedish clinical text.

This work is an extension of our earlier work [10] with a system for identification and expansion of abbreviations in clinical texts called Swedish Clinical Abbreviation Normalizer (SCAN). The system is rule-, heuristics- and lexicon-based, inspired by previous approaches taken for English and Swedish [26,27,19,12,6]. SCAN relies on word character lengths, heuristics for handling patterns such as hyphenation, and lexicons of known common words, abbreviations and medical terms for identifying abbreviation candidates in a corpus. The system was initially evaluated for the task of *identifying* abbreviations in Swedish clinical assessment entries from an emergency department. It's best performance was reported as 79% F1-measure (76% recall, 81% precision), a considerable improvement over a baseline where words were checked against lexicons only (51% F1-measure). In this work, we extend the evaluation to another clinical subdomain (radiology), and initiate evaluation on abbreviation expansion.

## 1.2   Aim and Objective

Our aim is to improve automated information access and information extraction from clinical text in EHR, for e.g. decision support systems and patients' access to reading their own records. The objective of this study is to characterise abbreviations in Swedish clinical text, improve the performance of SCAN, adapt it for the clinical sublanguage of radiologic reports, and to advance work on abbreviation expansion for Swedish clinical text by creating new lexical resources.

## 2   Method

This study consisted of three main steps: 1) data collection, analysis and characterization of abbreviation types and reference standard creation, 2) iterative development of SCAN, and 3) evaluation of system outputs, coverage analysis of expansion candidates in existing lexical resources along with new lexicon creation. These steps are further described below.

## 2.1  Data and Content Analysis

For each iteration (n=3) in the development of SCAN, we used subsets from the Stockholm EPR Corpus[2] [5]: 3×10 000 words from randomly selected assessment entries from an emergency department (ED), and 3×10 000 words from randomly selected radiology reports (X-ray). All notes are written in Swedish, and written by physicians. Entire notes with preserved context were used. Each subset was manually annotated for abbreviations by a domain expert (a clinician, MK), resulting in 3×2 reference standards (ED, X-ray). Furthermore, we performed a content analysis on abbreviations found in both text subtypes, resulting in a characterisation of types of abbreviations found in Swedish ED and X-ray notes.

## 2.2  SCAN: Iterative Development

We employed an iterative development of SCAN; an error analysis of the output from the first SCAN version (SCAN 1.0) was performed in order to identify common error types. New versions were subsequently developed based on the identified modification needs found through this error analysis, ending in a final version (SCAN 2.0). Three SCAN versions were evaluated on the created reference standards.

## 2.3  Evaluation: System Results, Expansion Coverage and Lexicon Creation

System results were evaluated with precision, recall and F1-measure as the main outcome measures on the held-out datasets, to approximate system performance on unseen data. We also evaluated the coverage (%) of abbreviation expansion candidates in the provided lexicons, and produced a lexicon with abbreviations and expansions for each clinical subtype (ED, X-ray) based on the actual abbreviations found in the datasets. Furthermore, we performed an extensive error analysis on the results from the first and the final iteration of SCAN, performed by a physician.

# 3  Results

We report the results from the content analysis and characterisation of the types of abbreviations found in the studied clinical subtypes ED and X-ray. The error analysis of SCAN 1.0 and the iterative development of SCAN 2.0 is described, followed by the abbreviation identification results from the three versions of SCAN. Finally, we report the coverage analysis of abbreviation expansion candidates from the provided lexicons, and describe the resulting lexicons.

## 3.1  Content Analysis and Characterization

The types of abbreviations are shown in Table 1. Of the abbreviated words, a fraction of 12% were part of compound words, consistently for both text types.

---

[2] This research was approved by the Regional Ethical Review Board in Stockholm (Etikprövningsnämnden i Stockholm), permission number 2012/2028-31/5.

**Table 1.** Characterization of abbreviations in EHR assessment fields from an emergency department (ED) and from radiology reports (X-ray). Numbers were calculated as averages of three datasets with 10 000 words in each set.

| Abbreviation type | ED (%) | X-ray (%) |
|---|---|---|
| Abbreviations, total | 11 | 7,1 |
| *Of these abbreviations:* | | |
| Acronyms | 37 | 62 |
| Shortened words or contractions | 63 | 38 |
| Compounds with abbreviation | 12 | 12 |

For compound words, it was very common that both parts of the word were abbreviated, e.g. *jnlant* (*journalanteckning* eng: record note). The abbreviated words were more often of the type shortened words (*pat* for *patient*) or contractions (*ssk* for *sjuksköterska*, eng: *nurse*) than acronyms (*ECG* for *electrocardiogram*) for the texts from the emergency department, with the proportions 63:37. For the radiology reports, the reverse was consistently seen as average in three sets of 10 000 words, with the proportions 38:62.

The content analysis (Figure 1) reflects the different tasks for physicians at the two respective departments. At the emergency department, the text is a narrative of events such as examinations, blood sampling and resulting lab results, prescribing medication and consultations with other physicians of various specialities. Administrative words denote different hospitals or wards. For radiologists, the task when writing is more descriptive of examinations and findings in the resulting images. A distinctive difference is that the patients are mentioned as a subject (abbr *pat*) at the emergency department whereas the patient is not mentioned as the subject in the radiology reports. In the emergency department assessment entries, the abbreviation of *pat, pats* (plural) is so extensive that this singular abbreviation make up 22% of the total number of abbreviations. Abbreviations for medications were for doses (ml=milliliter) or injections (i.v.= intravenous) but rarely of the medicine names or chemical compounds. Of all abbreviations, diagnostic expressions made up 5,2%. On the other hand, 14% of all diagnostic expressions were abbreviated. This is consistent with the findings of Skeppstedt et al. (2012) [21], where another subset of emergency department assessment entries from the Stockholm EPR Corpus was studied.

## 3.2   Error Analysis of SCAN 1.0 and Development of SCAN 2.0

The error analysis of SCAN 1.0 revealed that names, missing terminology and tokenization were the main sources of errors (Table 2). Names (people and locations) constituted the majority of errors (54%) as these were identified as unknown words and hence the names shorter than 6 characters were identified as abbreviations. Terms that were missing in lexicons were also mistakenly labeled as abbreviations (21%). Incorrect tokenization, making abbreviations

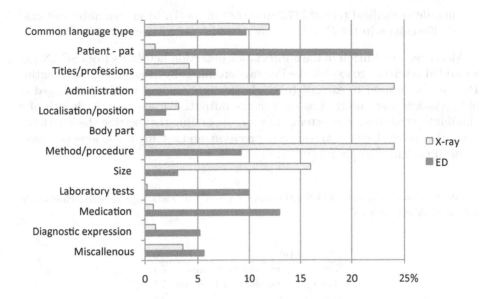

**Fig. 1.** Content analysis for abbreviations in Swedish emergency department assessment entries (ED) and radiology notes (X-ray). Numbers were calculated as averages of 3 datasets with 10 000 words in each set. For the category "Administration", during the iterations in this work, it was found that some administrative information in the end of the radiology texts was redundant and was subsequently removed (proportion dropped from 31% to 10%).

undetectable by e.g. breaking up an abbreviation into two different tokens after a punctuation character, made up 19% of the errors. Only 6% of the errors were due to ambiguity with common words, e.g. *hö*, abbreviation for *höger* (right) can also mean "hay", and was therefore not identified as an abbreviation.

When developing SCAN 2.0, we took these issues into consideration by modifying the following parts:

1. Tokenization: instead of tokenising with in-built heuristics and regular expressions, an existing tool for tokenization and Part-of-Speech (PoS) tagging developed for general Swedish was used (Stagger [17]). In order to better handle domain specific clinical abbreviations, the tokenization rules in Stagger were extended and modified to better handle domain-specific abbreviations found in the error analysis, e.g. handling different instantiations of the abbreviation *vb* (*vid behov* eng: when needed).

2. Names and missing terminology: we added several lexicons for better coverage. Lists of names (first and last) were added from Carlsson & Dalianis [3], totalling 404,899 lexicon entries. Furthermore, in addition to the lexicons used for SCAN 1.0, freely available online lexical resources were added to

handle a) medical terms[3] (17,380 entries in total), b) known abbreviations[4] (7,455 entries in total), and common words[5] (122,847 entries in total).

Moreover, in addition to the abbreviation detection heuristics from SCAN 1.0, we added heuristics to exploit the PoS tags produced by Stagger, e.g. punctuation PoS-tags were used to exclude tokens in the analysis and words PoS-tagged as abbreviations were marked as such in the output. We also set the length of a candidate word to six characters, based on the finding that setting the length too short (i.e. three characters) decreases precision, and setting it too long decreases recall (i.e. eight characters) [10].

**Table 2.** Error analysis: SCAN 1.0 output on Swedish radiology reports, characterization of false positives

| Error type | % |
|---|---|
| Names (people and locations) | 54 |
| Missing terminology in lexicons | 21 |
| Tokenization | 19 |
| Common words | 6 |
| $\sum$ | 100 |

### 3.3   Abbreviation Identification

The abbreviation identification results from three versions of SCAN (1.0, 1.5 and 2.0) are shown in Table 3. SCAN 1.0 is the original version of SCAN. The new tokenization as well as added and modified heuristics are used in SCAN 1.5 and 2.0. SCAN 1.5 uses the same lexicons as SCAN 1.0, while SCAN 2.0 also uses additional lexicons. The tokenization changes clearly leads to performance improvements, in particular for the X-ray data (from 61% to 83% F1-measure). Precision results are best when using SCAN 2.0, with the largest improvement observed for X-ray (from 66% using SCAN 1.5 to 78% using SCAN 2.0). Adding new lexicons does not improve recall (83% vs. 80% for ED, 92% vs. 89% for X-ray), but overall results are improved with the added lexicons (SCAN 2.0).

The false positives produced by SCAN 2.0 include medical terminology, e.g. *flavum*, misspellings, e.g. *västka* (*vätska*, eng: fluid), and unusual person names.

---

[3] Downloaded from: `anatomin.se`, `neuro.ki.se` `smittskyddsinstitutet.se`, `medicinskordbok.se`

[4] Resulting abbreviations from the error analysis, along with entries downloaded from `sv.wikipedia.org/wiki/Lista_över_förkortningar`, `karolinska.se/Karolinska-Universitetslaboratoriet/Sidor-om-PTA/ Analysindex-alla-enheter/Forkortningar/`

[5] Downloaded from `runeberg.org`, `g3.spraakdata.gu.se/saob`,

**Table 3.** Performance of SCAN 1.0, SCAN 1.5 and SCAN 2.0, evaluated with precision, recall and F1-measure. SCAN 1.0 = original SCAN, as reported in [10]. SCAN 1.5 = improved SCAN (new tokenization, added and modified heuristics), but using the same lexicons as SCAN 1.0. SCAN 2.0 = improved SCAN plus added lexicons.

|            | SCAN 1.0 | | SCAN 1.5 | | SCAN 2.0 | |
|------------|------|-------|------|-------|------|-------|
|            | ED   | X-ray | ED   | X-ray | ED   | X-ray |
| recall     | 0.79 | 0.83  | **0.83** | **0.92** | 0.80 | 0.89  |
| precision  | 0.81 | 0.48  | 0.85 | 0.66  | **0.92** | **0.78** |
| F1-measure | 0.80 | 0.61  | 0.84 | 0.77  | **0.85** | **0.83** |

False negatives include compounds, e.g. *lungrtgbilder* (*lung-röntgen-bilder*, eng: lung x-ray images) and ambiguous words, e.g. *sin* (could mean "his" or "her" as well as "sinister", Latin for left side).

### 3.4 Abbreviation Expansion Coverage Analysis and Lexicons

For both record types, a majority of the correct expansions are present in the lexicons[6] (Table 4): 79% for emergency department assessment entries (ED), and 60% for radiology notes (X-ray). However, for radiology, there were more cases where there were no suggestions for expansions in the lexicons (32%). Moreover, in many cases where the correct expansion was present in lexicons, there were many possible expansion candidates. As a result of this analysis, a comprehensive lexicon of abbreviations and their correct expansion in its context was created for each clinical subset (ED, X-ray). Some abbreviations were found in several different typographic variants, e.g. *ua, u.a., u a, u. a.* (*utan anmärkning*, eng: without remark). Moreover, abbreviations could in some cases be expanded to an inflected form, e.g. *us - undersökning* (examination) or *undersökningen* (the examination). The resulting lexicons from this analysis include all typographic variants and expansion inflections found in the data[7].

**Table 4.** Coverage analysis, abbreviation expansions in lexicons. Results from the evaluation of SCAN 2.0 on 10 000 words each of the two datasets are shown.

| Coverage type                               | ED (%) | X-ray (%) |
|---------------------------------------------|--------|-----------|
| Correct expansion in lexicons               | 79     | 60        |
| Missing the correct expansion in lexicons   | 8      | 8         |
| No suggestion for expansion in lexicons     | 13     | 32        |

---

[6] Note that one of the lexicons is the result of the analysis in one of the SCAN development iterations.

[7] *All* possible inflections for an abbreviation expansion are *not* included in the lexicons.

# 4   Analysis and Discussion

We characterized the abbreviations in two subsets of Swedish clinical text and further developed an abbreviation normalizer for Swedish clinical text, SCAN. We also adapted SCAN to the new sublanguage radiologic reports (X-ray) in addition to the previous development for emergency department assessment entries (ED). Our characterisation analysis shows that some abbreviations are from the general language but around 90% of the abbreviations are unique for the domain. The type of abbreviations differ between the subdomains; ED notes contain more references to the patient, medications and laboratory tests, while radiology reports contain abbreviations about methods/procedures and sizes. Acronyms are more prevalent in radiology reports, while shortened forms and contractions are more common in emergency department notes. This information could be informative features in future abbreviation detection systems.

Overall results of SCAN 2.0 are improved on ED data when compared to SCAN 1.0: 0.85 F1-measure as opposed to the initial 0.79. This was mainly due to high precision (0.92) with more extensive lexicons and improved tokenization. On X-ray data, both precision and recall was improved with the largest improvement seen on precision (from 0.48 to 0.78) and we obtained 0.83 F1-measure for SCAN 2.0. Compared to results for English clinical text, our system still has room for improvement. Excellent results (95.7% F1-measure) have been reached by Wu et al. [25] with a combination of machine learning techniques. In the 2013 ShARe/CLEFeHealth task 2 for abbreviation normalization [15], the top-performing system resulted in an Accuracy of 0.72. However, the task did not include the abbreviation detection part, i.e. this was only for normalizing a given abbreviation to its UMLS concept identifier. To our knowledge, there are no available abbreviation detection and/or normalizing tools for Swedish clinical text to which we could compare our results. For Swedish biomedical scientific text, there are results on acronym identification reaching 98% recall and 94% precision [6]. However, as mentioned previously, clinical text differs greatly from other types of texts, in particular the way abbreviations are used and created.

The coverage analysis revealed that existing Swedish lexical resources contain the majority of correct expansions (79%/61% ED/X-ray), but clearly more comprehensive resources are needed. Most importantly, many abbreviations found in the data are missing altogether in existing lexicons.

Part of our aim was to produce new resources. We have created two reference standards with abbreviation annotations that can be used for further studies on abbreviation detection in Swedish clinical text[8]. Moreover, we have created two lexical resources with abbreviations and their expansions as found in the clinical data (ED and X-ray), that are freely available[9].

---

[8] These datasets are available for research purposes upon request, although constrained by obtaining appropriate ethical approval and signing confidentiality agreements.

[9] Please contact the authors for access to the lexical resources.

## 4.1  Limitations and Future Work

This study has some limitations. Although we have created reference standards, they were only annotated by one annotator. SCAN is rule-based and relies on lexicons and heuristics. We depend on existing lexical resources, but do not claim to have included all possible available resources. SCAN was only evaluated with a word length of six characters. We intend to utilise the reference standards to build machine learning classifiers which we believe will lead to improved results for abbreviation detection. Moreover, for abbreviation normalization, we have only evaluated coverage in existing lexicons, and created new lexicons manually. We intend to extend our work also to include abbreviation normalization. Finally, a limitation with our rule-based approach is disambiguation, which is one of the sources for false negatives. Our plan is to extend our work to larger datasets and develop probabilistic classifiers for disambiguating words that could be either an abbreviation or a common word, as well as disambiguating abbreviation expansions when there are multiple candidates. Furthermore, we intend to map Swedish abbreviations to existing terminologies such as SNOMED CT, for future cross-language interoperability.

## 4.2  Significance of Study

To our knowledge, this is the first in-depth study on automatic detection of abbreviations in Swedish clinical text, which also covers two sublanguages (emergency department notes, radiology notes). Our tool, SCAN, is freely available upon request. The created lexicons are being made available online. These resources are a significant contribution to the research community, as they will enable other researchers to work on abbreviation detection and normalization in the Swedish clinical domain. Also, abbreviation detection with machine-learning is facilitated with the new reference standard.

## 5  Conclusions

In this study, we have successfully characterised abbreviations in two subdomains of Swedish clinical text and used the results to improve detection of abbreviations and acronyms with SCAN, resulting in an overall F1-measure of 0.85 for emergency department assessment entries and 0.83 for radiology notes. Further, we have created lexicons with abbreviations and their expansions as found in ED and X-ray reports, and we have evaluated the coverage of correct expansions found in existing lexical resources. For abbreviation normalization in clinical text, it is essential to understand the many irregular ways of ad hoc creativity in abbreviation generation and work closely with domain experts.

**Acknowledgments.** The study was partly funded by the Vårdal Foundation and Swedish Research Council (350-2012-6658), and supported by Swedish Fulbright Commission and the Swedish Foundation for Strategic Research through the project High-Performance Data Mining for Drug Effect Detection (ref. no. IIS11-0053).

# References

1. Aronson, A.R.: Effective mapping of biomedical text to the UMLS Metathesaurus: the MetaMap program. In: Proc. AMIA Symp., pp. 17–21 (2001)
2. Aronson, A., Lang, F.M.: An overview of MetaMap: historical perspective and recent advances. Journal of the American Medical Informatics Association: JAMIA 17(3), 229–236 (2010)
3. Carlsson, E., Dalianis, H.: Influence of Module Order on Rule-Based De-identification of Personal Names in Electronic Patient Records Written in Swedish. In: Proceedings of the Seventh International Conference on Language Resources and Evaluation, LREC 2010, Valletta, Malta, May 19–21, pp. 3071–3075 (2010)
4. Cederblom, S.: Medicinska förkortningar och akronymer. Studentlitteratur (2005) (in Swedish)
5. Dalianis, H., Hassel, M., Henriksson, A., Skeppstedt, M.: Stockholm EPR Corpus: A Clinical Database Used to Improve Health Care. In: Nugues, P. (ed.) Proc. 4th SLTC, Lund, October 25–26, pp. 17–18 (2012), http://nlp.lacasahassel.net/publications/dalianisetal12sltc.pdf
6. Dannélls, D.: Automatic acronym recognition. In: Proceedings of the 11th Conference on European Chapter of the Association for Computational Linguistics, EACL (2006)
7. Friedman, C., Alderson, P.O., Austin, J.H., Cimino, J.J., Johnson, S.B.: A general natural-language text processor for clinical radiology. J. Am. Med. Inform. Assoc. 1(2), 161–174 (1994)
8. Friedman, C., Kra, P., Rzhetsky, A.: Two biomedical sublanguages: a description based on the theories of Zellig Harris. Journal of Biomedical Informatics 35(4), 222–235 (2002)
9. Henriksson, A., Moen, H., Skeppstedt, M., Daudaravicius, V., Duneld, M.: Synonym Extraction and Abbreviation Expansion with Ensembles of Semantic Spaces. Journal of Biomedical Semantics 5, 6 (2014)
10. Isenius, N., Velupillai, S., Kvist, M.: Initial Results in the Development of SCAN: a Swedish Clinical Abbreviation Normalizer. In: Proceedings of the CLEF 2012 Workshop on Cross-Language Evaluation of Methods, Applications, and Resources for eHealth Document Analysis - CLEFeHealth2012. CLEF, Rome, Italy (September 2012)
11. Kvist, M., Velupillai, S.: Professional Language in Swedish Radiology Reports – Characterization for Patient-Adapted Text Simplification. In: Proceedings of the Scandinavian Conference on Health Informatics 2013, Linköping University Electronic Press, Linköpings Universitet, Copenhagen, Denmark (2013), http://www.ep.liu.se/ecp/091/012/ecp13091012.pdf
12. Larkey, L., Ogilvie, P., Price, M., Tamilio, B.: Acrophile: An Automated Acronym Extractor and Server. In: Proceedings of the Fifth ACM Conference on Digital Libraries, pp. 205–214 (2000)
13. Liu, H., Lussier, Y.A., Friedman, C.: Disambiguating Ambiguous Biomedical Terms in Biomedical Narrative Text: An Unsupervised Method. Journal of Biomedical Informatics 34, 249–261 (2001)
14. Lövestam, E., Velupillai, S., Kvist, M.: Abbreviations in Swedish Clinical Text – use by three professions. In: Proc. MIE 2014 (to be presented, 2014)
15. Mowery, D., South, B., Christensen, L., Murtola, L.M., Salanterä, S., Suominen, S., Martinez, D., Elhadad, N., Pradhan, S., Savova, G., Chapman, W.: Task 2: Share/clef ehealth evaluation lab 2013 (2013), http://www.clef-initiative.eu/documents/71612/599e4736-2667-4f59-9ccb-ab5178cae3c5

16. Mowery, D.L., South, B.R., Leng, J., Murtola, L., Danielsson-Ojala, R., Salanterä, S., Chapman, W.: Creating a Reference Standard of Acronym and Abbreviation Annotations for the ShARe/CLEF eHealth Challenge 2013. In: AMIA Annu. Symp. Proc. (2013)

17. Östling, R.: Stagger: an Open-Source Part of Speech Tagger for Swedish. Northern European Journal of Language Technology 3, 1–18 (2013)

18. Pakhomov, S., Pedersen, T., Chute, C.G.: Abbreviation and Acronym Disambiguation in Clinical Discourse. In: Proc. AMIA 2005, pp. 589–593 (2005)

19. Park, Y., Byrd, R.: Hybrid text mining for finding abbreviations and their definitions. In: Proceedings of Empirical Methods in Natural Language Processing, pp. 126–133 (2001)

20. Savova, G., Masanz, J., Ogren, P., Zheng, J., Sohn, S., Kipper-Schuler, K., Chute, C.: Mayo clinical Text Analysis and Knowledge Extraction System (cTAKES): architecture, component evaluation and applications. Journal of the American Medical Informatics Association 17(5), 507–513 (2010)

21. Skeppstedt, M., Kvist, M., Dalianis, H.: Rule-based Entity Recognition and Coverage of SNOMED CT in Swedish Clinical Text. In: Proceedings of the Eighth International Conference on Language Resources and Evaluation, LREC 2012, Istanbul, Turkey, May 23–25, pp. 1250–1257 (2012)

22. Smith, K.: Treating a case of the mumbo jumbos: What linguistic features characterize Swedish electronic health records? Master's thesis, Dept. of Linguistics and Philology, Uppsala University, Sweden (2014)

23. Tengstrand, L., Megyesi, B., Henriksson, A., Duneld, M., Kvist, M.: Eacl - expansion of abbreviations in clinical text. In: Proceedings of the 3rd Workshop on Predicting and Improving Text Readability for Target Reader Populations (PITR), pp. 94–103. Association for Computational Linguistics, Gothenburg (2014), http://www.aclweb.org/anthology/W14-1211

24. Wu, Y., Denny, J.C., Rosenbloom, S.T., Miller, R.A., Giuse, D.A., Xu, H.: A comparative study of current clinical natural language processing systems on handling abbreviations in discharge summaries. In: AMIA Annu. Symp. Proc., pp. 997–1003 (2012)

25. Wu, Y., Rosenbloom, S.T., Denny, J.C., Miller, R.A., Mani, S., Giuse, D.A., Xu, H.: Detecting Abbreviations in Discharge Summaries using Machine Learning Methods. In: AMIA Annu. Symp. Proc., pp. 1541–1549 (2011)

26. Xu, H., Stetson, P.D., Friedman, C.: A Study of Abbreviations in Clinical Notes. In: Proc. AMIA 2007, pp. 821–825 (2007)

27. Yeates, S.: Automatic Extraction of Acronyms from Text. In: Proc. Third New Zealand Computer Science Research Students' Conference, pp. 117–124 (1999)

# A Study of Personalised Medical Literature Search

Richard McCreadie[1], Craig Macdonald[1], Iadh Ounis[1], and Jon Brassey[2]

[1] University of Glasgow
{firstname.lastname}@glasgow.ac.uk
[2] TRIPDatabase.com
{jon.brassey@tripdatabase.com}

**Abstract.** Medical search engines are used everyday by both medical practitioners and the public to find the latest medical literature and guidance regarding conditions and treatments. Importantly, the information needs that drive medical search can vary between users for the same query, as clinicians search for content specific to their own area of expertise, while the public search about topics of interest to them. However, prior research into personalised search has so far focused on the Web search domain, and it is not clear whether personalised approaches will prove similarly effective in a medical environment. Hence, in this paper, we investigate to what extent personalisation can enhance medical search effectiveness. In particular, we first adapt three classical approaches for the task of personalisation in the medical domain, which leverage the user's clicks, clicks by similar users and explicit/implicit user profiles, respectively. Second, we perform a comparative user study with users from the TRIPDatabase.com medical article search engine to determine whether they outperform an effective baseline production system. Our results show that search result personalisation in the medical domain can be effective, with users stating a preference for personalised rankings for 68% of the queries assessed. Furthermore, we show that for the queries tested, users mainly preferred personalised rankings that promote recent content clicked by similar users, highlighting time as a key dimension of medical article search.

## 1 Introduction

Medical practitioners access recent articles and case studies published online in peer-reviewed medical literature to inform the treatments that they recommend to patients [1]. Moreover, increasingly, patients are independently researching their own conditions using resources available on the Web. Indeed, a study by the Pew Research Centre indicated that over 80% of Internet users use search tools to find medical information [2]. As a result, it is critical that the search technologies used to access medical resources are effective, such that medical practitioners and patients can access the most informative and up-to-date information available.

However, the user-base of a medical search engine can be very diverse, and may express very different information needs for the same query. For instance, for the query 'AAO', an ophthalmologist (a specialist focusing on diseases of the eye) might be looking for articles published by the American Association of Ophthalmology, while otolaryngologists (clinicians specialising in ear, nose, and throat disorders) might be searching for new articles from the American Academy of Otolaryngology instead.

E. Kanoulas et al. (Eds.): CLEF 2014, LNCS 8685, pp. 74–85, 2014.

In a Web search environment, this type of problem has been tackled using personalised search approaches (e.g. [3–17]), where the search results for a user are altered based upon an explicit or implicit representation of what the user is interested in.

However, to-date, personalisation has not been examined within the context of medical search. Moreover, due to the differences in the Web and medical search domains, it is unclear whether personalised search approaches that have been shown to be effective for Web search will remain effective. For instance, consider a doctor who consults a series of patients with different illnesses over time. Personalisation approaches that mine contextual information from a user's long-term search history (e.g. [18]) could potentially harm search effectiveness by promoting documents relevant to the wrong patient. Hence, in this paper, we investigate whether search personalisation remains effective when applied to the medical domain.

In particular, we adapt three classical personalisation approaches from the literature to the task of medical search, namely P-Click [19] that uses historical clicks by the user to suggest new documents to promote; G-Click [19], which leverages between-user similarity to identify documents clicked by similar users that are relevant; and a keyword vector-based approach [17] that uses both document and user-level evidence to identify relevant documents clicked by similar users. Using click data from TRIP-Database.com, in addition to a user preference study with volunteers from the user-base of that same provider, we evaluate whether personalisation can increase the effectiveness of medical search. Via automatic evaluation based upon click data, we show that personalised approaches can outperform a baseline production system that does not personalise by a statistically significant margin. Moreover, our user-study showed that for 68% of queries, users preferred the personalised rankings, illustrating that personalisation is remains an effective tool for use in the medical domain.

The remainder of this paper is structured as follows. Section 2 discusses prior works in the fields of medical article search and personalisation. In Section 3, we describe the three personalised medical search approaches that we examine later. Section 4 describes our experimental setup, including our dataset and measures, while in Section 5 we discuss our experimental results. We summarise our conclusions in Section 6.

## 2 Related Work

**Search in the Medical Domain:** Prior works in textual medical search have focused on how end-users make use of Web search engines to explore health-related topics. For instance, Cartright et al. [20] examined how general medical search differs from diagnosis seeking intents, showing that users follow distinct patterns during search, e.g. starting with symptoms and generalising to causes. Ayers and Kronenfeld [21] examined the relationship between chronic medical conditions and how often users search the Web on related topics. Their results indicate that a user's search behaviour changes based on the number of chronic conditions they suffer from and that the type of information they find can alter their subsequent behaviour. Meanwhile, White and Horvitz [22] investigated the related topic of search intent escalation by users from symptom search to finding related medical professionals or hospitals. Moreover, there are also a series of dedicated medical article search systems available on the Web, such as TRIPDatabase.com,

PubMed and Health on the Net. In general, this shows that end users commonly make use of search engines to satisfy medical information needs and that the results they find can impact their behaviour, hence there is a need for effective medical article search approaches.

However, there have been few approaches proposed for the dedicated searching of medical articles. Early work into medical article search using the MEDLINE database was examined during the Genomics track at the Text REtrieval Conference (TREC) [23], but focused only on core IR techniques such as field-based retrieval [24]. Later research into medical-related search has targeted the retrieval of semi-structured e-health records. For instance, the CLEF eHealth Evaluation Lab[3] examined search and exploration of eHealth data, while the TREC Medical Records track [25] examined cohort identification.

Relatedly, ImageCLEF currently runs a medical task that examines (among other topics) ad-hoc retrieval of medical images.[4] Indeed, a variety of medical image search engines such as Goldminer and Yottalook exist to enable medical practitioners to find relevant medical images for specified medical conditions. However, these systems are concerned with tagged medical images rather than medical articles examined here. Indeed, to the best of our knowledge, no prior research has examined how search personalisation can be used for medical article search, which is the focus of this paper.

**Personalised Search Approaches:** In contrast, there is a large volume of literature relating to personalisation in the Web search domain. Classical personalisation approaches involved users providing explicit feedback to the search system in the form of a user profile [8, 10]. However, while these approaches can be effective, it has been shown that users are reluctant to provide explicit profiles when searching [26]. Instead, a number of approaches that use previous user search interactions (queries and clicks) have been proposed, since such data can be collected easily and automatically [4, 5, 7, 11–17]. For instance, Sriram et al. [27] described a search engine that used only the current user session for personalisation, although session data proved to be too sparse to perform well for some queries. Personalisation using longer periods of user history has also been investigated [11, 14, 28]. Speretta and Gauch [14] and Qiu and Cho [11] leveraged the user's click history to classify them into topic hierarchies, using these hierarchies to re-rank the search results. Another popular approach to personalise search results is to train a general ranking function using personalised data from query and click logs [7, 12, 15, 16]. Of note is that Dou et al. [19] proposed two effective approaches named P-Click and G-Click. P-Click promotes documents previously clicked on by the same user for the same query. G-Click promotes documents clicked on by other users for the same query. In a similar manner to [29] and [17], we extend P-Click to consider all previously clicked documents by the user. We then use both P-Click and G-Click as personalised approaches in our later experiments. However, due to sparsity in the query/click logs for some queries, other approaches incorporate information from additional historical sources, rather than just the previous interactions by the current user [15, 17]. For example, Teevan et al. [17] created a combined model of user interests by generating keyword indices for queries issued, web-pages viewed

---

[3] http://clefehealth2014.dcu.ie/
[4] http://www.imageclef.org/2013/medical

and available local content such as emails. They then personalised the ranking produced for a query by up-weighting terms identified as personally relevant, identified from the user's interest model. Expanding on this concept for the medical domain, we test a similar approach that combines implicit click evidence with an interest model for each clinician. We summarise each of the three personalisation approaches that we use in the next section.

## 3    Personalisation Approaches

We experiment with three approaches from the personalisation literature for use in the medical domain, each representing different ways to describe the user's interests. In particular, we experiment with the P-Click and G-Click personalisation approaches proposed by Dou *et al.* [19], and propose a similar approach to that used by Teevan *et al.* [17], which builds an interest profile from all of the click and profile data we have on each user. We detail each of these approaches below.

### 3.1    P-Click

The idea underpinning the P-Click approach is that if a user has clicked on a document before, then they are likely to click on that document again later. Hence. when a user enters a query that they have previously entered, then documents they have previously clicked should be up-weighted. Hence, P-Click defines a document re-scoring function $score_{p-click}(Q,d,u)$ as follows:

$$score_{p-click}(Q, d, u) = \frac{|P_{clicks}(Q, d, u)|}{|P_{clicks}(Q, u)| + \beta} \tag{1}$$

where $Q$ is a query, $d$ is a document to be re-scored, $u$ is the user, $|P_{clicks}(Q, d, u)|$ is the number of previous clicks on document $d$ by user $u$ for query $Q$ and $|P_{clicks}(Q, u)|$ is the total number of documents that the user clicked on for query $Q$. $\beta$ is a normalisation factor that is set to 0.5, as per the original paper [19].

### 3.2    G-Click

One of the issues identified with P-Click was that the rankings produced will not be personalised the first time a user enters a new query, since they will have not have clicked on any documents for that query previously. The G-Click approach attempts to solve this issue by performing group-based personalisation. In particular, in the original paper, G-Click represented each user as a weighted vector of 67 pre-defined topic categories [19]. This weighted vector enables similar users to be identified. Under G-Click, each document is re-scored based upon the number of times similar users have clicked each document and the degree of similarity between the users. In this way, if similar users click a document, then that document is promoted in the ranking. The score for a document is calculated as follows:

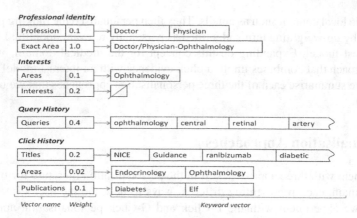

**Fig. 1.** Representation of a sample user comprised of eight keyword vectors

$$score_{g-click}(Q, d, u) = \frac{\sum_{u_i \in U} sim(u, u_i) \cdot |P_{clicks}(Q, d, u_i)|}{\sum_{u_i \in U} |P_{clicks}(Q, u_i)| + \beta} \qquad (2)$$

where $U$ is the set of the $k$ most similar users to $u$ and $sim(u, u_i)$ is the similarity between the users $u$ and $u_i$. However, in the medical domain, we do not have pre-defined topic categories for each user. Instead, we build an interest profile based upon the titles of the documents that each user has previously clicked, where each profile is represented as a term vector, denoted $\rho_u$. User similarity is calculated as the cosine similarity between the two user profiles:

$$sim(u, u_i) = cosine(\rho_u, \rho_{u_i}) \qquad (3)$$

### 3.3 Medical Interest Profiling

As described earlier in Section 2, Teevan *et al.* [17] previously proposed an effective approach that built rich interest profiles for each user using any and all information that the system had access to. Under this approach multiple keyword vectors are constructed, one per information source (e.g. queries or clicked documents), representing the different interests of a user. The interest profiles are used to personalise the document ranking by promoting those documents that share terms with the user's interest profile. We propose a similar approach for medical search personalisation that uses enriched user interest profiles as described below.

First, we represent each user as a weighted series of eight keyword vectors, spread over four aspects, namely: Professional Identity, Interests, Query History and Click History. An example user is illustrated in Figure 1. As can be seen from the figure, each of the four aspects contains one or more keyword vectors. The Professional Identity and Interests aspects come from an explicit profile created when the user registers with the medical search provider. The Query/Click History aspects are generated from an associated query and click log. For example, the 'Areas' vector contains the medical domains that any articles clicked by the user were from, while the 'Publications' vector contains the titles of the publications those clicked articles were published within.

Each keyword vector is assigned a weight, indicating the contribution of that vector to the overall similarity calculation. In our example, the 'Professional Identity' aspect contains two keyword vectors, 'Profession' and 'Exact Area', where the 'Profession' vector has weight 0.1 and contains the keywords 'doctor' and 'physician'. Notably, by weighting each keyword vector, we are able to emphasise aspects of the profile that are important when identifying similar users in the medical domain, e.g. by focusing on the Professional Identity aspects, the algorithm will rank users that come from the same medical background more highly. Furthermore, due to sparsity in the data available, one or more of the keyword vectors may be empty for a given user. For instance, in Figure 1, the 'Interests' vector is empty, indicating that this user did not specify any interests when they registered. Notably, since the search engine we have access to only logs of users who have logged in before querying, the query and click history aspects can also be sparse.

In a similar manner to G-Click described earlier, we define a similarity function between two users $sim(u, u_i)$, such that we can better identify other users with similar interest profiles. We calculate similarity between two users as the sum of the similarities between the each of the eight keyword vectors as shown below:

$$sim(u, u_i) = \sum_{0 \leq j \leq |V|} weight(v_j) \cdot sim(v_j^u, v_j^{u_i}) \tag{4}$$

where $u$ and $u_i$ are users, $v_j^u$ is the $j$'th keyword vector for $u$, $weight(v_j)$ is the weight assigned to that vector, where $0 \leq weight(v_j) \leq 1$ and $|V|$ is the number of vectors (eight). We use the cosine measure to calculate the similarity between vectors. In this way, we are able to arrive at a combined estimate of user similarity between medical search engine users that combines both implicit query/click information with explicit information about the user's interests and profession. The weights for each keyword vector are trained using volunteer clinicians on a separate training set (see Section 4).

Using this similarity function, we then re-score each document based both the user's interest profile and the profiles of similar users. In particular, we define a re-scoring function $score_{MIP}(Q, d, u)$ as follows:

$$score_{MIP}(Q, d, u) = \sum_{u_i \in U} score(d, Q) \cdot \begin{cases} \lambda \cdot sim(u, u_i) & \text{if } |P_{clicks}(Q, d, u_i)| > 0 \\ 0 & \text{otherwise} \end{cases} \tag{5}$$

where $d$ is a document to be scored, $Q$ is the user query, $u$ is the user, $U$ is the set of top $k$ similar users ranked for $u$, $score(d, Q)$ is the original score assigned to document $d$ for the query $Q$ and $|P_{clicks}(Q, d, u_i)|$ is the number of times user $u_i$ clicked on document $d$ for the query $Q$. For our experiments, we use the PL2 [30] weighting model to calculate $score(d, Q)$ as it was the most effective based on prior testing on a hold-out training set. We refer to this approach in our later experiments as medical interest profiles (MIP). In the next section, we describe our experimental setup for evaluation of these three personalisation approaches within a medical search scenario.

## 4 Experimental Setup

**Methodology.** We evaluate our proposed personalisation approach to medical article search in two manners, both based upon a medical document collection containing

1,418,996 medical articles from the period of June 1855 to April 2013 (although over 90% of these articles were published during the last 10 years) provided by the TRIP-Database.com medical article search engine. We use this dataset since it comes with an associated query/click log and user profiling information from that search engine. First, inspired by prior literature [19], we attempt to evaluate in a fully automatic manner using the aforementioned query/click log. Second, we evaluate as part of a preference user study with volunteers from the aforementioned search engine. We describe the preparation of each evaluation below.

**Query-Log Evaluation.** For our query-log evaluation, we use medical search queries and clicks issued to TRIPDatabase.com since 2010. In particular, for each user that registered with the search engine, a query log lists that user's search queries and the documents they clicked, grouped into search sessions. Each user also has a profile containing their profession and clinical areas of interest. To create our test topics, we sampled 968 users who had used the search engine for more than one month and had issued one or more queries during the month of April 2013 (our chosen test month). For each of these users, we selected the last search session they made. The first query in that session for each user is used as a topic query, forming a test set comprised of 968 topics. The document(s) that the user clicked upon during the last session are considered to be relevant, similarly to [5]. All queries and clicks made by the user prior to the last session are used as training data, i.e. to calculate $P_{clicks}$ in Equation 1,2 and 5, as well as generate the user interest profiles under G-Click and MIP. However, for 897 of the 968 test topics, the click data available in the test session was sufficiently sparse that none of the documents promoted by the personalised approaches had clicks. This is to be expected, since the personalised approaches (particularly G-Click and MIP that use other similar user's interaction history to re-rank the results) are likely to promote documents that the user did not originally see/click on. As a result, we further down sample the test set to the 71 topics where the performance of the baseline and personalised approaches differ.

**User-Study Evaluation.** To mitigate the limitations of the query-log evaluation, we also perform a user-study using volunteers from the user-base of TRIPDatabase.com. We recruited 17 users and then had each suggest queries that we then use to test personalisation. A total of 90 queries were suggested, which we use as topics. These topics do not overlap with the 71 used in the query-log evaluation. For each query and the user that suggested it, we produce both personalised and unpersonalised rankings. We then performed a blind side-by-side evaluation [31] to determine whether the users preferred the personalised rankings over the unpersonalised ones. Our evaluation interface is shown in Figure 2. As can be seen, we render each ranking side-by-side in a pair-wise manner per-query, the user selects their preferred ranking using the buttons at the top of each. The positioning of the personalised and unpersonalised rankings (left or right position) are randomised. This ordering is hidden from the assessors. To further investigate why users preferred one ranking approach over another, for each ranking pair, we also had the volunteer fill a questionnaire, where they select zero or more reasons for choosing that ranking as follows:

Query: 'Lipodystrophy in ARV treatment'

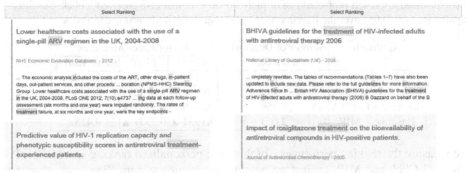

Fig. 2. User study preference assessment interface

- The selected ranking was more relevant to the query.
- Documents within the selected ranking were more informative.
- The selected ranking provided better coverage of the topic.
- The documents within the selected ranking were more recent.

**Parameter Training.** The MIP approach requires weights for the $\lambda$ parameter and each keyword vector ($weight(v_j)$ in Equation 4). To generate these weights, we had volunteers from the user-base of TRIPDatabase.com score each document ranked by MIP on a separate set of 18 topics (this does not overlap with either the two other topic sets used above). Volunteers labelled each document as relevant or not to the topic for a given user profile. The optimal value for the $\lambda$ parameter and each keyword vector weight was optimised via a parameter scan over each (where $0 \leq weight(v_j) \leq 1$, $0 \leq \lambda \leq 10$ and increments of size 0.1 were tested).

**Measures.** For evaluation using the query log, we report the classical IR ranking metrics mean average precision (MAP), Precision at rank 5 (P@5) and the Rank Scoring metric from the collaborative filtering literature [32].

# 5   Results

To determine whether personalisation is effective when applied to the task of medical article search, we investigate the following two research questions, each in a separate section.
- Can personalisation approaches more effectively rank medical documents than the unpersonalised baseline? (Section 5.1)
- Do end-users prefer the (MIP) personalised rankings to the unpersonalised baseline? (Section 5.2)

## 5.1   Evaluating Using Click-Logs

We begin by investigating our first research question, i.e. can personalisation approaches more effectively rank medical documents than the unpersonalised baseline? To do so,

**Table 1.** Ranking performance of the medical search approaches tested using the 71 topics where a personalised approach promoted one or more documents that also received a click. Statistical significance (p<0.05) over the Baseline approach using the paired t-test is denoted ▲.

| Approach | Number of Documents Promoted | Performance Measures | | |
|---|---|---|---|---|
| | | P@5 | MAP | Rank Scoring |
| Baseline | n/a | 0.1250 | 0.1651 | 0.3101 |
| Baseline + P-Click | 1,291 | 0.1361 | 0.1769 | 0.3334 |
| Baseline + G-Click | 8,459 | 0.1694 | **0.2731 ▲** | 0.3851 |
| Baseline + MIP | 2,063 | **0.1951 ▲** | 0.2571 ▲ | **0.4282** |

we measure the ranking performance of the three personalised ranking approaches (P-Click, G-Click and MIP) against the baseline production system (Baseline) using the 71 topics sampled from our medical query-log. Table 1 reports the performance of the baseline and personalised approaches in terms of the MAP, P@5 and Rank Scoring metrics. Higher scores indicate that the approaches are ranking the documents clicked by users higher in the ranking.

From Table 1, we observe the following. First, all of the personalised approaches outperform the production system. Indeed, P-Click provides the smallest increase in performance of 1.21% absolute P@5, while the largest increase in performance was observed from the MIP approach, with a statistically significant +6.94% absolute P@5. Second, we see that under the precision-orientated metrics, P@5 and Rank Scoring, MIP personalisation outperformed the unpersonalised baseline and both the personalised P-Click and G-Click approaches. This shows that in the high ranks, using rich user interest profiles to find similar users is more effective than using the user-profile or user-click data alone when identifying additional documents that the user might be interested in. For instance, one topic where MIP outperformed G-Click was for the query 'personality disorder' when the user was interested in 'antisocial behaviour' and had selected the clinical area 'Psychiatry'. For this query, the MIP approach used its user interest profiles to find a similar clinician who had previously clicked on two documents relevant to the current user, i.e. 'Antisocial personality disorder, treatment, management and prevention' and 'Psychological interventions for antisocial personality disorder', which were then ranked higher. For the same topic, G-Click failed to find these two documents, because the current user had not clicked on documents about antisocial behaviour before.

However, we also see from Table 1 that G-Click evidences higher performance than MIP under MAP. This result is to be expected, since MIP is by its nature more conservative in how it promotes documents from similar users, since its more granular between-user similarity function (Equation 4) limits the contribution of users where only a sub-set of the interest profile vectors match. This contrasts with G-Click, where only the (cosine) similarity between the clicked document titles are is used to weight the emphasis placed on each previously clicked document. Indeed, from the second column of Table 1, we can see that G-Click promoted more than 4 times the number of documents than MIP did. Hence, MIP can be characterised as a more precision-orientated approach than G-Click. To answer our first research question, based upon the click-based assessments available, personalised approaches appear to be effective, significantly outperforming the baseline production system in the case of MIP. Indeed,

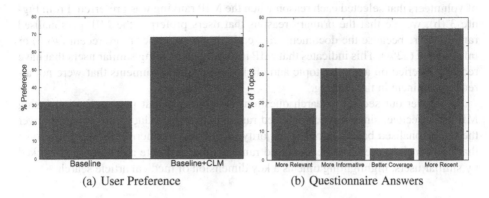

(a) User Preference                    (b) Questionnaire Answers

**Fig. 3.** Proportion of queries that users prefer the MIP personalised ranking in comparison to the baseline and the reasons provided for that preference

the MIP approach that uses richer user interest profiles is able to markedly outperform both other personalised approaches in terms of precision at rank 5 (P@5) and provides close-to G-Click's performance under mean average precision (MAP).

### 5.2   Evaluating via User-Study

Having shown that the personalised approaches are effective using the click data available to us, we next evaluate our second research question, i.e. do end-users prefer the (MIP) personalised ranking to the production system currently deployed by the search engine?[5] To this end, we perform a user study, where we have users state their preference for either the unpersonalised baseline or the MIP personalised rankings for the 90 query topics that they themselves suggested.

Figure 3 (a) shows the proportion of users that preferred the MIP personalised ranking in comparison to the production system over the 90 topics suggested by volunteer clinicians in our user study. From Figure 3 (a), we see that the personalised ranking was preferred over the unpersonalised baseline for the majority (68%) of queries tested, supporting our earlier observations on the click data indicating that MIP is effective. To illustrate, one example where the MIP ranking was preferred was for the query 'temporomandibular joint dysfunction' (about the jaw joint in humans) where the user had specified the clinical area 'Otolaryngology' (a field dealing with the ear, nose, and throat) and an interest about hearing aids. From this information, the MIP component identified a clinician from the same field who had been searching about anti-inflammatory drugs to treat people with hearing aids, thereby promoting a study about anti-inflammatory drugs that the volunteer clinician found informative.

However, also of interest is why users prefer the MIP ranking. To evaluate this, recall that for each ranking pair, the volunteer clinicians also filled a questionnaire regarding why they preferred that ranking in terms of 4 criteria, namely: relevance, informativeness, topical coverage and recency (see Section 4). Figure 3 (b) reports the proportion

---

[5] Note that we compare against MIP only here, since we showed previously that MIP outperforms P-Click and G-Click.

of volunteers that selected each reason when the MIP ranking was preferred. From Figure 3 (b), we see that the primary reasons that users preferred the MIP-personalised ranking were because the documents ranked highly were either more recent (46%) or informative (32%). This indicates that MIP is mainly identifying similar users that have recently queried on a similar topic and clicked on useful documents that were not already prominent in the ranking.

To answer our second research question, we conclude that personalisation (using MIP) is effective, since the personalised rankings that it produced are preferred over the unpersonalised baseline for the majority of queries. Furthermore, we have shown that users mainly preferred personalised rankings that promote recent content clicked by similar users, highlighting time as a key dimension of medical article search.

## 6    Conclusions

In this paper, we examined whether personalisation approaches previously proposed for use in the Web search domain remain effective for the task of medical article search. We adapted three classical personalisation approaches from the literature for medical search that leverage the user's clicks, clicks by similar users and explicit/implicit user interest profiles, respectively. Through experimentation over a medical search query log, we showed that these approaches could outperform an unpersonalised baseline system, and that the approach that used explicit/implicit user interest profiles was the most effective, suggesting that using the affinity between clinicians is a useful source of evidence to use when finding additional relevant content. Moreover, through a user study with volunteer clinicians, we showed that users prefer the rankings produced through personalisation to the baseline in a blind test - showing that personalisation approaches are effective in the medical article search domain. Finally through a questionnaire with our volunteer users, we found that the main reasons that the personalised approach improved over the baseline ranking from the user perspective was that the personalised results contained additional informative and recent content - highlighting the importance of finding the most up-to-date medical content of interest to each clinician. For future work, we aim to investigate how the across-session and within-session search patterns of users can be used to further personalise the medical search results for a user.

## References

1. Guyatt, G., Rennie, D., Hayward, R., et al.: Users' guides to the medical literature: A manual for evidence-based. In: Clinical Practice, vol. 706
2. Susannah Fox: Report: Health, Digital Divide - Health Topics (2011),
   http://pewinternet.org/Reports/2011/HealthTopics.aspx
3. Chirita, P.A., Nejdl, W., Paiu, R., Kohlschütter, C.: Using ODP metadata to personalize search. In: Proc. of SIGIR (2005)
4. Daoud, M., Tamine-Lechani, L., Boughanem, M., Chebaro, B.: A session based personalized search using an ontological user profile. In: Proc. of SAC (2009)
5. Dou, Z., Song, R., Wen, J.R.: A large-scale evaluation and analysis of personalized search strategies. In: Proc. of WWW (2007)

6. Gauch, S., Chaffee, J., Pretschner, A.: Ontology-based personalized search and browsing. Web Intelligence and Agent Systems Journal (2003)
7. Joachims, T.: Optimizing search engines using clickthrough data. In: Proc. of SIGKDD (2002)
8. Liu, F., Yu, C., Meng, W.: Personalized Web search by mapping user queries to categories. In: Proc. of CIKM (2002)
9. Liu, F., Yu, C., Meng, W.: Personalized web search for improving retrieval effectiveness. IEEE Transactions on Knowledge and Data Engineering (2004)
10. Pretschner, A., Gauch, S.: Ontology based personalized search. In: Proc. of ICTAI (1999)
11. Qiu, F., Cho, J.: Automatic identification of user interest for personalized search. In: Proc. of WWW (2006)
12. Shen, X., Tan, B., Zhai, C.: Implicit user modeling for personalized search. In: Proc. of CIKM (2005)
13. Sieg, A., Mobasher, B., Burke, R.: Web search personalization with ontological user profiles. In: Proc. of CIKM (2007)
14. Speretta, M., Gauch, S.: Personalized search based on user search histories. In: Proc of WIC (2005)
15. Sugiyama, K., Hatano, K., Yoshikawa, M.: Adaptive Web search based on user profile constructed without any effort from users. In: Proc. of WWW (2004)
16. Sun, J.T., Zeng, H.J., Liu, H., Lu, Y., Chen, Z.: CubeSVD: A novel approach to personalized web search. In: Proc. of WWW (2005)
17. Teevan, J., Dumais, S.T., Horvitz, E.: Personalizing search via automated analysis of interests and activities. In: Proc. of SIGIR (2005)
18. Tan, B., Shen, X., Zhai, C.: Mining long-term search history to improve search accuracy. In: Proc. of SIGKDD (2006)
19. Dou, Z., Song, R., Wen, J.R.: A large-scale evaluation and analysis of personalized search strategies. In: Proc. of WWW (2007)
20. Cartright, M.A., White, R.W., Horvitz, E.: Intentions and attention in exploratory health search. In: Proc. of SIGIR (2011)
21. Ayers, S., Kronenfeld, J.: Chronic illness and health-seeking information on the Internet. Health Journal (2007)
22. White, R.W., Horvitz, E.: Web to world: Predicting transitions from self-diagnosis to the pursuit of local medical assistance in Web search. In: Proc. of AMIA (2010)
23. Hersh, W., Voorhees, E.: TREC Genomics special issue overview. Information Retrieval Journal (2009)
24. Fujita, S.: Revisiting Again Document Length Hypotheses TREC 2004 Genomics Track Experiments at Patolis. In: Proceedings of TREC (2004)
25. Voorhees, E., Hersh, W.: Overview of the TREC 2012 Medical Records Track. In: Proc. of TREC (2012)
26. Carroll, J.M., Rosson, M.B.: Paradox of the active user. The MIT Press (1987)
27. Sriram, S., Shen, X., Zhai, C.: A session-based search engine. In: Proc. of SIGIR (2004)
28. Tan, B., Lv, Y., Zhai, C.: Mining long-lasting exploratory user interests from search history. In: Proc. of CIKM (2012)
29. Matthijs, N., Radlinski, F.: Personalizing web search using long term browsing history. In: Proc. of WSDM (2011)
30. Amati, G.: Probabilistic Models for Information Retrieval based on Divergence from Randomness. PhD thesis, University of Glasgow (2003)
31. Benjamin, C.A.: Low-Cost and Robust Evaluation of Information Retrieval Systems. PhD thesis, University of Massachusetts Amherst (2009)
32. Breese, J.S., Heckerman, D., Kadie, C.: Empirical analysis of predictive algorithms for collaborative filtering. In: Proc. of UAI (1998)

# A Hybrid Approach for Multi-faceted IR in Multimodal Domain

Serwah Sabetghadam, Ralf Bierig, and Andreas Rauber

Institute of Software Technology and Interactive Systems
Vienna University of Technology

**Abstract.** We present a model for multimodal information retrieval, leveraging different information sources to improve the effectiveness of a retrieval system. This method takes into account multifaceted IR in addition to the semantic relations present in data objects, which can be used to answer complex queries, combining similarity and semantic search. By providing a graph data structure and utilizing hybrid search in addition to structured search techniques, we take advantage of relations in data to improve retrieval. We tested the model with ImageCLEF 2011 Wikipedia collection, as a multimodal benchmark data collection, for an image retrieval task.

**Keywords:** Multimodal, Information Retrieval, Graph, Hybrid Search, Facet, Spreading Activation.

## 1   Introduction

The web is increasingly turning into a multimodal content delivery platform. This trend creates severe challenges for information retrieval. Using different modalities —text, image, audio or video—to improve an IR System is challenging since each modality has a different concept of similarity underneath.

There are numerous related works in this area, e.g., in combination of text and images, given the massive web data, relevant web images can be readily obtained by using keyword based search [7,5]. Utilizing intermodal analysis for automatic document annotation [11] is another possibility.

In addition to the observation that data consumption today is highly multimodal, it is also clear that data is now heavily semantically interlinked. This can be through social networks (text, images, videos of users on LinkedIn, Facebook or the like), or through the nature of the data itself (e.g. patent documents connected by their metadata - inventors, companies). Connected data poses structured IR as an option for retrieving more relevant data objects.

We observe, since 2005, a trend towards hybrid search, leveraging both structured and un-structured IR [8,4,6]. Combining the two search methods is challenging because of their respective diversity. In unstructured IR we have multimodality – the diverse nature of the data objects, while in structured IR we have multi-connectivity – the diverse nature of the links of the graph.

E. Kanoulas et al. (Eds.): CLEF 2014, LNCS 8685, pp. 86–97, 2014.

In this paper, we propose a model, named Astera, to leverage hybrid search in order to handle the diverse nature of the nodes and edges in the multimodal content domain. We model domain specific collections with the help of different relation types, and enrich the available data by extracting inherent information in the form of facets. Our model is a triangle of hybrid search, faceted search and multimodal data.

We show the applicability of this model on the multimodal domain by using the ImageCLEF 2011 Wikipedia collection dataset [17]. We perform a basic yet thorough evaluation and show that our model matches the efficiency of non-graph based indexes, while having the potential to exploit different facets for better retrieval. We show that the result of multimodal faceted approach, excels baseline results.

The paper is structured as follows: in the next section, we address the related work, followed in Section 3 by the basic definition of our model, graph traversal and weighting. The experiment design is shown in Section 4. The results are discussed in Section 5, and finally, conclusions and future work are presented in Section 6.

## 2   Related Work

Astera is at the crossroad of different related work areas: multimodal retrieval, hybrid search, faceted and semantic search. We try in this section to clarify the differentiation of Astera towards each category and highlight its new message.

There are many efforts in multimodal retrieval, e.g. in combining textual and visual modalities. Martinent et al. [11] propose to generate automatic document annotations from inter-modal analysis. They consider visual feature vectors and annotation keywords as binary random variables. Srinivasan and Slaney [16] add content based information to image characteristics as visual information to improve their performance. Their model is based on random walks on bipartite graphs of joint model of images and textual content. I-Search, as a multimodal search engine [9], defines relations between different modalities of an information object, e.g. a lion's image, its sound and its 3D representation. They define neighbourhood relation between two multimodal objects which are similar in at least one of their modalities. However, in I-Search, the semantic relation between objects (e.g. a dog and a cat object) is not considered.

In combining structured and unstructured IR, Magatti [10] provides a combination of graph and content search. For example, in an organization, members have hierarchal relations by their roles, meanwhile there are related documents to them. The structured search engine NAGA [8], provides the results of a structured (not keyword) query by using subgraph pattern on an Entity-Relationship graph. Rocha et al. [12] use spreading activation for relevance propagation applied to a semantic model of a given domain. Targeting RDF data, SIREn [4] supports both keywords and structured queries. Elbassuoni and Blanco [6] select subgraphs to match the query and do the ranking by means of statistical language models. We build upon these works and complement them with the concept of faceted search.

We extend the common notion of faceted search in order to enable a more flexible information access model. We connect extracted facets to their information objects and treat them as individual nodes. This provides various possibilities for both early and late fusion.

Another aspect of Astera is that the data model is a graph which relates it to work done in the semantic web domain. Search in the semantic web is keyword-based. Some research is particularly concerned with generating adequate interpretations of user queries [15]. In addition to semantic search, Astera is able to consider similarity computations (between object facets) for searching an information object. Furthermore, we generalize the query and provide a list of highly related neighbours for a user, rather than simply providing an exact response.

Related research on the ImageCLEF 2011 Wikipedia collection is generally based on a combination of text and image retrieval [17]. To our best knowledge, there is no approach that has modelled the collection as a graph structure and no approach has therefore leveraged the explicit links between objects and between objects and their features.

## 3    Model Representation

We define a model to represent information objects and their relationships, together with a general framework for computing similarity. We see the information objects as a graph $G = (V, E)$, in which $V$ is the set of vertices (including data objects and their facets) and $E$ is the set of edges. By facet we mean inherent information of an object, otherwise referred to as a representation of the object. For instance, an image object may have several facets (e.g. color histogram, texture representation). Each of these is a node linked to the original image object. Each object in this graph may have a number of facets. We define four types of relations between the objects in the graph. The relations and their characteristics are discussed in detail in [13]. We formally define the relation types and their weights as follows:

- **Semantic** ($\alpha$): any semantic relation between two objects in the collection (e.g. the link between lyrics and a music file). The edge weight $w_{uv}$ is made inversely proportional to the $\alpha$-out-degree of the source node $u$ (the number of outgoing $\alpha$ links from $u$). Thus $w_{uv} = 1/N_u^{(\alpha)}$. This reduces the effect of very connected nodes on the spreading process and simulates fanout constraint[3] to decrease the distributed energy to very low for popular nodes.
- **Part-of** ($\beta$): a specific type of semantic relation, indicating an object as part of another object, e.g. an image in a document. This is a containment relation as an object is part of another one, and therefore we set the default weight to 1.

- **Similarity** ($\gamma$): relation between objects with the same modality. This relation is defined just between the facets of the same type of two information objects, and the weight is the similarity value between the facets according to some facet-specific metric. For instance, we can compute the similarity between Edge Histogram facet of two images.
- **Facet** ($\delta$): linking an object to its representation(s). In our graph traversal, we can reach an object from its facet and go to other objects but we do not walk from an object to its facets. The edge in the direction of the object to the facet is weighted 0. On the other direction, from facet to the object, weights are given by perceived information content of features, with respect to the query type. For instance, with a query like "blue flowers", the color histogram is a determining facet that should be weighted higher. These weights should be learned for a specific domain, and even for a specific query if we were to consider relevance feedback.

In addition to the edge weights just defined, we consider the use of a self-transitivity value ($st$) to emphasize remaining on a specific state. This value leaves part or all of the initial energy with the current node.

$$W_{v|u} = \begin{cases} (1 - st)w_{uv} & u \neq v \\ st & u = v \end{cases} \tag{1}$$

where $W_{v|u}$ is the weight of going from node $u$ to $v$.

### 3.1 Traversal Method - Spreading Activation

For traversing the graph and finding the relevant result for a query, we propose to use spreading activation (SA). The SA procedure, always starts with an initial set of activated nodes, usually the result of a first stage processing of the query. During propagation, surrounding nodes are activated and ultimately, a set of nodes with respective activation are obtained. After $t$ steps, we use the method provided by Berthold et al. [2], to compute the nodes' activation value :

$$a^{(t)} = a^{(0)} \cdot W^t \tag{2}$$

where $a^{(0)}$ is the initial activation vector, $W$ is the weight matrix—containing different edge type weights—, and $a^{(t)}$ is the final nodes' activation value used for ranking.

### 3.2 Hybrid Search

The use of results from independent modality indexing neglect a) that data objects are interlinked through different relations and b) that many relevant images can be retrieved from a given node by following semantic or 'part-of' relations. Our hybrid ranking method consists of two steps: 1) In the first step, we perform an initial search with Lucene and/or Lire to obtain a set of activation nodes. 2) In the second step, using the initial result set of data objects (with normalized scores) as seeds, we exploit the graph structure and traverse it.

We follow the weighted edges from the initiating points for t steps. We perform the spreading activation and at the end recompute the ranked result based on the activation value nodes received via propagation (Equation 2).

The number of transitions is determined by imposing different stop rules: distance constraint [3], fan-out constraint [3] or type constraint[12]. In this version of our model, we use the distance constraint to stop the traversal.

## 4   Experiment Design

In this section, we describe the dataset and different retrieval methods. We used ImageCLEF 2011 Wikipedia collection to evaluate the indexing of multi-modal multimedia content and to test the functionality and performance of our hybrid search method.

### 4.1   Data Collection

We applied the ImageCLEF 2011 Wikipedia collection as a benchmark. This collection is based on Wikipedia pages and their associated images. It is a multimodal collection and an appropriate choice for testing the rich and diverse set of relations in our model. The goal in the setting of this particular test collection is to retrieve images. Each image has one metadata file that provides information about name, location, one or more associated parent documents in up to three languages (English, German and French), and textual image annotations (i.e. caption, description and comment). The collection consists of 125,828 documents and 237,434 images. We parsed the image metadata and created nodes for all parent documents, images and corresponding facets. We created different relation types: the $\beta$ relation between parent documents and images (as part of the document), and $\delta$ relation between information objects and their facets. We use the 50 English query topics.

### 4.2   Standard Text and Image Search

In the indexed search approach, as first phase of our hybrid search, we use Lucene indexing results both for documents and images. The computed scores in both modalities are normalized per topic between (0,1). Different indexings based on different facets are:

- **Document tf.idf facet**: We utilize default Lucene indexer, based on tf.idf, as document facet. We refer the result set of this facet as R1.
- **CEDD facet**: For image facets, we selected the Color and Edge Directivity Descriptor (CEDD) feature since it is considered the best method to extract purely visual results [1]. We refer to the image results of the CEDD facet as R2.

– **Image textual annotation tf.idf facet**: We use metadata information of the images (provided by the collection), as image textual facets (Tags). Metadata XML files of ImageCLEf 2011 Wikipedia collection, includes textual information (caption, comment and description) of images. Using Lucene we can index them as separate fields, and search based on a multi-field indexing. Tags search result make R3 result set.

*Weighting Strategy.* Each information object (e.g. image, document or any other type of information object) may have many facets. They can receive at maximum, the score of 1 from facets. We weight visual facets with 0.3 and textual facets with 0.7 as an experimental parametrization based on a set of previous empirical tests [14].

The formula for the combined scoring is like: $obj\_score = \sum_{i=0}^{n} w_i.f_i$ where $\sum_{i=0}^{n} w_i = 1$. Variable $n$ is the number of the facets, and $w_i$ is the weight of facet $f_i$.

For images, we have visual facet of CEDD, and metadata information as textual facet. Mapped to the score formula, it is $(0.7 * Tags + 0.3 * CEDD)$. For document objects, we have textual facet tf.idf and we give $(1.0 * tf.idf)$ as weighting. The weights are fixed based on the experiments, but should be learned.

### 4.3   Graph Search

In this section we describe how we manage facet fusion and graph traversal.

**Subgraph Traversal.** The ImageCLEF 2011 Wikipedia collection contains the total size of 363,262 information objects (images and documents without considering the facet nodes). With matrix in this size, we need about 983GB RAM to perform matrix multiplication. In order to make the calculation feasible for large collections, our strategy in Astera is to only contain the set of nodes that will be potentially reachable after N steps, and generate a smaller adjacency matrix only for them. However, this set of reachable nodes depends on the query . Therefore, for different query topic and different number of steps, we work with different subgraphs of the whole graph.

Starting from top ranked nodes for a query topic, we visit next round neighbours in each step. After visiting all neighbours to the specific step in the graph, we create the adjacency matrix $W$ out of that. The cell values of the adjacency matrix are the edge weights between different visited nodes.

As shown in Equation 2, we compute the steps in the graph by matrix multiplication. The $a^{(0)}$ vector is composed of top ranked nodes of R1,R2 and R3 (as non-zero elements), and visited neighbours through traversal (as zero elements). The final vector, $a^t$, provides the final activation value of all nodes. We filter out the images and calculate precision and recall based on their scores. We chose 9 steps to show spreading activation behaviour in primary steps in Astera. We are visiting on average about 15,000 nodes per topic.

**Maximum Nodes Searchable from Text.** With adding one facet for images and documents, we add about 363,262 nodes to the collection which results in 726,524 node graph. Starting from text indexing results, we continued the traversal in the graph up to visiting no new node. This happened in average after 40 steps and visiting about 170,000 nodes of total 726,524 nodes. This shows that starting just from documents provides limited view to the collection and we miss related objects in the other parts of the graph.

**Facet Fusion.** In practice, we are making a form of late facet fusion by combination of different scores and giving one score to the parent information object. However, it is not in the traditional way of late fusion. Since we are not making the result rank list out of top ranked nodes. We initiate their scores in graph nodes and then start propagation. In Astera, facet fusion is implicitly calculated by matrix multiplication and final vector computation.

## 5   Results and Discussion

### 5.1   Experiment 1: Baseline

The evaluation of this experiment represents our baseline and applies a standard Lucene index in combination with a standard Lucene search. For each ranked document result, we extracted its associated images and ranked them based on the score of the document. The result is shown in the first row of Table 1 (e.g. 0.311 for p@10). We additionally refine the baseline by computing the similarity between each of the query images and each of the result list images and keep the value of the maximum similarity SV as reference as shown in the following formula:

$$SV_{q_{imgs}, res_{img}} = max(Sim(q_{img_i}, res_{img})), 1 \leq i \leq 5$$

Now each image result has two scores, the text scores and the image similarity score. By applying a range of different weightings for their linear combination, we discovered the best result is obtained by weighting text with 0.7 and images with 0.3 (see second row of Table 1)[14]. Results purely obtained from image-only searches had very low recall and are not presented here.

**Table 1.** Results for baseline

| txt weight | img weight | p@10 | r@10 | p@20 | r@20 |
|------------|------------|-------|-------|-------|-------|
| 1          | 0          | 0.311 | 0.105 | 0.247 | 0.129 |
| 0.7        | 0.3        | 0.345 | 0.109 | 0.281 | 0.133 |

### 5.2   Experiment 2: Graph Modelled Data

Having modelled the collection in a graph, we designed several experiments based on tf.idf, CEDD and Tags facets, and *st* values. We aim to examine the effect of adding image facets and combination of document and image facets with different *st* values in our graph search.

**Search with Document Facet (R1).** In this experiment we use tf.idf facet results as initiating points in the graph. We do not include any visual or textual facet of the images. From Table 2, we observe that we are receiving better precision by using the graph structured data. We are receiving about the 0.34 of baseline result for P@10.

As the activation is propagated further up to 9 steps, we observe a decrease in precision. We are receiving almost the same precision in even steps compared to their prior odd steps. The reason is that $st$ holds the value of 0.9, and we count all images visited up to current state in the calculation.

**Table 2.** Result for documents without image facets, $st$:0.9

| steps | st | p@10 | r@10 | p@20 | r@20 |
|-------|-----|-------|-------|-------|-------|
| 1 | 0.9 | **0.34** | 0.136 | 0.25 | 0.161 |
| 2 | 0.9 | 0.34 | 0.136 | 0.25 | 0.161 |
| 3 | 0.9 | 0.286 | 0.114 | 0.208 | 0.158 |
| 4 | 0.9 | 0.28 | 0.112 | 0.206 | 0.149 |
| 5 | 0.9 | 0.252 | 0.104 | 0.188 | 0.144 |
| 6 | 0.9 | 0.244 | 0.104 | 0.18 | 0.138 |
| 7 | 0.9 | 0.218 | 0.095 | 0.176 | 0.138 |
| 8 | 0.9 | 0.194 | 0.081 | 0.158 | 0.124 |
| 9 | 0.9 | 0.19 | 0.08 | 0.148 | 0.115 |

*Bipartite Graph.* We observe that, the collection modelled is a bipartite graph combined of images on one side and documents on the other side. There is no relation between images or between documents. Therefore, without self-transitivity ($st$) value, energy flows totally from one side to the other. Facets are not included in this interpretation, since there is the way just from facet to the images and the way back is blocked by weight 0 on the edge from the information object to its facet.

**Search with CEDD Facet Added (R1 and R2).** In this experiment, top images, based on CEDD similarity are added to the $a^{(0)}$ vector to activate the graph. The activation vector is therefore a combination of indexed documents and images results. We first consider no $st$ value. In comparison to R1 result, we are receiving the worst results specially in even steps (Figure 2). The reason is that starting from top image nodes, we are visiting more images in even steps and they are mostly non relevant.

*Self-Transitivity Added.* In order to increase inertia, and include image results in all steps, from here we give $st$ value to all nodes. The same iterations with $st$ values 0.1 and 0.9 are shown in Figure 2. This time, we see high decrease in precision, especially for value 0.9. With high $st$ value, the CEDD results have a

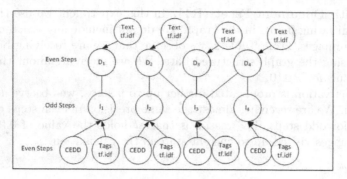

**Fig. 1.** Graph model: Starting from documents, we visit images in odd steps. Each image may have different facets.

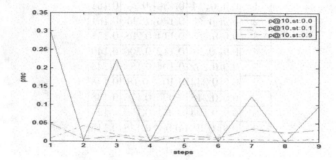

**Fig. 2.** Prec@10 for documents and images with CEDD facet

high impact in the selection of the top images. This shows that our model follows the proved claim in literature that pure image results are poorer compared with text-based results and should receive less weight.

**Weighted Document and CEDD Facets (R1 and R2).** In order to remove the high influence of top image results in the propagation, we weight the document and image score results. In order to compare with the best result we had in baseline search (with 0.7 weight to the documents and 0.3 to the images), we perform the same here. In Table 3 we observe that the weighted result is much better in even steps than Figure 2 with $st=0.9$, because the scores of the images are reduced to match their perceived importance for retrieval. We observe almost the same precision with R1 result experiment, however, with better recall in first four steps. Going further in the graph we see more number of images which decrease the efficiency of the system.

**Search with Document and Metadata Facets (R1 and R3).** In this experiment we search based on document and metadata facet results. We see

**Table 3.** Result for documents and images CEDD facet, $st$:0.9

| steps | st | p@10 | r@10 | p@20 | r@20 |
|-------|-----|-------|-------|-------|-------|
| 1 | 0.9 | 0.344 | 0.135 | 0.25 | **0.188** |
| 2 | 0.9 | 0.338 | 0.133 | 0.257 | **0.193** |
| 3 | 0.9 | 0.29 | 0.115 | 0.207 | **0.163** |
| 4 | 0.9 | 0.266 | 0.101 | 0.175 | **0.131** |
| 5 | 0.9 | 0.234 | 0.093 | 0.165 | 0.122 |
| 6 | 0.9 | 0.136 | 0.052 | 0.098 | 0.068 |
| 7 | 0.9 | 0.11 | 0.039 | 0.077 | 0.055 |
| 8 | 0.9 | 0.094 | 0.032 | 0.065 | 0.042 |
| 9 | 0.9 | 0.084 | 0.056 | 0.062 | 0.038 |

an increase of 0.06 in the first step (Table 4). Also in third step we have better precision, which shows that we visit related documents, not only after one step, but also after three steps. We see that using metadata facet we have better recall in the first three steps as well. In these experiments the $st$ value is 0.9 which means energy is partially remained in the nodes as well. Therefore, all image nodes visited in the traversal, participate in our calculations. Without $st$ value, no energy is remained in the nodes previously visited.

**Table 4.** Result for documents and image metadata facet, $st$:0.9

| steps | st | p@10 | r@10 | p@20 | r@20 |
|-------|-----|-------|-------|-------|-------|
| 1 | 0.9 | **0.362** | 0.139 | 0.265 | **0.189** |
| 2 | 0.9 | **0.346** | 0.132 | 0.259 | **0.175** |
| 3 | 0.9 | **0.308** | 0.119 | 0.224 | **0.165** |
| 4 | 0.9 | 0.24 | 0.088 | 0.187 | 0.135 |
| 5 | 0.9 | 0.212 | 0.081 | 0.164 | 0.118 |
| 6 | 0.9 | 0.158 | 0.06 | 0.133 | 0.097 |
| 7 | 0.9 | 0.164 | 0.06 | 0.128 | 0.091 |
| 8 | 0.9 | 0.144 | 0.56 | 0.113 | 0.085 |
| 9 | 0.9 | 0.084 | 0.027 | 0.062 | 0.038 |

**Search with Document, CEDD and Metadata Facets (R1, R2 and R3)**
We included all three result sets in this experiment. Receiving higher recall than previous experiment with R1 and R2 shows that the combination of R2 and R3 hit points helps visiting more related nodes. Precision in the first step is the same as combination of R1 and R3 result. This means that CEDD top ranked nodes did not help. In the second step (according to Figure 1), starting from document hit nodes (R1) we visit documents again which do not affect the result of this stage. However starting from images (R2 and R3), we visit new images in second step. Precision increase to 0.372, demonstrates visiting related documents from R2 and R3 points in first step, that in second step lead to more related images.

We observe that CEDD could have positive effect in combination with Tags to increase the precision in second step (Table 5), while in the combination of R1 and R2 experiment, it was not effective (Table 3).

**Table 5.** Result for documents and images CEDD and metadata facets, $st$:0.9

| steps | st | p@10 | r@10 | p@20 | r@20 ($) |
|-------|-----|-------|-------|-------|----------|
| 1 | 0.9 | **0.358** | 0.14 | 0.27 | **0.195** |
| 2 | 0.9 | **0.372** | 0.137 | 0.272 | **0.193** |
| 3 | 0.9 | **0.308** | 0.12 | 0.22 | **0.166** |
| 4 | 0.9 | 0.25 | 0.093 | 0.186 | 0.127 |
| 5 | 0.9 | 0.218 | 0.083 | 0.162 | 0.113 |
| 6 | 0.9 | 0.114 | 0.037 | 0.088 | 0.06 |
| 7 | 0.9 | 0.114 | 0.037 | 0.085 | 0.056 |
| 8 | 0.9 | 0.138 | 0.056 | 0.113 | 0.085 |
| 9 | 0.9 | 0.068 | 0.055 | 0.107 | 0.083 |

## 6     Conclusion

We presented a multifaceted model for hybrid search in a multimodal domain. In this model, data collections can be described based on different link types. We enriched the modeled connections by extracting inherent information of data objects as facets. The preliminary results of combination of text and image facets show the correct functionality in the combined modalities. However, we were able to improve these results by using a weighted combination of document and image results. Furthermore, the Astera model enabled us to search the collection from different points of view by using different facets. Utilizing image textual facet increased precision and recall. Further, combination of two different facets of images (CEDD and Tags) gave better result than the sum of their individual results. This demonstrates the positive effect of the combination of different facets in Astera.

Our future work will focus on the following: 1) Learning the weight of different facets through supervised learning methods. 2) Further exploring the semantic relations between the ImageCLEF 2011 Wikipedia collection and DBPedia. For example, traversing the graph starting from the collection and spreading through DBPedia until returning to the collection, considering the effect of semantic links. 3) Using concept extraction to create additional, more meaningful semantic links between query topics and image textual annotations(caption, comment and description of the image).

# References

1. Berber, T., Vahid, A.H., Ozturkmenoglu, O., Hamed, R.G., Alpkocak, A.: Demir at imageclefwiki 2011: Evaluating different weighting schemes in information retrieval. In: CLEF (2011)
2. Berthold, M.R., Brandes, U., Kotter, T., Mader, M., Nagel, U., Thiel, K.: Pure spreading activation is pointless. In: CIKM (2009)
3. Crestani, F.: Application of spreading activation techniques in information retrieval. Artificial Intelligence Review, 11 (1997)
4. Delbru, R., Toupikov, N., Catasta, M., Tummarello, G.: A node indexing scheme for web entity retrieval. In: Aroyo, L., Antoniou, G., Hyvönen, E., ten Teije, A., Stuckenschmidt, H., Cabral, L., Tudorache, T. (eds.) ESWC 2010, Part II. LNCS, vol. 6089, pp. 240–256. Springer, Heidelberg (2010)
5. Duan, L., Li, W., Tsang, I.W.-H., Xu, D.: Improving web image search by bag-based reranking. IEEE Transactions on Image Processing 20(11) (2011)
6. Elbassuoni, S., Blanco, R.: Keyword search over RDF graphs. In: CIKM (2011)
7. Fergus, R., Fei-Fei, L., Perona, P., Zisserman, A.: Learning object categories from google's image search. In: Proc. of Intl. Conf. on Computer Vision (2005)
8. Kasneci, G., Suchanek, F., Ifrim, G., Ramanath, M., Weikum, G.: Naga: Searching and ranking knowledge. In: ICDE (2008)
9. Lazaridis, M., Axenopoulos, A., Rafailidis, D., Daras, P.: Multimedia search and retrieval using multimodal annotation propagation and indexing techniques. Signal Processing: Image Comm. (2012)
10. Magatti, D., Steinke, F., Bundschus, M., Tresp, V.: Combined Structured and Keyword-Based Search in Textually Enriched Entity-Relationship Graphs. In: Proceedings of the Workshop on Automated Knowledge Base Construction (2011)
11. Martinet, J., Satoh, S.: An information theoretic approach for automatic document annotation from intermodal analysis. In: Workshop on Multimodal Information Retrieval (2007)
12. Rocha, C., Schwabe, D., Aragao, M.P.: A hybrid approach for searching in the semantic web. In: WWW (2004)
13. Sabetghadam, S., Lupu, M., Rauber, A.: Astera - a generic model for multimodal information retrieval. In: Proc. of Integrating IR Technologies for Professional Search Workshop (2013)
14. Sabetghadam, S., Lupu, M., Rauber, A.: A combined approach of structured and non-structured IR in multimodal domain. In: ICMR (2014)
15. Shekarpour, S., Auer, S., Ngomo, A., Gerber, D., Hellmann, S., Stadler, C.: Keyword-driven sparql query generation leveraging background knowledge. In: Web Intelligence and Intelligent Agent Technology (WI-IAT), IEEE/WIC/ACM International Conference on Web Intelligence, vol. 1. IEEE (2011)
16. Srinivasan, S., Slaney, M.: A bipartite graph model for associating images and text. In: Workshop on Multimodal Information Retrieval (2007)
17. Tsikrika, T., Popescu, A., Kludas, J.: Overview of the wikipedia image retrieval task at imageclef 2011. In: CLEF (2011)

# Discovering Similar Passages within Large Text Documents

Demetrios Glinos

[1] Computer Science, University of Central Florida, Orlando, Florida, United States
[2] Advanced Text Analytics, LLC, Orlando, Florida, United States

**Abstract.** We present a novel general method for discovering similar passages within large text documents based on adapting and extending the well-known Smith-Waterman dynamic programming local sequence alignment algorithm. We extend that algorithm for large document analysis by defining: (a) a recursive procedure for discovering multiple non-overlapping aligned passages within a given document pair; (b) a matrix splicing method for processing long texts; (c) a chaining method for combining sequence strands; and (d) an inexact similarity measure for determining token matches. We show that an implementation of this method is computationally efficient and produces very high precision with good recall for several types of order-based plagiarism and that it achieves higher overall performance than the best reported methods against the PAN 2013 text alignment test corpus.

**Keywords:** passage retrieval, text alignment, plagiarism detection.

## 1 Introduction

The task of text alignment is to identify passages in one text document that correspond to passages in another document according to some measure of similarity. Text alignment is used in plagiarism detection, document deduplication, and passage retrieval for textual entailment determination, among other uses. Thus, depending on the context, it may be important to recognize that the passage *"This article discusses the famous Hamlet monologue of the main themes of the game."* may be a paraphrase of the passage *"This essay discusses Hamlet's famous soliloquy in relation to the major themes of the play."*

It should not be surprising that finding such a pair of passages is not a trivial task in general, even for the relatively simple case of identifying passages that are identical in both documents. Suppose we are given two 5,000-word documents, both of which contain the second sentence above. Suppose further that we are asked to find the common sentence but we have no information at all about it. Thus, we do not know how many words the sentence may have, nor its punctuation, nor even the topic of the sentence. How are we to find it?

A brute-force search to locate identical passages would involve comparing every possible passage of every valid length in one document with all possible passages of equal length in the other document. Moreover, since the documents

E. Kanoulas et al. (Eds.): CLEF 2014, LNCS 8685, pp. 98–109, 2014.
© Springer International Publishing Switzerland 2014

could be complete duplicates, all passage lengths up to and including the common document length must be included in the search. Such a search will have a computational complexity of $O(n^3)$. Thus, for the 16-token second sentence above, there are 4,985 possible shingles of 16 consecutive words in the first document that will need to be compared against the same number of shingles in the second document, resulting in a total of approximately 25 million comparisons. A similar number of calculations would be required for each of the approximately 5,000 other valid passage lengths which, at an average number of 2,500 shingles, will require a total of over 60 billion passage comparisons.

The problem is all the more difficult when the given documents may not contain any similar passages at all, or where corresponding passages do exist, they differ due to paraphrasing, reordering, additions and deletions of words or phrases, and the use of synonyms and alternative grammatical constructions. Considering only that the corresponding passages may be of different lengths, computational complexity jumps to $O(n^4)$ for the brute-force search.

As a result, practical text alignment methods must employ different methods for exploring the search space.

Current implementations typically involve layers of heuristics in a *seeding-extending-filtering* approach [5]. At the first level, heuristics are used to identify the anchor points in each document for possible corresponding passages. A second set of heuristics is then used to extend and merge these anchor points to form passages. A final set of heuristics filters the resulting passages to remove overlapping alignments, short passages, and passages that do not meet certain other criteria.

Thus, Torrejón and Ramos [9] find anchor points using a comprehensive set of 3-grams obtained by various transformations (termed "Contextual N-grams", "Surrounding Context N-grams", and "Odd-Even N-grams") on three-word shingles from which short and stop words have been eliminated and the remaining words have been stemmed. Extension is performed using an algorithm that takes into account common n-grams that appear within threshold distances from each other in the two documents, the distance depending on document length and various tuning parameters. Final filtering is performed using a "Granularity Filter" that joins adjacent passages that appear in both documents.

In a similar manner, Suchomel et al. [8] use word 4-grams, but also supplement them with stop word 8-grams to find the anchor points. This presents an ordering problem at the extension step, since in general there is no natural ordering of the combination of the two types of n-grams, which the authors term "features". For example, a stop word 8-gram can span multiple sentences, and hence overlap several word 4-grams. The authors resolve this using an algorithm that merges features into non-overlapping intervals using their character offsets and then retains intervals containing at least four features [7].

A different approach is is used by Kong et al. [3], for whom anchor points are sentences that exceed a given cosine similarity threshold after elimination of whitespace, punctuation, stop words, case transformation and stemming. The set of candidate sentence pairs is further winnowed based on the relative numbers of similar words in each sentence. At the extension step, adjacent sentence pairs that are within a threshold distance are merged using a "Bilateral Alternating Sorting" algorithm [4].

A problem closely related to the text alignment problem discussed here is the *sequence alignment* problem in bioinformatics, which involves matching biological sequences such as amino-acid chains in proteins and nucleotide sequences in DNA strands. The sequences for comparison typically involve thousands of bases in the query sequences and potentially millions in the database strings to which they are compared. The problem has been well studied and current practice is dominated by heuristically-based methods, such as BLAST ("Basic Local Alignment Search Tool") [1].

Prior to such heuristic methods, however, the dominant algorithm for sequence alignment was the Smith-Waterman algorithm [6], particularly as it was improved for efficiency by Gotoh [2]. The Smith-Waterman algorithm is of interest to us since it is a dynamic programming method, and as such, it has the desirable feature that it is guaranteed to find a maximal length alignment. Moreover, algorithm time complexity is low-order polynomial, as it is roughly $O(nm)$ for comparing a sequence of length $n$ against one of length $m$.

Our approach takes advantage of the fact that while typical text documents for comparison may be long, they are considerably shorter than the biological sequences that prompted the migration to heuristic methods in that domain. As a result, even for long text documents, we feel that using Smith-Waterman is both optimal and tractable, provided it is adapted to the text analysis environment.

We have therefore adapted and extended the algorithm in a number of ways. In particular, we have extended the algorithm by defining a recursive procedure for discovering multiple non-overlapping passages for a given document pair. We have also defined a matrix splicing procedure for dividing the computational task so that the method will scale with document size without exceeding memory constraints. And we have extended the algorithm to merge adjacent sequence strands and to cover inexact matches.

We believe our extensions and our approach are novel and have not been reported elsewhere.

We have tested an implementation of this approach against the 2103 PAN Workshop series text alignment test corpus [5]. PAN[1] is an evaluation lab, now in its eleventh year, for uncovering plagiarism, authorship, and social software misuse. The 2013 text alignment test corpus is a comprehensive collection of document pairs exhibiting different types of plagiarism, including direct copies, random obfuscation, cyclic translations, and summarization. This corpus includes test cases that are suitable for our algorithm, as well as non-order preserving plagiarism cases. Document sizes within the collection vary widely, and many large documents are included. Test results for our implementation are very encouraging and show that the proposed method performs well under evaluation test conditions, and indeed overall performance tops the best reported results from the 2013 evaluation despite addressing only a subset of the problem types.

---

[1] http://pan.webis.de

Although we have tested the method in a plagiarism detection context, the method is sufficiently general that it can be applied in other contexts readily, as it does not involve any plagiarism-specific tuning parameters.

In the sections that follow, we present the details of the method and the experimental results. Section 2 explains how the basic alignment algorithm works, with baseline extensions. Section 3 describes the recursive method for discovering multiple passages. Section 4 describes the matrix splicing procedure. Section 5 describes the corpus, measures, and results of the evaluation experiments. And finally, Section 6 presents our conclusions.

## 2 Basic Alignment Algorithm

Given two text documents $A$ and $B$, we first read the documents as UTF-8 bytes and tokenize them into words, retaining all punctuation as separate tokens, except for " 's", which is retained as a single token. We also convert all non-printing ASCII characters to spaces, convert all newlines, tabs, and returns to spaces, and finally reduce all remaining tokens to lower case. The result is two sequences of tokens of generally different lengths, $A = a_0, a_1, ..., a_m$ and $B = b_0, b_1, ..., b_n$.

We then apply the basic Smith-Waterman algorithm [8], as simplified by Gotoh [9], to build up recursively a match matrix $M$, as follows[2]:

$$M(i, j) = max \begin{cases} M(i-1, j-1) + match(a_i, b_j) \\ M(i-1, j) + gap \\ M(i, j-1) + gap \\ 0 \end{cases} \qquad (1)$$

where $match(a_i, b_j) = +2$, if $a_i = b_j$; and $-1$ otherwise; and where $gap = -1$ is the gap penalty.

The algorithm produces a matrix of non-negative integer values from which the maximal alignment is obtained using a straightforward traceback procedure that starts from the largest value in the matrix and simply reverses the matrix generation algorithm above to recover the path that produced the maximal value. If the alignment sequence that is produced contains at least 40 tokens of each input sequence, it is retained as an alignment detection.

We adapt the algorithm for text alignment by extending it in two ways. First, we provide a mechanism for joining directly adjacent subsequences. We do this by defining a parameter *chain*, which is configured to some small number. This parameter represents the number of "jumps" that are permitted in the traceback process, where a jump represents moving from a zero-value cell to an adjacent nonzero-value cell according to the traceback algorithm. This feature permits merging sequence strands in both documents that are separated by only one token in each document string. We use a chain value of 2 for our implementation,

---

[2] The matrix is of dimension $(m+1)$ by $(n+1)$ and is initialized with all zeroes in the first row and first column. The matrix is built row by row, proceeding left to right.

which we arrived at informally during development against the training corpus, thus permitting two such jumps in building up our alignment sequences.

We also extend the basic algorithm by relaxing the equality requirement for a match and using a similarity determination instead. While the similarity function can include synonymy, we have elected for this study to use a simpler implementation in which we equate the determiners *the*, *a*, and *an*, and where we also equate these twenty-five commonly occurring prepositions: *of, in, to, for, with, on, at, from, by, about, as, into, like, through, after, over, between, out, against, during, without, before, under, around,* and *among*.

Table 1 shows the matrix elements that are generated using our modified algorithm for the two sample sentences in the introductory section. Except for the first row and column, which are all initialized to zeroes to prime the recursion, the rows and columns in the table correspond to the tokens in the two documents. The shaded cells in the table show the traceback path that is produced by backtracking from the maximal element at the lower right. No jumps were involved in traceback in this example. The table also includes additional elements at the end of each token sequence to show how the operation of the algorithm exhibits a tapering effect once past the maximal element.

**Table 1.** Match matrix elements for two sample sentences showing traceback defining maximal-length alignment and tapering effect past the maximal element

| | | This | essay | discusses | Hamlet | 's | famous | soliloquy | in | relation | to | the | major | themes | of | the | play | . | tempus | fugit |
|---|---|---|---|---|---|---|---|---|---|---|---|---|---|---|---|---|---|---|---|---|
| | 0 | 0 | 0 | 0 | 0 | 0 | 0 | 0 | 0 | 0 | 0 | 0 | 0 | 0 | 0 | 0 | 0 | 0 | 0 | 0 |
| This | 0 | 2 | 1 | 0 | 0 | 0 | 0 | 0 | 0 | 0 | 0 | 0 | 0 | 0 | 0 | 0 | 0 | 0 | 0 | 0 |
| article | 0 | 1 | 1 | 0 | 0 | 0 | 0 | 0 | 0 | 0 | 0 | 0 | 0 | 0 | 0 | 0 | 0 | 0 | 0 | 0 |
| discusses | 0 | 0 | 0 | 3 | 2 | 1 | 0 | 0 | 0 | 0 | 0 | 0 | 0 | 0 | 0 | 0 | 0 | 0 | 0 | 0 |
| the | 0 | 0 | 0 | 2 | 2 | 1 | 0 | 0 | 0 | 0 | 0 | 2 | 1 | 0 | 0 | 2 | 1 | 0 | 0 | 0 |
| famous | 0 | 0 | 0 | 1 | 1 | 1 | 3 | 2 | 1 | 0 | 0 | 1 | 1 | 0 | 0 | 1 | 1 | 0 | 0 | 0 |
| Hamlet | 0 | 0 | 0 | 0 | 3 | 2 | 2 | 2 | 1 | 0 | 0 | 0 | 0 | 0 | 0 | 0 | 0 | 0 | 0 | 0 |
| monologue | 0 | 0 | 0 | 0 | 2 | 2 | 1 | 1 | 1 | 0 | 0 | 0 | 0 | 0 | 0 | 0 | 0 | 0 | 0 | 0 |
| of | 0 | 0 | 0 | 0 | 1 | 1 | 1 | 0 | 3 | 2 | 2 | 1 | 0 | 0 | 2 | 1 | 0 | 0 | 0 | 0 |
| the | 0 | 0 | 0 | 0 | 0 | 0 | 0 | 0 | 2 | 2 | 1 | 4 | 3 | 2 | 1 | 4 | 3 | 2 | 1 | 0 |
| main | 0 | 0 | 0 | 0 | 0 | 0 | 0 | 0 | 1 | 1 | 1 | 3 | 3 | 2 | 1 | 3 | 3 | 2 | 2 | 0 |
| themes | 0 | 0 | 0 | 0 | 0 | 0 | 0 | 0 | 0 | 0 | 0 | 2 | 2 | 5 | 4 | 3 | 2 | 2 | 1 | 0 |
| of | 0 | 0 | 0 | 0 | 0 | 0 | 0 | 0 | 2 | 1 | 2 | 1 | 1 | 4 | 7 | 6 | 5 | 4 | 3 | 2 |
| the | 0 | 0 | 0 | 0 | 0 | 0 | 0 | 0 | 1 | 1 | 1 | 4 | 3 | 3 | 6 | 9 | 8 | 7 | 6 | 5 |
| game | 0 | 0 | 0 | 0 | 0 | 0 | 0 | 0 | 0 | 0 | 0 | 3 | 3 | 2 | 5 | 8 | 8 | 7 | 6 | 5 |
| . | 0 | 0 | 0 | 0 | 0 | 0 | 0 | 0 | 0 | 0 | 0 | 2 | 2 | 2 | 4 | 7 | 7 | 10 | 9 | 8 |
| carpe | 0 | 0 | 0 | 0 | 0 | 0 | 0 | 0 | 0 | 0 | 0 | 1 | 1 | 1 | 3 | 6 | 6 | 9 | 9 | 8 |
| diem | 0 | 0 | 0 | 0 | 0 | 0 | 0 | 0 | 0 | 0 | 0 | 0 | 0 | 0 | 2 | 5 | 5 | 8 | 8 | 8 |

# 3  Discovering Multiple Passages

It is quite possible that two text documents may contain more than one set of corresponding passages. Moreover, it is not generally possible to know *a priori* how many there may be, if indeed there are any at all. Further, corresponding passages may not possess the same relative ordering in one document that they possess in the other.

We therefore define a recursive procedure for finding multiple aligned passages. This procedure makes use of two auxiliary linear arrays corresponding to the tokens for each document. The arrays are initialized to indicate that at the start, all tokens in each document are available for inclusion in the next found alignment sequence. However, as each sequence is found, the array elements for the tokens that have been used are marked to block off those tokens from further consideration. This ensures that there can be no overlapping alignments.

The recursive procedure is illustrated in Figure 1. The matrix sketch on the left depicts a first maximal alignment that has been found in matrix region *A*. By construction, the alignment includes all tokens in the first sequence that run from the top row to the bottom row of region *A*. Similarly, the alignment also includes all tokens from the second sequence that run from the leftmost column to the rightmost column of region *A*. Because the tokens used for this alignment may not be used again, the sketch on the left shows in white the remaining regions of the matrix that may contain additional alignments. These are searched in recursive fashion.

Similarly, the sketch on the right shows the situation after a second maximal alignment is found in region *B*. This results in blocking off from further consideration additional tokens, as shown by the additional shaded regions.

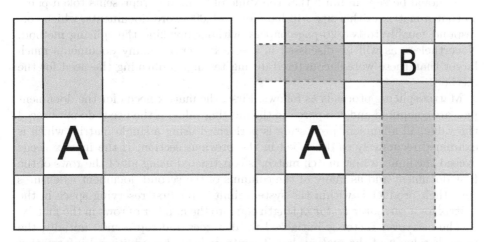

**Fig. 1.** Sketch of match matrix regions showing in white the remaining regions that may contain additional aligned passages after an alignment is first found in region A and subsequently an alignment is found in region B

As may be observed from Figure 1, it is the case in general that whenever an alignment is found within a region of the matrix, four subregions remain where additional alignments may potentially be found. These are searched in recursive fashion, adding to the auxiliary linear arrays each time a fresh alignment is found. The recursion ends when all regions have been searched.

# 4   Handling Long Documents

Because our method involves generating and processing a match matrix of a size equal to the product of the numbers of tokens in each of the two source documents, we recognize that there may be some text document pairs whose matrix requirements may exceed the available memory for storing such a data structure. Therefore, to ensure that our method scales with document size, we have devised a procedure for processing very large matrices, and by extension, very large documents, which we term *matrix splicing*.

Matrix splicing uses a system configuration parameter that represents the largest matrix size in terms of the total number of matrix elements that will be processed at one time. This value is system dependent and represents the memory available on the host system for the match matrix. It does not reflect any characteristic of the text documents themselves or the text analysis domain. We used a value of 50 million during initial development, which was adequate for our system, but we subsequently decreased it to 25 million to ensure that the matrix slicing component was exercised adequately. And since the system performed well on all test data with that value, we retained that value in the tests described in the next section.

It should be kept in mind that the value of 25 million represents token pairs, so that a matrix of this size will handle two 5,000-word documents, which correspond roughly to two 20-page papers, without invoking the splicing method. Nevertheless, as will be discussed in the next section, many documents much larger than these were encountered during testing, confirming the need for the method.

Matrix splicing proceeds as follows. First, the matrix needs for the document pair are computed and compared to the limiting value. If the needs do not exceed the value, all alignment processing is performed using a single matrix, which is examined recursively as described in the previous section. If the matrix needs exceed the limit, a first match matrix is constructed using all of the rows of the first document and as many of the columns of the second document as ensures that their product is within the system limit, after first reserving space in the matrix for a *carryover vector* of length equal to the number of rows in the matrix.

The carryover vector is initialized to all zeroes and represents, initially, the zeroeth column of the matrix, but it contains fields for additional information that may be needed later to stitch together two sequence segments that cross the boundary between two adjacent match matrices for the document pair.

Given an initialized carrover vector, the first match matrix is processed recursively as described in the previous section to identify valid text alignments within its boundaries. All detected alignments that do not begin at the rightmost boundary of the matrix are treated as strictly internal and are saved to be reported as a group with all other alignments for the document pair. However, all sequences, however short, that begin on the rightmost boundary of the current matrix are preserved in the carryover vector since they may be the beginnings of alignments that are completed in the next match matrix for the pair. It should be noted that only the matrix value and the row and column indices of the head of each such subsequence are needed to fully specify such a sequence, as they define the upper left corner of the bounding rectangle and the value that is used for applying the modified Smith-Waterman algorithm in the next match matrix.

Thus, after the first match matrix is processed, any fully internal alignments will be saved to be reported later, and any sequences that begin on the right boundary will be preserved in the corresponding entries of the carryover vector, which will also have zero values for all other entries. The next match matrix is then generated. However, this time, instead of all zeroes in the leftmost column, as in the simplest case, any nonzero values specified by the carryover vector will be used for values in the leftmost column in the matrix algorithm. During traceback, any alignment sequences that reach the leftmost column of the match matrix are then augmented by the information stored in the carryover vector at the boundary location. In this manner, alignment sequences are spliced together to form the combined sequences that would have been produced had the two documents been processed using a single match matrix. This process then repeats for however many match matrices are needed to process the matrix needs for the two documents.

## 5 Experiments and Results

### 5.1 Test Corpus

To evaluate the performance of the method and algorithms described in the preceding sections, we selected the PAN Workshop 2013 test corpus. As described in [5], the corpus consists of document pairs on 145 topics that were processed both automatically and manually to produce document pairs that involve the following types of plagiarism: (i) no plagiarism; (ii) no obfuscation; (iii) random obfuscation; (iv) cyclic translation obfuscation; and (v) summary obfuscation. The corpus includes both order-preserving plagiarism problems suitable for testing our algorithm, as well as plagiarism problems (such as summarization) that our algorithm does not address.

Full details of the construction of the corpus are contained in [5]. Briefly, however, the document categories are described as follows: The no plagiarism category is self-explanatory. The no-obfuscation category represents cut-and-paste copying, although some differences in whitespace and line breaks are introduced. The random obfuscation category includes some amount of random text operations, such as word shuffling, adding or deleting words or phrases, and word replacement using synonyms. Cyclic translation involves translations of a document using automated translation services into two successive languages other than English, and then back into English. Finally, the summary category includes documents obtained from the Document Understanding Conference (DUC) 2006 corpus that have been processed to introduce noisy areas in addition to the summaries in the test documents.

The actual 2013 PAN text alignment test corpus comprises 5,185 document pairs from 3,169 source documents and 1,826 documents that contain suspected plagiarism. The test corpus includes 1,185 document pairs from the summary category and 1,000 from each of the other categories. The basic characteristics of the corpus are summarized in Table 2. The word counts in the table were obtained in each case by dividing the number of characters observed by five, which is the average word length for English.

**Table 2.** PAN 2013 Text Analysis Test Corpus basic characteristics

| PAN 2013 Test Corpus | Chars | Words |
|---|---|---|
| Suspect Documents | | |
| Min length | 657 | 131 |
| Max length | 101,484 | 20,297 |
| Mean length | 14,650 | 2,930 |
| Source Documents | | |
| Min length | 520 | 104 |
| Max length | 61,385 | 12,277 |
| Mean length | 4,570 | 914 |

## 5.2   Performance Measures

Full details for evaluating plagiarism detection performance are contained in [1]. We summarize them here.

The traditional measures of precision and recall for information retrieval systems are retained, but are adapted to the plagiarism detection context so that both measures reflect how well a detected alignment corresponds to the gold standard character offsets and lengths for both source and suspected documents.

The measures involve plagiarism *cases* and *detections*, which are defined as follows. A plagiarism *case* is a 4-tuple $s = \langle r_{off}, r_{len}, s_{off}, s_{len} \rangle$ that represents the gold standard offsets and lengths for the corresponding passages in the suspect document (”$r$”) and the source document (”$s$”), respectively. Similarly, a *detection* is represented by the 4-tuple $r = \langle r'_{off}, r'_{len}, s'_{off}, s'_{len} \rangle$ . All offsets and lengths are represented in characters.

Now, if both the suspect and source intervals of the detection have nonempty intersections with the corresponding intervals of the gold standard case, then we say that the case has been detected by the reported detection.

If we further define $S$ to be the union of all gold standard cases and $R$ to be the union of all reported detections, then we can define precision and recall as follows:

$$\text{precision(S,R)} = \frac{1}{|R|} \sum \frac{\bigcup(s \sqcap r)}{|r|} \text{ and recall(S,R)} = \frac{1}{|S|} \sum \frac{\bigcup(s \sqcap r)}{|s|} \qquad (2)$$

$$\text{where } s \sqcap r = \begin{cases} s \cap r, \text{ if } r \text{ detects } s \\ \emptyset, \text{otherwise} \end{cases} \qquad (3)$$

An additional measure called *granularity* is also used to reflect that it is undesirable for a detector to report multiple detections where there should be only one, thus:

$$granularity(S, R) = \frac{1}{|S_R|} \sum |R_S| \qquad (4)$$

where $S_R \subseteq S$ are the subset of cases that are detected and $R_S$ are the subset of reported detections that detect cases.

Finally, all of the above measures are combined in a composite measure called the *plagiarism detection score*, as follows:

$$plagdet(S, R) = \frac{F_1}{log_2(1 + granularity(S, R))} \qquad (5)$$

where $F_1$ is the balanced harmonic mean of precision and recall.

## 5.3   Experimental Results

Our system implementation was run first against the the entire PAN 2013 text alignment test corpus in a test in which the source and suspect document plagiarism database categories were not known. Subsequent runs were then made against the document pairs for each of the individual categories. Table 3 below summarizes aggregate performance for the test runs. Table 4 presents the corresponding raw detection and plagiarism case information.

We examine first the runtime performance of the system. Overall, the system processed the 5,185 document pairs in approximately 23.5 minutes, corresponding to an average of 0.2590 seconds per document pair. This is quite respectable performance for a natural language processing system, although not real time. Our code was written in Java and was executed in a Linux virtual machine environment on a dual-core 2.66 GHz machine with 4 GB RAM. We anticipate that improved runtime performance can be obtained from migrating to a compiled language and better hardware. Runtime performance against the individual category types varied, with approximately equal time consumed for the three categories for which substantial numbers of alignments were detected.

Next, we turn to the functional performance of the system. Overall, the 0.8404 composite plagiarism detection score achieved by the system was 1.8% higher than the best reported result against the test corpus [5] despite poor performance against the summary obfuscation category. Nevertheless, overall precision was 0.9690, which exceeded the best reported by 7.4%. Overall recall, however, was dragged down by performance against the summary category and falls within the middle of the pack for reported results (see [5]).

**Table 3.** Aggregate performance against PAN 2013 test corpus

| Target Corpus | PlagDet | Recall | Precision | Granularity | Runtime |
|---|---|---|---|---|---|
| No plagiarism | undefined | undefined | 0.0000 | undefined | 1:41.2013 |
| No obfuscation | 0.9624 | 0.9603 | 0.9644 | 1.0000 | 6:47.717 |
| Random obfuscation | 0.7958 | 0.7073 | 0.9732 | 1.0413 | 5:09.562 |
| Cyclic obfuscation | 0.8441 | 0.7506 | 0.9730 | 1.0056 | 6:55.170 |
| Summary obfuscation | 0.0984 | 0.0560 | 0.9794 | 1.1099 | 2:52.770 |
| | | | | | |
| Overall | 0.8404 | 0.7588 | 0.9690 | 1.0177 | 22:23.481 |

**Table 4.** Case and detection counts for test runs against PAN 2013 test corpus

| Target Corpus | Document Pairs | Reports | Detections | Cases | Cases Detected |
|---|---|---|---|---|---|
| No plagiarism | 1,000 | 5 | 0 | 0 | 0 |
| No obfuscation | 1,000 | 1,160 | 1,159 | 1,206 | 1,159 |
| Random | 1,000 | 1,114 | 1,109 | 1,292 | 1,065 |
| Cyclic | 1,000 | 1,093 | 1,084 | 1,308 | 1,078 |
| Summary | 1,185 | 103 | 101 | 236 | 91 |
| | | | | | |
| Overall | 5,185 | 3,475 | 3,453 | 4,042 | 3,393 |

The anomalous performance against pairs in the summary obfuscation category is explained easily given the nature of our method and the type of obfuscation involved. Our method is for the detection of aligned texts. The key feature for any alignment is, by definition, that order is preserved. Summarization, by contrast, has an entirely different character. It is the nature of summarization that terms and concepts are taken from various locations within the source document, and there is no requirement that such terms and concepts appear in the summary in any particular order. Accordingly, summarization is inherently non-order preserving, and as such, an alignment method such as ours will generally fail to find an alignment. Nevertheless, we observe that the system did in fact detect 91 out of 236 summarization cases, and a manual examination of a number of these detections revealed source passages that appeared to us to indicate that perhaps some summaries were prepared by essentially paraphrasing coherent sections of the source text. While true summarization in context may be considered plagiarism, it does not present in our view a text alignment problem. Some of the random obfuscation and cyclic translation cases also exhibited these characteristics, although we did not have the opportunity to quantify the extent in this initial effort.

Overall, the test results show that our method performs best against the no-obfuscation category, where order is necessarily preserved, and that performance remains high and degrades only somewhat for the cyclic and random categories, which involve some measure of reordering of terms and concepts.

# 6    Conclusions

We have presented a general method for detecting text alignments across documents and have shown that it possesses both adequate runtime performance and is robust against alignment problems of varying difficulty. The method is capable of finding multiple algnments within a given document pair. The method is also scalable to handle very long documents. Based on our investigations, we believe that the method can serve as a component of a full plagiarism detection system, and can also be applied in a variety of other document processing contexts.

# References

1. Altschul, S.F., Gish, W., Miller, W., Myers, E.W., Lipmanl, D.J.: Basic local alignment search tool. Journal of Molecular Biology 215(2), 403–410 (1990)
2. Gotoh, O.: An Improved Algorithm for Matching Biological Sequences. Journal of Molecular Biology 162, 705–708 (1981)
3. Kong, L., Qi, H., Wang, S., Du, C., Wang, S., Han, Y.: Approaches for Candidate Document Retrieval and Detailed Comparison of Plagiarism Detection. In: Forner, P., Karlgren, J., Womser-Hacker, C. (eds.) CLEF (Online Working Notes/Labs/Workshop) (2012)
4. Kong, L., Qu, H., Du, C., Wang, M., Han, Z.: Approaches for Source Retrieval and Text Alignment of Plagiarism Detection–Notebook for PAN at CLEF 2013. In: Forner, P., Navigli, R., Tufis, D. (eds.) Working Notes Papers of the CLEF 2013 Evaluation Labs (September 2013)
5. Potthast, M., Gollub, T., Hagen, M., Tippmann, M., Kiesel, J., Rosso, P., Stamatatos, E., Stein, B.: Overview of the 5th International Competition on Plagiarism Detection. In: Forner, P., Navigli, R., Tufis, D. (eds.) Working Notes Papers of the CLEF 2013 Evaluation Labs (September 2013)
6. Smith, T., Waterman, M.: Identification of common molecular subsequences. Journal of Molecular Biology 147(1), 195–197 (1981)
7. Suchomel, S., Kasprzak, J., Brandejs, M.: Three Way Search Engine Queries with Multi-feature Document Comparison for Plagiarism Detection. In: Forner, P., Karlgren, J., Womser-Hacker, C. (eds.) CLEF (Online Working Notes/Labs/Workshop) (2012)
8. Suchomel, Š., Kasprzak, J., Brandejs, M.: Diverse Queries and Feature Type Selection for Plagiarism Discovery–Notebook for PAN at CLEF 2013. In: Forner, P., Navigli, R., Tufis, D. (eds.) Working Notes Papers of the CLEF 2013 Evaluation Labs (September 2013)
9. Torrejón, D., Ramos, J.: Text Alignment Module in CoReMo 2.1 Plagiarism Detector–Notebook for PAN at CLEF 2013. In: Forner, P., Navigli, R., Tufis, D. (eds.) Working Notes Papers of the CLEF 2013 Evaluation Labs (September 2013)

# Improving Transcript-Based Video Retrieval Using Unsupervised Language Model Adaptation

Thomas Wilhelm-Stein, Robert Herms, Marc Ritter, and Maximilian Eibl

Technische Universität Chemnitz, 09107 Chemnitz, Germany
{wilt,robeh,ritm,eibl}@hrz.tu-chemnitz.de

**Abstract.** One challenge in automated speech recognition is to determine domain-specific vocabulary like names, brands, technical terms etc. by using generic language models. Especially in broadcast news new names occur frequently. We present an unsupervised method for a language model adaptation, which is used in automated speech recognition with a two-pass decoding strategy to improve spoken document retrieval on broadcast news. After keywords are extracted from each utterance, a web resource is queried to collect utterance-specific adaptation data. This data is used to augment the phonetic dictionary and adapt the basic language model. We evaluated this strategy on a data set of summarized German broadcast news using a basic retrieval setup.

**Keywords:** language modeling, out-of-vocabulary, spoken document retrieval, unsupervised adaptation.

## 1 Introduction

Today, there is a growing amount of videos. These videos, after being produced and published, need to be made accessible. Spoken document retrieval tries to improve the access to content, which is not properly annotated [1]. By employing automatic speech recognition (ASR) videos are transcribed so they can be processed using classical information retrieval.

In the domain of broadcast news there is a challenge, because new words, particularly named entities, are a very common phenomenon. When these words are unknown to the automatic speech recognition engine, it is unable to recognize them correctly. This problem is called out-of-vocabulary (OOV). Out of vocabulary has a serious impact on the information retrieval performance, because names, which were not recognized, cannot be searched for subsequently.

To add a word to an ASR system, which is yet unknown, three essential steps are required: At first the missing word must be identified, second a phonetic notation for the word is needed and third the language models must be adapted to include the word. Even though all three steps can be assisted manually, we want to focus on a fully automatic solution to this problem.

The required data to adapt the language model can be acquired by using the result of preliminary ASR transcripts as queries to an information retrieval

E. Kanoulas et al. (Eds.): CLEF 2014, LNCS 8685, pp. 110–115, 2014.

(IR) system [2, 3]. Web-resources like standard web pages [3, 4, 5], RSS feeds or Twitter [6] provide easy available and accessible sources for the information retrieval system.

However, the enrichment of the language model with external data, in particular with out-of-domain data, does not necessarily results in an improved recognition [7]. Saykham et al. [8] showed minor improvements by adapting a language model using recent online news texts.

## 2 Method

Our approach is based on the assumption that utterances in speech, which appear in temporal proximity to each other, have a common topic and share some vocabulary. Therefore we performed a block-based, unsupervised adaptation of a general language model. Additionally the base dictionary is enriched with the new phonetically transcribed vocabulary.

Our method utilizes an ASR system with a two-pass decoding strategy. First a transcript of the speech was generated by the ASR system. The segmentation of the transcript into several units was performed by the recognizer of this system. It divides segments when silences occur for an extended time. Segments ranged from short statements to whole sentences. The segments were separated into blocks of specific sizes. All segments of each block were processed and used as web queries for retrieving the adaptation data to build a block-specific dictionary and language model. Finally, the speech was transcripted again using the adapted dictionaries and language models for the corresponding blocks.

We employed a keyword extraction algorithm based on natural language processing (NLP) to reduce the word count and to narrow down the web query. The following prioritized constraints were used:

1. Nouns and named entities are directly applied to the web query.
2. If 1. returns no results, only the named entities are used as a web query.
3. If 2. returns no results, the sequence of named entities is recursively decomposed into two parts until there is any retrieved result.

The articles of the retrieved HTML pages were extracted and special characters, acronyms and numbers are converted in order to be conform to the conventions of the adaptation process and the ASR system. For example numbers are transformed to their corresponding words, because otherwise it cannot be used for the next step, where the phonetic dictionary is amended.

The phonetic dictionary adaptation aims to enrich a basic dictionary with new vocabulary of the adaptation corpus. Vocabulary from the adaptation corpus was extracted and compared to the basic dictionary. Then, the new vocabulary was phonetically transcribed using a grapheme-to-phoneme (G2P) decoder and merged into a temporary dictionary. Finally, the temporary and the basic dictionary are merged to the adapted dictionary.

Our basic language model is a general model trained on topic-independent data collection. On basis of the adaption corpus an intermediate language model was trained, which was merged with our basic language model. The vocabulary of the resulting model is finally a superset of the vocabulary of both models.

Our training set was created using short video clips of a popular German news broadcast show called "Tagesschau". The full show is aired each day on the German television station "Das Erste". It covers a variety of topics including politics, economy, sports and weather. There is an additional format called "Tagesschau in 100 Sekunden", which is a summary of the most important video clips. Each show is separately produced and has a length of about 100 seconds with approximately 20 sentences and is publicly available as a webcast, which can easily be downloaded. Since 2011 we have collected various of these web clips. Our experiments were performed using a training set of the years 2011 and 2012 and a test set of 2013 and the first quarter of 2014. Therefore, we are able to investigate the out-of-vocabulary problem concerning the more recent data. The training set for acoustic as well as language modeling consists of 208 clips with a vocabulary of 8,300 words and more than 6 hours of speech. The test set is a sequence of 30 chronological combined clips with a vocabulary size of 2,500 and a total duration of 1 hour.

We used CMU Sphinx to perform acoustic modeling and train a gender-dependent triphone Hidden-Markov-Models together with eight Gaussian mixture models. The application of gender detection right before the speech recognition event allows us to apply the appropriate acoustic model. To train the basic language model, the MITLM toolkit with Kneser-Ney smoothing was used. The adaptation of the intermediate and the basic language model was performed using a linear interpolation with fixed weights.

The adaptation corpus was constructed by parsing web articles from the "Tagesschau" news portal. Even though this is the same source as for the video clips, these articles did not include transcripts of the broadcasted news and were edited independent from the video clips. Therefore they can be regarded as different. To acquire relevant articles the search function of this website was used and the results were prioritized with respect to relevance and date according to the requirements of the test set.

We tested different block sizes to determine an optimal size. For each test we increased the block size by 10 utterances. The experiments were continued until the result of the word error rate [9] (WER) was below the baseline or no further improvements were observable.

To evaluate our approach for improving spoken document retrieval we indexed all recognized statements using the Xtrieval Framework [10]. An unaltered and standard Apache Lucene version 4.3.1 was used as search and retrieval component. During the pre-processing step 231 common German stop words[1] were removed and the German Snowball stemmer was applied. Each utterance was indexed as a single document.,The resulting index contained 583 documents. For the retrieval test we created 18 topics based on knowledge of the documents. Some were especially aimed at out-of-vocabulary issues. The topics cover different scopes like political news, sports, and weather (e.g. "edathy affäre",

---

[1] Retrieved from http://snowball.tartarus.org/algorithms/german/stop.txt

"olympische winterspiele in sotschi", and "regen oder schnee"). All topics were formulated into keyword queries using OR as conjunction operator.

For each block size a new index was built. All topics were searched in these indices and a list of candidate results was assembled. Each result was checked against the transcript corpus for its relevance. The result was a list of relevant and non-relevant results returned by the search. In the last step the mean average precision (MAP) was calculated for each block size.

## 3  Results and Discussion

The results in Table 1 show that the best word error rate of 38.1 percent was achieved at a block size of 30 utterances. Compared to the baseline, where no adaptation was performed, this is an improvement of 7.5 percent.

The mean average precision of the manually generated transcripts outperformed the baseline with 90.14 versus 55.66 percent. The automatically generated speech transcripts perform better than the baseline, but are still inferior to the manual transcripts. Our best result was at a block size of 50 utterances and achieved a mean average precision of 67.33 percent. This is 11.69 percent above the baseline, but 22.81 percent below the manual transcripts. The reduction of the word error rate has a positive effect on the mean average precision.

As the video clips have a size of approximately 20 utterances and are processed in chronological order, the block sizes of 30 and 50 indicate that consecutive video clips support each other. This is probably due to shared topics and thus some common vocabulary.

With increasing block size the OOV-rate is reduced. The best result is at the maximum block size of 200 with 3.7 percent and could therefore be reduced

**Table 1.** Mean Perplexity (MPPL), out-of-vocabulary (OOV), word error rate (WER), and mean average precision (MAP) for the test set (Reference), Baseline, and different block sizes (BS)

| Configuration | MPPL | OOV (%) | WER (%) | MAP |
|---|---|---|---|---|
| Reference | - | - | - | 0.9014 |
| Baseline | 103.7 | 13.4 | 45.6 | 0.5567 |
| BS10 | 116.6 | 8.9 | 39.2 | 0.6073 |
| BS20 | 117.7 | 7.1 | 38.4 | 0.6484 |
| BS30 | 119.1 | 6.3 | 38.1 | 0.6572 |
| BS40 | 119.5 | 6.1 | 38.9 | 0.6686 |
| BS50 | 120.1 | 5.7 | 39.3 | 0.6733 |
| BS60 | 118.9 | 5.4 | 39.3 | 0.6171 |
| BS70 | 120.8 | 5.3 | 41.0 | 0.6056 |
| BS80 | 119.1 | 5.0 | 41.3 | 0.6329 |
| BS90 | 122.1 | 4.9 | 39.7 | 0.5809 |
| BS100 | 120.6 | 4.4 | 41.0 | 0.5834 |
| BS150 | 121.7 | 4.0 | 43.4 | 0.5689 |
| BS200 | 122.6 | 3.7 | 42.0 | 0.5843 |

by 9.7 percent compared to the baseline. This can be explained by the fact that adaptation data based on utterances which are more distant in time is considered in larger block sizes.

The mean perplexity rose slowly for growing block sizes, probably because out-of-domain data got increasingly included in the language model. For small block sizes the perplexity on the utterance level varies more than for big block sizes. For instance, at a block size of 10 the perplexity for a certain block was as low as 56.5 but for another block it was as high as 241.0. Whereas at a block size of 200 it ranged from 117.3 to 132.1.

## 4  Conclusions

We presented an unsupervised method for a language model adaptation, which is used in automated speech recognition with a two-pass decoding strategy to improve spoken document retrieval on broadcast news. The experiments showed an out-of-vocabulary reduction and as a result a better performing document retrieval by applying the new models to the corresponding blocks.

The biggest improvement of mean average precision in comparison to the baseline was about 11.7 percent at a block size of 50 utterances. The best word error rate of 38.1 percent was achieved at a block size of 30. Both values were close together and show that the retrieval benefits from an improved recognition.

The remaining gap compared to the manually generated transcripts could be further reduced by using appropriate context dependent acoustic models. Further improvements may comprise an adjustment of the weights of linear interpolation of the language models. Since the test set was of German language a decomposition strategy could be beneficial towards a better mean average precision. Additionally, resources like RSS feeds or Web 2.0 might be useful as adaptation data. We intend to evaluate this method using different types of speech, e.g. a mixture of broadcast news, advertisement and talk shows. Furthermore, it would be interesting to use additional resources from the web, like Twitter and RSS Feeds as adaptation data.

**Acknowledgements.** This work was realized as part of the project Chrooma+ supported by the Sächsische Aufbaubank within the European Social Fund in the Free State of Saxony, Germany and the project ValidAX funded by the Federal Ministry of Education and Research, Germany.

## References

[1] Garofolo, J.S., Auzanne, C.G.P., Voorhees, E.M.: The trec spoken document retrieval track: A success story. In: Mariani, J.J., Harman, D. (eds.) RIAO, CID, pp. 1–20 (2000)
[2] Chen, L., Lamel, L., Gauvain, J.L., Adda, G.: Dynamic language modeling for broadcast news. In: 8th International Conference on Spoken Language Processing (INTERSPEECH), pp. 997–1000 (2004)

[3] Meng, S., Thambiratnam, K., Lin, Y., Wang, L., Li, G., Seide, F.: Vocabulary and language model adaptation using just one speech file. In: The IEEE International Conference on Acoustics Speech and Signal Processing (ICASSP), pp. 5410–5413 (2010)

[4] Lecorvé, G., Gravier, G., Sébillot, P.: An unsupervised web-based topic language model adaptation method. In: The IEEE International Conference on Acoustics Speech and Signal Processing (ICASSP), pp. 5081–5084 (2008)

[5] Tsiartas, A., Georgiou, P.G., Narayanan, S.: Language model adaptation using www documents obtained by utterance-based queries. In: The IEEE International Conference on Acoustics Speech and Signal Processing (ICASSP), pp. 5406–5409 (2010)

[6] Schlippe, T., Gren, L., Vu, N.T., Schultz, T.: Unsupervised language model adaptation for automatic speech recognition of broadcast news using web 2.0. In: The 14th Annual Conference of the International Speech Communication Association (INTERSPEECH), pp. 2698–2702 (2013)

[7] Iyer, R., Ostendorf, M.: Relevance weighting for combining multi-domain data for n-gram language modeling. Computer Speech and Language 13(3), 267–282 (1999)

[8] Saykham, K., Chotimongkol, A., Wutiwiwatchai, C.: Online temporal language model adaptation for a thai broadcast news transcription system. In: Calzolari, N., Choukri, K., Maegaard, B., Mariani, J., Odijk, J., Piperidis, S., Rosner, M., Tapias, D. (eds.) LREC. European Language Resources Association (2010)

[9] Klakow, D., Peters, J.: Testing the correlation of word error rate and perplexity. Speech Communication 38(1-2), 19–28 (2002)

[10] Kürsten, J., Wilhelm, T.: Extensible retrieval and evaluation framework: Xtrieval. In: Baumeister, J., Atzmüller, M. (eds.) LWA. Volume 448 of Technical Report, Department of Computer Science, University of Würzburg, Germany, 107–110 (2008)

# Self-supervised Relation Extraction Using UMLS

Roland Roller and Mark Stevenson

Department of Computer Science
University of Sheffield
Regent Court, 211 Portobello
S1 4DP Sheffield, England

**Abstract.** Self-supervised relation extraction uses a knowledge base to automatically annotate a training corpus which is then used to train a classifier. This approach has been successfully applied to different domains using a range of knowledge bases. This paper applies the approach to the biomedical domain using UMLS, a large biomedical knowledge base containing millions of concepts and relations among them. The approach is evaluated using two different techniques. The presented results are promising and indicate that UMLS is a useful resource for semi-supervised relation extraction.

## 1 Introduction

Medline is a large database which contains millions of biomedical articles and scientific abstracts. Every month several thousand new medical abstracts are published on Medline. The volume of documents available make it difficult to identify relevant document. Information Extraction can help with this problem by identifying pre-specified types of information within documents. Relation extraction is a sub-area of Information Extraction that tries to identify relationships between entities (words or concepts) within sentences. The output from relation extraction systems can be used to populate knowledge bases. For example, a relationship could be *DRUG-may_be_used_to_treat-DISEASE* and described in a sentence such as example 1.

*Example 1.* Dosing regimen effects of [**DRUG**:*modafinil*] for improving daytime wakefulness in patients with [**DISEASE**:*narcolepsy*]. *(PMID: 14520165)*

The goal of relation extraction is to identify pairs of entities within sentences that are connected by a pre-specified relation. Supervised learning approaches have proved successful for this problem. They require positive and negative training examples of the target relation and use machine learning techniques to train a classifier. These approaches have proved successful but require training data (annotated corpus) which is not always available. The generation of an appropriate corpus may require expert knowledge and can be time-consuming. Self-supervision (aka. distant supervision) avoids this bottleneck by using a knowledge base which contains information about the relation of interest to automatically annotate a data set. The baseline assumption is that a sentence which contains entity pairs representing (or not representing) a relation will also express the relationship as well.

E. Kanoulas et al. (Eds.): CLEF 2014, LNCS 8685, pp. 116–127, 2014.

Self-supervised learning has been used in different domains and for different data bases. The technique was originally developed for the biomedical domain by [8] who used the Yeast Protein Database to automatically annotate relation instances. The Unified Medical Language System (UMLS) is a large biomedical knowledge base which contains millions of medical concepts and the relations among them. This work explores the usage of this knowledge base for self-supervised relation extraction from biomedical publications. In particular it provides techniques to measure the efficiency of a self-supervised relation extractor using UMLS. The goal of this paper is to show, that it is possible to use UMLS for this purposes and to provide some baseline evaluation results which can be utilised as a benchmark for further work.

The paper is structured as follows: The next section presents related work. An overview of UMLS is provided in section 3. The following section 4 shows how the baseline data set is generated by matching known facts to the Medline repository. Section 5 explains the classification method used. Section 6 reports an analysis of the annotated examples generated by this process by comparing them against human judgements. The annotated examples are used to train a supervised relation extraction system, the evaluation of which is reported in Section 7. The paper's conclusions are reported in Section 8.

## 2   Related Work

Relation extraction is the task of detecting or extracting relationships between entities. Supervised relation extraction is a well studied method which uses machine learning techniques to address this problem. This method requires a sufficient amount of training data, consisting of positive and negative training examples. Performance normally improves when more training data is available and when that training data accurately describes the target relation. The support vector machine (SVM) [12] is a popular machine learning technique for relation extraction. A successful SVM-based approach for relation extraction is the TEES system of [3,4]. It was the winning system at the BioNLP Shared Task 2011 and one of the best systems at the BioNLP Shared Task 2013. Other successful approaches for relation extraction use particular kernel methods [19] or combine different models by stacking [17] or ensemble learning [22].

Supervised Machine Learning techniques require annotated training data. This data might be not always available for all different tasks. Furthermore, the generation of an annotated data set for training is time consuming and expensive. Depending on the domain it may even require expert knowledge to carry out the annotation. Self-supervised learning techniques face this problem and avoid using annotated data sets. Instead they utilise already known information and apply an automatic annotation, similar to seed and bootstrapping approaches such as [5] or [1]. While bootstrapping techniques are provided with limited information (in the form of seed examples), self-supervised learning uses a knowledge base with a large amount of information representing a relationship. There are many different data bases available which contain known entity pairs representing different relationships. [8] introduced self-supervision for relation extraction. The authors used the Yeast Protein Database (YPD) which includes subcellar localisation fields for many proteins. The knowledge base refers to certain PubMed articles which contain information about known relationships and were utilised to extract training examples. Some years later their idea of self-supervision for relation extraction was used outside the biomedical domain. [20] focussed on the identification of hypernyms (is-a relationship) using WordNet. [14] introduced self-supervision using Freebase, a large semantic database containing thousands of relations. For each entity pair of one of the main relations they find sentences in Wikipedia containing these entities and extract them. Negative data is produced by generating random pairs which do not appear in Freebase. Unlike previous approaches, this classifier takes the occurrence of an entity pair in several relations at the same time, into account. [11] use the infoboxes of Wikipedia as knowledge source and annotate the information the the articles of Wikipedia. [18] instead use Freebase but annotate the New York Times corpus with the entity pairs. Their work focuses on the three relations *nationality*, *place_of_birth* and *contains*. To train a classifier, the authors introduce the usage of a multi-instance learning [9] approach for this context. Later work still focuses on the same knowledge base and the same corpus, but try to consider the fact that information occur in different relations at once (overlapping relations) [10], try to reduce wrong annotations (labels) [21] or facing the problem of knowledge base gaps [24]. Knowledge base gaps for example can lead to information annotated as negative training data (false negatives) and will influence the classification results.

Applications of self-supervised approaches to relation extraction in the biomedical domain have been limited, the best known approach being [8]. [23] use self-supervision to train a classifier for protein-protein interactions (PPI). Similar to many other approaches in the biomedical domain, the authors use a SVM with a shallow linguistic kernel as classifier. The knowledge about interacting proteins is taken from the database IntAct. Different to for example [14] or other approaches, negative instance pairs are extracted from an additional knowledge base Negatome, which contains proteins which never interact with each other.

This work focuses on self-supervised relation extraction using the Unified Medical Language System (UMLS) as knowledge base. UMLS is a large biomedical knowledge base with millions of medical concepts and relations among them. This knowledge base is much more complex and contains many more relations between them than other self-supervised approaches in the biomedical domain. To our knowledge there is no data set annotated with UMLS relations which could be used to directly evaluate a UMLS-based relation extraction system. In this paper evaluation is carried out using two techniques. A first set of experiments uses a set of UMLS Metathesaurus relations based on the National Drug File - Reference Terminology (NDF-RT) vocabulary which provides information such as *diseases* treated by *drugs*. Evaluation in these experiments is carried out using a *held-out* approach. In addition, the system is also applied to a small set of sentences and the results evaluated manually.

## 3  Unified Medical Language System

The *Unified Medical Language System* (UMLS) is a set of files and software which combines different biomedical vocabularies, knowledge bases and standards. It includes three tools: Metathesaurus, Semantic Network and SPECIALIST Lexicon. The UMLS

Metathesaurus is a knowledge source containing several million biomedical and health related names and concepts and relationships among them. For this work just the Metathesaurus (version 2013AA) is utilised. The knowledge in the Metathesaurus is a unification of different data sources (source vocabularies) such as the National Drug File (NDFRT), the Medical Subject Heading (MSH) or Authorized Osteopathic Thesaurus (AOT) for example. The utilised UMLS version contains 121 different source vocabularies (including different language variations). UMLS is growing with every new release in terms of further concepts, relations and also source vocabularies. The different source vocabularies have a certain amount of overlap to each other. Overall UMLS is a large knowledge base trying to unify different medical knowledge sources and bring it to a common standard.

The information within UMLS Metathesaurus is spread across different files. The most important ones for this work are MRCONSO and MRREL. MRCONSO contains all medical concepts with all its different names, variants and spellings and unifies them with the **Concept Unique Identifiers** (CUI). The concepts are taken across all different vocabularies. MRREL uses these CUIs and defines binary relations between them. Many of these relations are child-parent relationships, express a synonymy or are vaguely defined as broader or narrower relation. Some other relationships define a better defined relation name (RELA) between two CUIs, such as *moved_from*, *has_location*, *mechanism_of_action_of* or *drug_contraindicated_for*. In general each relationship between two CUIs is defined in both ways, e.g. if there is a relations such as has_location(CUI-A,CUI-B), then there is also a relation location_of(CUI-B,CUI-A). MRREL contains in the UMLS version 2013AA, 52,388,978 instance pairs (relations).

## 4 Generation of Annotated Corpus

The corpus used to generate annotated data is the Medline repository, which contains abstracts of millions of publications from medicine and related fields. Sentences from Medline containing information of interest are used to generate training examples for distant supervision. Therefore it is necessary to process the Medline abstracts to identify related information. In UMLS relations are expressed by a pair of CUIs. To find out whether a sentence contains two possibly related CUIs, a mapping of UMLS concepts to the sentences of Medline is required. Manual annotation would be impractical so the MetaMap system[1] [2] is used. MetaMap identifies concepts mentioned in text in the form of UMLS CUIs (Concept Unique Identifiers). It first divides the text into segments and then identifies possible UMLS concepts for each segment. This is carried out by identifying the possible CUIs that could related to the sentence (known as *candidates*). Depending on the context and the different possible candidates, MetaMap will provide different possible *mappings* to annotate the sentence with the previously found UMLS concepts. A mapping will always involve only concepts of the candidate list, but it just selects the most probable (or best) ones depending on the context. That means that a mapping usually involves fewer concepts than the candidates. MetaMap can be configured to provide several possible different mappings. For this work the mapping MetaMap considers to be the best is taken as the annotation and all other

---

[1] http://metamap.nlm.nih.gov/

candidates ignored since using all possible mappings could generate false annotations. For the experiments a MetaMapped version of the year 2012 (using UMLS release 2011AB) was used, which was provided by the Medline Baseline Repository[2] (MBR). Altogether 3,000,000 abstracts from 1997-2003 of this MetaMapped Medline Repository were utilised. All extracted instance pairs for distant supervision base on the UMLS release 2013AA.

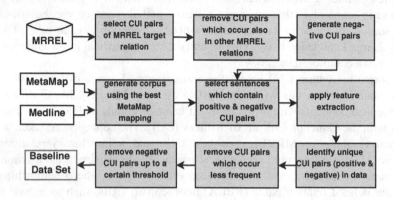

**Fig. 1.** Processing pipeline to generate the baseline data set

Training examples are based on the relations from the UMLS' MRREL table. To train a self-supervised classifier for a particular UMLS relation, self-supervised training examples have to be generated (positive and negative examples). To generate a classifier for a certain target relation, all CUI pairs for that relation are extracted from MRREL and taken as a set of positive instance pairs. Self-supervision uses the baseline assumption that the occurrence of a positive entity pair in a sentence will describe the relation of interest. Any CUI pairs which also occur in another MRREL relations are removed from the list of positive instance pairs. In the next step, negative instance pairs will be generated. Based on the positive instance pair set, new CUI pair combinations will be generated (combining all CUIs from the first position with all CUIs from the second position). Only if a newly generated CUI pair is not in the positive list and not contained in another MRREL relation, it will be used as negative instance pair. This random generation of new negative instance pairs can usually generate many more CUI combinations than the known positive instance pairs. On the other hand, it might happen that many of these negative instance pairs are not found together within a sentence and are therefore less useful to generate negative training examples.

In the next step sentences of the MetaMapped Medline repository are scanned for positive and negative instance pairs. If a sentence contains a positive (or a negative) CUI pair, it will be taken and processed to be a positive (or negative) training example. The generated examples serve as baseline training set of positive and negative training examples to train the MRREL relational classifier. Figure 1 visualises the different processing steps to generate the baseline data set. Table 1 shows the amount of instance

---

[2] http://mbr.nlm.nih.gov/Download/MetaMapped_Medline/2012/

pairs which are available to generate the baseline data set. Furthermore, it shows that just a small number of instance pairs can be found in the utilised subset of the Medline repository. The MRREL relation *drug_contraindicated_for* for instance contains 36,251 CUI pairs. After the removal of CUI pairs (due to the occurrence in other MRREL tables), 28,867 pairs remain. These remaining positive instance pairs can generate 4,103,724 different negative combinations. In the given MetaMapped Medline repository 2,015 sentences containing positive instance pairs have been found. These 2,015 sentences contain just 566 unique CUI pairs.

**Table 1.** Amount of CUI pairs for the generation of the baseline data set (all); #given: amount of CUI pairs in MRREL, #pos: amount of positive CUI pairs, #neg (g): amount of negative CUI pairs generated from the positive pairs, #u-pos: unique positive pairs, #u-neg: unique negative pairs

| MRREL relation | instance pairs | | | CUI pairs found in baseline data set | | | |
|---|---|---|---|---|---|---|---|
| | #given | #pos | #neg (g.) | #pos | #u-pos | #neg | #u-neg |
| may_treat | 48,298 | 35,271 | 8,826,775 | 10,819 | 2,062 | 58,719 | 24,148 |
| drug_contraindicated_for | 36,251 | 28,867 | 4,103,724 | 2,015 | 566 | 61,609 | 20,340 |
| physiologic_effect_of | 27,684 | 21,356 | 4,863,838 | 694 | 110 | 11,612 | 1,850 |
| mechanism_of_action_of | 16,696 | 12,321 | 3,265,878 | 1,091 | 233 | 9,252 | 3,465 |
| may_prevent | 6,048 | 2,337 | 722,584 | 2,787 | 215 | 16,770 | 5,383 |
| contraindicating_class_of | 2,228 | 1,756 | 90,991 | 1,090 | 167 | 20,412 | 2,668 |
| may_diagnose | 967 | 791 | 51,535 | 1,070 | 61 | 2,462 | 570 |

Depending on the evaluation, further methods to select more useful training examples will be applied. First unique CUI pairs are identified. Sentences with pairs which occur less frequently are removed (for these experiments the threshold is set to 2). Since the amount of unique positive and unique negative CUI pairs are often strongly biased, some unique negative CUIs with their sentences are removed. For the following experiments the amount of utilised unique negative CUI pairs is reduced to a maximum of three times the amount of different unique positive CUI pairs.

## 5 Relation Classifier

For the self-supervised relation extraction a support vector machine (SVM) is used. This work utilises SVM-Light [12] with the implementation SVM-Light-TK 1.2[3] [15] which takes a combination of a Subset-Tree Kernel (SST) [7] and a polynomial kernel as input. The Charniak-Johnson Parser [6] is used to generate part of speech tags and a syntax tree. The Stanford parser [13] takes this data as input and generates a dependency tree. In addition, words of the sentence are reduced to their stem using the Porter Stemmer [16]. Next the features will be extracted. The syntax tree is used to generate the input for the SST-kernel. Words in the two related entities are replaced with a place-holder and the smallest sub-tree which contains the two entities is extracted. This sub-tree will be used as input for the SST-kernel.

---

[3] http://disi.unitn.it/moschitti/Tree-Kernel.htm

The polynomial kernel takes token features and dependency chain features as input, similar to those described in [3]. To adjust the SVM the parameters *cost*, *d* (for the polynomial kernel) and *decay factor* have to be defined.

## 6  Data Analysis

To analyse the quality of the training examples and automatic annotation, a set of 100 positive examples were selected at random and examined in more detail. Each of the positively annotated entity pairs and sentences will be examined to determine whether they express the relation or not. The examination was carried out by one author, a Computer Science PhD student and biomedical non-expert. To reduce the amount of annotation errors, a simple UMLS relations has been selected: *may_treat*. Some sentences are easy to understand and clearly contain the relation of interest, such as in examples 1 and 2. Sentences which do not contain the relations are more difficult to detect. In some cases the mentioned drug stands in another relationship to the disease, than the relation *may_treat* (such as example 3). Sometimes the sentences express, that a certain drug is not useful to treat a certain disease (see example 4). In that case the sentence is also annotated as negative.

*Example 2.* We retrospectively studied 9 children (6 with [**DISEASE:***congenital adrenal hyperplasia*], CAH) receiving [**DRUG:***hydrocortisone*] replacement after switching to prednisolone (dose ratio, 1:5). *(PMID: 14517528)*

*Example 3.* Among the remaining cases, probable [**DISEASE:***type 2 diabetes*] was defined when a child had one or more of the following characteristics: weight per age > or =95th percentile or acanthosis nigricans at diagnosis, elevated C-peptide or [**DRUG:***insulin*], family history of type 2 diabetes; *(PMID: 14517522)*

*Example 4.* Oral [**DRUG:***insulin*] doesn't prevent [**DISEASE:***type 1 diabetes*]. *(PMID: 14528584)*

Overall, 64 sentences were annotated as positive and 36 as negative. This shows that the data contains many false positive and that filtering methods to remove false training examples are required. Furthermore, that amount of false positives in the given set is comparable to the manual examined data set in [18] for the context of Freebase relations.

## 7  Evaluation Methods

In this section two evaluation methods for self-supervised relation extraction using UMLS are presented. First different relational classifiers are trained and evaluated using the held-out approach (Section 7.1). Next the classifiers are evaluated on a small gold standard evaluation set (Section 7.2).

## 7.1  Held-Out

Held-out is an evaluation technique which uses part of the data in the knowledge base to train the self-supervised classifier. The remaining parts of the data are used for the evaluation. After removing the less frequent unique CUI pairs and reduction of the negative CUI pairs, the remaining pairs will be divided into a set of training pairs and evaluation pairs. For this work, 3/4 of the remaining positive and negative CUI pairs will be used to generate the training set. The remaining 1/4 of the pairs are used to generate the evaluation set. After splitting into sets of training and evaluation CUI pairs, sentences containing these pairs are sorted into the training and evaluation set.

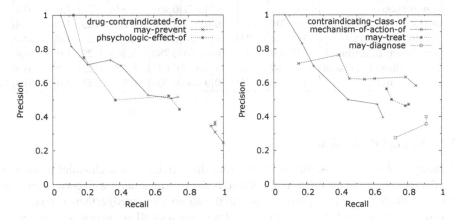

**Fig. 2.** Held-out evaluation graphs

The relation classifier is trained using the training set and evaluated on the evaluation set. The approach is evaluated as follows: The evaluation set contains different CUI pairs. Some are known (according to MRREL) to describe the target relation. It is assumed, that the other CUI pairs which are not found in the MRREL target relation do not describe the relationship. In the ideal case, sentences containing the positive CUI pairs describe the relation of interest and sentences containing negative CUI pairs do not describe the target relation. The task of the relational classifier is to detect the CUI pairs which are supposed to describe the relation. If a CUI pair is predicted at least once as positive (CUI pairs often occur several times), it will be considered as predicted positive. Otherwise the CUI pair will be considered as predicted as negative.

Figure 2 shows the relation between precision and recall using different configurations in terms of SVM parameter *cost*, *d* and *decay factor* (DF). Depending on the configuration of the decay factor, the different classifiers vary from a high precision with low recall to a low precision with a high recall. Three of the relations (*may_treat*, *may_diagnose* and *may_prevent*) only provide a good recall with a lower precision, but not the other way. This could be an indicator that the chosen training examples contain too many false positives and false negatives. Table 2 presents the best held-out results for the different relations. The evaluation set of the relation *may_prevent* for instance, contains 41 positive and 125 negative unique CUI pairs. 105 different CUI pairs have been predicted at least once as positive and 39 of them have been predicted correct.

The results in the table are compared to a naive baseline approach, which classifies every instance as positive. Compared to the naive results, all self-supervised result provide much better results. The improvements vary between 34% and 75% in terms of F-Score.

**Table 2.** Best results using held-out

| MRREL relation | Unique CUI pairs | | | | Results | | | Naive Baseline | | |
|---|---|---|---|---|---|---|---|---|---|---|
| | #pos | #neg | #pred | #cor | Prec. | Rec. | F-Score | Prec. | Rec. | F-Score |
| may_treat | 200 | 597 | 239 | 135 | 0.565 | 0.675 | 0.615 | 0.25 | 1.0 | 0.4 |
| may_prevent | 41 | 125 | 105 | 39 | 0.371 | 0.951 | 0.534 | 0.25 | 1.0 | 0.4 |
| drug_contraindicated_for | 81 | 246 | 116 | 60 | 0.517 | 0.741 | 0.609 | 0.25 | 1.0 | 0.4 |
| physiologic_effect_of | 16 | 48 | 21 | 11 | 0.524 | 0.688 | 0.595 | 0.25 | 1.0 | 0.4 |
| mechanism_of_action_of | 33 | 100 | 41 | 26 | 0.634 | 0.788 | 0.703 | 0.25 | 1.0 | 0.4 |
| contraindicating_class_of | 29 | 87 | 38 | 18 | 0.474 | 0.621 | 0.537 | 0.25 | 1.0 | 0.4 |
| may_diagnose | 11 | 33 | 25 | 10 | 0.400 | 0.909 | 0.556 | 0.25 | 1.0 | 0.4 |

## 7.2   Manual Evaluation

Although held-out is a useful way to measure the efficiency of a classifier it relies on the data representing the relation of interest. A data set annotated with correct relations is preferable for evaluation purposes. But, to the authors knowledge, there is no existing data set with annotated relations of UMLS. Therefore a small evaluation set is generated manually by one of the authors, a biomedical non-expert and Computer Science PhD student. 100 sentences from the baseline data set for a simple target relation (*may_treat*) are chosen and annotated. The resulting manual annotations are compared with the automatic annotation of the baseline data set in table 3. It shows, that just 3 of the 20 instances automatically annotated as positive were also annotated manually as positive. Further on, 8 instances of the automatic negative annotation were changed to positive instances. The resulting evaluation set contains 11 positive and 89 negative instances.

**Table 3.** *may_treat:* manual versus automatic annotation

| | | annotation based on UMLS | | |
|---|---|---|---|---|
| | | positives | negatives | |
| manual annotation | positives | 3 | 8 | 11 |
| | negatives | 17 | 72 | 89 |
| | | 20 | 80 | |

It is important to mention that some sentences are difficult to annotate. Their annotation highly depends on the view of the annotator. The sentence in example 5 for instance was annotated as negative in the evaluation set but could conceivably be annotated differently. The sentence expresses that there is an effect on the disease *Parkinson's disease* using the drug *pramipexole*. It is not clear whether is has a positive or negative effect and whether the author of the underlying sentences suggests the treatment of the disease using *pramipexole*.

*Example 5.* We compared the antitremor effect of [**DRUG**:*pramipexole*], pergolide, or placebo in [**DISEASE**:*Parkinson's disease*] (PD). *(PMID: 14639675)*

A further experiment was carried out in which the relation classifier was trained using examples of the *may_treat* relation created using the self-supervision process and evaluated against the manually annotated corpus. Similar to the previous experimental setup, all CUI pairs which occur fewer than two times are removed from the set and the set of negative CUI pairs is reduced to a maximum of three times the number of positive CUI pairs. Since the *may_treat* baseline set contains around 70,000 instances, the set was reduced to decrease the runtime of the classifier before identifying the unique CUI pairs. Table 4 presents the results of this experiment. The *naive* method is a simple baseline technique which predicts that each instance is positive. The best configuration of the basic self-supervised approach with an restriction of the baseline data set to 10,000, easily outperforms the naive approach, with a F-Score of 0.571. This resulting F-score is very close to the result of the *may_treat* classifier within the held-out experiment.

Table 4. Results on evaluation set using *may_treat*

| method | Precision | Recall | F-Score |
|---|---|---|---|
| naive | 0.110 | 1.000 | 0.198 |
| basic DS (max 5,000 training instances) | 0.273 | 0.273 | 0.273 |
| basic DS (max 10,000 training instances) | 0.600 | 0.545 | 0.571 |
| basic DS (max 20,000 training instances) | 0.417 | 0.455 | 0.435 |

# 8   Conclusion

This work presented a self-supervised relation extraction system which uses information from the UMLS to generate training examples. The results of this approach are highly promising. They show that UMLS relations can be used to train a relational classifier and extract related entities of biomedical publications. Results based on a standard self-supervised relation extraction platform provide an average F-Score of around 0.6.

This paper demonstrates that, in general, it is possible to use relations from UMLS for self-supervised relation extraction. It also reports evaluation of this approach using two techniques. The results reported here serve as a baseline against which future approaches can be compared.

**Acknowledgements.** The authors are grateful to the Engineering and Physical Sciences Research Council for supporting the work described in this paper (EP/J008427/1).

# References

1. Agichtein, E., Gravano, L.: Snowball: extracting relations from large plain-text collections. In: Proceedings of the Fifth ACM Conference on Digital libraries, DL 2000, pp. 85–94 (2000)
2. Aronson, A., Lang, F.: An overview of MetaMap: historical perspective and recent advances. Journal of the American Medical Association 17(3), 229–236 (2010)
3. Björne, J., Salakoski, T.: Generalizing biomedical event extraction. In: Proceedings of BioNLP Shared Task 2011 Workshop, pp. 183–191. Association for Computational Linguistics, Portland (2011)
4. Björne, J., Salakoski, T.: Tees 2.1: Automated annotation scheme learning in the bionlp 2013 shared task. In: Proceedings of the BioNLP Shared Task 2013 Workshop, pp. 16–25. Association for Computational Linguistics, Sofia (2013)
5. Brin, S.: Extracting patterns and relations from the world wide web. In: Atzeni, P., Mendelzon, A.O., Mecca, G. (eds.) WebDB 1998. LNCS, vol. 1590, pp. 172–183. Springer, Heidelberg (1999)
6. Charniak, E., Johnson, M.: Coarse-to-fine n-best parsing and maxent discriminative reranking. In: Proceedings of the 43rd Annual Meeting on Association for Computational Linguistics, ACL 2005, pp. 173–180 (2005)
7. Collins, M., Duffy, N.: New ranking algorithms for parsing and tagging: Kernels over discrete structures, and the voted perceptron. In: Proceedings of 40th Annual Meeting of the Association for Computational Linguistics, pp. 263–270. Association for Computational Linguistics, Philadelphia (2002)
8. Craven, M., Kumlien, J.: Constructing biological knowledge bases by extracting information from text sources. In: Proceedings of the Seventh International Conference on Intelligent Systems for Molecular Biology (ISMB), pp. 77–86. AAAI Press (1999)
9. Dietterich, T.G., Lathrop, R.H., Lozano-Perez, T., Pharmaceutical, A.: Solving the multiple-instance problem with axis-parallel rectangles. Artificial Intelligence 89, 31–71 (1997)
10. Hoffmann, R., Zhang, C., Ling, X., Zettlemoyer, L., Weld, D.S.: Knowledge-based weak supervision for information extraction of overlapping relations. In: Proceedings of the 49th Annual Meeting of the Association for Computational Linguistics, ACL 2011, pp. 541–550 (2011)
11. Hoffmann, R., Zhang, C., Weld, D.S.: Learning 5000 relational extractors. In: Proceedings of the 48th Annual Meeting of the Association for Computational Linguistics, ACL 2010, pp. 286–295 (2010)
12. Joachims, T.: Making Large-scale Support Vector Machine Learning Practical. In: Advances in Kernel Methods, pp. 169–184 (1999)
13. Klein, D., Manning, C.D.: Accurate unlexicalized parsing. In: Proceedings of the 41st Annual Meeting of the Association for Computational Linguistics, pp. 423–430 (2003)
14. Mintz, M., Bills, S., Snow, R., Jurafsky, D.: Distant supervision for relation extraction without labeled data. In: Proceedings of the Joint Conference of the 47th Annual Meeting of the ACL and the 4th International Joint Conference on Natural Language Processing of the AFNLP: ACL 2009, vol. 2, pp. 1003–1011 (2009)
15. Moschitti, A.: Making tree kernels practical for natural language learning. In: EACL, pp. 113–120 (2006)
16. Porter, M.F.: An Algorithm for Suffix Stripping. In: Readings in Information Retrieval, pp. 313–316 (1997)
17. Riedel, S., McClosky, D., Surdeanu, M., McCallum, A.: D. Manning, C.: Model combination for event extraction in bionlp 2011. In: Proceedings of BioNLP Shared Task 2011 Workshop, pp. 51–55. Association for Computational Linguistics, Portland (2011)

18. Riedel, S., Yao, L., McCallum, A.: Modeling relations and their mentions without labeled text. In: Balcázar, J.L., Bonchi, F., Gionis, A., Sebag, M. (eds.) ECML PKDD 2010, Part III. LNCS, vol. 6323, pp. 148–163. Springer, Heidelberg (2010)
19. Segura-Bedmar, I., Martínez, P., de Pablo-Sánchez, C.: Using a shallow linguistic kernel for drug-drug interaction extraction. Journal of Biomedical Informatics 44(5), 789–804 (2011)
20. Snow, R., Jurafsky, D., Ng, A.Y.: Learning syntactic patterns for automatic hypernym discovery. In: Advances in Neural Information Processing Systems (NIPS 2004) (November 2004)
21. Takamatsu, S., Sato, I., Nakagawa, H.: Reducing wrong labels in distant supervision for relation extraction. In: Proceedings of the 50th Annual Meeting of the Association for Computational Linguistics: Long Papers, ACL 2012, vol. 1, pp. 721–729 (2012)
22. Thomas, P., Neves, M., Solt, I., Tikk, D., Leser, U.: Relation extraction for drug-drug interactions using ensemble learning. In: DDIExtraction2011: First Challenge Task: Drug-Drug Interaction Extraction at SEPLN 2011, vol. 4, pp. 11–18 (2011)
23. Thomas, I.P., Solt, Klinger, R., Leser, U.: Learning protein protein interaction extraction using distant supervision. In: Proceedings of Robust Unsupervised and Semi-Supervised Methods in Natural Language Processing, pp. 34–41 (2011)
24. Xu, W., Hoffmann, R., Zhao, L., Grishman, R.: Filling knowledge base gaps for distant supervision of relation extraction. In: Proceedings of the 51st Annual Meeting of the Association for Computational Linguistics (Volume 2: Short Papers), pp. 665–670. Association for Computational Linguistics, Sofia (2013)

# Authorship Identification
# Using Dynamic Selection of Features
# from Probabilistic Feature Set*

Hamed Zamani, Hossein Nasr Esfahani, Pariya Babaie, Samira Abnar,
Mostafa Dehghani, and Azadeh Shakery

School of Electrical and Computer Engineering, College of Engineering,
University of Tehran, Tehran, Iran
{h.zamani,h_nasr,pariya.babaie,s.abnar,mo.dehghani,shakery}@ut.ac.ir

**Abstract.** Authorship identification was introduced as one of the important problems in the law and journalism fields and it is one of the major techniques in plagiarism detection. In this paper, to tackle the authorship verification problem, we propose a probabilistic distribution model to represent each document as a feature set to increase the interpretability of the results and features. We also introduce a distance measure to compute the distance between two feature sets. Finally, we exploit a KNN-based approach and a dynamic feature selection method to detect the features which discriminate the author's writing style.

The experimental results on PAN at CLEF 2013 dataset show the effectiveness of the proposed method. We also show that feature selection is necessary to achieve an outstanding performance. In addition, we conduct a comprehensive analysis on our proposed dynamic feature selection method which shows that discriminative features are different for different authors.

**Keywords:** authorship identification, dynamic feature selection, k-nearest neighbors, probabilistic feature set.

## 1 Introduction

Authorship identification is an important problem in many fields such as law and journalism. During the last decade, automatic authorship identification was considered as an applicable problem in Computer Science. As a result, many approaches related to machine learning, information retrieval, and natural language processing have been proposed for this purpose [15]. Authorship identification includes two separate problems: authorship attribution and authorship verification, where the latter is the most realistic interpretation of the authorship

---

* A simplified version of the approach proposed in this paper participated in PAN at CLEF 2014 Authorship Identification competition. In PAN 2014, we did not consider knee detection technique for feature selection and only selected the best two features. It is worth mentioning that the achieved results on English Novels and Dutch Reviews datasets were promising.

E. Kanoulas et al. (Eds.): CLEF 2014, LNCS 8685, pp. 128–140, 2014.

identification task [9]. Authorship verification has a considerable overlap with plagiarism detection, especially in intrinsic plagiarism detection, where the goal is to determine whether a given paragraph (or a part of a document) is written by a given author or not [6,16].

Many research studies have been conducted on authorship identification and plagiarism detection until now, especially in the "evaluation labs on uncovering plagiarism, authorship, and social software misuse" (PAN)[1]. The authorship identification task of PAN at CLEF 2013 and 2014 focused on authorship verification [2]. The authorship verification task is to verify whether an unknown authorship document is written by a given author or not, when there are only a limited number of documents written by this author are available.

Authorship verification can be simply considered as a binary classification task. However, there are many challenges in this task, such as limited number of positive documents, unbalanced number of negative and positive documents, and existence of many features for each document. Moreover, each author has his/her own writing style and detecting the discriminative features of the writing style of each author is a challenge.

In most of the previous studies in this field, a vector of features is defined for each document [15]. This approach brings two problems. First of all, different features are put together in one vector, and thus the values in a vector are not interpretable and are meaningless in comparison with each other (e.g., a vector containing frequency of stopwords and punctuations). The second problem is about the dimensionality of the feature vector, which may be quite high. In order to solve this problem, feature selection algorithms are used. The output of most of the feature selection algorithms, such as principal component analysis, is a new vector that is the original vector with some eliminated or/and combined cells. Although this solution may decrease the input vector's dimensionality, the result vector is less interpretable for further analysis. The interpretability is essential in this task, especially when the authorship verification problem is designed as a human-in-the-loop system. To tackle these problems, we propose to define a feature set, instead of using a global vector including all feature values. Each element of the feature set is a probabilistic distribution (e.g., the probabilistic distribution of stopwords in the document). Since all features are extracted and stored in a probabilistic format, we do not have to worry about the variability of document lengths. Additionally, there are some well-defined mathematical comparison measures for probabilistic distributions which may perform better than the heuristic ones used extensively in the existing authorship identification methods.

To verify whether an unknown authorship document is written by a given author or not, we use k-nearest neighbors (KNN) technique which can outperform learning-based classification methods, when the amount of training data is limited. In addition, KNN is fast and we can use it repeatedly in our algorithm without worrying about efficiency.

---

[1] http://pan.webis.de/

Each author has his/her own writing style; hence, in authorship verification, we should focus on the discriminative features for each author. To detect the writing styles, we propose a dynamic feature selection method which uses leave-one-out technique to determine the discriminative features of each author.

We use the dataset of PAN at CLEF 2013 authorship identification task in our evaluations. The experimental results indicate that the proposed method outperforms all the methods presented in PAN at CLEF 2013.

The remaining of this paper is structured as follows: Section 2 reviews the related research studies and Section 3 includes our proposed methodology to verify the authorship of documents. We evaluate our methodology and discuss the results in Section 4, and finally we conclude our paper and illustrate future works in Section 5.

## 2   Related Work

Two general approaches are mainly used for author verification task: profile-based and instance-based approaches[15]. In the profile-based methods, documents of each author are considered as a single document. Concatenation of each author's documents results in a profile which represents the author's general writing style. Therefore, the concatenated document is used for extracting the writing style features. The likelihood of the unseen document being written by the given author is determined by a defined distance measure [12].

In the instance-based methods, documents are considered as independent samples. The known authorship instances, represented by a feature vector, are fed to a classifier as the training data. In order to achieve a general and accurate model, each author should have sufficient numbers of sample instances. Hence, in the case of availability of a limited number of instances, possibly long ones, the idea is to segment each document to shorter ones with equal size. Nevertheless, the limited amount of training data continues to be a challenge [11]. It has been proposed that with multiple training instances, each having a different length per author, the documents length must be normalized [13].

Instance-based methods generally include a classifier. The feature selection method, the classification algorithm, and the comparison method affect the performance of the model. Numerosity of attributes within a document's content further add to the importance of both feature extraction and selection. Since feature extraction and selection can solve the problem of overfitness on the training data, considering them potentially can improve the performance significantly [15].

The classification algorithm is chosen based on the application of author identification. Two types of algorithms are generally used in this task, learning-based algorithms, such as neural networks [4,8], SVM [11,13], and Bayesian regression [1,3] and memory-based algorithms, such as k-nearest neighbors [5,17]. Learning-based algorithms require sufficient amount of training data, which is not always available. K-nearest neighbors is used to calculate style deviation score between documents of a known authorship and an unseen document. Based on the calculated score and the defined threshold, the unseen document may belong to this class [5]. In this paper, we also use a KNN-based approach to cope with the authorship verification problem.

# 3  Methodology

In this section, we first introduce our probabilistic feature set for each document. Then, we propose a distance measure to compute the distance of two different feature sets. After that, we introduce the proposed KNN-based approach for classification and finally we state our feature selection technique which selects the most discriminant features of each author's documents dynamically. Dynamic feature selection is used to improve the performance of authorship verification.

## 3.1  Probabilistic Feature Set

In the author verification task, features should be defined such that they can discriminate authors' writing styles. Several previous studies have introduced features which represent the authors' writing styles using a single number (e.g., number of different words); however, these features are not highly effective. It is notable that the previous methods store all of the features in a single vector. This kind of feature gathering suffers from lack of interpretation. In other words, when all features (e.g., lexical, stylish, and content-based features) are stored in a single vector, analysing the features is difficult. In addition, all the features are counted as equally important. Another point is that when feature selection techniques are applied on a single feature vector, the result may be meaningless; because some features (e.g., stopwords) may contain more than one value in the feature vector and feature selection techniques may omit some of them.

To tackle the mentioned problems, we store a set of features where each of the elements is a probabilistic distribution of one of the defined features. In other words, we define a feature set for each document, which includes probabilistic distributions. The probabilistic distribution of feature $F$ are estimated using Maximum Likelihood Estimation (MLE) for each feature element $f$, such that the probability of each feature element is calculated as follows:

$$p(f|d) = \frac{count(f, d)}{\sum_{f' \in F} count(f', d)} \tag{1}$$

where $count(f, d)$ indicates the frequency of feature element $f$ in document $d$. In other words, $f$ is one of the elements of probabilistic distribution $F$. These features are defined below:

1. **Probabilistic distribution of stopword usage**: Each element of this feature indicates the percentage of using a specific stopword. This feature is almost independent of the topic the author is writing about. Hence, it could show the writing style of the authors.

2. **Probabilistic distribution of punctuation usage**: Each element of this distribution shows the percentage of using a given punctuation mark. It is obvious that this feature is almost independent of the context.
3. **N-gram probabilistic distribution**: This feature shows the usage frequency of N-grams in the content. This feature can help us detect the phrases which are frequently used by an author. In addition, this feature can be effective when an author always writes about a few subjects.
4. **Probabilistic distribution of sentence length**: Sentence length is referred to the number of words used in a given sentence. Since, complex sentences are longer, this feature shows the writing complexity of each author.
5. **Probabilistic distribution of paragraph length**: Paragraph length can be considered as one of the discriminative features of writing styles. Thus, this feature is defined as the number of sentences which are used in a paragraph to obtain the distribution of the paragraph length.
6. **Part of Speech (POS) tag probabilistic distribution**: POS tags distribution shows how much a given author uses each POS tag. The intuition behind this feature is that the pattern of using POS tags is a good representation of the grammatical manner in writing. Since grammar is one of the key features of the writing styles, exploiting this feature could be beneficial.
7. **Word length probabilistic distribution**: The $i^{th}$ element of this feature shows how many of the words in a document contains exactly $i$ characters. Long words are commonly more complex than the short ones. Therefore, this feature may show the expertise of the author in vocabulary knowledge.

The difference between the size of the documents may cause some problems during the authorship verification process. For instance, long documents contain more stopwords. Since all of the mentioned features are probabilistic distributions, they do not depend on the document's length.

It is worth mentioning that we will exclude some of the features during the feature selection phase. To avoid the zero probabilities and to solve the sparseness problem (for further usages in calculating the distance between two feature sets), smoothing methods can be used. In this paper, we use Laplace smoothing approach [10].

## 3.2   Distance Measure

To measure the distance of two documents, we compare their probabilistic feature sets. This comparison is based on the divergence of two corresponding feature distributions. In other words, if $FS_i$ and $FS_j$ are the feature sets of documents $i$ and $j$, respectively, the distance of these two feature sets is calculated as:

$$distance(i,j) = \mathcal{F}\left(Dist(FS_i \| FS_j)\right) \qquad (2)$$

where $\mathcal{F}$ is a function whose input is inputs a list of numbers and it outputs a single number representing the distance between documents $i$ and $j$. In Equation 2, $Dist(FS_i \| FS_j)$ is a vector whose $k^{th}$ element shows the divergence of

$k^{th}$ probabilistic distributions of feature sets $FS_i$ and $FS_j$. The $k^{th}$ element of $Dist(FS_i||FS_j)$ is computed as:

$$Dist_k(FS_i||FS_j) = JSD(FS_{ik}||FS_{jk}) \tag{3}$$

where $JSD(FS_{ik}||FS_{jk})$ is the Jensen-Shannon divergence (JS-divergence) of $k^{th}$ distributions of feature sets $FS_i$ and $FS_j$, which is given by:

$$JSD(FS_{ik}||FS_{jk}) = \frac{1}{2} * D(FS_{ik}||\overline{FS_k}) + \frac{1}{2} * D(FS_{jk}||\overline{FS_k}) \tag{4}$$

where $\overline{FS_k}$ is the average of $FS_{ik}$ and $FS_{jk}$ distributions and $D$ demonstrates the Kullback-Leibler divergence (KL-divergence) [7] between two distributions, that is calculated as:

$$D(P||Q) = \sum_{i=1}^{m} P_i \log \frac{P_i}{Q_i} \tag{5}$$

where $P_i$ and $Q_i$ are the $i$th elements of distributions $P$ and $Q$ respectively and $m$ is the number of elements in both distributions.

JS-divergence is one of the metrics used to compare two distributions which have commutative property. In this context, it means that the distance of documents A and B is equal to the distance of B and A, which is reasonable and is one of our reasons to use this measure, instead of KL-divergence.

In our experiments, we consider the sum operation as the function $\mathcal{F}$ in Equation 2. In other words, we calculate the divergence of each pair of the corresponding features in two feature sets and consider the summation of them as the distance measure.

### 3.3 Authorship Verification Using a KNN-Based Approach

The most trivial solution to determined whether a document is written by a given author or not, is using a binary classifier, in which the positive class means that the given author is the writer of the document and the negative class means not. However, there are two main challenges in this solution:

- In most of the cases, the number of features in author identification task is large and classifiers require huge amounts of training data for their learning phase. However, this amount of training data is not always available.
- The number of documents which are not written by an author (negative documents) is extremely larger than the number of documents written by him/her. If we choose all of the negative documents to learn a classifier, unbalance in training data leads to learning a biased model. Although random sampling of negative documents could be a naive solution, it may eventuate wrong results in some cases.

Considering the aforementioned facts, we use an algorithm that is described in Algorithm 1. In this algorithm, we use the k-nearest neighbors (KNN) method.

---

**Algorithm 1:** KNN-based Authorship Classification Algorithm

---

**Input**: The set of documents $D$ written by a given author, the set $L$ including
the sets of documents of all authors having the same language as the
given author, and an unknown document $d_u$

**Output**: The estimated probability that the document $d_u$ is written by the
given author

$p \leftarrow 0$

**foreach** $D' \in L \ \& \ D' \neq D$ **do**

    $k \leftarrow \min(|D|, |D'|)$

    $C \leftarrow \{k \ nearest \ documents \ of \ \{D \cup D'\} \ to \ d_u\}$

    **if** $|C \cap D| > k/2$ **then**

        $p = p + 1/(|L| - 1)$

    **end**

**end**

**return** $p$

---

To verify that a document is written by author A or not, we take all of the other authors into account. In each step, we consider the documents of author A as instances of the positive class and the documents of one of the other authors (i.e. author B) as instances of the negative class and determine the class of the unknown document using KNN. We set the parameter $k$ of KNN algorithm as the minimum of number of documents written by A and number of documents written by B. We repeat this procedure with other authors as class B and calculate in how many of them, the unknown document is assigned to A.

The output of Algorithm 1 is the fraction of times the unknown authorship document is assigned to the questioned author. If the output of Algorithm 1 is greater than a threshold, we decide that the unknown document is written by A.

### 3.4   Dynamic Feature Selection

The idea behind dynamic feature selection is that discriminative features could be different for each author. For example, there could be an author that uses stopwords with a special writing style, but uses punctuation like other authors. Thus, for this author we need to emphasize stopword feature instead of considering all features similarly. Therefore, unlike previous methods that use all features to verify authors, we try to select discriminative features for each author. Dynamic feature selection consists of two main parts. First, we assign a score to each feature for each author and then we decide how many features we should use for each author and select the high score features. In the following, we describe these two parts in detail.

**Assigning Score to Each Feature for Each Author.** In feature selection, we consider each element of the probabilistic feature set individually. In other words, we assume that the features are independent. Although, this assumption is not always true, but it helps us have a faster algorithm; since, without this assumption, we should consider all subsets of the feature sets and select the most discriminant one, which is extremely time-consuming and costly. Assume that $C_j$ is a classifier that only uses the $j^{th}$ feature. Using a single feature can help us understand the effectiveness of each feature individually, considering the independence assumption between features.

To select the top most discriminative features, we try to assign a score $S_j$ to each feature. In order to calculate this score we apply the leave-one-out technique on the documents of each author (the known authorship documents). As an example, suppose that an author has $k$ known documents $\{d_1, d_2, ..., d_k\}$. For each document $d_i$, we exclude $d_i$ from the known document set and consider it as an unknown authorship document. Next we apply every $C_j$ on the new unknown document ($d_i$). Each $C_j$ will return a score between zero and one, indicating the probability of considering this document as a relative document to the corresponding author. Score zero means that this unknown document is completely irrelevant to this author and score one means that this new unknown authorship document is definitely relevant to the author. As we know that this document was written by this author, we expect that the score would be close to one. Therefore, the higher the score returned by the classifier $C_j$, the more effective and discriminative the $j$th feature will be. Hence, we add the score returned by $C_j$ to $S_j$. $S_j$ is calculated as:

$$S_j = \sum_{i=1}^{k} C_j(d_i) \tag{6}$$

$C_j(d_i)$ donates applying our classification using only $j^{th}$ feature where the unknown authorship document is $d_i$. Hence, we assign a score to each document for each author. Note that since, $S_j$s are independents, we can parallelize the calculation of these scores to increase the efficiency.

**Selecting Effective Features.** To select the effective features, we use knee detection as described as follows: First we sort all $S_j$s in descending order so that $S_o(l)$ means the $l^{th}$ greatest element of all scores. Then, we find the $l^*$ as follow:

$$l^* = \arg\max_{1 \leq l < k} \{S_o(l)/S_o(l+1)\} \tag{7}$$

This means that if we order features by their scores, the distance between $l^{*th}$ feature and $(l^*+1)^{th}$ feature is greater than any other adjacent scores. We select the first $l^*$ features as the most effective features and use them in classification.

After selecting effective features, we apply our classifier on the unknown authorship document, using only selected features and get the assigned score for the unknown authorship document by the classifier. This score is the final score for relativeness of this document to the corresponding author.

# 4 Experiments

In this section, we first describe the dataset which is used in our the experiments and then we briefly describe the experimental setup. We report the experimental results and discussions. It should be noted that we use F1-measure as the evaluation metric in our experiments.

## 4.1 Dataset

We use author identification dataset provided by the $9^{th}$ evaluation lab on uncovering plagiarism, authorship, and social software misuse (PAN) at CLEF[2] 2013. The dataset includes a number of questions each containing up to 10 documents from an author and exactly one document with unknown authorship. The goal is to determine whether the unknown document is written by the given author or not. All documents of each question are in one of the English, Spanish, and Greek languages. The dataset is separated into two different parts:

- **Training set**: This part of dataset is provided for training the proposed models and parameter tuning. Training set contains 10 questions in English, 5 questions in Spanish, and 20 questions in Greek.
- **Evaluation set**: In the evaluation set, there are 30 questions in English, 25 questions in Spanish, and 30 questions in Greek. This part of the dataset was used in the final evaluations of PAN 2013.

It is notable that we have made the assumption that authors of known authorship documents are not same person in different questions. Therefore, in processing each question, we consider the known authorship documents of other questions as negative instances.

## 4.2 Experimental Setup

In our experiments, we divide each document to two separate ones to increase the number of documents and to avoid the overfitting problem. To extract the features from documents, we use Apache OpenNLP toolkit[3] in our experiments for sentence detection, tokenization, and also POS tagging. Since we do not have access to POS taggers in Spanish and Greek, we avoid this feature for these two languages. In addition, we do not apply any text normalization technique on the texts and consider them in their original format. It is noteworthy that we have considered $n = 2$ for the N-gram feature and for the stopword distribution feature, we have used a standard set of stopwords for each language, containing around 500 words in that language.

---

[2] Conference and Labs of the Evaluation Forum.
[3] https://opennlp.apache.org/

## 4.3   Results and Discussion

In this subsection, we first demonstrate the effectiveness of the proposed feature selection technique. Then we discuss about the selected features in different languages on the evaluation set. After that we compare our results with the results of PAN 2013 winners.

**Feature Selection.** In order to investigate the effectiveness of our proposed feature selection method, we compare different feature selection methods. In Table 1, "w/o FS" refers to using all defined features without any feature selection. "Top1", "Top2", and "Top3" refer to using the one, two, and three features with the highest scores, respectively. "KD" is used for the dynamic feature selection using knee detection technique described in Subsection 3.4. Table 1 reports F1-measure for the mentioned feature selection methods on the evaluation set.

According to Table 1, dynamic feature selection achieves the highest score in all languages and its results are equal to Top3 and Top2 in Spanish and Greek languages, respectively. Table 1 also shows that the feature selection is necessary for author detection when we exploit a KNN-based classifier. Also, the results of knee detection technique shows the effectiveness of this method in selecting the best features among all defined features.

**Table 1.** Performance of different feature selection methods on the evaluation set in terms of F1-measure

|        | Overall | English | Spanish | Greek |
|--------|---------|---------|---------|-------|
| w/o FS | 0.635   | 0.700   | 0.760   | 0.466 |
| Top1   | 0.611   | 0.766   | 0.760   | 0.333 |
| Top2   | 0.717   | 0.766   | 0.720   | **0.666** |
| Top3   | 0.705   | 0.700   | **0.840** | 0.600 |
| KD     | **0.776** | **0.833** | **0.840** | **0.666** |

**Table 2.** Selected features frequency

|                  | English | Spanish | Greek |
|------------------|---------|---------|-------|
| stopwords        | 18      | 15      | 11    |
| punctuation      | 7       | 17      | 16    |
| N-gram           | 30      | 19      | 30    |
| sentence length  | 5       | 8       | 5     |
| paragraph length | 0       | 8       | 4     |
| POS tag          | 5       | –       | –     |
| word length      | 7       | 8       | 12    |
| average          | 2.4     | 3       | 2.6   |

Table 3. Comparison with winners of PAN 2013 in terms of F1-measure

|         | Overall | English | Spanish | Greek |
|---------|---------|---------|---------|-------|
| KNN-DFS | **0.776** | **0.833** | **0.840** | 0.666 |
| IM      | 0.753   | 0.800   | 0.600   | **0.833** |
| KNNE    | 0.718   | 0.700   | **0.840** | 0.633 |

**Selected Features.** In this part, we take a closer look at the selected features in different languages. Table 2 demonstrates how many times each aforementioned feature is selected using dynamic feature selection technique. According to Table 2, N-gram probabilistic distribution is the most selected feature in all languages. This feature is selected in all English and Greek questions. Another discriminant feature for most English documents is stopwords distribution. This feature is also one of the discriminative ones in Spanish.

Another point which is shown in Table 2 is that we cannot select a specific set of features for a given language as the discriminative feature set. It demonstrates that each author may have his/her own writing style and the features cannot be selected for each language generally. In addition, the average number of features selected for each question is less than half of all features. This shows the importance of feature selection in authorship verification.

**Comparison with Bests of PAN 2013.** We compare our results on the evaluation set with the winners of PAN at CLEF 2013 competition in each language. Impostors Method (IM) [14] was the winner of PAN and achieved the best results on English and Greek languages. k-nearest neighbors estimation (KNNE) [5] also had the best results on Spanish language in the final evaluation. Table 3 shows the comparison of the proposed method with IM and KNNE.

As shown in Table 3, KNN-DFS outperforms the best results of PAN on English and also its result in Spanish is equal to the best results of PAN. However, KNN-DFS has lower F1-measure in comparison with the winners of PAN in Greek. The reason may be the lack of text normalization and pre-processing.

## 5  Conclusions and Future Work

In this paper, we proposed a novel probabilistic feature set to model the features of each document. We further introduced a distance measure to compare two different feature sets and proposed a KNN-based approach to verify the authorship of unknown authorship documents. A dynamic feature selection technique was also used to detect the discriminant features per each author.

We evaluated our approaches on PAN at CLEF 2013 dataset. The experiments showed that the proposed method outperforms the approaches proposed by the winners of PAN at CLEF 2013 in terms of F1-measure. Also, we showed that the proposed feature selection technique can improve the results significantly. In our experiments, N-gram probabilistic distribution was selected as the most discriminant feature, especially in English and Greek languages. We illustrated that each author has his/her own writing style and feature selection should be based on each author, not the languages.

Future research studies can focus on weighting the features for each author. In other words, in addition to selecting some features, a weight can be assigned to each author and these weights can be considered in $\mathcal{F}$ function used in the defined distance measure. Moreover, defining effective features (e.g., some language-dependant features) may improve the performance.

# References

1. Argamon, S., Koppel, M., Pennebaker, J.W., Schler, J.: Automatically profiling the author of an anonymous text. Commun. ACM 52(2), 119–123 (2009)
2. Forner, P., Navigli, R., Tufis, D. (eds.): CLEF 2013 Evaluation Labs and Workshop–Working Notes Papers (2013)
3. Genkin, A., Lewis, D.D., Madigan, D.: Large-scale bayesian logistic regression for text categorization. Technometrics 49, 291–304 (2007)
4. Graham, N., Hirst, G., Marthi, B.: Segmenting documents by stylistic character. Nat. Lang. Eng. 11(4), 397–415 (2005)
5. Halvani, O., Steinebach, M., Zimmermann, R.: Authorship verification via k-nearest neighbor estimation - notebook for pan at clef 2013. In: Forner et al [2]
6. Joula, P., Stamatatos, E.: Overview of the author identification task at pan 2013. In: Information Access Evaluation. Multilinguality, Multimodality, and Visualization. vol. 8138 (2013)
7. Kullback, S., Leibler, R.A.: On information and sufficiency. Annals of Mathematical Statistics 22, 49–86 (1951)
8. Li, J., Zheng, R., Chen, H.: From fingerprint to writeprint. Commun. ACM 49(4), 76–82 (2006)
9. Luyckx, K., Daelemans, W.: Authorship attribution and verification with many authors and limited data. In: Proceedings of the 22nd International Conference on Computational Linguistics, COLING 2008, pp. 513–520 (2008)
10. Manning, C.D., Raghavan, P., Schütze, H.: Introduction to Information Retrieval. Cambridge University Press, New York (2008)
11. Mohtasseb, H., Ahmed, A.: Two-layered blogger identification model integrating profile and instance-based methods. Knowl. Inf. Syst. 31(1), 1–21 (2012)
12. Potha, N., Stamatatos, E.: A profile-based method for authorship verification. In: Likas, A., Blekas, K., Kalles, D. (eds.) SETN 2014. LNCS, vol. 8445, pp. 313–326. Springer, Heidelberg (2014)
13. Sanderson, C., Guenter, S.: Short text authorship attribution via sequence kernels, markov chains, and author unmasking: An investigation. In: Proceedings of the 2006 Conference on Empirical Methods in Natural Language Processing, EMNLP 2006, pp. 482–491 (2006)
14. Seidman, S.: Authorship verification using the impostors method - notebook for pan at clef 2013. In: Forner et al. [2]
15. Stamatatos, E.: A survey of modern authorship attribution methods. J. Am. Soc. Inf. Sci. Technol. 60(3), 538–556 (2009)

16. Stamatatos, E., Koppel, M.: Plagiarism and authorship analysis: introduction to the special issue. Language Resources and Evaluation 45(1), 1–4 (2011)
17. Zhao, Y., Zobel, J.: Searching with style: Authorship attribution in classic literature. In: Proceedings of the Thirtieth Australasian Conference on Computer Science, ACSC 2007, pp. 59–68 (2007)

# A Real-World Framework for Translator as Expert Retrieval

Navid Rekabsaz[1] and Mihai Lupu[2]

[1] Faculty of Informatics, Vienna University of Technology
navid.rekabsaz@student.tuwien.ac.at
[2] Information and Software Engineering Group Vienna University of Technology
A-1040 Vienna, Austria
lupu@ifs.tuwien.ac.at

**Abstract.** This article describes a method and tool to identify expert translators in an on-demand translation service. We start from existing efforts on expert retrieval and factor in additional parameters based on the real-world scenario of the task. The system first identifies topical expertise using an aggregation function over relevance scores of previously translated documents by each translator, and then a learning to rank method to factor in non-topical relevance factors that are part of the decision-making process of the user, such as price and duration of translation. We test the system on a manually created test collection and show that the method is able to effectively support the user in selecting the best translator.

## 1 Introduction

We look at the technology of Information Retrieval from the perspective of a real-world user scenario involving the selection of human translators based on a combination of expertise and practical factors. It has become more and more common place to consider search technology in a series of applications previously served only by database technology, if at all by a computer system [1]. In such cases, new data, new users, and new scenarios need to be observed, existing methods have to be adapted to the task at hand, and new evaluation procedures have to be devised.

This paper addresses the problem of searching translators as experts. We offer a novel translator-expert retrieval platform and evaluate different expert retrieval methods based on a multilingual dataset. In contrast to common expert retrieval systems, we also include non-topical factors involved in the search for a translator (such as price and delivery time). The proposed method has two distinct components: A proficiency estimation phase, in which different aggregation algorithms related to documents of translators are studied based on the proof-readers' assessments as gold standard; and a Learning-to-Rank phase in which different features are tested under different Learning-to-Rank methods based on a manually created ground truth, which we make available together with the

E. Kanoulas et al. (Eds.): CLEF 2014, LNCS 8685, pp. 141–152, 2014.
© Springer International Publishing Switzerland 2014

gold standard and the document similarities, under GPL[1]. The contributions of the report are three-fold:

1. the application and adaptation of state-of-the-art IR methods to a new use-case
2. extensive evaluation in a realistic scenario, including non-topical relevance criteria as part of the evaluation
3. creation of a publicly available test collection for both of the steps involved in the retrieval framework

The remainder of the paper is organised as follows: In Section 2, the use-case is presented and the Translator-Expert Retrieval framework is described in detail. Then, Section 3 explains the methods used in the study. Section 4 shows the result of applied methods on the framework. We discuss these results and conclude the study in Section 5.

## 2    Translator Recommendation

### 2.1    Use-Case

The user model for this application is that of an online user in possession of a document in a language other than a desired one. The need for a different language comes either from an internal need to know the contents of the document, or from an external requirement to provide the document in a high-quality translation in the desired language. However, the document is not simply an official document (e.g. a birth certificate) since the platform does not provide legal translation services. Therefore, we can assume that the document to be translated has a particular narrative and a certain topic.

The task of this user is to identify a translator who balances translation quality with non-functional requirements such as cost and delivery time.

The system is therefore charged to estimate the proficiency of the translator on the topic of the document at hand by considering previously translated documents, and to learn a preference model that a typical user will have in combining this proficiency estimation with the other aspects involved in the decision making process (monetary, temporal and social). A reasonable hypothesis, which we will verify in what follows, is that a high-proficiency, low-cost, fast-delivery, professionally known translator will be preferred.

### 2.2    The Platform

Essential components of the platform as well as the workflow of searching for the translators are depicted in Figure 1. The platform consists of four main components: *Ranking*, *Proficiency Estimator*, *Scheduler* and *Profiles*.

The *Profiles* component stores translator profile information i.e. source and target languages, offered price and translation duration per word, as well as the number of translations the translator has performed for the same client.

---

[1] https://github.com/neds/expert-retrieval-translators

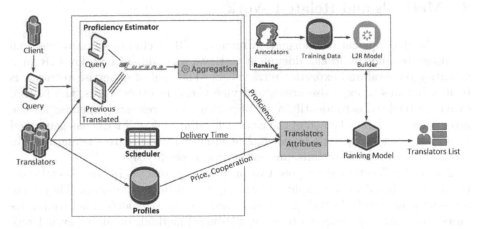

**Fig. 1.** Translator-Expert Search Workflow

The *Scheduler* system calculates the delivery time based on the timetable of each translator. The scheduler builds an efficient data structure to calculate the delivery time in a reasonable response time. The details of the process are out of scope of the paper. In this report we focus on the Proficiency Estimator and the Ranking elements.

The *Proficiency Estimator* sub-system stores the previously-translated documents of each translator and indexes them using Lucene. The similarity between query and indexed documents is used as a basis for the estimation of translator's proficiency for the task at hand. The proficiency score is obtained by aggregating the documents' similarity scores. Different aggregation functions are analyzed in Section 4. Finally, the *Ranking* sub-system uses all the data generated in the previous steps to create the ranking model. It uses Learning to Rank techniques to return the most relevant candidate translators. The training data is provided by a group of annotators familiar with the business of the company, using an evaluation system created specifically for generating this ground truth. The evaluation system presents three translators and the annotators rank them based on the values of each of their attributes (i.e. proficiency, delivery time, price, cooperation). In order to prevent bias in evaluation, the translators are suggested randomly and without name and picture. The applied learning to rank methods and their results are described in Section4.

Separately from the mentioned workflow, after finishing the translation, another expert (a proofreader) revises the translation. The proofreader is selected by the client and guarantees the quality of the final translation. As well as revising, the proofreader assesses the quality of translator's task from different points of view (grammar, style, accuracy, content and language). The assessment value can be from 1 (very bad) to 5 (perfect). In Section 4 we use these assessments to evaluate and compare aggregation algorithms.

# 3    Methods and Related Work

With the development of information retrieval (IR) techniques, many research efforts go beyond traditional document retrieval and address high-level IR such as entity retrieval and expertise retrieval [2]. The goal of expertise retrieval is to link humans to expertise areas, and vice versa. In other words, the task of expertise retrieval is to identify a set of persons with relevant expertise for the given query [3,4]. The launch of the Expert Finding task at TREC has generated a lot of interest in expertise retrieval, following by rapid progress being made in terms of modeling, algorithms, and evaluation aspects [5,4].

Cao and colleagues [5] propose two principal approaches in the expertise retrieval area based on probabilistic language modeling techniques. They were formalized as so-called *candidate models* and *document models*. The candidate-based approach, also referred to as profile-based method, builds a textual representation of candidate experts and then ranks them based on the query. The document models first find documents relevant to the topic and then locate the experts associated with these documents [3].

In either of the two models, aggregation functions have a significant effect on the performance of expert retrieval systems. Aggregate tasks are those where documents' similarities are not the final outcome, but instead an intermediary component. In expert search, a ranking of candidate persons with relevant expertise to a query is generated after aggregation of their related documents [6].

Ranking techniques are an essential part of each IR framework. In recent years, Learning to Rank (L2R) has been studied extensively especially for document retrieval. It refers to machine learning techniques for training the model in a ranking task [3]. In essence, expert search is a ranking problem and thus the existing L2R techniques can be naturally applied to it [7].

For the task at hand, we found that the two methods have to be used in two different steps. Aggregation can be used to bring together in one value elements essentially of the same nature. In this case - query similarity scores of different documents. The test collection at hand relies for its topical similarity exclusively on term frequencies, as there are no hyperlinks, metadata, or other sources of information in the documents. As a second step, in order to bring in attributes orthogonal to topical similarity, learning to rank methods are an obvious choice. In the following, we describe related work related to these two aspects, and in doing so prepare the ground for our experiments, which we present in the next section.

## 3.1    Aggregation Functions

The aggregation function has a significant impact on the performance of Expert Retrieval system [8]. As a usual scenario in expert retrieval systems, first each document related to an expert is scored and ranked regarding to query. Then, the top $N$ document scores associated with a candidate expert are aggregated in order to rank the experts.

MacDonald and Ounis [9] consider expert search as a voting problem, where documents vote for the candidates with relevant expertise. Eleven data fusion methods as well as three statistically different document weighting models were tested in their experiments. In practice, the approach considers both the number of documents and expert features regarding to the ranking score of the documents. The results show that while some of adapted voting techniques most likely outperform others, the proposed approach is effective when using the appropriate one.

Cummins and colleagues [8] study the effect of different features on the aggregation function. They show that the number of documents is an important factor, in that the performance of different queries are optimal for different values of $N$. Comparing query-based features using statistical measures, they infer that the document features (such as TF, IDF) may not, in general, be able to predict the optimal number of documents to aggregate for each query. In contrast, individual Expert Features have been shown to be more informative such that relevant experts are associated with a higher ranked document than non-relevant experts. More interestingly, relevant experts are associated with less documents on average.

Focusing on these features Cummins et al. [8] introduce a new aggregation method. It uses genetic programming to learn a formula for the weights of document associations within the candidate profiles. The formula, denoted as $GP2$, is as follows:

$$GP2 = \frac{\sqrt{\sqrt{2/no\_docs_{xi}}/(\sqrt{(10/R)} + R)}}{\sqrt{sq(10/R) + R + sq(10/R) + \sqrt{R*2}}}$$

where $R$ is the rank of the document in the initial ranking and $no\_docs_{xi}$ is the total number of documents associated with expert $x_i$.

## 3.2   Learning to Rank

Learning to rank refers to machine learning techniques for training a model in a ranking task. Due to importance of ranking problems, learning to rank has been drawing broad attention in the machine learning community recently.

In the learning to rank approach, the ranking problem is transformed to classification, regression and ordinal classification, and existing methods and techniques for solving machine learning problems are applied. As Hang [7] points out, the relation between learning to rank and ordinal classification is that, in ranking, one cares more about accurate ordering of objects, while in ordinal classification, one cares more about accurate ordered-categorization of objects.

The first step in accumulating data required for learning to rank, is relevance judgments, normally done by human annotators. Lie [10] presents the three main strategies in learning to rank:

- *Relevance degree*: In this method, the annotator specifies whether an object is relevant or not to the query. It can be either in binary judgment or by specifying the degree of relevance (e.g., Perfect, Excellent, Good, Fair, or Bad).
- *Pairwise preference*: The annotator compares a pair of objects in order to specify which one is more relevant with regards to a query.
- *Total order*: The annotator specifies the total order of all objects with respect to a query by rating each object.

Among the three mentioned kinds of judgments, the first one is the most popularly used judgment since is the easiest to obtain, while the third one is more accurate but laborious for human annotators. In our case, we have used the total order method because our ranked lists consisted of only 3 translators.

The learning to rank techniques are categorized in three main groups: *Pointwise*, *Pairwise* and *Listwise*.

In the pointwise approach, the ranking problem is transformed to classification, regression or ordinal classification. Therefore, the group structure of ranking is ignored in this approach [7]. Here, linear or polynomial regression are widely used methods.

The pairwise approach transforms the ranking problem into pairwise classification or regression. In fact, it cares about the relative order between two documents. Similar to the pointwise approach, the pairwise method also ignores the group structure of ranking [7]. Here is a brief explanation of some pairwise algorithms:

- *RankNet* [11]: Widely applied by commercial search engines, it uses gradient descent method and neural network to model the underlying ranking function.
- *RankBoost* [12]: It adopts AdaBoost algorithm for the classification over the object pairs.
- *LambdaRank* [13]: It considers the evaluation measures to set its pair weight. In particular, the evaluation measures (which are position based) are directly used to define the gradient with respect to each document pair in the training process.
- *LambdaMART* [14]: It combines the strengths of boosted tree classification and LambdaRank.

The listwise approach takes the entire set of documents associated with a query in the training data as the input and predicts their ground truth labels [10]. In contradiction to two previous approaches, it maintains the group structure of ranking. In addition, ranking evaluation measures can be more directly incorporated into the loss functions in learning [7]. In the following, two common listwise algorithms are briefly discussed:

- *AdaRank* [15]: It applies the evaluation measures on the framework of Boosting and focuses on effectively optimization.
- *ListNet* [16]: It uses different probability distributions in order to define the loss function.

Lie [10] compares the algorithms by applying on different data-sets. It concludes that listwise techniques are in general the most effective among the others. However, the choice of the learning evaluation measure and the rank cutoff may have a noticeable impact on the effectiveness of the learned model [17].

## 3.3 Evaluation

A critical point in all information retrieval systems is the evaluation of results. The evaluation on the performance of a ranking model is carried out by comparison between the ranking lists output of the model and the ranking lists given as the ground truth. Some common IR evaluation methods like Mean average precision (MAP), [Normalized] Discounted Cumulative Gain ([N]DCG), Mean Reciprocal Rank (MRR) are also widely user in leaning to rank evaluation. Among the mentioned metrics, DCG/NDCG is the only one used for graded relevance.

Recently, Chapelle and Zhang [18] have proposed Expected Reciprocal Rank (ERR) which claims to model user's satisfaction with search results better than the DCG metric. Their work addresses the underlying independence assumption of DCG that a document in a given position has always the same gain and discount independently of the documents shown above it. It asserts that based on research on modeling user click behavior [19,20], the likelihood a user examines the document at rank $i$ is dependent on how satisfied the user was with previously observed documents in the ranked list. In other words, it assumes that a user is more likely to stop browsing if they have already seen one or more highly relevant documents. Introducing the ERR formula, Chapelle and Zhang claim that results reflect real user browsing behavior better and quantifies user satisfaction more accurately than DCG.

## 4 Experimental Results

In this section, we applied the different approaches presented in the previous section within our platform. By comparing the methods, we aim to discover the most appropriate one considering to the project's characteristics and data.

### 4.1 Aggregation Functions

Translator's proficiency on the topic of the query is one of the attributes used for creating the ranking model. In order to obtain the value, we aggregate the similarity values of the previously translated documents with the query document. Selecting the most appropriate aggregation function is the objective of the current section.

In order to evaluate aggregation functions results, we use the assessment of the proof-readers after every translation. As mentioned before, the hypothesis is that a translator is likely to do a better job if she is familiar with the vocabulary of the query. In other words, when the query document is more similar to the translator's pre-translated documents, we expect higher assessment from the proof-reader. We can then use the proof-readers assessments as a gold standard and observe which of the three aggregation methods correlates more with the scores given by the proof-readers.

We repeat the experiment done by Cummins and colleagues [8] for the particular use-case and data at hand, comparing three aggregation algorithms: $GP2$, $Top5$ and $Top1$. $GP2$ is the state of the art, while $Top1$ and $Top5$ are two common forms of $TopN$ aggregation algorithm which refers to algorithm that summarizes the $N$ top documents. Furthermore, $Top1$ can be interpreted as the maximum similarity score, and follows the intuition that it is sufficient for a translator to have had only one highly similar translation job before in order to do a good job on the new task.

As input data we have 181 translation orders collected from the live system. For each of them, we know the translator who performed the translation (including all her previously translated documents), the text of the document to be translated, and the score given by the proof-reader. Because this is historical data, evaluating the aggregation method cannot be done by giving the same translation task to different translators. However, by calculating the value of each mentioned algorithm on all finished translations, we achieve three lists of translations each annotated with an additional aggregation value field. Then, in order to compare the algorithms, we test the correlation of each list with the list of translations annotated with proof-readers' assessments. Again, the assumption being that if we rank translation jobs by aggregation scores, the top elements would have high proof-reader scores, while the bottom elements lower scores. The distribution of data between the values of each aggregation function and the proof-reader's assessments is shown in Figure 2.

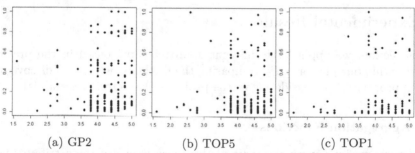

(a) GP2                    (b) TOP5                    (c) TOP1

**Fig. 2.** Data distribution of aggregation values against proof-readers' assessments. The x-axis shows the assessments of proof-readers, while the y-axis represents the values of the corresponding aggregation function

In order to calculate the correlation value, we applied Spearman Rank Order and Kendall Rank Correlation as two common methods. Table 1 shows the results of Spearman correlation coefficient ($r_s$) and Kendall's tau coefficient ($\tau$) using the 181 records of purchased orders. In addition, it represents the Significance Test of both methods. For Spearman's test, p-values are computed using algorithm AS 89 [21].

The outcome shows an approximately weak correlation between aggregation functions and assessments of proof-readers. In all the algorithms, the coefficient value of Spearman is slightly higher than Kendall's. Regarding to p-Value of significance test, a meaningful relation between $GP2$ and assessments can be considered. $Top1$ which has the worst values in the table shows a meaningless and near random correlation though.

Comparing the algorithms, $GP2$ outperforms the others in both correlation tests. In comparison to $Top1$, $Top5$ has slightly better performance. The results are also nearly the same when comparing based on language-pairs.

**Table 1.** Correlation test between algorithms and proof-readers' assessments as well as P-Value of significance of correlation test

|  |  | Top1 | Top5 | GP2 |
|---|---|---|---|---|
| $r_s$ | Correlation Test | 0.052 | 0.089 | 0.145 |
|  | p-Value | 0.4866 | 0.2295 | 0.05038 |
| $\tau$ | Correlation Test | 0.034 | 0.059 | 0.102 |
|  | p-Value | 0.5157 | 0.2562 | 0.05263 |

## 4.2 Learning to Rank

In order to accumulate data required for ranking model, we conduct a survey with eight human annotators. The questions of survey represent three translators each with four criteria (price, delivery time, proficiency and number of cooperation times). As mentioned before, in order to prevent bias in results, the name and the picture of the translators are hidden from the annotators. The annotators rate the questions from one to three based on *Total Order* strategy. The accumulated data consists of 400 annotated list and overall 1200 records.

We use the RankLib library[2] to apply a large set of Learning to Rank methods. The library provides the implementation of some Learning to Rank algorithms as well as evaluation measures in Java. By splitting the data in train, validation and test datasets, we use 5-Fold Cross-Validation on each run. One pointwise, three pairwise and two listwise methods are tested.

Since evaluation of the results should be applied on the entire result list (with 3 items), we have to use relevance grading evaluation measures like DCG, NDCG or ERR. In the current study, NDGC and ERR both with rank position at 3 are used.

Because of the short final predicted list (3 items), every measure returns a very high score. In order to understand the real benefit of our framework compared with just presenting the un-ranked set of three translators, we evaluate two random approaches. In the first approach, we run all the algorithms on data

---

[2] http://sourceforge.net/p/lemur/wiki/RankLib

with random generated labels. In order to increase the accuracy of results, the
process of generating randomized label is repeated 5 times. The second approach
is developing a simple ranker which randomly predicts the rank of each record.
In fact, the first tests whether there is anything to learn in the data and the
second examines if the learning algorithms learn from the data.

**Table 2.** Results of applying Learning to Rank methods based on NDCG and ERR
evaluation measures

| Method | NDCG@3 | | ERR@3 | |
|---|---|---|---|---|
| | Result | Random | Result | Random |
| Linear Regression | **0.935** | 0.833 | **0.451** | 0.375 |
| RankNet | 0.876 | 0.834 | 0.394 | 0.378 |
| RankBoost | 0.909 | 0.831 | 0.432 | 0.374 |
| LambdaMART | 0.93 | 0.832 | 0.447 | 0.373 |
| ListNet | 0.915 | 0.831 | 0.439 | 0.375 |
| AdaRank | 0.857 | 0.83 | 0.399 | 0.373 |
| Random Ranker | 0.832 | 0.832 | 0.375 | 0.378 |

**Table 3.** Coefficient value of features in Linear Regression model

| Feature | Value |
|---|---|
| Price | 2.002 |
| Duration | 0.057 |
| Proficiency | -0.048 |
| Number of Cooperation Times | -0.313 |

The result is shown in Table 2. Figure 3 depicts the corresponding data in
diagrams. As it is shown, random values define a base line for comparison
the goodness of methods. Among the applied methods, Linear Regression and
LambdaMART tend to have better results. In particular, Linear Regression
shows a narrower confidence interval and hence more stable. Furthermore, tra-
cing NDCG and ERR diagrams shows a considerable similarity in behavior of
both evaluation methods regarding to the data.

In addition to comparing the methods, features comparison can be an interesting point. Table 3 shows the coefficients of features, calculated in Linear
Regression model. The coefficient value is a measure for understanding the importance of each feature in comparison to the others.

As it is shown, price and delivery time seem to be the most effective features
while the number of cooperation times has the lowest importance. Surprisingly,
proficiency plays a small role in the ranking of the translators. It can be because
of the proposed business plan of the platform to the clients which guarantees
an acceptable quality of translation. In addition, we expect that by applying
the methods on much more amount of data, the proficiency feature gains more
importance.

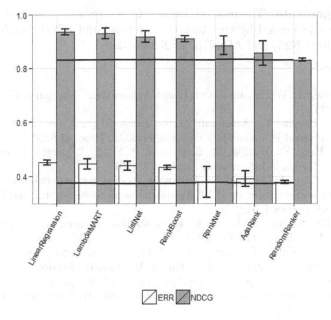

**Fig. 3.** Learning to Rank Results

## 5    Conclusion and Future Work

We propose a comprehensive solution for a translator-expert retrieval system. As well as system architecture, we thoroughly study the obstacles and pitfalls in implementing such a system. Multilingual IR tools are adapted to solve two essential steps in a practical system: Estimating the translators proficiency on a particular topic (document aggregation), ranking translators based on real-world factors (learning to rank).

To address the first issue we have compared three commonly used aggregation methods. The aggregation methods estimate the proficiency of each translator based on the similarity values of the previous translated documents with the query document. Using the assessment of the proof-readers on the final translation as the gold standard, we compare three aggregation methods. We found that the GP2 method shows better performance in comparison to the others with reasonable good results. Future work in addressing the estimation of translators' proficiency will allow us to increase the correlation between the aggregation and proof-readers' scores.

The second issue tackles the problem of experts ranking. By applying different learning to rank algorithms, we obtain a ranking model based on linear regression with a very high performance. The model's performance is tested with both NDCG and ERR evaluation measures. Feature analysis of data shows that real users consider price and delivery time much more important than the other features. This is relatively disappointing, but in retrospective not surprising for a real-world system.

**Acknowledgements.** The research leading to the results presented in this paper was partially funded by the Austrian Science Fund (FWF) under projects MUCKE (I 1094-N23) and ADmIRE (P25905-N23).

# References

1. Grefenstette, G., Wilber, L.: Search Based Applications. Morgan & Claypool Publishers (2011)
2. Balog, K., Bogers, T., Azzopardi, L., de Rijke, M., van den Bosch, A.: Broad expertise retrieval in sparse data environments. In: Proc. of SIGIR (2007)
3. Balog, K., Fang, Y., de Rijke, M., Serdyukov, P., Si., L.: Expertise retrieval. Foundations and Trends in Information Retrieval 6 (2012)
4. Deng, H., King, I., Lyu, M.R.: Enhanced models for expertise retrieval using community-aware strategies. IEEE Transactions on Systems Man and Cybernetics Part B: Cybernetics (2012)
5. Cao, Y., Liu, J., Bao, S., Li, H.: Research on expert search at enterprise track of trec 2005. In: Proc. of TREC (2005)
6. Macdonald, C., Ounis, I.: Learning Models for Ranking Aggregates. In: Clough, P., Foley, C., Gurrin, C., Jones, G.J.F., Kraaij, W., Lee, H., Mudoch, V. (eds.) ECIR 2011. LNCS, vol. 6611, pp. 517–529. Springer, Heidelberg (2011)
7. Hang, L.I.: A short introduction to learning to rank. Transactions on Information and Systems (2011)
8. Cummins, R., Lalmas, M., O'Riordan, C.: Learning aggregation functions for expert search. In: Proc. of ECAI (2010)
9. Macdonald, C., Ounis, I.: Voting for candidates: adapting data fusion techniques for an expert search task. In: Proc. of CIKM (2006)
10. Lie, T.Y.: Learning to rank for information retrieval. Foundations and Trends in Information Retrieval. Springer (2011)
11. Burges, C., Shaked, T., Renshaw, E., Lazier, A., Deeds, M., Hamilton, N., Hullender, G.: Learning to rank using gradient descent. In: Proc. of ICML (2005)
12. Freund, Y., Iyer, R., Schapire, R.E., Singer, Y.: An efficient boosting algorithm for combining preferences (1998)
13. Burges, C.C.J., Ragno, R., Le, V.Q.: Learning to rank with nonsmooth cost functions. MIT Press (2006)
14. Wu, Q., Burges, C.J.C., Svore, K.M., Gao, J.: Adapting boosting for information retrieval measures. Springer Science (2009)
15. Xu, J., Li, H.: Adarank: A boosting algorithm for information retrieval. In: Procs of SIGIR (2007)
16. Cao, Z., Qin, T., Liu, T.Y., Tsai, M.F., Li, H.: Learning to rank: From pairwise approach to listwise approach. In: Procs of ICML (2007)
17. Macdonald, C., Santos, R.L., Ounis, I.: The whens and hows of learning to rank for web search. Inf. Retr. 16 (2013)
18. Chapelle, O., Zhang, Y.: Expected reciprocal rank for graded relevance. In: Proc. of CIKM (2009)
19. Craswell, N., Zoeter, O., Taylor, M., Ramsey, B.: An experimental comparison of click position-bias models. In: Proc. of WSDM (2008)
20. Büttcher, S., Clarke, C.L.A., Yeung, P.C.K., et al.: Reliable information retrieval evaluation with incomplete and biased judgements (2007)
21. Best, D.J., Roberts, D.E.: Algorithm as 89: The upper tail probabilities of spearman's rho. Journal of the Royal Statistical Society. Series C (Applied Statistics) 24 (1975)

# Comparing Algorithms for Microblog Summarisation

Stuart Mackie, Richard McCreadie, Craig Macdonald, and Iadh Ounis

School of Computing Science, University of Glasgow, G12 8QQ, UK
s.mackie.1@research.gla.ac.uk, {firstname.lastname}@glasgow.ac.uk

**Abstract.** Event detection and tracking using social media and user-generated content has received a lot of attention from the research community in recent years, since such sources can purportedly provide up-to-date information about events as they evolve, e.g. earthquakes. Concisely reporting (summarising) events for users/emergency services using information obtained from social media sources like Twitter is not a solved problem. Current systems either directly apply, or build upon, classical summarisation approaches previously shown to be effective within the newswire domain. However, to-date, research into how well these approaches generalise from the newswire to the microblog domain is limited. Hence, in this paper, we compare the performance of eleven summarisation approaches using four microblog summarisation datasets, with the aim of determining which are the most effective and therefore should be used as baselines in future research. Our results indicate that the SumBasic algorithm and Centroid-based summarisation with redundancy reduction are the most effective approaches, across the four datasets and five automatic summarisation evaluation measures tested.

## 1 Introduction

Microblogging services (e.g. Twitter[1]) provide a platform for people and organisations to share up-to-date information about many topics, particularly news and current events. Such social media services are facilitating a shift towards real-time news reporting and discussion of events by the public and organisations. As a result, end-users and journalists leverage social media to monitor and track events as they evolve over time [2, 14]. However, due to the high volume and velocity of messages posted to social media streams[2], there may be vastly more posts published than users could ever read. This means that users would find it very difficult to keep up-to-date with events of interest.

To tackle this problem, summarisation algorithms have been proposed such as Sum-Basic [10] or Hybrid TF-IDF [12]. Automatic text summarisation techniques [9, 13] must algorithmically decide what is the essential information from the input text(s) that should be reported to the user as a summary. However, to-date, there has been little research regarding how different summarisation algorithms compare in terms of absolute performance, for the task of microblog summarisation. The only recent comparison of summarisation algorithms for microblog summarisation was performed by Sharifi *et al.* [12]. This study indicated that relatively simple term-frequency algorithms, such as

---

[1] http://twitter.com/

[2] https://blog.twitter.com/2014/celebrating-sb48-on-twitter

E. Kanoulas et al. (Eds.): CLEF 2014, LNCS 8685, pp. 153–159, 2014.

**Table 1.** Categorised summarisation algorithms

| Category | Approach | Representation | Scoring | Novelty | Selection |
|---|---|---|---|---|---|
| | | Components | | | |
| Random | Random | - | Random | - | Top k |
| Temporal | Temporal | - | By time | - | Top k |
| | SimEarliest | $tf-idf$ | $cosine(t_1,t_i)$ | - | Top k |
| Term Statistical | tfIDFSum | $tf-idf$ | $\sum_{0<j<\lvert t_i\rvert} tf-idf(t_{ij})$ | - | Top k |
| | TFIDFSum | $TF-idf$ | $\sum_{0<j<\lvert t_i\rvert} TF-idf(t_{ij})$ | - | Top k |
| Term Statistical +Novelty | tfIDFSum$_N$ | $tf-idf$ | $\sum_{0<j<\lvert t_i\rvert} tf-idf(t_{ij})$ | Similarity threshold | Top k |
| | TFIDFSum$_N$ | $TF-idf$ | $\sum_{0<j<\lvert t_i\rvert} TF-idf(t_{ij})$ | Similarity threshold | Top k |
| | SumBasic [10] | Language Model | $\sum_{0<j<\lvert t_i\rvert} Prob(t_{ij})$ | Down-scoring terms | Top k |
| | Hybrid-TFIDF [12] | $TF-idf$ | $Norm(t_i)\cdot\sum_{0<j<\lvert t_i\rvert} TF-idf(t_{ij})$ | Similarity threshold | Top k |
| Cohesiveness | Centroid [11] | $tf-idf$ | $cosine(centroid(T),t_i)$ | - | Top k |
| Cohesiveness+Novelty | Centroid$_N$ [11] | $tf-idf$ | $cosine(centroid(T),t_i)$ | Similarity threshold | Top k |

Hybrid-TFIDF, offered reasonable summary effectiveness – but was limited in scope, evaluating using a single dataset. Furthermore, there is not a generally accepted baseline for microblog summarisation, against which researchers may compare new summarisation algorithms, making it difficult to quantify the gains each new approach brings over those that came before it.

Hence, as a step towards tackling these issues, we perform a comparison of 11 microblog summarisation algorithms to determine which is the most effective. We compare the effectiveness of these algorithms for microblog summarisation using 4 Twitter datasets, and analyse their performance under both model-summary and input-summary automatic evaluation paradigms (using ROUGE [3] and SIMetrix [7], respectively). Our results confirm that summarisation algorithms that use term statistics to select tweets for inclusion into the summary are effective, supporting observations from [12], but also show that centroid-based summarisation [11] can outperform SumBasic and Hybrid TF.IDF. The remainder of this paper is organised as follows: In Section 2, we describe algorithms for microblog summarisation. We report our experimental setup in Section 3. In Section 4, we present our experimental results. Finally, Section 5 summarises our conclusions.

## 2   Summarisation Algorithms

Given a set of tweets, $T = \{t_1, t_2, \ldots, t_n\}$, about a topic, the task of microblog summarisation is to produce a summary composed of tweets from $T$, $S = \{s_1, s_2, \ldots, s_k\}$, that captures the maximum amount of essential information about the topic, within a desired summary length $k$ (e.g. 5 or 10 tweets). Prior literature in the field of text summarisation identifies three stages that extractive summarisation algorithms typically follow [9]. First, an intermediate representation of the input documents is generated, e.g. *tf.idf* vectors. Second, each sentence is scored with respect to its preference for inclusion into the summary, where more salient or important sentences are scored highest. Third, summary sentences are selected from a ranked list (produced using the scored sentences), either by simply selecting the top $k$ sentences for a desired summary length, or employing a redundancy filter (e.g. based on a cosine similarity threshold to previously selected sentences). We use a similar characterisation to describe the approaches to microblog summarisation examined in this paper, listed in Table 1.

Table 1 reports the 11 different summarisation approaches that we compare in our later experiments and the components that they are comprised of. $t_i$ is a tweet to be ranked and $t_{ij}$ is a term in $t_i$. $t_1$ is the earliest tweet in the timeline. $cosine()$ returns the cosine similarity between two tweets. $tf - idf()$ returns the score for the term $t_{ij}$ using the classical tf-idf weighting model. $TF - idf()$ on the other hand, returns the classical tf-idf score, with the exception that the $tf$ component is calculated over the whole set of input tweets (with all tweets combined into a virtual document), rather than just the frequency of $t_{ij}$ in $t_i$. $centroid()$ is a pseudo tweet calculated as the $tf - idf$ centroid of all tweets in the input tweet set $T$. $Norm()$ is a short text normalisation factor designed to avoid biasing toward longer tweets [12].

Furthermore, based upon how the different algorithms select tweets for inclusion into the summary, Table 1 also provides a categorisation of the different algorithms into six broad classes, namely: Random, Temporal, Term Statistical-Only, Term Statistical+Novelty, Cohesiveness and Cohesiveness+Novelty. We use this categorisation in our later experiments to characterise which types of algorithm are the most effective for microblog summarisation. In the next section, we describe our experimental setup, including the datasets and measures we use to evaluate microblog summarisation.

# 3  Experimental Setup

**Evaluation Metrics:** We evaluate the effectiveness of summaries, produced under each of the summarisation algorithms, using evaluation metrics from the literature: ROUGE-1 Recall; ROUGE-1 Precision; ROUGE-1 F-score; Jensen-Shannon Divergence; and Fraction of Topic Words. These metrics are implemented within the ROUGE[3] [3] and SIMetrix[4] [7] automatic summarisation evaluation tool-kits. We note, ROUGE evaluation requires a gold-standard, whereas evaluation using SIMetrix (Jensen-Shannon Divergence, and Fraction of Topic Words) does not require human authored gold-standard reference summaries (i.e. SIMetrix permits *model free* summary evaluation). We briefly describe each of the automatic summarisation evaluation metrics below:

*ROUGE-N* is an n-gram similarity measure between two pieces of text, from which precision, recall and f-scores are derived. In our experiments, we use ROUGE-1, which measures uni-gram overlap between a reference summary (model) and the automatically generated summary (peer) we wish to evaluate. ROUGE-1 is commonly used to measure effectiveness of microblog summarisation, due to its reported agreement with manual evaluation for short summaries [5].

*Jensen-Shannon Divergence (JSD)* is a measure of two probability distributions over words: the text of the original document and the text of the summary being evaluated. Low divergence [6] from the input document(s) by the produced summary is taken as a signal of an effective summary.

---

[3] http://www.berouge.com
[4] http://homepages.inf.ed.ac.uk/alouis/IEval2.html

**Table 2.** The four tweet datasets used and their statistics

| Dataset | Source | Number of Topics | Avg. Number of Tweets Per topic | Gold Standard Summaries |
|---------|--------|------------------|----------------------------------|-------------------------|
| trending-topics-2010 (50) | Crawled via the Twitter API | 50 | 100 | ✗ |
| trending-topics-2010 (25) | Crawled via the Twitter API | 25 | 100 | ✔ |
| twitter-topics-2011/12 | TREC Microblog Track 2011/12 | 50 | 167 | ✗ |
| trending-topics-2014 | Crawled via the Twitter API | 50 | 100 | ✗ |

*Fraction of Topic Words (FoTW)* measures the quotient of topic words (or topic signatures [4]) of the input document(s) present in the produced summary. Effective summaries contain more topic words (from the input) in the produced summary text.

**Evaluation Datasets:** To compare the different microblog summarisation algorithms, discussed in the previous section, we use four microblog summarisation datasets to ensure that our results are generalisable. Each dataset is comprised of sets of tweets, where each set contains tweets about Twitter trending topics or events being discussed on Twitter. Per dataset, each topic has an associated set of relevant tweets, $T$, which are to be summarised (i.e. the tweets are the input to the summarisation algorithms). Table 2 gives information about the four datasets, and we describe each in turn below:

*trending-topics-2010 (50/25)* – This dataset was obtained from Sharifi *et al.* [12]. It consists of tweets from 50 trending topics collected from the Twitter API during 2010. Notably, this dataset contains ROUGE gold-standard summaries (of length 4 tweets) for 25 of the 50 topics. As such, in our later experiments, we count this as two datasets: 'trending-topics-2010 (50)' that contains all 50 topics; and 'trending-topics-2010 (25)' that contains only the 25 topics with a gold-standard. Tweet timestamps were not provided with this dataset, hence temporal ranking approaches cannot be tested using them.

*twitter-topics-2011/12* – We use a subset of the Tweets2011 corpus from the TREC Microblog track [8], taking only tweets judged relevant to the topics by NIST assessors. Ordering the collection by the number of relevant tweets per topic, we take the first 50 topics with the most tweets. The tweets are from late January to early February 2011.

*trending-topics-2014* – For this dataset, we poll the Twitter API for tweets about 50 trending topics (trends in the United Kingdom). We remove non-English tweets, subsequent tweets from the same user, and filter re-tweets and near-duplicate tweets (Levenshtein distance $< 5$). The tweets are from late January to early February 2014.

**Configuration:** For both SIMetrix and ROUGE, we evaluate with stopwords removed and Porter stemming applied, to obtain a more accurate picture of textual similarity. Random performance is averaged over 10 runs. When reporting JSD and FoTW, we evaluate with a summary length of 5 tweets. When reporting ROUGE-based metrics, we evaluate at summary length 4, such that the gold-standard summaries and output summaries are the same length. Parameters within each approach are trained using a 5-fold cross validation within each dataset.

**Table 3.** Microblog summarisation performance using SIMetrix and ROUGE. For JSD, lower is better. For FoTW and ROUGE, higher is better. '-' denotes that the approach could not be tested on that dataset due to a lack of tweet timestamps. ∗ denotes statistical significance from random. † denotes statistically significant improvements over SumBasic by $Centroid_N$. Statistical significance is computed using the t-test, with $p < 0.05$.

| Approach | SIMetrix-only | | | | | | SIMetrix and ROUGE | | | | |
| | trending-topics-2010 (50) | | twitter-topics-2011/12 | | trending-topics-2014 | | trending-topics-2010 (25) | | | | |
| | JSD | FoTW | JSD | FoTW | JSD | FoTW | JSD | FoTW | Recall | Precision | $F_1$ |
|---|---|---|---|---|---|---|---|---|---|---|---|
| Random | 0.3025 | 0.2636 | 0.2653 | 0.2961 | 0.2822 | 0.3072 | 0.3147 | 0.2236 | 0.3436 | 0.3020 | 0.3149 |
| Temporal | - | - | 0.2850∗ | 0.2660 | 0.3084∗ | 0.2848 | - | - | - | - | - |
| SimEarliest | - | - | 0.2739 | 0.2556∗ | 0.2788 | 0.2944 | - | - | - | - | - |
| tfIDFSum | 0.3503∗ | 0.2705 | 0.2997∗ | 0.3659∗ | 0.3499∗ | 0.2625∗ | 0.3725∗ | 0.1929 | 0.3054 | 0.1797∗ | 0.2212∗ |
| TFIDFSum | 0.3079 | 0.3649∗ | 0.2635 | 0.4360∗ | 0.3015 | 0.3481∗ | 0.3217 | 0.2997∗ | 0.3915 | 0.2289∗ | 0.2835 |
| tfIDFSum$_N$ | 0.3451∗ | 0.2784 | 0.3221∗ | 0.2554∗ | 0.3446∗ | 0.2712∗ | 0.3694∗ | 0.1727∗ | 0.2401∗ | 0.1827∗ | 0.1959∗ |
| TFIDFSum$_N$ | 0.2966 | 0.3936∗ | 0.2519 | 0.3845∗ | 0.2720 | 0.4171∗ | 0.3168 | 0.3140∗ | 0.4023 | 0.2357∗ | 0.2921 |
| SumBasic [10] | **0.2526**∗ | 0.3176∗ | **0.2180**∗ | 0.3449∗ | **0.2354**∗ | 0.3791∗ | **0.2512**∗ | 0.2581 | 0.3787 | **0.4596**∗ | **0.4022**∗ |
| Hybrid-TFIDF [12] | 0.2892 | 0.3353∗ | 0.2472∗ | 0.3825∗ | 0.2628∗ | **0.4223**∗ | 0.2907 | 0.2876∗ | 0.3911 | 0.3665∗ | 0.3707 |
| Centroid [11] | 0.2755∗ | 0.3282∗ | 0.2519 | 0.2995 | 0.2715 | 0.3057 | 0.2835∗ | 0.3066∗ | 0.3906 | 0.2912 | 0.3237 |
| Centroid$_N$ [11] | **0.2572**∗ | **0.4202**∗† | **0.2143**∗ | **0.4008**∗† | **0.2303**∗ | **0.4325**∗† | **0.2657**∗ | **0.3847**∗† | **0.4572**∗ | 0.3197† | 0.3702 |

## 4 Results

In this section, we investigate which of the different summarisation algorithms, discussed in Section 2, are the most effective for the task of microblog summarisation. Table 3 reports the performance of each of the 11 summarisation algorithms, in terms of JSD and FoTW for all four datasets, then including ROUGE-1 Recall, Precision and $F_1$ for the trending-topics-2010 (25) dataset. The best performing approach under each measure/dataset pair is highlighted in bold. If two of the best approaches offer similar performances then both are highlighted. From Table 3, we observe the following.

First, comparing each approach to the random baseline, we see not all approaches outperform it. In particular, the temporal approaches (those that rank by time) and the tfIDFSum approaches produce less effective summaries than the random baseline (in some cases by a statistically significant margin, denoted ∗). For the case of the temporal approaches, this can be explained in terms of the distribution of informative information over time. By selecting tweets either by time or with respect to their similarity with the earliest tweet, informative tweets that were posted later are unlikely to be selected. The poor performance of tfIDFSum, and its novelty-enhanced version tfIDFSum$_N$, highlights the lack of discriminative information provided by the $tf$ component in the microblog domain, supporting observations in [1].

Next, we compare the random baseline with the remaining approaches under the SIMetrix measures (JSD and FoTW) for the four datasets. For JSD, SumBasic and $Centroid_N$ are the highest performing, i.e. the language model of the summaries produced by these systems diverge the least from the language model of the input tweet set $T$. Meanwhile, under FoTW, $Centroid_N$ is the highest performing, i.e. the summaries produced by this system cover the largest number of important topic words. Comparing these results to the only other recent study of summarisation systems for use on microblogs [12], we observe the following. First, the high performance of term-statistic-based SumBasic approach is expected, since it was previously been shown to be one of the top three systems tested in [12]. Second, the high performance of Centroid$_N$ which focuses on cohesiveness and novelty is surprising, since its clustering approach is similar to the classical MEAD summarisation system that was previously reported to perform poorly (it was ranked 7th out of 10 in [12]). Third, we see that the Hybrid-TFIDF approach, previously reported to be one of the best summarisation approaches is consistently outperformed by the SumBasic algorithm under JSD and ROUGE-1 Precision, and by the Centroid$_N$ algorithm under JSD, FoTW and ROUGE-1 Recall.

Finally, comparing the best approaches, i.e. SumBasic and Centroid$_N$ under the ROUGE metrics (Precision, Recall and F$_1$), we observe that these approaches perform well under different metrics. In particular, SumBasic performs well under precision, while Centroid$_N$ performs well under recall. This indicates that SumBasic is producing more concise summaries, while Centroid$_N$'s summaries tend to better cover the information in the gold-standard.

## 5 Conclusions

Effective summarisation of social media and user-generated content is an important research problem, since there are many use-cases where such sources can provide up-to-date information to end users. However, as a relatively new research topic, there has been little prior work comparing the effectiveness of summarisation algorithms specifically for the microblog domain. Hence, in this paper, we compared eleven different summarisation algorithms from the literature, over four microblog datasets, evaluating their effectiveness using five automatic summarisation evaluation metrics. Our results indicate that the SumBasic algorithm and Centroid-based summarisation with redundancy reduction were the most effective. As such, we recommend that future works report the performance of these algorithms as baselines.

**Acknowledgements.** All authors acknowledge the support of EC SMART project (FP7-287583). McCreadie, Macdonald and Ounis acknowledge the support of EPSRC project ReDites (EP/L010690/1).

## References

[1] Amati, G., Amodeo, G., Bianchi, M., Marcone, G., Bordoni, F.U., Gaibisso, C., Gambosi, G., Celi, A., Di Nicola, C., Flammini, M.: FUB, IASI-CNR, UNIVAQ at TREC 2011 Microblog Track. In: Proc. of TREC 2011 (2011)

[2] Kwak, H., Lee, C., Park, H., Moon, S.: What is Twitter, a Social Network or a News Media? In: Proc. of WWW 2010 (2010)

[3] Lin, C.Y.: ROUGE: a Package for Automatic Evaluation of Summaries. In: Proc. of ACL 2004 (2004)

[4] Lin, C.Y., Hovy, E.: The automated acquisition of topic signatures for text summarization. In: Proc. of ACL 2000 (2000)

[5] Lin, C.Y., Hovy, E.: Automatic Evaluation of Summaries using N-gram Co-occurrence Statistics. In: Proc. of NAACL-HLT 2003 (2003)

[6]  Lin, J.: Divergence Measures based on the Shannon Entropy. IEEE Transactions on Information Theory 37(1) (1991)

[7]  Louis, A., Nenkova, A.: Automatically Assessing Machine Summary Content without a Gold Standard. Computational Linguistics 39(2) (2013)

[8]  McCreadie, R., Soboroff, I., Lin, J., Macdonald, C., Ounis, I., McCullough, D.: On Building a Reusable Twitter Corpus. In: Proc. of SIGIR 2012 (2012)

[9]  Nenkova, A., McKeown, K.: Automatic Summarization. Foundations and Trends in Information Retrieval 5(2-3) (2011)

[10]  Nenkova, A., Vanderwende, L.: The Impact of Frequency on Summarization. MSR-TR-2005-101 (2005)

[11]  Rosa, K.D., Shah, R., Lin, B., Gershman, A., Frederking, R.: Topical Clustering of Tweets (2011)

[12]  Sharifi, B.P., Inouye, D.I., Kalita, J.K.: Summarization of Twitter Microblogs. The Computer Journal (2013)

[13]  Spärck Jones, K.: Automatic Summarizing: Factors and Directions. In: Advances in Automatic Text Summarization (1999)

[14]  Teevan, J., Ramage, D., Morris, M.R.: #TwitterSearch: a Comparison of Microblog Search and Web search. In: Proc. of WSDM 2011 (2011)

# The Effect of Dimensionality Reduction
# on Large Scale Hierarchical Classification

Aris Kosmpoulos[1,2], Georgios Paliouras[1], and Ion Androutsopoulos[2]

[1] Institute of Informatics and Telecommunications,
National Center for Scientific Research "Demokritos"9, Athens, Greece
https://www.iit.demokritos.gr/skel
[2] Department of Informatics,
Athens University of Economics and Business, Greece
http://nlp.cs.aueb.gr

**Abstract.** Many classification problems are related to a hierarchy of classes, that can be exploited in order to perform hierarchical classification of test objects. The most basic way of hierarchical classification is that of cascade classification, which greedily traverses the hierarchy from root to the predicted leaf. In order to perform cascade classification, a classifier must be trained for each node of the hierarchy. In large scale problems, the number of features can be prohibitively large for the classifiers in the upper levels of the hierarchy. It is therefore desirable to reduce the dimensionality of the feature space at these levels. In this paper we examine the computational feasibility of the most common dimensionality reduction method (Principal Component Analysis) for this problem, as well as the computational benefits that it provides for cascade classification and its effect on classification accuracy. Our experiments on two benchmark datasets with a large hierarchy show that it is possible to perform a certain version of PCA efficiently in such large hierarchies, with a slight decrease in the accuracy of the classifiers. Furthermore, we show that PCA can be used selectively at the top levels of the hierarchy in order to decrease the loss in accuracy. Finally, the reduced feature space, provided by the PCA, facilitates the use of more costly and possibly more accurate classifiers, such as non-linear SVMs.

**Keywords:** Hierarchical Classification, Dimensionality Reduction, Principal Component Analysis.

## 1 Introduction

In most classification problems the predefined categories are assumed to be independent. In hierarchical classification problems, a hierarchy is also given, which contains the relations between the categories. In the simplest case which we study in this paper, these relations are of is-a type and the hierarchy is a tree. We also assume that each instance belongs to only one category (single-label classification) and that this category is always a leaf.

E. Kanoulas et al. (Eds.): CLEF 2014, LNCS 8685, pp. 160–171, 2014.

Many researchers ignore the hierarchy and treat hierarchical classification of this type using flat classifiers, while others use mildly hierarchical approaches [1]. In most flat approaches, a binary classifier is trained for each category, using all the instances belonging to that category as positive examples and all or some of the other instances as negative examples (one-versus-all). The simplest form of hierarchical classification is that of cascade classification, where a binary classifier is trained for each node of the hierarchy, in order to separate it from its siblings. Then each test instance is guided through the hierarchy from root to leaf, choosing each time the most probable descendant.

In large scale hierarchical classification problems, the number of training instances and features can be very high (thousands or even millions). A flat classification approach can deal with the high dimensionality by performing instance and/or feature selection for each one-versus-all classifier. For hierarchical classification, however, feature selection is more complicated. Classifiers at the upper levels of the hierarchy need to deal with instances of all of their numerous descendant classes and any kind of intense feature selection could lead to a situation where many test instances cannot be represented adequately by the selected features. For example, in text classification with binary bag-of-word features (each indicating if a particular word is present in a text or not), there may be many test texts (belonging to very different descendant categories) that do not contain any of the words corresponding to the selected features of the upper level classifiers. These texts will have identical (all-zero) feature vectors and, hence, the upper level classifiers will be unable to distinguish them. Since intense feature selection is impossible in the upper levels of the hierarchy, classifier training can be very computationally expensive, because both the number of training instances and the number of features is high.

In order to facilitate hierarchical classification, we examine the use of a principal component (PCA) transformation, reducing the dimensionality at the top levels of the hierarchy. In this way, hierarchical classifiers can be trained on much fewer dimensions, leading to faster training and testing and to lower memory demands. At the same time, the use of a linear transformation of the initial feature set, instead of a discrete feature selection, reduces the risk that test instances will not be represented in the new space.

However, the use of PCA is not without difficulties. First, one needs to use a version of PCA that can handle the scale of the data. In this paper we select one such method and show that it can be used for large scale hierarchical classification. Additionally, we study the effect of dimensionality reduction on the computational performance of the classifier and its classification accuracy. In particular, we show that the combination of classifiers trained on a reduced feature space at the top levels of the hierarchy with classifiers trained on the original space at the lower levels provides the highest benefit for the lowest cost. We experiment with two popular hierarchical text classification datasets in this paper, but our approach should be useful in any hierarchical classification problem with many dimensions and sparse feature vectors.

In Section 2, we present the proposed approach and give advice on the selection of the most appropriate PCA method. Section 3 shows experimentally the effect of our approach on the computational cost and the accuracy of the hierarchical classifiers. Finally Section 4 concludes and points to future work.

## 2    Cascade Classification with PCA

In cascade classification a classifier must be trained for each node of the hierarchy. In this paper we focus on tree hierarchies, where instances belong only to the leaves of the hierarchy. An example of such a hierarchy is presented in Figure 1. In this example, a text classifier must be trained for each of the following nodes: *Arts, Health, Music, Dance, Fitness* and *Medicine*. A classifier of a node $U$ is trained with all instances belonging to the leaf descendants of $U$ as positive examples and all instances belonging to the leaf descendants of the siblings of $U$ as negative ones. The classifier of node *Arts*, for example, would use instances of *Music* and *Dance* as positive examples and instances of *Fitness* and *Medicine* as negative ones.

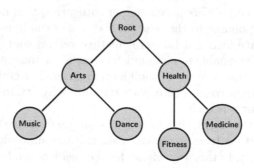

**Fig. 1.** Tree hierarchy example

Assuming again bag-of-word features, if we do not perform any feature selection the classifier of node Arts would use features for all the words of its positive and negative instances. In large datasets, where the hierarchy is composed of thousands of categories, the number of initial features can be hundreds of thousands (or even millions in text classification, if stemming or other similar preprocessing techniques are not used). Training a classifier for each node of the hierarchy using all these features can be very computationally demanding. On the other hand, an intense feature selection at the upper levels of the hierarchy would lead to inaccurate classifiers, since the few selected features would be unlikely to represent the test instances adequately, as already discussed.

Instead of feature selection, we suggest dimensionality reduction with principal component analysis (PCA) applied to each set of siblings of the hierarchy. In Figure 1, for example, we would need to perform PCA three times:

- for the nodes *Arts* and *Health*
- for the nodes *Music* and *Dance*
- for the nodes *Fitness* and *Medicine*.

The two classifiers of nodes *Arts* and *Health* would use the same feature space, and similarly for the siblings *Music* and *Dance* and *Fitness* and *Medicine*. Hence, PCA needs to be performed only once for each set of siblings. We note that performing PCA on all the leaves (as if we had a flat classification problem) would require a very large number of principal components to distinguish the leaves, drastically reducing the benefit of applying PCA.

Even applying PCA to sets of siblings, however, is not trivial at the scale that we are considering. In regular PCA an eigen decomposition of the covariance matrix $YY^T$ ($p \times p$) must be performed, where $Y$ is the $p \times n$ matrix of the observed data. Most of the times a Singular Value Decomposition (SVD) of $Y$ is performed instead:

$$Y = U\Sigma V^T \tag{1}$$

where $U$ is the square ($n \times n$) matrix whose columns contain the left singular vectors of Y, $\Sigma$ is a $n \times p$ rectangular diagonal matrix containing the singular values and $V$ is the square ($p \times p$) matrix whose columns contain the right singular vectors of Y.

The number of features ($p$) and instances ($n$) can by too large to perform a regular PCA. In [2] an Expectation Maximization (EM) algorithm for PCA is proposed, where the number $k$ of principal components must be set from the beginning. The steps of the EM are the following:

$$\text{E-step: } X = (C^T C)^{-1}C^T Y$$
$$\text{M-step: } C^{new} = YX^T(XX^T)^{-1} \tag{2}$$

where $X$ is a $k \times n$ matrix and $C$ is $p \times k$ matrix. These quantities are much easier to compute than those of the regular PCA, since $k$ can be set to a much smaller value than $p$. In order to compute the final eigenvectors and eigenvalues, we only need to project the observed data $Y$ to the orthonormal basis for the range of matrix $C$ ($orth(C)^T Y$) and perform a regular PCA in this $k$-dimensional subspace.

Adopting this approach we can perform PCA in very large datasets, where normal PCA would be very computationally demanding, especially in terms of memory. Even with this approach, PCA remains computationally expensive, but in practice it only needs to be performed once per dataset, greatly reducing the time needed to perform subsequent experiments with many different classifiers.

The only disadvantage is that we need to choose the value of $k$ (number of principal components) prior to performing PCA. In Section 3 we present results which show that by using only a few hundreds of principal components one can achieve similar results as when thousands of initial features are used.

Various linear and nonlinear dimensionality reduction approaches exist [3]. In this paper we focus on linear approaches, because of the large scale factor. Another linear approach that we could use is that of Simple PCA [4], but we chose EM since the principal components in Simple PCA are calculated approximately.

The most similar one is the extension of the Stochastic Gradient Ascent (SGA) neural network, proposed in [5]. The disadvantage of this method compared to EM PCA is that it requires a rate parameter to be set and also converges less quickly. Another approach would be to use the implicitly restarted Arnoldi method to compute the SVD of the data matrix [6]. However the EM approach seems more straightforward. We also examined the idea of using Sparse Principal Component Analysis [7], which was not suitable, as our focus was more on solving computational issues, instead of computing more accurate eigenvectors. In [8], the Fisher vector could not be directly used in large scale (but not hierarchical) image classification; hence, three different compression techniques were proposed to reduce the dimensionality.

## 3 Experimental Results

### 3.1 Experimental Set-Up

In order to assess the effect of combining PCA with cascade classification, we used both the dry-run and the large datasets form Task 1 of the first Large Scale Hierarchical Text Classification Challenge (LSHTC1).[1]

The dry-run dataset contains 6,323 instances (split into train and validation files), composed of 55,765 distinct features and belonging to 1,139 categories. An extra set of 1,858 test instances is also provided for evaluation. The large dataset contains 93,505 instances (split into train and validation files), composed of 381,581 distinct features and belonging to 12,294 categories. The test instances in this dataset are 34,880.

In both datasets, every instance has to be classified in a single leaf of the hierarchy, and the hierarchy is a tree. The systems are evaluated using the evaluation measures of the challenge, which are: Accuracy, Macro F-measure, Macro Precision, Macro Recall and Tree Induced Error [9].

As statistical significance tests, we used p-test ($p < 0.01$) for accuracy and S-test ($p < 0.01$) for macro F-measure. More information regarding these tests can be found in [10].

In the experiments we report, we used an L2 Regularized Logistic Regression [11], with the regularization parameter C set to 1 (usually the default value). We also conducted experiments with other regularization methods and other values of C, but the results were similar. We experimented with TF and TF-IDF bag-of-word features, but we report mostly experimental results with TF-IDF features, since led to better performance.

For each node of the hierarchy we trained two binary classifiers. One using all the initial features and one using $k$ principal components. R-analysis requires

---

[1] http://lshtc.iit.demokritos.gr/node/1

that $k < n$ [12], but for computational reasons we set a much smaller value for $k$. In practice, we observed that in both datasets for values of $k$ greater than a certain point the computational cost increased a lot, without significant gains in terms of classification accuracy. For the dry-run dataset, we set $k$ equal to 390, i.e. 390 components. In cases where $390 > n$ we set $k$ equal to $n - 1$ in order to satisfy $k < n$. In Figure 2 we present accuracy at the first top level of the hierarchy (children classes of the Root node) of the dry-run dataset, for various numbers of principal components. The figure illustrates the decreasing gains in accuracy as the number of components increases. Similarly for the large dataset we set $k$ equal to 490.

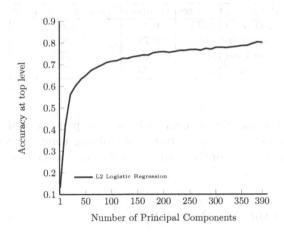

**Fig. 2.** Accuracy at top level of the hierarchy of the dry-run dataset, using $k$ Principal Components for various values of $k$

## 3.2   Feature Selection Results

In this section we present results showing that feature selection at the top levels of the hierarchy can heavily decrease the accuracy of the classifiers. In Tables 1 and 2 we present results in terms of accuracy and training time at the first level of the hierarchy of the dry-run and the large dataset, using feature selection. For each category the best features were selected according to the Chi-square statistic $\chi^2$ [13]. These experiments were conducted using an i7 3.2 GHz CPU (single thread).

Although the best features are selected for each binary classifier of the top level, many instances cannot be represented adequately by the selected features (empty feature vectors). As a result, in both datasets the accuracy falls significantly with the reduced feature sets. Since these errors at the top level will be carried to the leaves of the hierarchy, any form of intense feature selection will lead to inferior final results compared to keeping all the features. On the

**Table 1.** Accuracy and training time at the top level of the hierarchy of the dry-run dataset using $\chi^2$ feature selection

| Number of Features | Accuracy | Training Time (sec) |
|---|---|---|
| 55,765 (100%) | 0.82 | 7 |
| 27,882 (50%) | 0.76 | 5 |
| 5,576 (10%) | 0.56 | 0.84 |
| 557 (1%) | 0.29 | 0.18 |

**Table 2.** Accuracy and training time at the top level of the hierarchy of the large dataset using $\chi^2$ feature selection

| Number of Features | Accuracy | Training Time (sec) |
|---|---|---|
| 381,580 (100%) | 0.83 | 328 |
| 190,790 (50%) | 0.78 | 182 |
| 38,158 (10%) | 0.63 | 57 |
| 3,815 (1%) | 0.33 | 7 |

other hand, the training times seem to be almost proportional to the number of features. Therefore, we gain in terms of training times, as well as memory requirments, since the size of the training models is correlated to the number of features.

## 3.3   Results on the Dry-Run Dataset

Since feature selection is ineffective at the top levels of the hierarchy, we reduce the number of features using PCA. In Table 3, we present the results of four different systems on the dry-run dataset, using the five evaluation measures of Section 3.1. The first system (*Cascade*) uses all features (TF-IDF) in order to train each binary classifier. The second system (*PCA Cascade*) uses only classifiers trained with PCA features in all levels of the hierarchy (with PCA applied to sibling classes). In the system *Combo Cascade*, the classifiers at the top two levels of the hierarchy are trained using PCA features, while the ones at the lower levels are trained using the initial features. Finally we also provide results of flat classifiers (*Flat*) trained using all the initial features.

The first observation is that the *Cascade* system performs better than all the other systems, including the popular flat classifier. Flat classifiers perform well enough according to the four flat evaluation measures, but they have the worst performance according to the Tree Induced Error (lower number indicates better performance), which is the only hierarchical evaluation measure. This means that when the flat classifier fails to predict the exact category, its mistake is further from the correct category compared to the hierarchical systems. This is particularly important in hierarchical classification problems. Another disadvantage of flat classification is that on large scale problems, the use of traditional classifiers, such as SVMs or Logistic Regression, can be prohibitively expensive

**Table 3.** Results using the dry-run dataset for each approach per evaluation measure, using TF-IDF features. The best performing approach per evaluation measure appears in bold. Since Tree Induced Error is an error rate, lower values are better. Results with no statistically significant difference are marked with a ⋆ symbol.

| Evaluation Measure | Cascade | PCA Cascade | Combo Cascade | Flat |
|---|---|---|---|---|
| Accuracy | **0.444**⋆ | 0.419⋆ | 0.436⋆ | 0.438⋆ |
| Macro F-measure | **0.312**⋆ | 0.276 | 0.302⋆ | 0.304⋆ |
| Macro Precision | **0.284** | 0.250 | 0.275 | **0.284** |
| Macro Recall | **0.346** | 0.307 | 0.336 | 0.326 |
| Tree Induced Error | **3.588** | 3.754 | 3.673 | 3.976 |

computationally [14], since a binary classifier must be trained for each leaf using all instances.

Comparing *PCA Cascade* and *Cascade* we see that the latter is more accurate according to all evaluation measures. However, the difference is relatively small and in *PCA Cascade* the classifier is trained with 305 features instead of a few tens of thousands. Furthermore, we can improve the performance of *PCA Cascade* by using PCA only at the top levels of the hierarchy, where training is most expensive. As can be seen in Table 3, *Combo Cascade* achieves classification performance that is less than one precedence point smaller than that of *Cascade*.

Therefore, the combination of PCA at the top levels with training on the original feature space at the lower levels, provides high classification accuracy, while making cascading scalable to large datasets. The choice of the level at which the method should stop reducing the dimensionality of the feature space is largely an issue of computational cost. However, it is important to assess the effect of dimensionality reduction at each level. The results of this experiment are presented in Table 4. At each level of the hierarchy, we assume that the preceding (higher-level) classifiers have predicted the correct category and we measure only the accuracy at the corresponding level. According to the results in Table 4, it seems safe to assume that PCA affects classification accuracy similarly in all the levels of the hierarchy.

**Table 4.** Accuracy for cascade classification on the dry-run dataset, using the original and the reduced dimensions (PCA) per level of the hierarchy. Results with no statistically significant difference are marked with a ⋆ symbol.

| Level of the Hierarchy | Original Features | Reduced Dimensions (PCA) |
|---|---|---|
| 1 | 0.820⋆ | 0.814⋆ |
| 2 | 0.819⋆ | 0.812⋆ |
| 3 | 0.820⋆ | 0.807⋆ |
| 4 | 0.856⋆ | 0.849⋆ |
| 5 | 0.840⋆ | 0.834⋆ |

In Section 3.1 we mentioned that TF-IDF features provided better results than TF features. In Table 5 we present the results for *Cascade*, *PCA Cascade* and *Flat* using TF features. Not only *Cascade* and *Flat* systems performed worse with TF features, but also the *PCA Cascade* was greatly affected. Therefore we advise those who may use the proposed hierarchical PCA approach to perform a TF/IDF transformation.

**Table 5.** Results for each approach per evaluation measure, using TF features. The best performing approach per evaluation measure appears in bold. Since Tree Induced Error is an error rate, lower values are better. Results with no statistically significant difference are marked with a ⋆ symbol.

| Evaluation Measure | Cascade | PCA Cascade | Flat |
|---|---|---|---|
| Accuracy | **0.388**⋆ | 0.361⋆ | 0.385⋆ |
| Macro F-measure | **0.254**⋆ | 0.221 | 0.248⋆ |
| Macro Precision | 0.232 | 0.201 | **0.235** |
| Macro Recall | **0.281** | 0.246 | 0.262 |
| Tree Induced Error | **4.065** | 4.356 | 4.625 |

### 3.4 Results on the Large Dataset

In order to examine the scalability of our approaches, in Table 6 we present results for the large dataset using TF-IDF features. As in the dry-run data set *Cascade* uses all features in order to train each binary classifier. In *Combo Cascade* the classifiers at the top level of the hierarchy are trained using PCA features, while the ones at the lower levels using the initial features. Since the initial features are much more than the dry-run dataset (381,581 compared to 55,765), we used 100 more principal components (490) in the *Combo Cascade* system. We also provide results of flat classifiers (*Flat*) trained using all the initial features. Finally, we present the training times of the classifiers in each case.

**Table 6.** Results using the large dataset for each approach per evaluation measure and training time, using TF-IDF features. The best performing approach per evaluation measure appears in bold. Since Tree Induced Error is an error rate, lower values are better. Results with no statistically significant difference are marked with a ⋆ symbol.

| Evaluation Measure | Cascade | Combo Cascade | Flat |
|---|---|---|---|
| Accuracy | 0.404⋆ | 0.385 | **0.405**⋆ |
| Macro F-measure | **0.278**⋆ | 0.259 | 0.256⋆ |
| Macro Precision | **0.269** | 0.249 | 0.254 |
| Macro Recall | 0.289 | 0.268 | **0.302** |
| Tree Induced Error | **3.609** | 3.845 | 3.874 |
| Training Time | 8.66 min | 6.2 min | 1017.63 min |

According to Accuracy and Macro Recall, *Flat* is somewhat more accurate than *Cascade*, although the p-test detected no statistically significant difference between them in Macro Recall. On the other hand, as in the dry-run dataset, according to the hierarchical evaluation measure (tree induced error) *Cascade* performs better. *Cascade* also performs better in terms of Macro Precision and Macro F-measure, although the S-test for Macro F-measure detected no significant difference. Finally *Combo Cascade*, with PCA applied to the top level of the hierarchy, performs slightly worse. In terms of training times, *Flat* is very slow compared to *Cascade*. Between *Cascade* and *Combo Cascade*, we observe a speed up of about 30%. Performing PCA at lower levels would only mildly affect speed, since the initial feature vectors are already sparse enough.

Furthermore, computational cost could also affect the choice of the classifier used. For example, an RBF SVM [15] is very expensive at the top level of the hierarchy, if the original feature set is used. However, with PCA the use of such a costly classifier is made possible, as the number of features is reduced from 381,581 to a few hundreds. In Table 7 we present the time in minutes required to train L2 logistic regression and SVM with an RBF kernel using the original and the reduced (PCA) features at the top level of the hierarchy of the large dataset.

**Table 7.** Training time for L2 logistic regression and RBF SVM using the original and the reduced dimensions (PCA) at the top level of the hierarchy of the large dataset

|  | Original Features | Reduced Dimensions (PCA) | Gain |
|---|---|---|---|
| L2 Logistic Regression | 5.46 min | 2.84 min | 48% |
| SVM with RBF kernel | 691.2 min | 124.1 min | 82% |

Although in both cases the training times are reduced, the gain is much larger for the RBF SVM. In addition to the training time, complex classifiers require more parameter tuning, which is only made possible with the *Combo Cascade* method. In Table 8 we present results, using an RBF SVM classifier at the top

**Table 8.** Results using the large dataset for Cascade Combo with an SVM classifier at the top level, using TF/IDF features. Cascade results are repeated for ease of reference. The best performing approach, given each evaluation measure, appears in bold. Since Tree Induced Error is an error rate, lower values are better. Results with no statistically significant difference are marked with a ⋆ symbol.

| Evaluation Measure | Cascade | Combo Cascade with Tuned SVM | Combo Cascade with Default SVM |
|---|---|---|---|
| Accuracy | **0.404**⋆ | 0.402⋆ | 0.377 |
| Macro F-measure | **0.278**⋆ | 0.274⋆ | 0.252 |
| Macro Precision | **0.269** | 0.264 | 0.243 |
| Macro Recall | **0.289** | 0.283 | 0.262 |
| Tree Induced Error | **3.609** | 3.616 | 3.952 |

level of the hierarchy for the *Combo Cascade* method. In one case the SVM is trained using the default parameters, while in the other the parameters have been (non-exhaustively) tuned (c=100, g=0.01). As we can observe the tuned SVM performs much better than the default one. The p-test and S-test detected no statistically significant difference between *Cascade* and *Combo Cascade* with a tuned SVM. Given the training time cost in the initial feature space, this tuning would be much harder without the use of PCA.

## 4   Conclusion

In large scale hierarchical classification problems the number of features and instances to be used for training classifiers can be very large at the upper levels of the hierarchy. This can discourage the use of more complex, but more accurate classifiers and cause computational issues. In this paper we examined the use of dimensionality reduction (PCA) for hierarchical classification. This approach is independent of the classifier used and can be applied to all or some nodes of the hierarchy.

Even though performing PCA itself on such large scale datasets is not trivial, there are methods that can handle the complexity. We also showed experimentally that, although applying PCA to all levels of the hierarchy can decrease accuracy to some extent, this effect can be drastically limited, if we apply PCA only to the upper levels, which are the most computationally demanding. It would also be interesting to adaptively select the nodes were PCA should be used, instead of just applying it to the upper levels. We plan to examine such an adaptive selection method in the future.

The dimensionality reduction of the PCA procedure allows the use of more complex and possibly more accurate classifiers, such as non-linear SVMs. As future work, we also plan to compare the presented results with that of better tuned SVM classifiers. These classifiers are easier to train, using the reduced feature space provided by the PCA approach. We also plan to extend the presented PCA approach to Directed Acyclic Graphs (DAG) hierarchies, where it is unclear how the multiple inheritance of each node will affect the PCA for each set of siblings.

## References

1. Kosmopoulos, A., Gaussier, É., Paliouras, G., Aseervatham, S.: The ECIR 2010 large scale hierarchical classification workshop. In: SIGIR Forum. vol. 44, pp. 23–32 (2010)
2. Roweis, S.: EM Algorithms for PCA and SPCA. In: Advances in Neural Information Processing Systems, pp. 626–632 (1998)
3. Van der Maaten, L.J.P., Postma, E.O., van den Herik, H.J.: Dimensionality reduction: A comparative review. Journal of Machine Learning Research 10, 66–71 (2009)
4. Patridge, M., Calvo, R.: Fast dimensionality reduction and Simple PCA. Intelligent Data Analysis 2, 292–298 (1997)

5. Oja, E.: Principal components, minor components, and linear neural networks. In: Neural Networks, pp. 927–935 (1992)
6. Lehoucq, R.B., Sorensen, D.C., Yang, C.: ARPACK Users' Guide: Solution of Large-Scale Eigenvalue Problems with Implicitly Restarted Arnoldi Methods. Software, Environments, and Tools 6 (1998)
7. Grbovic, M., Dance, R.C., Vucetic, S.: Sparse Principal Component Analysis with Constraints. In: Proceedings of the Twenty-Sixth AAAI Conference on Artificial Intelligence (2012)
8. Perronnin, F., Liu, Y., Sánchez, J., Poirier, H.: Large-scale image retrieval with compressed Fisher vectors. In: The Twenty-Third IEEE Conference on Computer Vision and Pattern Recognition, pp. 3384–3391 (2010)
9. Dekel, O., Keshet, J., Singer, Y.: Large margin hierarchical classification. In: ICML 2004: Proceedings of the Twenty First International Conference on Machine Learning, p. 27 (2004)
10. Yang, Y., Liu, X.: A re-examination of text categorization methods, pp. 42–49. ACM Press (1999)
11. Fan, R.-E., Chang, K.-W., Hsieh, C.-J., Wang, X.-R., Lin, C.-J.: LIBLINEAR: A library for large linear classification. Journal of Machine Learning Research 9, 1871–1874 (2008)
12. Venables, K.V., Ripley, B.D.: Modern Applied Statistics with S. Springer (2002)
13. Setiono, R., Liu, H.: Chi2: Feature selection and discretization of numeric attributes. In: Proceedings of the Seventh IEEE International Conference on Tools with Artificial Intelligence (1995)
14. Liu, T., Yang, Y., Wan, H., Zeng, H., Chen, Z., Ma, W.: Support Vector Machines Classification with a Very Large-scale Taxonomy. In: SIGKDD Explor. Newsl., pp. 36–43 (2005)
15. Chang, C., Lin, C.: LIBSVM: a library for support vector machines. In: ACM Transactions on Intelligent Systems and Technology (2011)

# Overview of the ShARe/CLEF eHealth Evaluation Lab 2014*

Liadh Kelly[1], Lorraine Goeuriot[1], Hanna Suominen[2], Tobias Schreck[3],
Gondy Leroy[4], Danielle L. Mowery[5], Sumithra Velupillai[6],
Wendy W. Chapman[7], David Martinez[8], Guido Zuccon[9], and João Palotti[10]

[1] Dublin City University, Ireland
{Firstname.Lastname}@computing.dcu.ie
[2] NICTA, The Australian National University, University of Canberra,
and University of Turku, ACT, Australia
Hanna.Suominen@nicta.com.au
[3] University of Konstanz, Germany
tobias.schreck@uni-konstanz.de
[4] University of Arizona, Tucson, AZ, USA
gondyleroy@email.arizona.edu
[5] University of Pittsburgh, Pittsburgh, Pennsylvania, United States
dlm31@pitt.edu
[6] Stockholm University, Sweden
sumithra@dsv.su.se
[7] University of Utah, Salt Lake City, Utah, United States
wendy.chapman@utah.edu
[8] University of Melbourne, VIC, Australia
david.martinez@nicta.com.au
[9] Queensland University of Technology, Australia
g.zuccon@qut.edu.au
[10] Vienna University of Technology, Austria
palotti@ifs.tuwien.ac.at

**Abstract.** This paper reports on the 2nd ShARe/CLEFeHealth evaluation lab which continues our evaluation resource building activities for the medical domain. In this lab we focus on patients' information needs as opposed to the more common campaign focus of the specialised information needs of physicians and other healthcare workers. The usage scenario of the lab is to ease patients and next-of-kins' ease in understanding eHealth information, in particular clinical reports. The 1st ShARe/CLEFeHealth evaluation lab was held in 2013. This lab consisted of three tasks. Task 1 focused on named entity recognition and normalization of disorders; Task 2 on normalization of acronyms/abbreviations; and Task 3 on information retrieval to address questions patients may have when reading clinical reports. This year's lab introduces a new challenge in Task 1 on visual-interactive search and exploration of eHealth data. Its aim is to help patients (or their next-of-kin) in readability issues

---

* In alphabetical order, LK & LG co-chaired the lab & led Task 3; DLM, SV & WWC led Task 2; and DM, GZ & JP were the leaders of result evaluations. In order of contribution HS, TS & GL led Task 1.

E. Kanoulas et al. (Eds.): CLEF 2014, LNCS 8685, pp. 172–191, 2014.
© Springer International Publishing Switzerland 2014

related to their hospital discharge documents and related information search on the Internet. Task 2 then continues the information extraction work of the 2013 lab, specifically focusing on disorder attribute identification and normalization from clinical text. Finally, this year's Task 3 further extends the 2013 information retrieval task, by cleaning the 2013 document collection and introducing a new query generation method and multilingual queries. De-identified clinical reports used by the three tasks were from US intensive care and originated from the MIMIC II database. Other text documents for Tasks 1 and 3 were from the Internet and originated from the Khresmoi project. Task 2 annotations originated from the ShARe annotations. For Tasks 1 and 3, new annotations, queries, and relevance assessments were created. 50, 79, and 91 people registered their interest in Tasks 1, 2, and 3, respectively. 24 unique teams participated with 1, 10, and 14 teams in Tasks 1, 2 and 3, respectively. The teams were from Africa, Asia, Canada, Europe, and North America. The Task 1 submission, reviewed by 5 expert peers, related to the task evaluation category of Effective use of interaction and targeted the needs of both expert and novice users. The best system had an Accuracy of 0.868 in Task 2a, an F1-score of 0.576 in Task 2b, and Precision at 10 (P@10) of 0.756 in Task 3. The results demonstrate the substantial community interest and capabilities of these systems in making clinical reports easier to understand for patients. The organisers have made data and tools available for future research and development.

**Keywords:** Information Retrieval, Information Extraction, Information Visualisation, Evaluation, Medical Informatics, Test-set Generation, Text Classification, Text Segmentation.

# 1 Introduction

Laypeople find eHealth clinical reports, such as discharge summaries and radiology reports, difficult to understand. Clinicians also experience difficulties in understanding the jargon of other professional groups even though laws and policies emphasise patients' right to be able to access and understand their clinical documents. A simple example from a US discharge document is "*AP: 72 yo f w/ ESRD on HD, CAD, HTN, asthma p/w significant hyperkalemia & associated arrythmias*". As described in [1], there is much need for techniques which support individuals in understanding such eHealth documents.

The usage scenario of the CLEF eHealth lab is to ease patients and next-of-kins' ease in understanding eHealth information. eHealth documents are much easier to understand after expanding shorthand, correcting misspellings and normalising all health conditions to standardised terminology. This would result in "*Description of the patient's active problem: 72 year old female with dependence on hemodialysis, coronary heart disease, hypertensive disease, and asthma who is currently presenting with the problem of significant hyperkalemia and associated arrhythmias.*" The patient's and her next-of-kin's understanding of health conditions can also be supported by linking discharge summary terms to a patient-centric search on the Internet. The search engine could, for example, link hyperkalemia and its synonyms to definitions in Wikipedia, Consumer Health Vocabulary, and other patient-friendly sources[1]. This would explain the connection between hyperkalemia and arrhythmia: *Extreme hyperkalemia (having too much potassium in the blood) is a medical emergency due to the risk of potentially fatal arrhythmias (abnormal heart rhythms)*. The engine should also assess the reliability of information (e.g., guidelines by healthcare service providers vs. uncurated but insightful experiences on discussion forums).

Natural language processing (NLP), computational linguistics and machine learning are recognised as ways to process textual health information. Several evaluation campaigns have been organised to share benchmarks and improve techniques such as information retrieval (IR), text mining, image retrieval and processing, etc. We described these campaigns in detail in [1].

This paper presents an overview of the ShARe/CLEFeHealth2014 evaluation lab[2] to support development of approaches which support patients' and their next-of-kins' information needs stemming from clinical reports. Towards this, this second year of the novel lab aimed to build on the resource building and evaluation approaches offered by the first year of the lab. The first year of the lab contained two tasks which focused on named entity recognition and normalization of disorders and acronyms/abbreviations in clinical reports [2,3], and one task which explored supporting individuals' information needs stemming from clinical reports through IR technique development [4]. This years' lab expands our year one efforts and supports evaluation of information visualisation (Task 1), information extraction (Task 2) and information retrieval (Task 3) approaches for the space. Specifically, Task 1 [5] aims to help patients (or their next-of-kin) in readability issues related to their hospital discharge documents and related information search on the Internet. Task 2 [6] continues the information extraction work of the 2013 CLEFeHealth lab, specifically focusing on information extraction of disorder attributes from clinical text. Task 3 [7] further extends the 2013 information retrieval task, by cleaning the 2013 document collection and introducing a new query generation method and multilingual queries.

In total the 2014 edition of the CLEFeHealth lab attracted 24 teams to submit 105 systems[3]; demonstrated the capabilities of these systems in contributing to patients' understanding and information needs; and made data, guidelines, and tools available for future research and development. The lab workshop was held at CLEF in September 2014.

---

[1] http://en.wikipedia.org/ and http://www.consumerhealthvocab.org/

[2] http://clefehealth2014.dcu.ie/,     Shared     Annotated     Resources, http://clinicalnlpannotation.org, and Conference and Labs of the Evaluation Forum, http://www.clef-initiative.eu/

[3] Note: in this paper we refer to systems, experiments, and runs as *systems*.

## 2    Materials and Methods

### 2.1    Text Documents

For Tasks 2 and 3, de-identified clinical reports were from US intensive care and originated from the ShARe corpus which has added layers of annotation over the clinical notes in the version 2.5 of the MIMIC II database[4]. The corpus consisted of discharge summaries, electrocardiogram, echocardiogram, and radiology reports. They were authored in the intensive care setting. Although the clinical reports were de-identified, they still needed to be treated with appropriate care and respect. Hence, all participants were required to register to the lab, obtain a US human subjects training certificate[5], create an account to a password-protected site on the Internet, specify the purpose of data usage, accept the data use agreement, and get their account approved. Six of these clinical reports were further de-identified for use in Task 1. This was done by organisers manually removing any remaining potentially identifying information, e.g. treatment hospital, from the reports.

For Tasks 1 and 3, an updated version of the CLEFeHealth 2013 Task 3 large crawl of health resources on the Internet was used. In this updated crawl, the 2013 Task 3 crawl was further cleaned, by removing some errors in HTML, duplicate documents, etc. It contained about one million documents [8] and originated from the Khresmoi project[6]. The crawled domains were predominantly health and medicine sites, which were certified by the HON Foundation as adhering to the HONcode principles (appr. 60–70 per cent of the collection), as well as other commonly used health and medicine sites such as Drugbank, Diagnosia and Trip Answers.[7] Documents consisted of pages on a broad range of health topics and were targeted at both the general public and healthcare professionals. They were made available for download on the Internet in their raw HTML format along with their URLs to registered participants on a secure password-protected server. [8]

### 2.2    Human Annotations, Queries, and Relevance Assessments

For Task 1 the input data provided to participants consists of *six carefully chosen cases* from the CLEFeHealth2013 data set. Using the first case was mandatory

---

[4] Multiparameter Intelligent Monitoring in Intensive Care, Version 2.5,
   http://mimic.physionet.org
[5] The course was available free of charge on the Internet, for example, via the CITI Collaborative Institutional Training Initiative at
   https://www.citiprogram.org/Default.asp or the US National Institutes of Health (NIH) at http://phrp.nihtraining.com/users/login.php
[6] Medical Information Analysis and Retrieval, http://www.khresmoi.eu
[7] Health on the Net, http://www.healthonnet.org,
   http://www.hon.ch/HONcode/Patients-Conduct.html, http://www.drugbank.ca,
   http://www.diagnosia.com, and http://www.tripanswers.org
[8] HyperText Markup Language and Uniform Resource Locators.

for all participants and the other five cases were optional. Each case consisted of a discharge summary, including the disease/disorder spans marked and mapped to *Systematized Nomenclature of Medicine Clinical Terms, Concept Unique Identifiers* (SNOMED-CT), and the shorthand spans marked and mapped to the *Unified Medical Language System* (UMLS). Each discharge summary was also associated with a *profile* to describe the patient, a *narrative* to describe her information need, a *query* to address this information need by searching the Internet documents, and the list of *returned relevant documents*. To access the data set on the *PhysioNetWorks workspaces*, the participants had to first register to CLEF2014 and agree to our data use agreement. The dataset was accessible to authorized users from December 2013. The data set is to be opened for all registered PhysioNetWorks users in October 2014.

For Task 2, the annotations were created as part of the ongoing Shared Annotated Resources (ShARe) project. For this year's evaluation lab, the annotations extended the existing disorder annotations from clinical text from Task 1 ShARe/CLEF eHealth 2013 by focusing on template filling for each disorder mention[9]. As such, each disorder template consisted of 10 different attributes including *Negation Indicator, Subject Class, Uncertainty Indicator, Course Class, Severity Class, Conditional Class, Generic Class, Body Location, DocTime Class,* and *Temporal Expression*. Each attribute contained two types of annotation values: normalization and cue detection value with the exception of the *DocTime Class* which did not contain a cue detection value. Each note was annotated by two professional coders trained for this task, followed by an open adjudication step. The initial development set contained 300 documents of 4 clinical report types - discharge summaries, radiology, electrocardiograms, and echocardiograms. The unseen test set contained 133 documents of only discharge summaries.

From the ShARe guidelines, for a <u>disorder mention</u>, an **attribute** *cue* is a span of text that represents a non-default normalization value (*default normalization value):

**Negation Indicator:** def. indicates a disorder was negated: *no, *yes*
Ex. *No* <u>cough</u>.

**Subject Class:** def. indicates who experienced a disorder: *patient, *family_ member*, donor_family_member, donor_other, null, other
Ex. *Dad* had <u>MI</u>.

**Uncertainty Indicator:** def. indicates a measure of doubt about the disorder: *no, *yes*
Ex. *Possible* <u>pneumonia</u>.

**Course Class:** def. indicates progress or decline of a disorder: *unmarked, changed, increased, decreased, improved, worsened, *resolved*
Ex. <u>Bleeding</u> *abated*.

---

[9] http://clefehealth2014.dcu.ie/task-2/2014-dataset

**Severity Class:** def. indicates how severe a disorder is: *unmarked, slight, moderate, *severe*
Ex. Infection is *severe*.

**Conditional Class:** def. indicates existence of disorder under certain circumstances: *false, *true*
Ex. Return *if* nausea occurs.

**Generic Class:** def. indicates a generic mention of disorder: *false, *true*
Ex. Vertigo *while* walking.

**Body Location:** def. represents an anatomical location: *NULL, *CUI: C0015450*, CUI-less
Ex. *Facial* lesions.

**DocTime Class:** def. indicates temporal relation between a disorder and document authoring time: *before*, after, overlap, before-overlap, *unknown
Ex. Stroke in *1999*.

**Temporal Expression:** def. represents any TIMEX (TimeML) temporal expression related to the disorder: *none, *date*, time, duration, set
Ex. Flu on *March 10*.

For Task 3, queries and the respective result sets were associated with the text documents. Two Finnish nursing professionals created 55 queries from the main disorders diagnosed in discharge summaries provided in Task 1 (semi-automatically identified). Participants were provided with the mapping between queries and discharge summaries, and were free to use the discharge summaries. Relevance assessments were performed by domain experts and technological experts using the Relevation system[10] [9] for collecting relevance assessments of documents contained in the assessment pools. Documents and queries were uploaded to the system via a browser-based interface; judges could browse documents for each query and provide their relevance judgements. The domain experts included two Indian medical professionals, and two Finnish nursing professionals. The technological experts included six Irish, five Czech, one Austrian and one Australian senior researcher in clinical NLP and machine learning (ML). Assessments compared the query and its mapping to the content of the retrieved document on a four-point scale. These graded relevance assessments yielded 0: 3,044, 1: 547, 2: 974, 3: 2,235 documents. The relevance of each document was assessed by one expert. The 55 queries were divided into 5 training and 50 test queries. Assessments for the 5 training queries were performed by the same two Finnish nursing professionals who generated the queries. As we received 65 systems, we had to limit the pool depth for the test set of 50 queries and distribute the relevance assessment workload between domain experts and technological

---

[10] https://github.com/bevankoopman/relevation, open source, based on Python's Django Internet framework, uses a simple Model-View-Controller model that is designed for easy customisation and extension

experts. System outputs for 35 test queries were assessed by the domain experts and the remaining 15 test queries by the technological experts.

## 2.3  Evaluation Methods

The following evaluation criteria were used: In Task 1, each final submission was assessed by a team of four evaluation panellists, supported by an organizer. Primary evaluation criteria included the effectiveness and originality of the presented submissions. More precisely, submissions were judged on usability, visualization, interaction, and aesthetics. In Task 2 evaluation was based on correctness in assigning normalization values to ten semantic attributes attributes (2a), and correctness in assigning cue values to the nine semantic attributes with cues (2b), and in Task 3 relevance of the retrieved documents to patients or their representatives based on English queries (3a) or non-English queries translated into English (3b).

In Task 1, teams were asked to submit the following mandatory items by 1 May 2014:

1. a concise report of the design, implementation (if applicable), and application results discussion in the form of an extended abstract that highlights the obtained findings, possibly supported by an informal user study or other means of validation and
2. two demonstration videos illustrating the relevant functionality of the functional design or paper prototype in application to the provided task data.

In the first video, the user should be a person who knows the system functionalities and in the second video, the user should be a novice with no previous experience of these functionalities. The video should also explain how the novice was trained to use the functionality.

In Tasks 2a and 2b, each participating team was permitted to upload the outputs of up to two systems. Task 2b was optional for Task 2 participants. In Task 3a, teams were asked to submit up to seven ranked outputs (typically called *runs*): a mandatory baseline (referred to as {team}.run1): only title and description in the query could be used without any additional resources (e.g., clinical reports, corpora, or ontologies); up to three outputs from systems which use the clinical reports (referred to as {team}.run2–{team}.run4); and up to three outputs from systems which do not use the clinical reports (referred to as {team}.run5–{team}.run7). One of the runs 2–4 and one of the runs 5–7 needed to use only the fields title and description from the queries. The ranking corresponded to priority (referred to as {team}.{run}.{rank} with ranks 1–7 from the highest to lowest priority). In Task 3b, teams could submit a similar set of ranked outputs for each of the cross-lingual languages.

Teams received data from December 2013 to April 2014. In Task 1, all data was accessible to authorized users from December, 2013. In Tasks 2 and 3, data was divided into training and test sets; the evaluation for these tasks was conducted using the blind, withheld test data (reports for Task 2 and queries for Task

3). Teams were asked to stop development as soon as they downloaded the test data. The training set and test set for Tasks 2 and 3 were released from December 2013 and April 2014 respectively. Evaluation results were announced to the participants for the three tasks from end May to early June.

In Tasks 2a and 2b, participants were provided with a training set containing clinical text as well as pre-annotated spans and CUIs for diseases/disorders in templates along with 1) normalized values for each of the ten attributes of the disease/disorder (Task 2a) and cue slot values for nine of the attributes (Task 2b). For Task 2a, participants were instructed to develop a system that kept or updated the normalization values for the ten attributes. For Task 2b, participants were instructed to develop a system that kept or updated the cue values for the nine attributes. The outputs needed to follow the annotation format. The corpus of reports was split into 300 training and 133 testing.

In Task 3, post-submission relevance assessment of systems trained on the 5 training queries and the matching result set was conducted on the 50 test queries to generate the complete result set. The outputs needed to follow the TREC format. The top ten documents obtained from the participants' baseline, the two highest priority runs from the runs 2–4, and the two highest priority output from the runs 5–7[11] were pooled with duplicates removed. This resulted in a pool of 6,040 documents, with a total of 6,800 relevance judgements.[12] Pooled sets for the training queries were created by merging the top 30 ranked documents returned by the two IR models (Vector Space Model [10] and BM25 [11]) and removing duplicates.

The system performance in the different tasks was evaluated against task-specific criteria. Task 1 aimed at providing a visual-interactive application to help users explore data and understand complex relationships. As such, an evaluation in principle needs to consider multiple dimensions regarding the system design, including effectiveness and expressiveness of the chosen visual design, and criteria of usability by different user groups. Specifically, in Task 1 participants were asked to demonstrate that their design addresses the posed user tasks, gives a compelling use-case driven discussions, and highlight obtained findings. Furthermore, we devised a set of usability and visualization heuristics to characterize the quality of the solution.

Tasks 2 and 3 system performance was evaluated using Accuracy in Task 2a and the F1-score in Task 2b, and Precision at 10 (P@10) and Normalised Discounted Cumulative Gain at 10 (NDCG@10) in Task 3. We relied on the Wilcoxon test [12] in Task 3 to better compare the measure values for the systems and benchmarks.

In Task 2a, the Accuracy was defined as the number of correctly predicted normalization value slots divided by the total number of gold standard normalization slot values.

In Task 2b, the F1 score was defined as the harmonic mean of Precision (P) and Recall (R); P as $n_{TP}/(n_{TP} + n_{FP})$; R as $n_{TP}/(n_{TP} + n_{FN})$; $n_{TP}$ as the

---

[11] Runs 1, 2, 3, 5 and 6 for teams who submitted the maximum number of runs.

[12] This means that some documents have been retrieved for several queries.

number of instances, where the spans identified by the system and gold standard were the same; $n_{FP}$ as the number of spurious spans by the system; and $n_{FN}$ as the number of missing spans by the system. We referred to the Exact (Relaxed) F1-score if the system span is identical to (overlaps) the gold standard span.

In Task 2b, the Exact F1-score and Relaxed F1-score were measured. In the Exact F1-score for Task 2b, the predicted cue slot span was identical to the reference standard span. In the Relaxed F1-score, the predicted cue slot span overlapped with reference standard span.

In Task 3, the official primary and secondary measures were P@10 and NDCG@10 [13], respectively. Both measures were calculated over the top ten documents retrieved by a system for each query, and then averaged across the whole set of queries. To compute P@10, graded relevance assessments were converted to a binary scale; NDCG@10 was computed using the original relevance assessments on a 4-point scale. The `trec_eval` evaluation tool[13] was used to calculate these evaluation measures[14]. Participants were also provided with other standard measures calculated by `trec_eval`[15].

The organisers provided the following evaluation tools on the Internet: a evaluation script for calculation of the evaluation measures of Task 2; a Graphical User Interface (GUI) for visualisation of gold standard annotations; and a pointer to the `trec_eval` evaluation tool for Task 3.

# 3    Results

The number of people who registered their interest in Tasks 1, 2, and 3 was 50, 79, and 91, respectively, and in total 24 teams with unique affiliations submitted to the shared tasks (Table 1). No team participated in all three tasks. One team participated in Tasks 2 and 3 (Table 2). Teams represented Canada, Czech Republic, France, Germany, India, Japan, Portugal, Spain, South Korea, Taiwan, Thailand, The Netherlands, Tunisia, Turkey, Vietnam, and USA.

In total 105 systems were submitted to the challenge (Table 2).

In Task 1, one final submission was received from a team from the USA called *FLPolytech*. This submission was also assessed during our optional draft submission round in March 2014. The team was a partnership between *Florida Polytechnic University's Department of Advanced Technology* and the commercial information science firm *Retrivika*. The submission addressed both Tasks *1a: Discharge Resolution Challenge* and *1b: Visual Exploration Challenge* together with their integration as the *Grand Challenge* solution. It related to the task evaluation category of *Effective use of interaction*. Although the submission did not describe tests with real expert and/or novice users, the described system

---

[13] http://trec.nist.gov/trec_eval/

[14] NDCG was computed with the standard settings in `trec_eval`, and by running the command `trec_eval -c -M1000 -m ndcg_cut qrels runName`.

[15] including P@5, NDCG@5, Mean Average Precision (MAP), and rel_ret (i.e., the total number of relevant documents retrieved by the system over all queries).

**Table 1.** Participating teams

| ID Team | Affiliation | Location |
|---------|-------------|----------|
| 1 ASNLP | iis, sinica | Taiwan |
| 2 CORAL | University of Alabama at Birmingham | USA |
| 3 CSKU/COMPL | Kasetsart University - Department of Computer Science | Thailand |
| 4 CUNI | Charles University in Prague | Czech Republic |
| 5 DEMIR | DEMIR-Dokuz Eyhul University, Multimedia Information Retrieval Group | Turkey |
| 6 DFKI-Medical | DFKI | Germany |
| 7 ERIAS | ISPED/UniversitÃ𝑓 of Bordeaux | France |
| 8 FLPolytech | Florida Polytechnic University'd Department of Advanced Technology and Retrivika | USA |
| 9 GRIUM | Departement of Computer Science and Operations Research, University of Montreal | Canada |
| 10 HCMUS | HCM City University of Science | Vietnam |
| 11 HITACHI | Research and Development Centre, Hitachi India Pvt Ltd, Hitachi, Ltd., Central Research Laboratory, Japan, International Institute of Information Technology Hyderabad, India | India, Japan |
| 12 HPI | Hasso Plattner Institute | Germany |

**Table 1.** (*Continued*)

| ID | Team | Affiliation | Location |
|---|---|---|---|
| 13 | IRLabDAIICT | DAIICT | India |
| 14 | KISTI | Korea Institute of Science and Technology Information | South Korea |
| 15 | LIMSI | LIMSI-CNRS | France |
| 16 | Miracl | Multimedia Information Systems and Advanced Computing Laboratory | Tunisia |
| 17 | Nijmegen | Information Foraging Lab, Institute for Computing and Information Sciences | The Netherlands |
| 18 | RelAgent | RelAgent Tech Pvt Ltd | India |
| 19 | RePaLi | Inria - IRISA - CNRS | France |
| 20 | SNUMEDINFO | Seoul National University | South Korea |
| 21 | UEvora | Universidade de ÁLvora | Portugal |
| 22 | UHU | Universidad de Huelva | Spain |
| 23 | UIOWA | The University of Iowa | USA |
| 24 | YORKU | York University | Canada |

**Table 2.** The tasks that the teams participated in

| ID | Team | Number of submitted systems per task | | | |
|---|---|---|---|---|---|
| | | 1 | 2a 2b | 3a | 3b |
| 1 | ASNLP | | 1 | | |
| 2 | CORAL | | 1 | | |
| 3 | CSKU/COMPL | | | 2 | |
| 4 | CUNI | | | 4 | 4 runs/language |
| 5 | DEMIR | | | 4 | |
| 6 | DFKI-Medical | | 2 | | |
| 7 | ERIAS | | | 4 | |
| 8 | FLPolytech | 1 | | | |
| 9 | GRIUM | | 1 | 4 | |
| 10 | HCMUS | | 1  1 | | |
| 11 | HITACHI | | 2  2 | | |
| 12 | HPI | | 1  1 | | |
| 13 | IRLabDAIICT | | | 6 | |
| 14 | KISTI | | | 7 | |
| 15 | LIMSI | | 2 | | |
| 16 | Miracl | | | 1 | |
| 17 | Nijmegen | | | 7 | |
| 18 | RelAgent | | 2 | | |
| 19 | RePaLi | | | 4 | |
| 20 | SNUMEDINFO | | | 7 | 4 runs/language |
| 21 | UEvora | | 1 | | |
| 22 | UHU | | | 4 | |
| 23 | UIOWA | | | 4 | |
| 24 | YORKU | | | 4 | |
| | Systems: | 1 | 14  4 | 62 | 24 | Total: 105 |
| | Teams: | 1 | 10  3 | 14 | 2 | |

**Table 3.** Evaluation in Task 2a: predict each attribute's normalization slot value. Accuracy: overall

| Attribute | System ID ({team}.{system}) | Accuracy |
|---|---|---|
| Overall | TeamHITACHI.2 | 0.868 |
| Average | TeamHITACHI.1 | 0.854 |
| | RelAgent.2 | 0.843 |
| | RelAgent.1 | 0.843 |
| | TeamHCMUS.1 | 0.827 |
| | DFKI-Medical.2 | 0.822 |
| | LIMSI.1 | 0.804 |
| | DFKI-Medical.1 | 0.804 |
| | TeamUEvora.1 | 0.802 |
| | LIMSI.2 | 0.801 |
| | ASNLP.1 | 0.793 |
| | TeamCORAL.1 | 0.790 |
| | TeamGRIUM.1 | 0.780 |
| | HPI.1 | 0.769 |

**Table 4.** Evaluation in Task 2a: predict each attribute's normalization slot value. Accuracy per attribute type - Attributes Negation Indicator, Subject Class, Uncertainty Indicator, Course Class, Severity Class, Conditional Class.

| Attribute | System ID | Accuracy | Attribute | System ID | Accuracy |
|---|---|---|---|---|---|
| Negation Indicator | TeamHITACHI.2 | 0.969 | Subject Class | TeamHCMUS.1 | 0.995 |
| | RelAgent.2 | 0.944 | | TeamHITACHI.2 | 0.993 |
| | RelAgent.1 | 0.941 | | TeamHITACHI.1 | 0.990 |
| | TeamASNLP | 0.923 | | TeamUEvora.1 | 0.987 |
| | TeamGRIUM.1 | 0.922 | | DFKI-Medical.1 | 0.985 |
| | TeamHCMUS.1 | 0.910 | | DFKI-Medical.2 | 0.985 |
| | LIMSI.1 | 0.902 | | LIMSI.1 | 0.984 |
| | LIMSI.2 | 0.902 | | RelAgent.2 | 0.984 |
| | TeamUEvora.1 | 0.901 | | RelAgent.1 | 0.984 |
| | TeamHITACHI.1 | 0.883 | | LIMSI.2 | 0.984 |
| | DFKI-Medical.2 | 0.879 | | TeamHPI | 0.976 |
| | DFKI-Medical.1 | 0.876 | | TeamCORAL.1 | 0.926 |
| | TeamCORAL.1 | 0.807 | | TeamASNLP | 0.921 |
| | TeamHPI | 0.762 | | TeamGRIUM.1 | 0.611 |
| Uncertainty Indicator | TeamHITACHI.1 | 0.960 | Course Class | TeamHITACHI.2 | 0.971 |
| | RelAgent.2 | 0.955 | | TeamHITACHI.1 | 0.971 |
| | RelAgent.1 | 0.955 | | RelAgent.1 | 0.970 |
| | TeamUEvora.1 | 0.955 | | RelAgent.2 | 0.967 |
| | TeamCORAL.1 | 0.941 | | TeamGRIUM.1 | 0.961 |
| | DFKI-Medical.1 | 0.941 | | TeamCORAL.1 | 0.961 |
| | DFKI-Medical.2 | 0.941 | | TeamASNLP | 0.953 |
| | TeamHITACHI.2 | 0.924 | | TeamHCMUS.1 | 0.937 |
| | TeamGRIUM.1 | 0.923 | | DFKI-Medical.1 | 0.932 |
| | TeamASNLP | 0.912 | | DFKI-Medical.2 | 0.932 |
| | TeamHPI | 0.906 | | TeamHPI | 0.899 |
| | TeamHCMUS.1 | 0.877 | | TeamUEvora.1 | 0.859 |
| | LIMSI.1 | 0.801 | | LIMSI.1 | 0.853 |
| | LIMSI.2 | 0.801 | | LIMSI.2 | 0.853 |
| Severity Class | TeamHITACHI.2 | 0.982 | Conditional Class | TeamHITACHI.1 | 0.978 |
| | TeamHITACHI.1 | 0.982 | | TeamUEvora.1 | 0.975 |
| | RelAgent.2 | 0.975 | | RelAgent.2 | 0.963 |
| | RelAgent.1 | 0.975 | | RelAgent.1 | 0.963 |
| | TeamGRIUM.1 | 0.969 | | TeamHITACHI.2 | 0.954 |
| | TeamHCMUS.1 | 0.961 | | TeamGRIUM.1 | 0.936 |
| | DFKI-Medical.1 | 0.957 | | LIMSI.1 | 0.936 |
| | DFKI-Medical.2 | 0.957 | | TeamASNLP | 0.936 |
| | TeamCORAL.1 | 0.942 | | LIMSI.2 | 0.936 |
| | TeamUEvora.1 | 0.919 | | TeamCORAL.1 | 0.936 |
| | TeamHPI | 0.914 | | DFKI-Medical.1 | 0.936 |
| | TeamASNLP | 0.912 | | DFKI-Medical.2 | 0.936 |
| | LIMSI.1 | 0.900 | | TeamHCMUS.1 | 0.899 |
| | LIMSI.2 | 0.900 | | TeamHPI | 0.819 |

**Table 5.** Evaluation in Task 2a: predict each attribute's normalization slot value. Accuracy per attribute type - Attributes Generic Class, Body Location, DocTime Class and Temporal Expression.

| Attribute | System ID | Accuracy | Attribute | System ID | Accuracy |
|---|---|---|---|---|---|
| Generic | TeamGRIUM.1 | 1.000 | Body | TeamHITACHI.2 | 0.797 |
| Class | LIMSI.1 | 1.000 | Location | TeamHITACHI.1 | 0.790 |
| | TeamHPI | 1.000 | | RelAgent.2 | 0.756 |
| | TeamHCMUS.1 | 1.000 | | RelAgent.1 | 0.753 |
| | RelAgent.2 | 1.000 | | TeamGRIUM.1 | 0.635 |
| | TeamASNLP | 1.000 | | DFKI-Medical.2 | 0.586 |
| | RelAgent.1 | 1.000 | | TeamHCMUS.1 | 0.551 |
| | LIMSI.2 | 1.000 | | TeamASNLP | 0.546 |
| | TeamUEvora.1 | 1.000 | | TeamCORAL.1 | 0.546 |
| | DFKI-Medical.1 | 1.000 | | TeamUEvora.1 | 0.540 |
| | DFKI-Medical.2 | 1.000 | | LIMSI.1 | 0.504 |
| | TeamHITACHI.2 | 0.990 | | LIMSI.2 | 0.504 |
| | TeamCORAL.1 | 0.974 | | TeamHPI | 0.494 |
| | TeamHITACHI.1 | 0.895 | | DFKI-Medical.1 | 0.486 |
| DocTime | TeamHITACHI.2 | 0.328 | Temporal | TeamHPI | 0.864 |
| Class | TeamHITACHI.1 | 0.324 | Expression | RelAgent.2 | 0.864 |
| | LIMSI.1 | 0.322 | | RelAgent.1 | 0.864 |
| | LIMSI.2 | 0.322 | | TeamCORAL.1 | 0.864 |
| | TeamHCMUS.1 | 0.306 | | TeamUEvora.1 | 0.857 |
| | DFKI-Medical.1 | 0.179 | | DFKI-Medical.2 | 0.849 |
| | DFKI-Medical.2 | 0.154 | | LIMSI.1 | 0.839 |
| | TeamHPI | 0.060 | | TeamHCMUS.1 | 0.830 |
| | TeamGRIUM.1 | 0.024 | | TeamASNLP | 0.828 |
| | RelAgent.2 | 0.024 | | TeamGRIUM.1 | 0.824 |
| | RelAgent.1 | 0.024 | | LIMSI.2 | 0.806 |
| | TeamUEvora.1 | 0.024 | | TeamHITACHI.2 | 0.773 |
| | TeamASNLP | 0.001 | | TeamHITACHI.1 | 0.766 |
| | TeamCORAL.1 | 0.001 | | DFKI-Medical.1 | 0.750 |

appeared to be rather good. The final submission was evaluated by four evaluation panellists and one organizer. The draft submission was reviewed by five organizers.

In total, ten teams submitted systems for Task 2a. Four teams submitted two runs. For Task 2b, three teams submitted systems, one of them submitted two runs. See Table 2. The best system had an Accuracy of 0.868 in Task 2a and an F1-score of 0.576 in Task 2b. See Tables 3 - 6 for details.

Fourteen teams participated in Task 3a. Two of these teams also participated in Task 3b. The number of submissions per team ranged from 1-7. See Table 2. The best system in Task 3a had P@10 of 0.756 and NDCG@10 of 0.7445; and the best system in Task 3b had P@10 of 0.7551 and NDCG@10 of 0.7011. See Tables 7 - 9 for details.

**Table 6.** Evaluation in Task 2b: predict each attribute's cue slot value. Strict and Relaxed F1-score, Precision and Recall (overall and per attribute type).

| Attribute | System ID | Strict | | | Relaxed | | |
|---|---|---|---|---|---|---|---|
| | | F1-score | Precision | Recall | F1-score | Precision | Recall |
| Overall | TeamHITACHI.2 | 0.676 | 0.620 | 0.743 | 0.724 | 0.672 | 0.784 |
| Average | TeamHITACHI.1 | 0.671 | 0.620 | 0.731 | 0.719 | 0.672 | 0.773 |
| | TeamHCMUS.1 | 0.544 | 0.475 | 0.635 | 0.648 | 0.583 | 0.729 |
| | HPI.1 | 0.190 | 0.184 | 0.197 | 0.323 | 0.314 | 0.332 |
| Negation | TeamHITACHI.2 | 0.913 | 0.955 | 0.874 | 0.926 | 0.962 | 0.893 |
| Indicator | TeamHITACHI.1 | 0.888 | 0.897 | 0.879 | 0.905 | 0.912 | 0.897 |
| | TeamHCMUS.1 | 0.772 | 0.679 | 0.896 | 0.817 | 0.735 | 0.919 |
| | HPI.1 | 0.383 | 0.405 | 0.363 | 0.465 | 0.488 | 0.444 |
| Subject | TeamHCMUS.1 | 0.857 | 0.923 | 0.800 | 0.936 | 0.967 | 0.907 |
| Class | TeamHITACHI.1 | 0.125 | 0.068 | 0.760 | 0.165 | 0.092 | 0.814 |
| | TeamHITACHI.2 | 0.112 | 0.061 | 0.653 | 0.152 | 0.085 | 0.729 |
| | HPI.1 | 0.106 | 0.059 | 0.520 | 0.151 | 0.086 | 0.620 |
| Uncertainty | TeamHITACHI.2 | 0.561 | 0.496 | 0.647 | 0.672 | 0.612 | 0.746 |
| Indicator | TeamHITACHI.1 | 0.514 | 0.693 | 0.408 | 0.655 | 0.802 | 0.553 |
| | TeamHCMUS.1 | 0.252 | 0.169 | 0.494 | 0.386 | 0.275 | 0.646 |
| | HPI.1 | 0.166 | 0.106 | 0.376 | 0.306 | 0.209 | 0.572 |
| Course | TeamHITACHI.1 | 0.645 | 0.607 | 0.689 | 0.670 | 0.632 | 0.712 |
| Class | TeamHITACHI.2 | 0.642 | 0.606 | 0.682 | 0.667 | 0.632 | 0.705 |
| | TeamHCMUS.1 | 0.413 | 0.316 | 0.594 | 0.447 | 0.348 | 0.628 |
| | HPI.1 | 0.226 | 0.153 | 0.435 | 0.283 | 0.196 | 0.510 |
| Severity | TeamHITACHI.2 | 0.847 | 0.854 | 0.839 | 0.850 | 0.857 | 0.843 |
| Class | TeamHITACHI.1 | 0.843 | 0.845 | 0.841 | 0.847 | 0.848 | 0.845 |
| | TeamHCMUS.1 | 0.703 | 0.665 | 0.746 | 0.710 | 0.672 | 0.752 |
| | HPI.1 | 0.364 | 0.306 | 0.448 | 0.396 | 0.336 | 0.483 |
| Conditional | TeamHITACHI.1 | 0.638 | 0.744 | 0.559 | 0.801 | 0.869 | 0.743 |
| Class | TeamHITACHI.2 | 0.548 | 0.478 | 0.643 | 0.729 | 0.669 | 0.800 |
| | TeamHCMUS.1 | 0.307 | 0.225 | 0.484 | 0.441 | 0.340 | 0.625 |
| | HPI.1 | 0.100 | 0.059 | 0.315 | 0.317 | 0.209 | 0.658 |
| Generic | TeamHITACHI.1 | 0.225 | 0.239 | 0.213 | 0.304 | 0.320 | 0.289 |
| Class | TeamHITACHI.2 | 0.192 | 0.385 | 0.128 | 0.263 | 0.484 | 0.181 |
| | HPI.1 | 0.100 | 0.058 | 0.380 | 0.139 | 0.081 | 0.470 |
| | TeamHCMUS.1 | 0.000 | 0.000 | 0.000 | 0.000 | 0.000 | 0.000 |
| Body | TeamHITACHI.2 | 0.854 | 0.880 | 0.829 | 0.874 | 0.897 | 0.853 |
| Location | TeamHITACHI.1 | 0.847 | 0.866 | 0.829 | 0.868 | 0.885 | 0.852 |
| | TeamHCMUS.1 | 0.627 | 0.568 | 0.700 | 0.750 | 0.701 | 0.807 |
| | HPI.1 | 0.134 | 0.298 | 0.086 | 0.363 | 0.611 | 0.258 |
| Temporal | TeamHCMUS.1 | 0.287 | 0.313 | 0.265 | 0.354 | 0.383 | 0.329 |
| Expression | TeamHITACHI.2 | 0.275 | 0.226 | 0.354 | 0.370 | 0.310 | 0.458 |
| | TeamHITACHI.1 | 0.269 | 0.217 | 0.356 | 0.364 | 0.300 | 0.461 |
| | HPI.1 | 0.000 | 0.000 | 0.000 | 0.000 | 0.000 | 0.000 |

**Table 7.** Evaluation in Task 3 (a) – part 1; baseline results are also provided. The best P@10 value for each team is emphasised.

| Run ID | P@5 | P@10 | NDCG@5 | NDCG@10 | MAP | rel_ret |
|---|---|---|---|---|---|---|
| baseline.bm25 | 0.6080 | 0.5680 | 0.6023 | 0.5778 | 0.3410 | 2346 |
| baseline.dir | 0.7240 | *0.6800* | 0.6926 | 0.6790 | 0.3789 | 2427 |
| baseline.jm | 0.4400 | 0.4480 | 0.4417 | 0.4510 | 0.2832 | 2399 |
| baseline.tfidf | 0.604 | 0.5760 | 0.5733 | 0.5641 | 0.3137 | 2326 |
| COMPL_EN_Run.1 | 0.5184 | 0.4776 | 0.4896 | 0.4688 | 0.1775 | 1665 |
| COMPL_EN_Run.5 | 0.5640 | *0.5540* | 0.5601 | 0.5471 | 0.2076 | 1828 |
| CUNI_EN_RUN.1 | 0.5240 | 0.5060 | 0.5353 | 0.5189 | 0.3064 | 2562 |
| CUNI_EN_RUN.5 | 0.5320 | *0.5360* | 0.5449 | 0.5408 | 0.3134 | 2556 |
| CUNI_EN_RUN.6 | 0.5080 | 0.5320 | 0.5310 | 0.5395 | 0.2100 | 1832 |
| CUNI_EN_RUN.7 | 0.5120 | 0.4660 | 0.5333 | 0.4878 | 0.1845 | 1676 |
| DEMIR_EN_Run.1 | 0.6720 | 0.6300 | 0.6536 | 0.6321 | 0.3644 | 2479 |
| DEMIR_EN_Run.5 | 0.7080 | 0.6700 | 0.6960 | 0.6719 | 0.3714 | 2493 |
| DEMIR_EN_Run.6 | 0.6840 | *0.6740* | 0.6557 | 0.6518 | 0.3049 | 2281 |
| DEMIR_EN_Run.7 | 0.6880 | 0.6120 | 0.6674 | 0.6211 | 0.3261 | 2404 |
| ERIAS_EN_Run.1 | 0.5040 | 0.5080 | 0.4955 | 0.5023 | 0.3111 | 2537 |
| ERIAS_EN_Run.5 | 0.5440 | 0.5280 | 0.547 | 0.5376 | 0.2217 | 2061 |
| ERIAS_EN_Run.6 | 0.5720 | *0.5460* | 0.5702 | 0.5574 | 0.2315 | 2148 |
| ERIAS_EN_Run.7 | 0.5960 | 0.5320 | 0.5905 | 0.5556 | 0.2333 | 2033 |
| GRIUM_EN_Run.1 | 0.7240 | 0.7180 | 0.7009 | 0.7033 | 0.3945 | 2537 |
| GRIUM_EN_Run.5 | 0.7680 | *0.7560* | 0.7423 | 0.7445 | 0.4016 | 2550 |
| GRIUM_EN_Run.6 | 0.7480 | 0.7120 | 0.7163 | 0.7077 | 0.4007 | 2549 |
| GRIUM_EN_Run.7 | 0.6920 | 0.6540 | 0.6772 | 0.6577 | 0.3495 | 2398 |
| IRLabDAIICT_EN_Run.1 | 0.7120 | *0.7060* | 0.6926 | 0.6869 | 0.4096 | 2503 |
| IRLabDAIICT_EN_Run.2 | 0.7040 | 0.7020 | 0.6862 | 0.6889 | 0.4146 | 2558 |
| IRLabDAIICT_EN_Run.3 | 0.5480 | 0.5640 | 0.5582 | 0.5658 | 0.2507 | 2032 |
| IRLabDAIICT_EN_Run.5 | 0.6680 | 0.6540 | 0.6523 | 0.6363 | 0.3026 | 2250 |
| IRLabDAIICT_EN_Run.6 | 0.7320 | 0.6880 | 0.7174 | 0.6875 | 0.3686 | 2529 |
| IRLabDAIICT_EN_Run.7 | 0.3160 | 0.2940 | 0.3110 | 0.2943 | 0.1736 | 1837 |
| KISTI_EN_Run.1 | 0.7400 | 0.7300 | 0.7195 | 0.7235 | 0.3978 | 2567 |
| KISTI_EN_Run.2 | 0.7320 | *0.7400* | 0.7191 | 0.7301 | 0.3989 | 2567 |
| KISTI_EN_Run.3 | 0.7240 | 0.7160 | 0.7187 | 0.7171 | 0.3959 | 2567 |
| KISTI_EN_Run.4 | 0.7560 | 0.7380 | 0.7390 | 0.7333 | 0.3971 | 2567 |
| KISTI_EN_Run.5 | 0.7440 | 0.7280 | 0.7194 | 0.7211 | 0.3977 | 2567 |
| KISTI_EN_Run.6 | 0.74400 | 0.7240 | 0.7218 | 0.7187 | 0.3971 | 2567 |
| KISTI_EN_Run.7 | 0.7480 | 0.7260 | 0.7271 | 0.7233 | 0.3949 | 2567 |
| miracl_en_run.1 | 0.6080 | *0.5460* | 0.6018 | 0.5625 | 0.1677 | 1189 |

**Table 8.** Evaluation in Task 3 (a) – part 2; baseline results are also provided. The best P@10 team value for each team is emphasised.

| Run ID | P@5 | P@10 | NDCG@5 | NDCG@10 | MAP | rel_ret |
|---|---|---|---|---|---|---|
| NIJM_EN_Run.1 | 0.5400 | 0.5740 | 0.5572 | 0.5708 | 0.3036 | 2330 |
| NIJM_EN_Run.2 | 0.6240 | *0.6180* | 0.6188 | 0.6149 | 0.2825 | 2190 |
| NIJM_EN_Run.3 | 0.5760 | 0.5960 | 0.5594 | 0.5772 | 0.2606 | 2154 |
| NIJM_EN_Run.4 | 0.5760 | 0.5960 | 0.5594 | 0.5772 | 0.2606 | 2154 |
| NIJM_EN_Run.5 | 0.5760 | 0.5880 | 0.5657 | 0.5773 | 0.2609 | 2165 |
| NIJM_EN_Run.6 | 0.5120 | 0.5220 | 0.5332 | 0.5302 | 0.2180 | 1939 |
| NIJM_EN_Run.7 | 0.5120 | 0.5220 | 0.5332 | 0.5302 | 0.2180 | 1939 |
| RePaLi_EN_Run.1 | 0.6980 | 0.6612 | 0.6691 | 0.652 | 0.4054 | 2564 |
| RePaLi_EN_Run.5 | 0.6920 | *0.6740* | 0.6927 | 0.6793 | 0.4021 | 2618 |
| RePaLi_EN_Run.6 | 0.6880 | 0.6600 | 0.6749 | 0.6590 | 0.3564 | 2424 |
| RePaLi_EN_Run.7 | 0.6720 | 0.6320 | 0.6615 | 0.6400 | 0.3453 | 2422 |
| SNUMEDINFO_EN_Run.1 | 0.7720 | 0.7380 | 0.7337 | 0.7238 | 0.3703 | 2305 |
| SNUMEDINFO_EN_Run.2 | 0.7840 | *0.7540* | 0.7502 | 0.7406 | 0.3753 | 2307 |
| SNUMEDINFO_EN_Run.3 | 0.7320 | 0.6940 | 0.7166 | 0.6896 | 0.3671 | 2351 |
| SNUMEDINFO_EN_Run.4 | 0.6880 | 0.6920 | 0.6562 | 0.6679 | 0.3514 | 2302 |
| SNUMEDINFO_EN_Run.5 | 0.8160 | 0.7520 | 0.7749 | 0.7426 | 0.3814 | 2305 |
| SNUMEDINFO_EN_Run.6 | 0.7840 | 0.7420 | 0.7417 | 0.7223 | 0.3655 | 2305 |
| SNUMEDINFO_EN_Run.7 | 0.7920 | 0.7420 | 0.7505 | 0.7264 | 0.3716 | 2305 |
| UHU_EN_Run.1 | 0.5760 | 0.5620 | 0.5602 | 0.5530 | 0.2624 | 2138 |
| UHU_EN_Run.5 | 0.6040 | *0.5860* | 0.6169 | 0.5985 | 0.3152 | 2465 |
| UHU_EN_Run.6 | 0.4880 | 0.5140 | 0.4997 | 0.5163 | 0.2588 | 2364 |
| UHU_EN_Run.7 | 0.5560 | 0.5100 | 0.5378 | 0.5158 | 0.3009 | 2432 |
| UIOWA_EN_Run.1 | 0.6880 | *0.6900* | 0.6705 | 0.6784 | 0.3589 | 2359 |
| UIOWA_EN_Run.5 | 0.6840 | 0.6600 | 0.6579 | 0.6509 | 0.3226 | 2385 |
| UIOWA_EN_Run.6 | 0.6760 | 0.6820 | 0.6380 | 0.6520 | 0.3259 | 2280 |
| UIOWA_EN_Run.7 | 0.7000 | 0.6760 | 0.6777 | 0.6716 | 0.3452 | 2435 |
| YORKU_EN_Run.1 | 0.4640 | 0.4360 | 0.4470 | 0.4305 | 0.1725 | 2296 |
| YORKU_EN_Run.5 | 0.5840 | *0.6040* | 0.5925 | 0.5999 | 0.3207 | 2549 |
| YORKU_EN_Run.6 | 0.0640 | 0.0600 | 0.0566 | 0.0560 | 0.0625 | 2531 |
| YORKU_EN_Run.7 | 0.0480 | 0.0680 | 0.0417 | 0.0578 | 0.0548 | 2194 |

**Table 9.** Evaluation in Task 3 (b). Results for the cross lingual submissions are reported along with the corresponding English results. The best P@10 for each team-language is emphasised.

| Run ID | P@5 | P@10 | NDCG@5 | NDCG@10 | MAP | rel_ret |
|---|---|---|---|---|---|---|
| CUNI_EN_RUN.1 | 0.5240 | 0.5060 | 0.5353 | 0.5189 | 0.3064 | 2562 |
| CUNI_EN_RUN.5 | 0.5320 | *0.5360* | 0.5449 | 0.5408 | 0.3134 | 2556 |
| CUNI_EN_RUN.6 | 0.5080 | 0.5320 | 0.5310 | 0.5395 | 0.2100 | 1832 |
| CUNI_EN_RUN.7 | 0.5120 | 0.4660 | 0.5333 | 0.4878 | 0.1845 | 1676 |
| CUNI_CS_RUN.1 | 0.4400 | 0.4340 | 0.4361 | 0.4335 | 0.2151 | 1965 |
| CUNI_CS_RUN.5 | 0.4920 | *0.4880* | 0.4830 | 0.4810 | 0.2399 | 2112 |
| CUNI_CS_RUN.6 | 0.4680 | 0.4560 | 0.4928 | 0.4746 | 0.1573 | 1591 |
| CUNI_CS_RUN.7 | 0.3360 | 0.3020 | 0.3534 | 0.3213 | 0.1095 | 1186 |
| CUNI_DE_RUN.1 | 0.3837 | 0.400 | 0.3561 | 0.3681 | 0.1872 | 1806 |
| CUNI_DE_RUN.5 | 0.4160 | *0.4280* | 0.3963 | 0.4058 | 0.2014 | 1935 |
| CUNI_DE_RUN.6 | 0.3880 | 0.3820 | 0.4125 | 0.4024 | 0.1348 | 1517 |
| CUNI_DE_RUN.7 | 0.3520 | 0.3200 | 0.3590 | 0.3330 | 0.1308 | 1556 |
| CUNI_FR_RUN.1 | 0.4640 | 0.4720 | 0.4611 | 0.4675 | 0.2344 | 2056 |
| CUNI_FR_RUN.5 | 0.4840 | *0.4840* | 0.4766 | 0.4776 | 0.2398 | 2064 |
| CUNI_FR_RUN.6 | 0.4600 | 0.4560 | 0.4772 | 0.4699 | 0.1703 | 1531 |
| CUNI_FR_RUN.7 | 0.3520 | 0.3240 | 0.3759 | 0.3520 | 0.1300 | 1313 |
| SNUMEDINFO_EN_Run.1 | 0.7720 | 0.7380 | 0.7337 | 0.7238 | 0.3703 | 2305 |
| SNUMEDINFO_EN_Run.5 | 0.8160 | *0.7520* | 0.7749 | 0.7426 | 0.3814 | 2305 |
| SNUMEDINFO_EN_Run.6 | 0.7840 | 0.7420 | 0.7417 | 0.7223 | 0.3655 | 2305 |
| SNUMEDINFO_EN_Run.7 | 0.7920 | 0.7420 | 0.7505 | 0.7264 | 0.3716 | 2305 |
| SNUMEDINFO_CZ_Run.1 | 0.7837 | 0.7367 | 0.7128 | 0.6940 | 0.3473 | 2147 |
| SNUMEDINFO_CZ_Run.5 | 0.7592 | *0.7551* | 0.6998 | 0.7011 | 0.3494 | 2147 |
| SNUMEDINFO_CZ_Run.6 | 0.7388 | 0.7469 | 0.6834 | 0.6871 | 0.3395 | 2147 |
| SNUMEDINFO_CZ_Run.7 | 0.7510 | 0.7367 | 0.6949 | 0.6891 | 0.3447 | 2147 |
| SNUMEDINFO_DE_Run.1 | 0.7673 | *0.7388* | 0.6986 | 0.6874 | 0.3184 | 2087 |
| SNUMEDINFO_DE_Run.5 | 0.7388 | 0.7347 | 0.6839 | 0.6790 | 0.3222 | 2087 |
| SNUMEDINFO_DE_Run.6 | 0.7429 | 0.7286 | 0.6825 | 0.6716 | 0.3144 | 2087 |
| SNUMEDINFO_DE_Run.7 | 0.7388 | 0.7122 | 0.6866 | 0.6645 | 0.3184 | 2087 |
| SNUMEDINFO_FR_Run.1 | 0.7673 | 0.7429 | 0.7168 | 0.7077 | 0.3412 | 2175 |
| SNUMEDINFO_FR_Run.5 | 0.7633 | *0.7469* | 0.7242 | 0.7090 | 0.344 | 2175 |
| SNUMEDINFO_FR_Run.6 | 0.7592 | 0.7306 | 0.7121 | 0.6940 | 0.3320 | 2175 |
| SNUMEDINFO_FR_Run.7 | 0.7469 | 0.7327 | 0.7078 | 0.6956 | 0.3363 | 2175 |

## 4　Conclusions

In this paper we provided an overview of the second year of the ShARe/CLEF eHealth evaluation lab. The lab aims to support the continuum of care by developing methods and resources that make clinical reports and related medical conditions easier to understand for patients. The focus on patients' information needs as opposed to the specialised information needs of healthcare workers is the main distinguishing feature of the lab from previous shared tasks on NLP, ML and IR in the space. Building on the first year of the lab which contained three tasks focusing on information extraction from clinical reports and a mono-lingual information retrieval, this years edition featured an information visualisation challenge, further information extraction challenges and multi-lingual information retrieval. Specifically this year's three tasks comprised: 1) Visual-Interactive Search and Exploration of eHealth Data; 2) Information extraction from clinical text; and 3) User-centred health information retrieval. The lab attracted much interest with 24 teams from around the world submitting a combined total of 105 systems to the shared tasks. Given the significance of the tasks, all test collections, etc associated with the lab have been made available to the wider research community.

**Acknowledgement.** The ShARe/CLEF eHealth 2014 evaluation lab has been supported in part by (in alphabetical order) MIMIC II Database; NICTA, funded by the Australian Government through the Department of Communications and the Australian Research Council through the ICT Centre of Excellence Program; PhysioNetWorks Workspaces; the CLEF Initiative; the Khresmoi project, funded by the European Union Seventh Framework Programme (FP7/2007-2013) under grant agreement no 257528; the ShARe project funded by the United States National Institutes of Health (R01GM090187); the US Office of the National Coordinator of Healthcare Technology, Strategic Health IT Advanced Research Projects (SHARP) 90TR0002; and the Swedish Research Council (350-2012-6658).

We acknowledge the generous support of time and expertise that the evaluation panelists (Chih-Hao (Justin) Ku, Assistant Professor in Text mining and information visualization, Lawrence Technological University, Southfield, MI, USA; Hilary Cinis, Senior User Experience Designer, NICTA, Sydney, NSW, Australia; Lin Shao, PhD student, in Computer and Information Science, University of Konstanz, Konstanz, Germany; and Mitchell Whitelaw, Associate Professor in Media Arts and Production, University of Canberra, Canberra ACT, Australia), annotators as well as members of the organising and mentoring committees have invested in this evaluation lab. We also acknowledge the contribution of George Moody, Harvard-MIT, Cambridge, MA, USA in proofing and supporting the release of our six double de-identified (manually and automatically) discharge summaries.

# References

1. Suominen, H., et al.: Overview of the shARe/CLEF eHealth evaluation lab 2013. In: Forner, P., Müller, H., Paredes, R., Rosso, P., Stein, B. (eds.) CLEF 2013. LNCS, vol. 8138, pp. 212–231. Springer, Heidelberg (2013)
2. Pradhan, S., Elhadad, N., South, B., Martinez, D., Christensen, L., Vogel, A., Suominen, H., Chapman, W., Savova, G.: Task 1: ShARe/CLEF eHealth Evaluation Lab 2013. In: Online Working Notes of CLEF, CLEF (2013)
3. Mowery, D., South, B., Christensen, L., Murtola, L., Salanterä, S., Suominen, H., Martinez, D., Elhadad, N., Pradhan, S., Savova, G., Chapman, W.: Task 2: ShARe/CLEF eHealth Evaluation Lab 2013. In: Online Working Notes of CLEF, CLEF (2013)
4. Goeuriot, L., Jones, G., Kelly, L., Leveling, J., Hanbury, A., Müller, H., Salanterä, S., Suominen, H., Zuccon, G.: ShARe/CLEF eHealth Evaluation Lab 2013, Task 3: Information retrieval to address patients' questions when reading clinical reports. In: Online Working Notes of CLEF, CLEF (2013)
5. Suominen, H., Schreck, T., Leroy, G., Hochheiser, H., Goeuriot, L., Kelly, L., Mowery, D., Nualart, J., Ferraro, G., Keim, D.: Task 1 of the CLEF eHealth Evaluation Lab 2014: visual-interactive search and exploration of eHealth data. In: CLEF 2014 Evaluation Labs and Workshop: Online Working Notes, Sheffield, UK (2014)
6. Mowery, D., Velupillai, S., South, B., Christensen, L., Martinez, D., Kelly, L., Goeuriot, L., Elhadad, N., Pradhan, S., Savova, G., Chapman, W.: Task 2 of the CLEF eHealth Evaluation Lab 2014: Information extraction from clinical text. In: CLEF 2014 Evaluation Labs and Workshop: Online Working Notes, Sheffield, UK (2014)
7. Goeuriot, L., Kelly, L., Lee, W., Palotti, J., Pecina, P., Zuccon, G., Hanbury, A., Gareth, J.F., Jones, H.M.: ShARe/CLEF eHealth Evaluation Lab 2014, Task 3: User-centred health information retrieval. In: CLEF 2014 Evaluation Labs and Workshop: Online Working Notes, Sheffield, UK (2014)
8. Hanbury, A., Müller, H.: Khresmoi – multimodal multilingual medical information search. In: MIE Village of the Future (2012)
9. Koopman, B., Zuccon, G.: Relevation! an open source system for information retrieval relevance assessment. arXiv preprint (2013)
10. Salton, G., Wong, A., Yang, C.S.: A vector space model for automatic indexing. Communications of the ACM 18(11), 613–620 (1975)
11. Robertson, S.E., Jones, S.: Simple, proven approaches to text retrieval. Technical Report 356, University of Cambridge (1994)
12. Smucker, M., Allan, J., Carterette, B.: A comparison of statistical significance tests for information retrieval evaluation. In: Proceedings of the 16th ACM Conference on Information and Knowledge Management (CIKM 2007), pp. 623–632 (2007)
13. Järvelin, K., Kekäläinen, J.: Cumulated gain-based evaluation of IR techniques. ACM Transactions on Information Systems 20(4), 422–446 (2002)

# ImageCLEF 2014: Overview and Analysis of the Results

Barbara Caputo[1], Henning Müller[2], Jesus Martinez-Gomez[3],
Mauricio Villegas[4], Burak Acar[5], Novi Patricia[6], Neda Marvasti[5],
Suzan Üsküdarlı[5], Roberto Paredes[4], Miguel Cazorla[7], Ismael Garcia-Varea[3],
and Vicente Morell[7]

[1] University of Rome La Sapienza, Italy
[2] University of Applied Sciences Western Switzerland in Sierre, Switzerland
[3] University of Castilla-La Mancha, Spain
[4] PRHLT, Universitat Politècnica de València, Spain
[5] Bogazici University, Turkey
[6] Idiap Research Institute, Switzerland
[7] University of Alicante, Spain

**Abstract.** This paper presents an overview of the ImageCLEF 2014 evaluation lab. Since its first edition in 2003, ImageCLEF has become one of the key initiatives promoting the benchmark evaluation of algorithms for the annotation and retrieval of images in various domains, such as public and personal images, to data acquired by mobile robot platforms and medical archives. Over the years, by providing new data collections and challenging tasks to the community of interest, the ImageCLEF lab has achieved an unique position in the image annotation and retrieval research landscape. The 2014 edition consists of four tasks: domain adaptation, scalable concept image annotation, liver CT image annotation and robot vision. This paper describes the tasks and the 2014 competition, giving a unifying perspective of the present activities of the lab while discussing future challenges and opportunities.

## 1 Introduction

Since its first edition in 2003, the ImageCLEF lab has aimed at providing an evaluation forum for the language independent annotation and retrieval of images [19]. Motivated by the need to support multilingual users from a global community accessing the ever growing body of visual information, the main goal of ImageCLEF is to support the advancement of the field of visual media analysis, indexing, classification and retrieval by developing the necessary infrastructure for the evaluation of visual systems operating in monolingual, language-independent and multi-modal contexts, providing reusable resources for benchmarking. To meet its objectives, ImageCLEF organises tasks that benchmark the annotation and retrieval of diverse images such as general photographic, medical images and adapting knowledge across different domains, as well as domain-specific tasks such as robot vision. These tasks aim to support

E. Kanoulas et al. (Eds.): CLEF 2014, LNCS 8685, pp. 192–211, 2014.

and promote research that addresses key challenges in the field. ImageCLEF has had a significant influence on the visual information retrieval field by benchmarking various retrieval and annotation tasks and by making available the large and realistic test collections built in the context of its activities. Many research groups have participated over the years in its evaluation campaigns and even more have acquired its datasets for experimentation. The impact of ImageCLEF can also be seen by its significant scholarly impact indicated by the substantial numbers of its publications and their received citations [32].

The remainder of this paper is organized as follows: section 2 describes the four subtasks of the 2014 edition: the domain adaptation task (section 2.1), the scalable concept image annotation task (section 2.2), the liver CT image annotation task (section 2.3) and the robot vision task (section 2.4). We conclude with an overall discussion, and pointing towards the challenges ahead and possible new directions for ImageCLEF 2015.

## 2  ImageCLEF 2014: The Tasks, The Data and Participation

The 2014 edition of ImageCLEF consisted of four main tasks: the domain adaptation task, the scalable concept image annotation task, the liver CT image annotation task and the robot vision task. These tasks had the goal to benchmark the annotation and retrieval of diverse images such as general photographic, as well as domain-specific tasks such as liver CT annotation and robot vision. The overall aim is to support and promote research that addresses key challenges in the field including:

- visual image annotation with concepts at various levels of abstraction that relies not only on manual and thus reliable training data but also on automatically acquirednand thus noisy labelled samples,
- scientific multimedia data management through the particular case of liver CT image annotation,
- the ability of generic annotation algorithms to adapt robustly and effectively across domains, and
- the shift in the area of robot vision from visual place recognition to multimodal place recognition.

In the rest of the section, we give an overview account, for each task, of its historical perspective within ImageCLEF and/or within the state of the art in each respective field, of its 2014 objective and task, and of the task participation and relative results.

### 2.1  Domain Adaptation Task

The amount of freely available and annotated image collections has dramatically increased over the last years, thanks to the diffusion of high-quality cameras and also to the introduction of new and cheap annotation tools such as Mechanical

Turk. Attempts to leverage over and across such large data sources has proved challenging. Indeed, tools like Google Goggle are able to relaibly recognize limited classes of objects like books or wine labels, but are not able to generalize across generic objects like food items, clothing items and so on. Several authors showed that, for a given task, training on a dataset (e.g. Pascal VOC 07) and testing on another (e.g. ImageNet) produces very poor results, although the set of depicted object categories is the same [26,31]. In other words, existing object categorization methods do not generalize well across databases.

This problem is known in the literature as the domain adaptation challenge. Addressing this issue would have a tremendous impact on the generality and adaptability of any vision-based annotation system. Current research in domain adaptation focuses on a scenario where

- (a) the prior domain (source) consists of one or a maximum of two databases;
- (b) the labels between the source and the target domain are the same, and
- (c) the number of annotated training data for the target domain are limited.

The goal of the Domain Adaptation Task, initiated in 2014 under the Image-CLEF umbrella [2], is to push the state of the art in domain adaptation towards more realistic settings, relaxing these assumptions. Our ambition is to provide, over the years, stimulating problems and challenging data collections that might stimulate and support novel research in the field.

**Objective and Task for the 2014 Edition.** In the 2014 version (first edition) of the Domain Adaptation Task, we focused on the number of sources available to the system. Current experimental settings, widely used in the community, consider typically one source and one target [26], or at most two sources and one target [9,30]. This scenario is unrealistic: with the wide abundance of annotated resources and data collections that are made available to users, and with the fast progress that is being made in the image annotation community, it is likely that systems will be able to access more and more databases and therefore to leverage over a much larger number of sources than two, as considered in the most challenging settings today.

To push research towards more realistic scenarios, the 2014 edition of the domain adaptation task has proposed an experimental setup with four sources, where such sources were built by exploiting existing available resources. Participants were thus requested to build recognition systems for the target classes by leveraging over such source knowledge. We considered a semi-supervised setting, i.e. a setting where the target data, for each class, is limited but annotated.

Specifically, to define the source and target data, we considered five publicly available databases:

- the *Caltech-256* database, consisting of 256 object categories, with a total of 30.607 images;
- the *ImageNet ILSVRC2012* database, organized according to the WordNet hierarchy, with an average of 500 images per node;

- the *PASCAL VOC2012* database, an image data set for object class recognition with 20 object classes;
- the *Bing* database, containing all 256 categories from the Caltech-256 one, and augmented with 300 web images per category that were collected through textual search using Bing;
- and the *SUN* database, a scene understanding database that contains 899 categories and 130.519 images.

We then selected twelve classes, common to all the datasets listed above: aeroplane, bike, bird, boat, bottle, bus, car, dog, horse, monitor, motorbike, and people. Figure 1 illustrates the images contained for each class in each of the considered datasets. As sources, we considered 50 images represented the classes listed above from the databases Caltech-256, ImageNet, PASCAL and Bing. The 50 images were randomly selected from all those contained in each of the data collection, for a total of 600 images for each source. As target, we used images taken from the SUN database for each class. We randomly selected 5 images per class for training, and 50 images per class for testing. These data were given to all participants as validation set. The test set consisted of 50 images for each class, for a total of 600, manually collected by us using the class names as textual queries with standard search engines.

Instead of making the images directly available to participants, we decided to release pre-computed features only, in order to keep the focus on the learning aspects of the algorithms in this year's competition. Thus, we represented every image with dense SIFT descriptors (PHOW features) at points on a regular grid with spacing 128 pixels [1]. At each grid point the descriptors were computed over four patches with different radii, hence each point was represented by four SIFT descriptors. The dense features have been vector quantized into 256 visual words using k-means clustering on a randomly chosen subset of the Caltech-256 database. Finally, all images were converted to $2 \times 2$ spatial histograms over the 256 visual words, resulted in 1024 feature dimension. The software used for computing such features is available at www.vlfeat.org.

**Participation and Results.** While 19 groups registered to the domain adaptation task to receive access to the training and validation data, only 3 groups eventually submitted runs: the XRCE group, the Hubert Curien Lab group and the Idiap group (organizers). They submitted the following algorithms:

- the XRCE group submitted a set of methods based on several heterogeneous methods for domain adaptation, of which predictions were subsequently fused. By combining the output of instance based approaches and metric learning one with a brute force SVM prediction, they obtained a set of heterogeneous classifiers all producing class prediction for the target domain instances. These were combined through different versions of majority voting in order to improve the overall accuracy.
- The Hubert Curien Lab group did not submit any working notes, neither sent any detail about their algorithm. We are therefore not able to describe it.

**Fig. 1.** Exemplar images for the 12 classes from the five selected public databases

– The Idiap group submitted a baseline run using a recently introduced learning to learn algorithm [21]. The approach considers source classifiers as experts, and it combines their confidence output with a high-level cue integration scheme, as opposed to a mid-level one as proposed in [10]. The algorithm is called High-level Learning to Learn (H-L2L). As our goal was not to obtain the best possible performance but rather to provide an off the shelf baseline against which to compare results of the other participants, we did not perform any parameter tuning.

Table 1 reports the final ranking among groups. We see that XRCE obtained the best score, followed by the Hubert Curien lab. The Idiap baseline obtained the worst score, clearly pointing towards the importance of parameter selection in these kind of benchmark evaluations.

For the complete results, details and analysis, please refer to the task overview paper [3].

## 2.2   Scalable Concept Image Annotation Task

Automatic concept detection within images is a challenging research problem, and as of today unsolved. Despite considerable research efforts the so-called semantic gap has not been successfully breached, in terms of being able to detect semantic concepts within any kind of imagery for any kind of concept as accurately as humans can. Furthermore, the greatest achievements in this research area are characterized by the reliance on clean hand labeled training data, a fact that greatly limits the scalability of the developed approaches. ImageCLEF's Scalable Concept Image Annotation task aims to advance the state of the art in image concept detection by acting as a platform to foster interaction and collaboration between researchers and by providing a realistic and challenging benchmark with a particular incentive for the development of technologies that are able to scale concept-wise without the requirement of large amounts of human effort.

**Past Editions.** The Scalable Concept Image Annotation task is a continuation of the general image annotation and retrieval task that has been part of ImageCLEF since its very first edition in 2003. In the early years the focus was on retrieving relevant images from a web collection given (multilingual) queries, while from 2006 onwards annotation tasks were also held, initially aimed at object detection, but more recently also covering semantic concepts. In its current form, the 2014 Scalable Concept Image Annotation task is its third edition, having been organized in 2012 [35] and 2013 [37] as subtasks of the the general image annotation and retrieval task. This is the first year in which this scalable annotation aimed benchmark has been organized as a standalone main task.

**Objective and Task for the 2014 Edition.** Image concept detection generally has relied on training data that has been manually, and thus reliably annotated, an expensive and laborious endeavor that cannot easily scale, particularly as the number of concepts grow. However, images for any topic can be cheaply gathered from the web, along with associated text from the webpages that contain the images. The degree of relationship between these web images and the surrounding text varies greatly, i.e., the data is very noisy, but overall this data contains useful information that can be exploited to develop annotation systems. Figure 2 shows examples of typical images found by querying search engines. As can be seen, the data obtained are useful and furthermore a wider variety of images is expected, not only photographs, but also drawings and computer generated graphics. Likewise there are other resources available that can help to determine the relationships between text and semantic concepts, such as dictionaries or ontologies.

**Table 1.** Ranking and best score obtained by the three groups that submitted runs

| Rank | Group | Score |
|------|-------|-------|
| 1 | XRCE | 228 |
| 2 | Hubert Curien Lab Group | 158 |
| 3 | Idiap | 45 |

(a) Images from a search query of "rainbow"

(b) Images from a search query of "sun".

**Fig. 2.** Example of images retrieved by a commercial image search engine

The goal of this task was to evaluate different strategies to deal with the noisy data so that it can be reliably used for annotating images from practically any topic. Participants were provided with a training set composed of images and corresponding webpage text, and for the given development/test set they had to detect the corresponding concepts for each image using only the input image, the provided training set, other similar image datasets and any other automatically obtained resources. There were several differences in this task with respect to the previous edition. First the list of concepts to detect was increased from 116 to 207, but most importantly the concepts in the test set not seen during development increased from 21 to 100. Another difference was that each image of the test set had its own list of concepts to detect, so not all images had to be annotated for the 207 concepts. This permitted among other things to have exactly the same 2013 test set as a subset, and also to have subsets of images in which all of the concepts to detect were not seen during development. A final difference to mention was that the amount of training data provided was doubled.

The data used in this task was similar to the one from last year [37], in fact half of the training data provided were exactly the same. The training set was composed of 500,000 samples each of which included: the raw image, seven types of precomputed visual features and four types of textual features. These training images were obtained from the web by querying popular image search engines. The development and test sets had 1,940 and 7,291 samples, respectively, which only included the visual features and the corresponding hand labeled concepts ground truth. The ground truth for the test set was not released, it was kept secret so that the participants had to submit the annotation results which were then analyzed by the task organizers. For further details, please refer to the task overview paper [36].

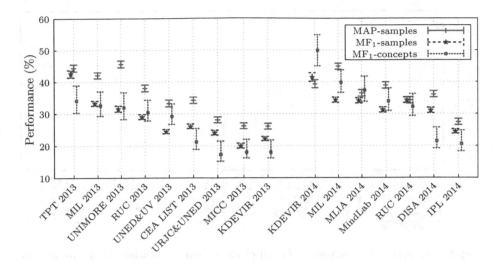

**Fig. 3.** The three performance measures for the best submission of each group for both this and last year's edition of the task. The results for both years are for the same test set (since the 2013 test set was included this year as a subset). Error bars correspond to the 95% confidence intervals computed using Wilson's method.

**Participation and Results.** Generally speaking, the participation was excellent, although there was a slight decrease in participation with respect to last year. In total, 11 groups took part in the task and submitted overall 58 system runs. Among the 11 participating groups, only 7 submitted a working notes paper, thus only for these there were specific details of their systems available. Last year the participation was 13 groups, 58 runs and 9 papers.

Last year it was decided that the ground truth for the test set would not be released, so that the same data could be reused every year and be able to observe the evolution of the developed systems overtime. Figure 3 presents the results, both for this and last year's edition of the task, in each case for the best system of each group that submitted a paper. The graph includes the three performance measures that were used to judge the systems, which were: the Mean Average Precision (MAP) computed for the samples, and the mean $F_1$-measure computed both for the samples and for the concepts. In the figure it can be observed that in general this year the participants obtained better systems, most of them achieving performances over 30% for the three measures.

One shortcoming found last year was that the number of concepts in the test set not seen during development was too small, so when comparing the performance of the different systems the confidence intervals were too wide, making it difficult to derive adequate conclusions. For this reason, an objective for this year was to increase the number of unseen concepts, and thus these were the most interesting results obtained this year, which are presented in Figure 4. In these results it can be clearly observed which systems outperform the others.

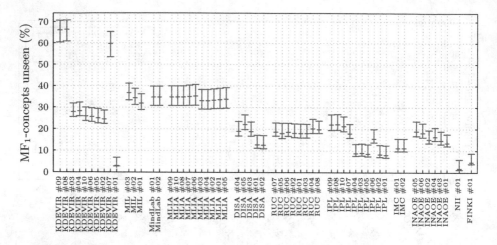

**Fig. 4.** The results for the test set for all of the submissions using the MF$_1$-concepts performance measure although only considering the concepts that were not seen during development. Error bars correspond to the 95% confidence intervals computed using Wilson's method.

Last year the best team TPT [27] obtained very good results by using learning techniques that take into account context, effectively finding a way to exploit the information available in the noisy webpage data. This year the best team KDEVIR [25] decided to follow the same line as TPT, however, on top of that they have developed techniques for automatically building ontologies for the concepts and using these both in training phase for better selecting the images used for optimizing the classifiers and in the testing phase for taking into account the relationships between the concepts.

It is curious to observe that the performance of the best system is significantly better for the unseen concepts ($\approx 65\%$) than overall ($\approx 50\%$). This is possibly because the unseen concepts are relatively easier, however when comparing with other systems it can indicate the importance of using automatically generated ontologies in this challenge.

For the complete results, details and analysis, please refer to the task overview paper [36].

## 2.3   Liver CT Image Annotation Task

Medical images present unique challenges in comparison to other images. A significant part of the medical image analysis tasks deal with a set of rather similar images, such as abdominal CT images, where the analysis is based on subtle differences between images. In a conventional setting, these subtle differences, such as the texture observed in the parenchyma of a liver, are observed by experts and translated into the medical vocabulary using medical terminology that constitutes image anotation. An annotation facilitates the high-level processing and communication of medical evidence derived from the images. In recognition of its importance, several standard terminologies are being developed/used, such as SNOMED-CT[1] (Systemized Nomenclature in Medicine), RadLex[2] (Radiology Lexicon), NCBO[3], UMLS[4] (Unified Medical Language System), etc. Despite its advantages, an expert annotation is a labor intensive task that can be performed by qualified individuals only and must be consistent among different individuals, sites, countries, etc. Hence, a key challenge in expert annotation is to translate computer generated objective low-level image observations (CoG) to high level semantic descriptions (ie. annotations) that comply with a standard terminology of choice. Such an automatic medical image annotation system can facilitate effective multi-site communication of medical information, semantic search and retrieval in (multi-site) medical databases, human-interpretable computer aided diagnosis, computer aided reporting, etc. The "Liver CT Image Annotation Task", introduced for the first time in ImageCLEF 2014, focused on the aforementioned challenge and is restricted to the liver CT image annotation, as a pilot application domain.

**Previous Work.** The automatic image annotation methods in the literature can be categorized as the classification based approaches [38] and the Bayesian methods [34]. In the classification based approaches, the annotation problems is addressed as a multi-class classification problem. Here, every semantic concept is treated as a class and a set of binary classification models are used to give yes-or-no votes. Conventional classifiers for this task include Support Vector Machines (SVM), Artificial Neural Networks (ANN), Decision Trees (DT), and Random Forest(RF). The majority of the proposed systems fall in this category. Shi et al.[29] trained an SVM with radial basis function kernel to annotate a set of images. They trained the SVM classifiers using the image features for every concept. Each classifier generates a probability value, fused with other SVM outputs producing the final label of that feature by applying majority voting. Goh et al. [8] pursued a similar approach and used a 3-level model to annotate a set of images. They used different sets of classifiers, estimated the decision for each set using majority voting and finally fused all decisions to get the final label. Qj et al. [24] have also used a three level classifier for two sets of SVM classifiers. The first group uses global features and the second group employs local features. Mueen et al. [18] have implemented the annotation using three-hierarchy-level SVM classification on X-ray images. Devrim et al. [33] used two approaches to automatically annotate X-ray images. In the first approach, they used a single SVM with 1-vs-all multi-class model and Gaussian radial basis function. In the second approach, they used separate SVM classifiers for each label and finally fused their classification results. Frat et al. [5] , Kim et al. [11], and Park et al. [20] have employed ANN to perform automatic image annotation. Data training

---

[1] http://www.ihtsdo.org/snomed-ct/

[2] http://www.radlex.org

[3] http://www.bioontology.org

[4] http://www.nlm.nih.gov/research/umls/

with ANN algorithms is time-consuming, but they can learn multiple classes simultaneuously. The number of layers and nodes of ANNs influence the performance. DT was employed by Friedl M.A. et al. [7], Wong R.C.F et al. [39], and Sethi I.K. et al. [28] to annotate land covers in the remote sensed data, real-world web images, and outdoor images into semantic concepts, respectively. A DT is a multi-stage decision making / classification tool, in which we have a set of root nodes, a set of terminal nodes, and a set of leaf nodes. DT divides the data into smaller non-overlapping subsets, according to if-then-rules. Byoung et al. [12] used a combination of RFs and wavelet-based center symmetric-local binary patterns for medical image classification to perform multiple keyword annotations. It has been shown that classification using RFs is much faster than SVMs. Bayesian probability rules can also be used to classify and annotate images. Particularly, in the training step the conditional probability of an image, being labeled by every class, is calculated using some parametric [40],[6] or non-parametric [34] methods. Then in test phase, the class/label of the image is defined by maximizing the posterior (MAP) criterion.

**Objective and Task for the 2014 Edition.** The participants were given a training set of 50 cropped liver CT images together with the liver, vessel and lesion masks, a set of 60 computer generated features (CoG) and a set of 73 manual semantic annotations (UsE) regarding the liver, the vessels and one selected lesion. The UsE features were generated by an expert radiologist as part of the CaReRa[5] (Case Retrieval in Radiology) project, using the opensource ONLIRA (Ontology Of Liver For Radiology) [13]. The test set had 10 cases, with all types of data available in the training set except the UsE features. The particpants were asked to estimate the missing 73 UsE features. They were allowed to use any subset or superset of the provided CoG features, giving them the option to compute and use any additional low-level features that they may extract from the CT images and the masks. The evaluation was based on the *Completeness* (defined as the percentage of all 73 UsE features that were estimated) and *Accuracy* (defined as the percentage of the estimated UsE features that were correct), geometric mean of which was used as the *Total Score*. Ideally, all metrics would be 1.00.

**Participation and Results.** Three groups participated in this task: BMET (University of Sydney), CASMIP (The Hebrew University of Jerusalem), piLab-VAVlab (Bogaziçi University).

Table 2 lists the results of all runs submitted. compares the results of different runs in predicting different groups of UsE features. We divide UsE features into 5 groups: liver, vessels and three lesion groups with area, lesion and component concepts. Results show that most of the methods predicted the vessel UsE features completely.

---

[5] TUBITAK-ARDEB grant no 110E264, PI: Burak Acar, PhD.
   http://www.vavlab.ee.boun.edu.tr/pages.php?p=research/CARERA/carera.html

**Table 2.** Results of the runs of Liver CT annotation task. CoG: The provided CoG features. CoG+: The extended set of CoG feature (Each group, when applicable, used a their own extension which is explained in the text). SVM: Support Vector Machine. IR-(no)FS: Image Retrieval w/o Feature Selection. TF: Tensor Factorization

| Group name | Run | Completeness | Accuracy | Total Score | method used | feature used |
|---|---|---|---|---|---|---|
| BMET | run1 | 0.98 | 0.89 | 0.935 | SVM-linear | CoG |
| BMET | run2 | 0.98 | 0.90 | 0.939 | SVM-linear | CoG+ |
| BMET | run3 | 0.98 | 0.89 | 0.933 | SVM-RBF | CoG |
| BMET | run4 | 0.98 | 0.90 | 0.939 | SVM-RBF | CoG+ |
| BMET | run5 | 0.98 | 0.91 | 0.947 | IR-noFS | CoG |
| BMET | run6 | 0.98 | 0.87 | 0.927 | IR-noFS | CoG+ |
| BMET | run7 | 0.98 | 0.91 | 0.947 | IR-FS | CoG |
| BMET | run8 | 0.98 | 0.87 | 0.926 | IR-FS | CoG+ |
| CASMIP | run1 | 0.95 | 0.91 | 0.93 | LDA+KNN | CoG+ |
| piLabVAVlab | run1 | 0.51 | 0.39 | 0.45 | TF-KL | CoG |
| piLabVAVlab | run2 | 0.51 | 0.89 | 0.677 | TF-EUC | CoG |
| piLabVAVlab | run3 | 0.51 | 0.88 | 0.676 | TF-KL | CoG |

The BMET group pursued two approaches: The classifier based approach and the retrieval based approach. They repeated all experiments with the provided CoG features and with an extended set of features where they added the bag of visual words (BoWD) to the CoG set. The classification based approach utilized a bank of SVMs, one for each UsE feature to be predicted, in two stages. The first stage used 1-vs-all classifiers, where, for a given concept, each label is learned against all other possible labels of that concept. In case the first stage cannot identify a single label, the second stage is applied where 1-vs-1 classifiers are used to break the tie. Linear and RBF kernels are used in the SVM classifiers. The retrieval based approach aimed at identifying $n$ ($n = 10$) taining cases that are closest to the test case in terms of the Euclidean distance in the feature space. A weighted voting scheme is applied to determine the UsE features of the test case using those of the identified training cases. The retrieval is applied with and without feature selection. Extending the CoG feature set did not improve the results significantly, it even decreased accuracy in the retrieval based approach. On the other hand, the retrieval based approach performed better than the classification based one.

The CASMIP group pursued a classification based approach in a lower dimensional feature space. They excluded 21 CoG features but added 9 new features describing the gray level of liver, lesion and the lesion boundary. They used 4 different classifiers in their experiments: Linear Discriminant Analysis (LDA), Logistic Regression (LR), K-Nearest Neighbours (KNN) and Support Vector Machines (SVM). All classifiers are trained on individual UsE features to be predicted and the best performing one of the 4 classifiers, is chosen for each UsE features separately. It turned out that LDA and KNN were the best performing classifiers for the majority of UsE features. Cluster_Size, Lesion_Lobe and Lesion_Segment were deterministically determined from the CoG features.

The piLabVAVlab group pursued a drastically different approach and assessed the use of Generalized Coupled Tensor Factorization (GCTF) [41]. The GCTF is a general framework where a high order tensor representation of the conditional probabilities (between CoG and UsE features) are used. KL-divergence and Euclidean distance is used in the tensor factorization problem modeling. Though the input UsE features are categorical, the output of GCTF is real valued, hence the method requires approapriate thresholding, which affects the results (as seen among different runs of this group). Furthermore, the piLabVAVlab group attempted to predict only the UsE features with 4 or 2 labels (categories), which set their completeness upper limit to 0.51. Their accuracy was not significantly different than the other groups', suggesting the GCTF as a promising method, which is totally blind to the domain knowledge.

Despite the small dataset size, the "Liver CT Image Annotation Task", introduced this year, demonstrated the feasibility of automatic medical image annotation from low level image features by means of retrieval, supervised machine learning and GCTF. None of the methods, specifically the GCTF, utilized the domain knowledge as represented with an ontology. It can be conjectured that using the domain knowledge would improve the results even further, paving the way for automatic radiology reporting and semantic search using low-level image features.

## 2.4    Robot Vision Task

The Robot Vision task addresses two problems in parallel: room classification and object recognition. Participants of the challenge are asked to classify rooms on the basis of visual and depth images captured by a Kinect sensor mounted on a mobile robot. Moreover, participants are also asked to detect the appearance or lack of a list of previously defined objects.

**Past Editions.** The first edition of the Robot Vision task started in 2009 [22], and since its origin, it has addressed the problem of place classification with application to robotics. This problem consists in answering the question "where am I?" from a semantic point of view. That is, using semantic information like I am in the office instead of metric one.

The procedure of the task has maintained similar from the first edition. Firstly, the organizers define the problem, the performance evaluation procedure, and release images annotated with semantic information for training. Participants are then expected to start developing their proposals using the provided information. Some time later, an annotated validation sequence is released. This sequence allows participants to estimate whether their algorithms perform well when facing new images not previously seen. Finally, an unannotated test sequence is released and participants have some days to process it. As a result of this processing, a submission file with the obtained annotations has to be uploaded. All the participant submissions are then evaluated (using the previously presented procedure) and ranked to determine the winner of the task.

Each new edition of the Robot Vision task has introduced new changes in the data provided to the participants as well as for the requested information. Some of the most important variations are enumerated in the following: the use of stereo images (2010@ICPR [23]), the inclusion of depth information (2012@ImageCLEF [15]), point cloud representation for depth information and object recognition problem (2013@ImageCLEF [16]).

**Objectives and Task for the 2014 Edition.** The sixth edition of the Robot Vision challenge [17] focuses on the use of multimodal information (visual images and point cloud files) with application to semantic localization and object recognition. It addresses the problem of robot localization in parallel to object recognition from a semantic point of view, and with a special interest in the capability of generalization. Both problems are inherently related: the objects present in a scene can help determine the room category and vice versa.

Participants were provided with visual and depth images in Point Cloud Data (PCD) format. In addition to all the image sequences, we created a Matlab script to be used as template for participants proposals. This script performs all the steps for generating solutions for the Robot Vision challenge: features generation, training, classification and performance evaluation. Fig. 5 shows the same scene represented in a visual image and a point cloud data file. Training, validation and test sequences were acquired within two different buildings with similar room distribution structure. All the room and object categories included in the test sequence were previously seen during training and validation. No subtasks were considered, and therefore all participants have to prepare their submissions using the same single test sequence where the temporal continuity is not represented.

Visual Image        Point Cloud File

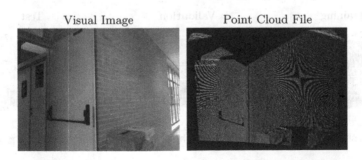

**Fig. 5.** Visual and 3D point cloud representation for a scene. Room class: corridor. List of objects: trash.

The 2014 dataset consists of three sequences (training, validation and test) of depth and visual images acquired within the following indoor environment: two department buildings at the University of Alicante, in Spain. Visual images were stored in PNG format while depth ones in PCD. Every image in the dataset is labelled with its corresponding room category and the list of eight objects to appear or not within it. The 10 room categories are: Corridor, Hall, ProfessorOffice, StudentOffice, TechnicalRoom, Toilet, Secretary, VisioConference, Warehouse and ElevatorArea. The 8 different objects are: Extinguisher, Phone, Chair, Printer, Urinal, Bookself, Trash and Fridge. The dataset has two labelled sequences used for training and validation with 5000 and 1500 images respectively. The unlabelled sequence used for test consists of 3000 different images. The frequency distribution for room categories and objects in the training, validation and test sequences are shown in Tables 6 and 7 respectively. Regarding the building used in the acquisition, all the 5000 training images were acquired in the building A. The validation sequence included 1000 images from building A but 500 new images from building B. Finally, all 3000 test images were acquired in building B.

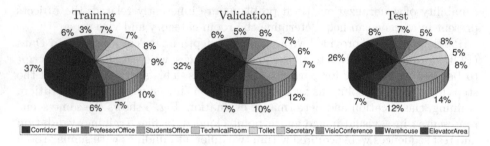

**Fig. 6.** Room distribution in training, validation and test sequences

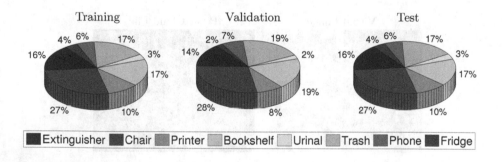

**Fig. 7.** Object distribution in training, validation and test sequences

Participant submissions were compared and sorted according to the obtained score. Every submission consisted of the room category assigned to each test image and the corresponding list of the 8 detected/non-detected objects within the image. The number of times a specific object appears in an image is not relevant to compute the score. Participants are allowed to not classify rooms, in which case the score is not affected. The total score was computed using the rules shown in Table 3.

**Table 3.** Rules used to calculate the final score for a test frame

| Room class/Category | |
|---|---|
| Room class/category correctly classified | +1.0 points |
| Room class/category wrongly classified | -0.5 points |
| Room class/category not classified | +0.0 points |
| Object Recognition | |
| For each object correctly detected (True Positive) | +1.0 points |
| For each object incorrectly detected (False Positive) | -0.25 points |
| For each object correctly detected as not present (True Negative) | +0.0 points |
| For each object incorrectly detected as not present (FalseNegative) | -0.25 points |

**Participation and Results.** In 2014, 28 participants registered to the Robot Vision task but only 4 submitted at least one run accounting for a total of 17 different runs. The scores obtained by all the submitted runs are shown in Fig. 8. The maximum score that could be achieved was 7004 (3000 from rooms and 4004 from objects) and the winner (NUDT) obtained a score of 4430,25 points.

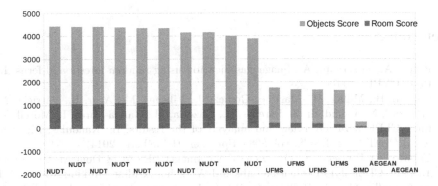

**Fig. 8.** Overall results of the runs submitted by the participant groups to the 2014 Robot Vision task

The NUDT proposal [42] that ranked first followed a spatial pyramid matching approach [14] based on gradients and dense SIFT features. The classification was performed using a multi-class SVM following the one versus all strategy. The CPPP/UFMS proposal [4] also uses dense SIFT descriptors and the spatial pyramid approach. However, this approach is based on a k-nearest neighbor classifier. The SIMD proposal was generated by the organizers of the task using the proposed Matlab script (Depth+RGB histograms descriptors and SVM for classification).

In view of the results, we can conclude that room classification remains an open problem when generalization is requested. On the other hand, we should point out the high performance of the submissions when facing the object recognition problem. This can be explained because generalization is not needed to recognize a specific object within a scene. Namely, phones or chairs will always be recognized as their type (a phone or a chair respectively) independently from the scene where they are placed.

## 3   Conclusions

This paper presents an overview of the activities in the 2014 edition of the ImageCLEF lab. The sustained interest in the lab, witnessed by the important number of registration and the number of groups actually participating in the lab, make ImageCLEF an important resource in the image annotation research landscape. The ever growing amount of data available through the Internet, and the growing demand of tools for accessing and exploiting them, will become one of the key focus for the 2015 edition of ImageCLEF.

**Acknowledgments.** This work has been partially supported by the tranScriptorium FP7 project under grant #600707 (M. V., R. P.).

## References

1. Bosch, A., Zisserman, A.: Image classification using random forests and ferns. In: Proc. CVPR (2007)
2. Caputo, B., Müller, H., Martinez-Gomez, J., Villegas, M., Acar, B., Patricia, N., Marvasti, N., Üsküdarlı, S., Paredes, R., Cazorla, M., Garcia-Varea, I., Morell, V.: ImageCLEF 2014: Overview and analysis of the results. In: Kanoulas, E., et al. (eds.) CLEF 2014. LNCS, vol. 8685, Springer, Heidelberg (2014)
3. Caputo, B., Patricia, N.: Overview of the ImageCLEF 2014 Domain Adaptation Task. In: CLEF 2014 Evaluation Labs and Workshop, Online Working Notes (2014)
4. de Carvalho Gomes, R., Correia Ribas, L., Antnio de Castro Jr., A., Nunes Gonalves, W.: CPPP/UFMS at ImageCLEF 2014: Robot Vision Task. In: CLEF 2014 Evaluation Labs and Workshop, Online Working Notes (2014)
5. Del Frate, F., Pacifici, F., Schiavon, G., Solimini, C.: Use of neural networks for automatic classification from high-resolution images. IEEE Transactions on Geoscience and Remote Sensing 45(4), 800–809 (2007)
6. Feng, S.L., Manmatha, R., Lavrenko, V.: Multiple bernoulli relevance models for image and video annotation. In: Proceedings of the 2004 IEEE Computer Society Conference on Computer Vision and Pattern Recognition, CVPR 2004, vol. 2, p. II–1002. IEEE (2004)

7. Friedl, M.A., Brodley, C.E.: Decision tree classification of land cover from remotely sensed data. Remote Sensing of Environment 61(3), 399–409 (1997)
8. Goh, K.-S., Chang, E.Y., Li, B.: Using one-class and two-class svms for multiclass image annotation. IEEE Transactions on Knowledge and Data Engineering 17(10), 1333–1346 (2005)
9. Gong, B., Shi, Y., Sha, F., Grauman, K.: Geodesic flow kernel for unsupervised domain adaptation. In: Proc. CVPR. Extended Version Considering its Additional Material
10. Jie, L., Tommasi, T., Caputo, B.: Multiclass transfer learning from unconstrained priors. In: Proc. ICCV (2011)
11. Kim, S., Park, S., Kim, M.: Image classification into object / non-object classes. In: Enser, P.G.B., Kompatsiaris, Y., O'Connor, N.E., Smeaton, A.F., Smeulders, A.W.M. (eds.) CIVR 2004. LNCS, vol. 3115, pp. 393–400. Springer, Heidelberg (2004)
12. Ko, B.C., Lee, J., Nam, J.Y.: Automatic medical image annotation and keyword-based image retrieval using relevance feedback. Journal of Digital Imaging 25(4), 454–465 (2012)
13. Kökciyan, N., Türkay, R., Üsküdarlı, S., Yolum, P., Bakır, B., Acar, B.: Semantic Description of Liver CT Images: An Ontological Approach. IEEE Journal of Biomedical and Health Informatics (2014)
14. Lazebnik, S., Schmid, C., Ponce, J.: Beyond bags of features: Spatial pyramid matching for recognizing natural scene categories. In: 2006 IEEE Computer Society Conference on Computer Vision and Pattern Recognition, vol. 2, pp. 2169–2178. IEEE (2006)
15. Martinez-Gomez, J., Garcia-Varea, I., Caputo, B.: Overview of the imageclef 2012 robot vision task. In: CLEF (Online Working Notes/Labs/Workshop) (2012)
16. Martinez-Gomez, J., Garcia-Varea, I., Cazorla, M., Caputo, B.: Overview of the imageclef 2013 robot vision task. In: CLEF 2013 Evaluation Labs and Workshop, Online Working Notes (2013)
17. Martinez-Gomez, J., Cazorla, M., Garcia-Varea, I., Morell, V.: Overview of the ImageCLEF 2014 Robot Vision Task. In: CLEF 2014 Evaluation Labs and Workshop, Online Working Notes (2014)
18. Mueen, A., Zainuddin, R., Baba, M.S.: Automatic multilevel medical image annotation and retrieval. Journal of Digital Imaging 21(3), 290–295 (2008)
19. Muller, H., Clough, P., Deselaers, T., Caputo, B.: ImageCLEF: experimental evaluation in visual information retrieval. Springer (2010)
20. Park, S.B., Lee, J.W., Kim, S.K.: Content-based image classification using a neural network. Pattern Recognition Letters 25(3), 287–300 (2004)
21. Patricia, N., Caputo, B.: Learning to learn, from transfer learning to domain adaptation: a unifying perspective. In: Proc. CVPR (2014)
22. Pronobis, A., Caputo, B.: The robot vision task. In: Muller, H., Clough, P., Deselaers, T., Caputo, B. (eds.) ImageCLEF. The Information Retrieval Series, vol. 32, pp. 185–198. Springer, Heidelberg (2010)
23. Pronobis, A., Christensen, H., Caputo, B.: Overview of the imageclef@ icpr 2010 robot vision track. In: Recognizing Patterns in Signals, Speech, Images and Videos, pp. 171–179 (2010)
24. Qi, X., Han, Y.: Incorporating multiple svms for automatic image annotation. Pattern Recognition 40(2), 728–741 (2007)

25. Reshma, I.A., Ullah, M.Z., Aono, M.: KDEVIR at ImageCLEF 2014 Scalable Concept Image Annotation Task: Ontology based Automatic Image Annotation. In: CLEF 2014 Evaluation Labs and Workshop, Online Working Notes. Sheffield, UK, September 15-18 (2014)

26. Saenko, K., Kulis, B., Fritz, M., Darrell, T.: Adapting visual category models to new domains. In: Daniilidis, K., Maragos, P., Paragios, N. (eds.) ECCV 2010, Part IV. LNCS, vol. 6314, pp. 213–226. Springer, Heidelberg (2010)

27. Sahbi, H.: CNRS - TELECOM ParisTech at ImageCLEF 2013 Scalable Concept Image Annotation Task: Winning Annotations with Context Dependent SVMs. In: CLEF 2013 Evaluation Labs and Workshop, Online Working Notes, Valencia, Spain, September 23-26 (2013)

28. Sethi, I.K., Coman, I.L., Stan, D.: Mining association rules between low-level image features and high-level concepts. In: Aerospace/Defense Sensing, Simulation, and Controls, pp. 279–290. International Society for Optics and Photonics (2001)

29. Shi, R., Feng, H., Chua, T.-S., Lee, C.-H.: An adaptive image content representation and segmentation approach to automatic image annotation. In: Enser, P.G.B., Kompatsiaris, Y., O'Connor, N.E., Smeaton, A.F., Smeulders, A.W.M. (eds.) CIVR 2004. LNCS, vol. 3115, pp. 545–554. Springer, Heidelberg (2004)

30. Tommasi, T., Caputo, B.: Frustratingly easy nbnn domain adaptation. In: Proc. ICCV (2013)

31. Tommasi, T., Quadrianto, N., Caputo, B., Lampert, C.H.: Beyond dataset bias: Multi-task unaligned shared knowledge transfer. In: Lee, K.M., Matsushita, Y., Rehg, J.M., Hu, Z. (eds.) ACCV 2012, Part I. LNCS, vol. 7724, pp. 1–15. Springer, Heidelberg (2013)

32. Tsikrika, T., de Herrera, A.G.S., Müller, H.: Assessing the scholarly impact of imageCLEF. In: Forner, P., Gonzalo, J., Kekäläinen, J., Lalmas, M., de Rijke, M. (eds.) CLEF 2011. LNCS, vol. 6941, pp. 95–106. Springer, Heidelberg (2011)

33. Ünay, D., Soldea, O., Akyüz, S., Çetin, M., Erçil, A.: Medical image retrieval and automatic annotation: Vpa-sabanci at imageclef 2009. In: The Cross-Language Evaluation Forum (CLEF) (2009)

34. Vailaya, A., Figueiredo, M.A., Jain, A.K., Zhang, H.J.: Image classification for content-based indexing. IEEE Transactions on Image Processing 10(1), 117–130 (2001)

35. Villegas, M., Paredes, R.: Overview of the ImageCLEF 2012 Scalable Web Image Annotation Task. In: Forner, P., Karlgren, J., Womser-Hacker, C. (eds.) CLEF 2012 Evaluation Labs and Workshop, Online Working Notes, Rome, Italy, September 17-20 (2012), http://mvillegas.info/pub/Villegas12_CLEF_Annotation-Overview.pdf

36. Villegas, M., Paredes, R.: Overview of the ImageCLEF 2014 Scalable Concept Image Annotation Task. In: CLEF 2014 Evaluation Labs and Workshop, Online Working Notes, Sheffield, UK, September 15-18 (2014), http://mvillegas.info/pub/Villegas14_ CLEF_Annotation-Overview.pdf

37. Villegas, M., Paredes, R., Thomee, B.: Overview of the ImageCLEF 2013 Scalable Concept Image Annotation Subtask. In: CLEF 2013 Evaluation Labs and Workshop, Online Working Notes, Valencia, Spain, September 23-26 (2013), http://mvillegas.info/pub/Villegas13_CLEF_Annotation-Overview.pdf

38. Villena Román, J., González Cristóbal, J.C., Goñi Menoyo, J.M., Martínez Fernández, J.L.: MIRACLE's naive approach to medical images annotation. IEEE Transactions on Pattern Analysis and Machine Intelligence 28(7), 1088–1099 (2005)

39. Wong, R.C., Leung, C.H.: Automatic semantic annotation of real-world web images. IEEE Transactions on Pattern Analysis and Machine Intelligence 30(11), 1933–1944 (2008)

40. Yang, C., Dong, M., Fotouhi, F.: Image content annotation using bayesian framework and complement components analysis. In: IEEE International Conference on Image Processing, ICIP 2005, vol. 1, pp. I–1193. IEEE (2005)

41. Yılmaz, K.Y., Cemgil, A.T., Simsekli, U.: Generalised coupled tensor factorisation. In: Advances in Neural Information Processing Systems, pp. 2151–2159 (2011)

42. Zhang, Y., Qin, J., Chen, F., Hu, D.: NUDTs Participation in ImageCLEF Robot Vision Challenge 2014. In: CLEF 2014 Evaluation Labs and Workshop, Online Working Notes (2014)

# Overview of INEX 2014

Patrice Bellot, Toine Bogers, Shlomo Geva[1], Mark Hall, Hugo Huurdeman,
Jaap Kamps[2], Gabriella Kazai, Marijn Koolen, Véronique Moriceau,
Josiane Mothe, Michael Preminger, Eric SanJuan, Ralf Schenkel[3],
Mette Skov, Xavier Tannier, and David Walsh

[1] INEX co-chair & QUT, Australia
[2] INEX co-chair & University of Amsterdam, The Netherlands
[3] INEX co-chair & University of Passau, Germany

**Abstract.** INEX investigates focused retrieval from structured documents by providing large test collections of structured documents, uniform evaluation measures, and a forum for organizations to compare their results. This paper reports on the INEX 2014 evaluation campaign, which consisted of three tracks: The *Interactive Social Book Search Track* investigated user information seeking behavior when interacting with various sources of information, for realistic task scenarios, and how the user interface impacts search and the search experience. The *Social Book Search Track* investigated the relative value of authoritative metadata and user-generated content for search and recommendation using a test collection with data from Amazon and LibraryThing, including user profiles and personal catalogues. The *Tweet Contextualization Track* investigated tweet contextualization, helping a user to understand a tweet by providing him with a short background summary generated from relevant Wikipedia passages aggregated into a coherent summary. INEX 2014 was an exciting year for INEX in which we for the third time ran our workshop as part of the CLEF labs. This paper gives an overview of all the INEX 2014 tracks, their aims and task, the built test-collections, the participants, and gives an initial analysis of the results.

## 1 Introduction

Traditional IR focuses on pure text retrieval over "bags of words" but the use of structure—such as document structure, semantic metadata, entities, or genre/topical structure—is of increasing importance on the Web and in professional search. INEX was founded as the *INitiative for the Evaluation of XML retrieval* and has been pioneering the use of structure for focused retrieval since 2002, by providing large test collections of structured documents, uniform evaluation measures, and a forum for organizations to compare their results. INEX 2014 was an exciting year for INEX in which we further integrated into the CLEF Labs structure in order to foster further collaboration and facilitate knowledge transfer between the evaluation forums.

In total three research tracks were included, which studied different aspects of focused information access:

E. Kanoulas et al. (Eds.): CLEF 2014, LNCS 8685, pp. 212–228, 2014.

**Interactive Social Book Search Track** investigates user information seeking behavior when interacting with various sources of information, for realistic task scenarios, and how the user interface impacts search and the search experience.

**Social Book Search Track** investigates the relative value of authoritative metadata and user-generated content for search and recommendation using a test collection with data from Amazon and LibraryThing, including user profiles and personal catalogues.

**Tweet Contextualization Track** investigates tweet contextualization, helping a user to understand a tweet by providing him with a short background summary generated from relevant Wikipedia passages aggregated into a coherent summary (in collaboration with the RepLab Lab).

Also a continuation of the Linked Data Track was announced (in collaboration with the CLEF QA Lab), in particular the Jeopardy Task running SPARQL queries on a DBpedia/Wikipedia corpus, but eventually the QALD task opted for a different corpus.

In the rest of this paper, we discuss the aims and results of the INEX 2014 tracks in relatively self-contained sections: the Interactive Social Book Search track (Section 2), the Social Books Search track (Section 3), and the Tweet Contextualization (Section 4) track.

## 2   Interactive Social Book Search Track

In this section, we will briefly discuss the INEX 2014 Interactive Social Book Search Track. Further details are in [4].

### 2.1   Aims and Tasks

The goal of the Interactive Social Book Search (ISBS) track is to investigate how book searchers use professional metadata and user-generated content at different stages of the search process. The purpose of this task is to gauge user interaction and user experience in social book search by observing user activity with a large collection of rich book descriptions under controlled and simulated conditions, aiming for as much "real-life" experiences intruding into the experimentation. The output will be a rich data set that includes both user profiles, selected individual differences (such as a motivation to explore), a log of user interactivity, and a structured set of questions about the experience.

The Interactive Social Book Search Track is a merger of the INEX Social Book Search Track (SBS, discussed in Section 3 below) and the Interactive task of CHiC [7, 9]. The SBS Track started in 2011 and has focused on system-oriented evaluation of book search systems that use both professional metadata and user-generated content. Out of three years of SBS evaluation arose a need to understand how users interact with these different types of book descriptions and how systems could support user to express and adapt their information needs during the search process. The CHiC Interactive task focused on interaction of users browsing and searching in the Europeana collection. One of the questions is what types of metadata searchers use to determine relevance and interest. The collection, use case and task were deemed not interesting and useful enough to users. The first year of the ISBS will focus on switching to the SBS collection and use case, with as few other changes as possible.

The goal of the interactive book search task is to investigate how searchers interact with book search systems that offer different types of book metadata. The addition of opinionated descriptions and user-supplied tags allows users to search and select books with new criteria. User reviews may reveal information about plot, themes, characters, writing style, text density, comprehensiveness and other aspects that are not described by professional metadata. In particular, the focus is on complex goal-oriented tasks as well as non-goal oriented tasks. For traditional tasks such as known-item search, there are effective search systems based on access points via formal metadata (i.e. book title, author name, publisher, year, etc). But even here user reviews and tags may prove to have an important role. The long-term goal of the task is investigate user behavior through a range of user tasks and interfaces and to identify the role of different types of metadata for different stages in the book search process.

For the Interactive task, the main research question is: *How do searchers use professional metadata and user-generated content in book search?* This can be broken down into a few more specific questions:

**RQ1.** *How should the system and user interface combine professional and user-generated information?*

**RQ2.** *How should the system adapt itself as the user progresses through their search task?*

## 2.2  Experimental Setup

The track builds on the INEX Amazon/LibraryThing (A/LT) collection [1, see also Section 3], which contains 1.5 million book descriptions from Amazon, enriched with content from LT. This collection contains both professional metadata and user-generated content. This collection is a subset of a larger collection of 2.8 million description, selecting all and only book descriptions that have a cover image.

Two tasks were created to investigate the impact of different task types on the participants interactions with the interfaces and also the professional and user-generated book meta-data. The first is a *goal-oriented* task, developed as a "simulated leisure task" [8] based on a topic derived from the LibraryThing discussion fora:

> Imagine you are looking for some interesting physics and mathematics books for a layperson. You have heard about the Feynman books but you have never really read anything in this area. You would also like to find an "interesting facts" sort of book on mathematics.

The LibraryThing collection contains discussion fora in which users asked other users for advice on which books to read for a given topic, question, or area of interest. From this list of discussion topics, a discussion on "layman books for physics and mathematics" was selected as the book collection contained a significant number of books on the topic, it is a neutral topic, it provides guidance, but it is also sufficiently flexible that participants can interpret it as needed.

The second is a *non-goal-oriented* task, based on the open-ended task used in the iCHiC task at CLEF 2013 [9]:

> Imagine you are waiting to meet a friend in a coffee shop or pub or the airport or your office. While waiting, you come across this website and explore it looking for any book that you find interesting, or engaging or relevant...

The aim of this task is to investigate how users interact with the system when they have no pre-defined goal in a more exploratory search context. It also allows the participants to bring their own goals or sub-tasks to the experiment in line with the "simulated work task" ideas [3].

The setup used extensive questionnaires as fascilitated by the SPIRE system [9]: *Consent* questionnaire: all participants had to confirm that they understood the tasks they would be asked to undertake and the types of data collected in the experiment, and also specified who had recruited them; *Demographics* questionnaire: the following factors were acquired in order to characterize the participants: gender, age, achieved education level, current education level, and employment status; *Culture* questionnaire: to quantify language and cultural influences, the following factors were collected: country of birth, country of residence, mother tongue, primary language spoken at home, languages used to search the web; *Post-Task* questionnaire: in the post task questions, participants were asked to judge how useful each of the interface components and meta-data parts that they had used in the task were, using 5-point Likert-like scales; and *Engagement* questionnaire: after participants had completed both tasks, they were asked to complete O'Brien and Toms [6]'s engagement scale.

Two distinct systems were developed. The first is a *Baseline* system representing a standard web-search interface, with the left column containing the task instructions, book-bag, and search history and the main area showing the results, see Figure 1.

The second is a *Multistage* system, having different views for three stages of the search process, see Figure 2. The initial *explore* stage aimed to support the initial exploration of the data-set and contains a very similar feature set to the baseline, including task instructions, search box, search results, book bag, and search history. The two main differences to the *baseline* interface were the navigation bar that allows the participants to switch between the stages and the dense, multi-column search results. The *focus* stage supports in-depth searching and provides detailed search results that directly include the full meta-data that in the other stages is shown via a popup. A category filter was also provided in the left column which provided a means to reduce and refine the search results. The *refine* stage supports the refining of the final list of books the participants want to choose. It thus focuses on the books the user has already added to their

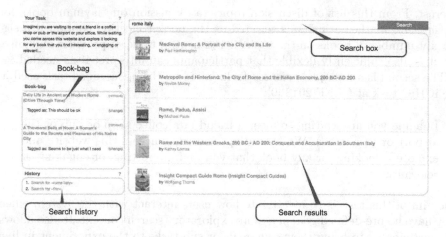

**Fig. 1.** Baseline interface's results view

**Table 1.** Overview of the participating teams and number of users per team

| Institute | # Test persons |
|-----------|----------------|
| Aalborg | 7 |
| Amsterdam | 7 |
| Edge Hill | 10 |
| Humboldt | 17 |
| Total | 41 |

book-bag and this stage cannot be entered until at least one book has been added to the book-bag.

## 2.3  Results

A total of four teams contributed 41 test persons to the experiments. In Table 1 we show which institutes participated in this track and the number of users that took part in their experiments.

Based on the participant responses and log data we have aggregated summary statistics for a number of basic performance metrics in Table 2.

*Session length* shows median and inter-quartile ranges in minutes and seconds for all interface and task combinations. While the results seem to indicate that participants spent longer in the *Baseline* interface and also longer on the *goal-oriented* task, the differences are not statistically significant (Wilcoxon signed-rank test). For the *non-goal* task, the median times are roughly similar to the session lengths in the iCHiC experiments This might indicate that that is the approximate time that participants can be expected to spend on any kind of open-ended leisure-task.

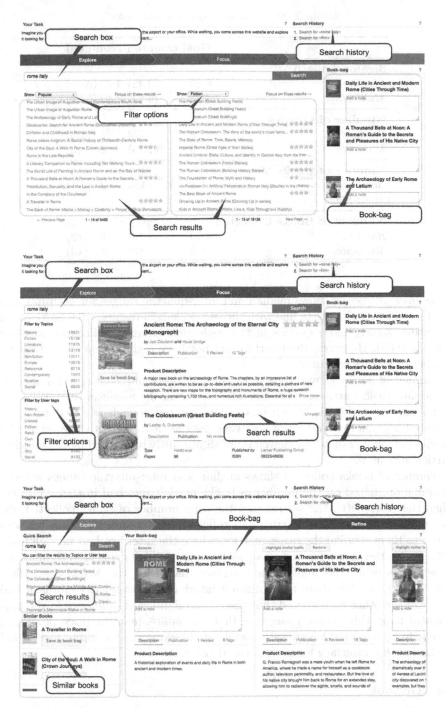

**Fig. 2.** Multistage interface: Explore view (top), Focus view (middle), and Refine view (bottom)

**Table 2.** Statistics over systems and tasks

|  | Goal-oriented | Non-goal | |
|---|---|---|---|
| **Session Length** | | | |
| *Baseline* | 6:25 | (3:42) 3:42 | (3:45) |
| *Multi-Stage* | 3:35 | (4:24) 2:40 | (6:21) |
| **Number of Queries** | | | |
| *Baseline* | 4 | (5.5) 2 | (4.5) |
| *Multi-Stage* | 3 | (2.75) 2 | (3) |
| **Number of Books Viewed** | | | |
| *Baseline* | 4 | (5.5) 2 | (4.5) |
| *Multi-Stage* | 3 | (2.75) 2 | (3) |
| **Number of Books Collected** | | | |
| *Baseline* | 3 | (3) 1 | (2) |
| *Multi-Stage* | 3.5 | (3) 2 | (3) |

*Number of queries* shows median and inter-quartile ranges for each interface and task. The results are in line with the session length results, with participants executing slightly more queries in the *goal-oriented* task (Wilcoxon rank-sum test $p < 0.05$). However, the interface did not have a significant impact on the number of queries executed.

*Number of books viewed* shows median and inter-quartile ranges for each interface and task. Participants viewed fewer books in the *non-goal* task (Wilcoxon rank-sum test $p < 0.05$), which was to be expected considering that they also executed less queries and spent less time on the task. As with the number of queries the number of books viewed is not significantly influenced by the interface participants used.

*Number of books collected* shows median and inter-quartile ranges for each combination, based on the number of books participants had in their book-bag when they completed the session, not the total number of books collected over the course of their session. Participants collected those books that they felt were of use to them. Unlike the other metrics, where the interface had no significant influence on the metric, in the *non-goal* task, participants collected significantly more books using the *multi-stage* interface than with the *baseline* interface. Considering that there are no significant interface effects for the *non-goal* task in any of the other metrics and that there is no significant difference in the *goal-oriented* task, this strongly suggests that the *multi-stage* interface provides a benefit to open-ended leisure tasks, while at the same time working just as well as the *baseline* interface for more focused tasks.

## 2.4   Outlook

As the focus on the INEX 2013 Interactive Social Book Search track was switching to the SBS collection and use case, in particular in terms of the experimental systems and the infrastructure to collect log and questionnaire data, the 2013 edition had the character of a pilot track. Next year, we are able to reap the benefits of these investments and continue with the ISBS track to further investigate how books searchers use professional metadata and user-generated content at different stages of the search process.

## 3  Social Book Search Track

In this section, we will briefly discuss the INEX 2014 Social Book Search Track. Further details are in [5].

### 3.1  Aims and Tasks

For centuries books were the dominant source of information, but how we acquire, share, and publish information is changing in fundamental ways due to the Web. The goal of the Social Book Search Track is to investigate techniques to support users in searching and navigating the full texts of digitized books and complementary social media as well as providing a forum for the exchange of research ideas and contributions. Towards this goal the track is building appropriate evaluation benchmarks, complete with test collections for social, semantic and focused search tasks. The track provides opportunities to explore research questions around two key areas: First, evaluation methodologies for book search tasks that combine aspects of retrieval and recommendation. Second, information retrieval techniques for dealing with professional and user-generated metadata.

The *Social Book Search* (SBS) task, framed within the scenario of a user searching a large online book catalogue for a given topic of interest, aims at exploring techniques to deal with complex information needs—that go beyond topical relevance and can include aspects such as genre, recency, engagement, interestingness, and quality of writing—and complex information sources that include user profiles, personal catalogues, and book descriptions containing both professional metadata and user-generated content.

The 2014 edition represents the fourth consecutive year the SBS task has run and once more the test collection used is the Amazon/LibraryThing collection of 2.8 million documents. LibraryThing forum requests for book suggestions, combined with annotation of these requests resulted in a topic set of 680 topics with graded relevance judgments. Compared to 2013, there are three important changes: (1) a much larger set of 94,000+ user profiles was provided to the participants this year; (2) an additional 300 forum topics were annotated, bringing the total number of topics up to 680; and (3) the *Prove It* task did not run this year. Prompted by the availability of large collections of digitized books, the Social Book Search Track aims to promote research into techniques for supporting users in searching, navigating and reading full texts of digitized books and associated metadata.

## 3.2  Test Collections

For the Social Book Search task a new type of test collection has been developed. Unlike traditional collections of topics and topical relevance judgements, the task is based on rich, real-world information needs from the LibraryThing (LT) discussion forums and user profiles. The collection consists of 2.8 million book descriptions from Amazon, including user reviews, and is enriched with user-generated content from LT. This collection was originally constructed by Beckers et al. [1], but extended and augmented in various ways, see [5].

For the information needs we used the LT discussion forums. Over the past two years, we had a group of eight different Information Science students annotate the narratives of a random sample of 2,646 LT forum topics. Of the 2,646 topics annotated by the students, 944 topics (36%) were identified as containing a book search information need. Because we want to investigate the value of recommendations, we use only topics where the topic creators add books to their catalogue both before (pre-catalogued) and after starting the topic (post-catalogued). Without the former, recommender systems have no profile to work with and without the latter the recommendation part cannot be evaluated. This leaves 680 topics. These topics were combined with all the pre-catalogued books of the topic creators' profiles and distributed to participating groups. An example of an annotated topic (topic 99309) is:

```
<topic id="99309">
  <query>Politics of Multiculturalism</query>
  <title>Politics of Multiculturalism Recommendations?</title>
  <group>Political Philosophy</group>
  <member>steve.clason</member>
  <narrative> I'm new, and would appreciate any recommended reading on
    the politics of multiculturalism. <a href="/author/parekh">Parekh
    </a>'s <a href="/work/164382">Rethinking Multiculturalism: Cultural
    Diversity and Political Theory</a> (which I just finished) in the end
    left me unconvinced, though I did find much of value I thought he
    depended way too much on being able to talk out the details later. It
    may be that I found his writing style really irritating so adopted a
    defiant skepticism, but still... Anyway, I've read
    <a href="/author/sen">Sen</a>, <a href="/author/rawles">Rawls</a>,
    <a href="/author/habermas">Habermas</a>, and
    <a href="/author/nussbaum">Nussbaum</a>, still don't feel like I've
    wrapped my little brain around the issue very well and would
    appreciate any suggestions for further anyone might offer.
  </narrative>
  <catalog>
    <book>
      <LT_id>9036</LT_id>
      <entry_date>2007-09</entry_date>
      <rating>0.0</rating>
      <tags></tags>
    </book>
    <book>
      ...
```

**Table 3.** User profile statistics of the topic creators and all other users

| Type | N | total | min | max | median | mean | stdev |
|---|---|---|---|---|---|---|---|
| Topic Creators | | | | | | | |
|    Pre-catalogued | 680 | 399,147 | 1 | 5,884 | 239 | 587 | 927 |
|    Post-catalogued | 680 | 209,289 | 1 | 5,619 | 114 | 308 | 499 |
|    Total catalogued | 680 | 608,436 | 2 | 8,563 | 432 | 895 | 1,202 |
| All users | | | | | | | |
|    Others | 93,976 | 33,503,999 | 1 | 41,792 | 134 | 357 | 704 |
| Total | 94,656 | 34,112,435 | 1 | 41,792 | 135 | 360 | 710 |

The relevance judgements come in the form of suggestions from other LT members in the same discussion thread and the additional annotations, translated into a graded relevance scale (see [5] for details).

In addition to information needs of social book search topics, LT also provides the rich user profiles of the topic creators and other LT users, which contain information on which books they have in their personal catalogue on LT, which ratings and tags they assigned to them and a social network of friendship relations, interesting library relations and group memberships. These profiles may provide important signals on the user's topical and genre interests, reading level, which books they already know and which ones they like and don't like. These profiles were scraped from the LT site, anonymised and made available to participants. Basic statistics on the number of books per user profile is given in Table 3. By the time users ask for book recommendations, most of them already have a substantial catalogue (pre-catalogued). The distribution is skewed, as the mean (587) is higher than the median (239). After posting their topics, users tend to add many more books (post-catalogued), but fewer than they have already added. Compared to the other users in our crawl (median of 134 books), the topic creators are the more active users, with larger catalogues (median of 432 books).

### 3.3 Results

A total of 64 teams registered for the track (compared with 68 in 2013, 55 in 2012 and 47 in 2011). At the time of writing, we counted 8 active groups (compared with 8 in 2013, 5 in 2012 and 10 in 2011) submitting a total of 40 runs, see Table 4.

The official evaluation measure for this task is nDCG@10. It takes graded relevance values into account and is designed for evaluation based on the top retrieved results. In addition, P@10, MAP and MRR scores will also be reported, with the evaluation results shown in Table 5.

The best performing run is *run6.SimQuery1000.rerank_all.L2R_RandomForest* by USTB, which used all topic fields combined against an index containing all available document fields. The run is re-ranked with 12 different re-ranking

**Table 4.** Active participants of the INEX 2014 Social Book Search Track and number of contributed runs

| ID | Institute | Acronym | Runs |
|----|-----------|---------|------|
| 4 | University of Amsterdam | UvA | 4 |
| 54 | Aalborg University Copenhagen | AAU | 3 |
| 65 | University of Minnesota Duluth | UMD | 6 |
| 123 | LSIS / Aix-Marseille University | SBS | 6 |
| 180 | Chaoyang University of Technology | CYUT | 4 |
| 232 | Indian School of Mines, Dhanbad | ISMD | 5 |
| 419 | Université Jean Monnet | UJM | 6 |
| 423 | University of Science and Technology Beijing | USTB | 6 |
| | Total | | 40 |

**Table 5.** Evaluation results for the official submissions (best run per team). Best scores are in bold. Runs marked with * are manual runs.

| Group | Run | nDCG@10 | P@10 | MRR | MAP | Profiles |
|-------|-----|---------|------|-----|-----|----------|
| USTB | run6.SimQuery1000.rerank_all.-L2R_RandomForest | **0.303** | **0.464** | **0.232** | 0.390 | No |
| UJM | 326 | 0.142 | 0.275 | 0.107 | 0.426 | No |
| LSIS | InL2 | 0.128 | 0.236 | 0.101 | 0.441 | No |
| AAU | run1.all-plus-query.all-doc-fields | 0.127 | 0.239 | 0.097 | **0.444** | No |
| CYUT | Type2QTGN | 0.119 | 0.246 | 0.086 | 0.340 | No |
| UvA | inex14.ti_qu.fb.10.50.5000 | 0.097 | 0.179 | 0.073 | 0.421 | No |
| UMD | Full_TQG_fb.10.50_0.0000227_50 | 0.097 | 0.188 | 0.069 | 0.328 | Yes |
| *ISMD | 354 | 0.067 | 0.123 | 0.049 | 0.285 | No |

strategies, which are then combined adaptively using learning-to-rank. The second group is UJM with run *326*, which uses BM25 on the title, mediated query and narrative fields, with the parameters optimised for the narrative field. The third group is lsis, with *InL2*. This run is based on the InL2 model, the index is built from all fields in the book xml files. The system uses the mediated query, group and narrative fields as a query.

There are 11 systems that made use of the user profiles, but they are not among the top ranking systems. The best systems combine various topic fields, with parameters trained for optimal performance. This is the first year that systems included learning-to-rank approaches, the best of which clearly outperforms all other systems.

Last year there were many (126 out of 380, or 33%) topics for which none of the systems managed to retrieve any relevant books. This year, there were only 56 of these topics (8%). There are 27 topics where the only books suggested in the thread are already catalogued or read by the topic creator, so all relevance values are zero. The other 39 topics where all systems fail to retrieve relevant books have very few (mostly 1 or 2) suggestions and tend to be very vague or broad topics where hundreds or thousands of books could be recommended. This drop is probably due to the restriction of selecting only topics of users who catalogue books. Many of the topics on which all systems fail are known-item topics posed by users who have either a private catalogue or who are new users with empty catalogues. These have been removed from this year's topic pool. By selecting topics from only active users, the evaluation moves further away from known-item search.

## 3.4  Outlook

This was the fourth year of the Social Book Search Track. The track ran only a single tasks: the system-oriented Social Book Search task, which continued its focus on both the relative value of professional and user-generated metadata and the retrieval and recommendation aspects of the LT forum users and their information needs. To promote the use of the profile and personal catalogue information for recommendation aspects, a related task is run as the data challenge of the ACM RecSys 2014 Workshop on New Trends in Content-based Recommender Systems (CBRecSys'14), see http://ir.ii.uam.es/cbrecsys2014/. The RecSys task is still ongoing at the time of writing, and will be reported on separated as part of ACM RecSys in October, 2014. Next year, we plan to shift the focus of the SBS task to the interactive nature of the topic thread and the suggestions and responses given by the topic starter and other members. We are also thinking of a pilot task in which the system not only has to retrieve relevant and recommendable books, but also to select which part of the book description—e.g. a certain set of reviews or tags—is most useful to show to the user, given her information need.

# 4  Tweet Contextualization Track

In this section, we will briefly discuss the INEX 2014 Tweet Contextualization Track. Further details are in [2].

## 4.1  Aims and Tasks

Tweets (or posts in social media) are 140 characters long messages that are rarely self-content. The Tweet Contextualization aims at providing automatically information—a summary that explains the tweet. This requires combining multiple types of processing from information retrieval to multi-document summarization including entity linking. Running since 2010, the task in 2014 was a slight variant of previous ones considering more complex queries from RepLab 2013. Given a tweet and a related entity, systems had to provide some context about the subject of the tweet from the perspective of the entity, in order to help the reader to understand it.

The Tweet Contextualization's task in 2014 is a slight variant of previous ones and it is complementary to CLEF RepLab. Previously, given a tweet, systems had to help the user to understand it by reading a short textual summary.

This summary had to be readable on a mobile device without having to scroll too much. In addition, the user should not have to query any system and the system should use a resource freely available. More specifically, the guideline specified the summary should be 500 words long and built from sentences extracted from a dump of Wikipedia. In 2014 a small variant of the task has been explored, considering more complex queries from RepLab 2013, but using the same corpus. The new use case of the task was the following: given a tweet and a related entity, the system must provide some context about the subject of the tweet from the perspective of the entity, in order to help the reader answering questions of the form "why this tweet concerns the entity? should it be an alert?"

In the remaining we give details about the English language tweets, and refer the reader to the overview paper [2] for the pilot task in Spanish.

## 4.2 Test Collection

The official document collection for 2014 was the same as in 2013. Between 2011 and 2013 the corpus did change every year but not the user case. In 2014, the same corpus was reused but the user case evolved. Since 2014 TC topics are a selection of tweets from RepLab 2013, it was necessary to use prior WikiPedia dumps. Some participants also used the 2012 corpus raising up the question of the impact of updating the WikiPedia over these tasks.

Let us recall that the document collection has been built based on yearly dumps of the English WikiPedia since November 2011. We released a set of tools to convert a WikiPedia dump into a plain XML corpus for an easy extraction of plain text answers. The same perl programs released for all participants have been used to remove all notes and bibliographic references that are difficult to handle and keep only non empty Wikipedia pages (pages having at least one section).

The resulting automatically generated documents from WikiPedia dump, consist of a title (`title`), an abstract (`a`) and sections (`s`). Each section has a subtitle (`h`). Abstract and sections are made of paragraphs (`p`) and each paragraph can contain entities (`t`) that refer to other Wikipedia pages.

As tweets, 240 topics have been collected from RepLab 2013 corpus. These tweets have been selected in order to make sure that:

- They contained "informative content" (in particular, no purely personal messages);
- The document collections from Wikipedia had related content, so that a contextualization was possible.

In order to avoid that fully manual, or not robust enough systems could achieve the task, all tweets were to be treated by participants, but only a random sample of them was to be considered for evaluation. These tweets were provided in XML and tabulated format with the following information:

- the category (4 distinct),
- an entity name from the wikipedia (64 distinct)
- a manual topic label (235 distinct).

The entity name was to be used as an entry point into WikiPedia or DBpedia. The context of the generated summaries was expected to be fully related to this entity. On the contrary, the usefulness of topic labels for this automatic task was and remains an open question at this moment because of their variety.

## 4.3  Evaluation

Tweet contextualization is evaluated on both informativeness and readability. Informativeness aims at measuring how well the summary explains the tweet or how well the summary helps a user to understand the tweet content. On the other hand, readability aims at measuring how clear and easy to understand the summary is.

The *informativeness* measure is based on lexical overlap between a pool of relevant passages (RPs) and participant summaries. Once the pool of RPs is constituted, the process is automatic and can be applied to unofficial runs. This year's topics included more facets and converting them into queries for a Research Engine was less straightforward. As a consequence, it was not possible to rely on a pooling from participant runs because it would have been too sparse and incomplete, and a thorough manual run by organizers based on the reference system that was made available to all participants. Unofficial runs based on this reference run can be reliably evaluated.

By contrast, *readability* is evaluated manually and cannot be reproduced on unofficial runs. In this evaluation the assessor indicates where he misses the point of the answers because of highly incoherent grammatical structures, unsolved anaphora, or redundant passages. Three metrics were used: **Relaxed metric**, counting passages where the T box has not been checked; **Syntax metric**, counting passages where the S box was not checked either (i.e, the passage has no syntactic problems), and the **Structure (or Strict) metric** counting passages where no box was checked at all. In all cases, participant runs were ranked according to the average, normalized number of words in valid passages.

## 4.4  Results

In the 2014 edition of the track, four combined teams from six countries (Canada, France, Germany, India, Russia, Tunesia) submitted 12 runs to the Tweet Contextualization track. Two other teams from Mexico and Spain participated to the pilot task in Spanish submitting three runs as detailed in the track overview paper [2]. The total number of submitted passages was $54,932$ with an average length of 32 tokens. The total number of tokens was $1,764,373$ with an average of $7,352$ per tweet. We also generated two reference runs based one the organizer's system made available to participants using 2013 and 2012 corpus respectively. These runs are based on top performing approaches in earlier years (hence a state of the art baseline) and use longer passages to promote the recall base of the resulting qrels.

Informativeness results are presented in Table 6, with passage t-rels on the left and NPs t-rels on the right. Note that the scores are divergences, and hence lower

**Table 6.** Informativeness results (official results are "with 2-gap")

| Rank | Passage t-rels Run | unigram | bigram | with 2-gap | Rank | NP t-rels Run | unigram | bigram | with 2-gap |
|------|------|---------|--------|-----------|------|------|---------|--------|-----------|
| 1 | ref2013 | 0.7050 | 0.7940 | 0.7960 | 1 | ref2013 | 0.7468 | 0.8936 | 0.9237 |
| 2 | ref2012 | 0.7528 | 0.8499 | 0.8516 | 2 | ref2012 | 0.7784 | 0.9170 | 0.9393 |
| 3 | 361 | 0.7632 | 0.8689 | 0.8702 | 3 | 361 | 0.7903 | 0.9273 | 0.9461 |
| 4 | 360 | 0.7820 | 0.8925 | 0.8934 | 4 | 368 | 0.8088 | 0.9322 | 0.9486 |
| 5 | 368 | 0.8112 | 0.9066 | 0.9082 | 5 | 369 | 0.8090 | 0.9326 | 0.9489 |
| 6 | 369 | 0.8140 | 0.9098 | 0.9114 | 6 | 370 | 0.8131 | 0.9360 | 0.9513 |
| 7 | 359 | 0.8022 | 0.9120 | 0.9127 | 7 | 360 | 0.8104 | 0.9406 | 0.9553 |
| 8 | 370 | 0.8152 | 0.9137 | 0.9154 | 8 | 359 | 0.8227 | 0.9487 | 0.9613 |
| 9 | 356 | 0.8415 | 0.9696 | 0.9702 | 9 | 356 | 0.8477 | 0.9710 | 0.9751 |
| 10 | 357 | 0.8539 | 0.9700 | 0.9712 | 10 | 357 | 0.8593 | 0.9709 | 0.9752 |
| 11 | 364 | 0.8461 | 0.9697 | 0.9721 | 11 | 364 | 0.8628 | 0.9744 | 0.9807 |
| 12 | 358 | 0.8731 | 0.9832 | 0.9841 | 12 | 358 | 0.8816 | 0.9840 | 0.9864 |
| 13 | 362 | 0.8686 | 0.9828 | 0.9847 | 13 | 363 | 0.8840 | 0.9827 | 0.9870 |
| 14 | 363 | 0.8682 | 0.9825 | 0.9847 | 14 | 362 | 0.8849 | 0.9833 | 0.9876 |

**Table 7.** Readability results

| Rank | Run | Relaxed | Strict | Syntax | Average |
|------|------|---------|--------|--------|---------|
| 1 | 358 | 0.948220 | 0.721683 | 0.722796 | 0.931005 |
| 2 | 356 | 0.952381 | 0.650917 | 0.703141 | 0.923958 |
| 3 | 357 | 0.948846 | 0.578212 | 0.713445 | 0.915750 |
| 4 | 362 | 0.836699 | 0.366561 | 0.608136 | 0.875917 |
| 5 | 363 | 0.836776 | 0.363954 | 0.611289 | 0.875500 |
| 6 | 364 | 0.880508 | 0.337197 | 0.639092 | 0.869167 |
| 7 | 359 | 0.930300 | 0.258563 | 0.535264 | 0.863375 |
| 8 | 360 | 0.925959 | 0.258658 | 0.588365 | 0.863274 |
| 9 | 361 | 0.932281 | 0.247883 | 0.501199 | 0.859749 |
| 10 | ref2013 | 0.917378 | 0.259702 | 0.605203 | 0.857958 |
| 11 | ref2012 | 0.913858 | 0.259584 | 0.606742 | 0.855583 |
| 12 | 369 | 0.912318 | 0.259539 | 0.549334 | 0.815625 |
| 13 | 368 | 0.908815 | 0.248981 | 0.565912 | 0.808750 |
| 14 | 370 | 0.901044 | 0.246893 | 0.538338 | 0.806958 |

scores are better. Both informativeness rankings in Table 6 are highly correlated, however discrepancies between the two rankings show that differences between top ranked runs rely on tokens outside NPs, mainly verbs since functional words are removed in the evaluation.

Readability results are presented in Table 7, revealing that the readability of reference runs is low, as they are made of longer passages than average to ensure local syntax correctness.

Since reference runs are using the same system and index as the manual run used to build the t-rels, they tend to minimize the informativeness divergence with the reference. However, average divergence remains high pointing out that selecting the right passages in the restricted context of an entity, was more difficult than previous more generic tasks. Considering readability, the fact that reference runs are low ranked confirms that finding the right compromise between readability and informativeness remains the main challenge in this task.

This year, the best participating system for informativeness used association rules. Since contextualization was restricted to some facet described by an entity, it could be that association rules helped to focus on this aspect. The best participating system for readability used an advanced summarization systems that introduced minor changes in passages to improve readability. Changing the content of the passages was not allowed, however this tend to show that to deal with readability some rewriting is required. Moreover, since this year evaluation did not include a pool of passages from participants, systems that provided modified passages have been disadvantaged in informativeness evaluation.

### 4.5 Outlook

The discussion on next year's track is only starting, and there are links to related activities in other CLEF labs that need to be further explored.

## 5 Envoi

This complete our walk-through of INEX 2014. INEX 2014 focused on three tracks. The *Interactive Social Book Search Track* investigated user information seeking behavior when interacting with various sources of information, for realistic task scenarios, and how the user interface impacts search and the search experience. The *Social Book Search Track* investigated the relative value of authoritative metadata and user-generated content for search and recommendation using a test collection with data from Amazon and LibraryThing, including user profiles and personal catalogues. The *Tweet Contextualization Track* investigated tweet contextualization, helping a user to understand a tweet by providing him with a short background summary generated from relevant Wikipedia passages aggregated into a coherent summary (in collaboration with the RepLab Lab).

The INEX tracks cover various aspects of focused retrieval in a wide range of information retrieval tasks. This overview has only touched upon the various approaches applied to these tasks, and their effectiveness. The online proceedings of CLEF 2014 contains both the track overview papers [2, 4, 5], as well as the papers of the participating groups. The main result of INEX 2014, however, is a great number of test collections that can be used for future experiments, and the discussion amongst the participants that happens at the CLEF 2014 conference in Sheffield and throughout the year on the discussion lists.

**Acknowledgments.** We thank the CLEF'15 lab chairs, Martin Halvey and Wessel Kraaij, the CLEF steering committee and its chair, Nicola Ferro, and in particular Linda Cappellato for her extraordinary work in the labs and working notes organization.

# References

[1] Beckers, T., Fuhr, N., Pharo, N., Nordlie, R., Fachry, K.N.: Overview and results of the INEX 2009 interactive track. In: Lalmas, M., Jose, J., Rauber, A., Sebastiani, F., Frommholz, I. (eds.) ECDL 2010. LNCS, vol. 6273, pp. 409–412. Springer, Heidelberg (2010)

[2] Bellot, P., Moriceau, V., Mothe, J., Sanjuan, E., Tannier, X.: Overview of the INEX 2014 tweet contextualization track. In: Cappellato, L., Ferro, N., Halvey, M., Kraaij, W. (eds.) CLEF 2014 Labs and Workshops, Notebook Papers. CEUR Workshop Proceedings, vol. 1180 (2014), http://ceur-ws.org/Vol-1180/

[3] Borlund, P., Ingwersen, P.: The development of a method for the evaluation of interactive information retrieval systems. Journal of Documentation 53(3), 225–250 (1997)

[4] Hall, M., Huurdeman, H., Koolen, M., Skov, M., Walsh, D.: Overview of the INEX 2014 interactive social book search track. In: Cappellato, L., Ferro, N., Halvey, M., Kraaij, W. (eds.) CLEF 2014 Labs and Workshops, Notebook Papers. CEUR Workshop Proceedings, vol. 1180 (2014), http://ceur-ws.org/Vol-1180/

[5] Koolen, M., Bogers, T., Kazai, G., Kamps, J., Preminger, M.: Overview of the INEX 2014 social book search track. In: Cappellato, L., Ferro, N., Halvey, M., Kraaij, W. (eds.) CLEF 2014 Labs and Workshops, Notebook Papers. CEUR Workshop Proceedings, vol. 1180 (2014), http://ceur-ws.org/Vol-1180/

[6] O'Brien, H.L., Toms, E.G.: The development and evaluation of a survey to measure user engagement. Journal of the American Society for Information Science and Technology 61(1), 50–69 (2009)

[7] Petras, V., Bogers, T., Toms, E., Hall, M., Savoy, J., Malak, P., Pawłowski, A., Ferro, N., Masiero, I.: Cultural heritage in CLEF (CHiC) 2013. In: Forner, P., Müller, H., Paredes, R., Rosso, P., Stein, B. (eds.) CLEF 2013. LNCS, vol. 8138, pp. 192–211. Springer, Heidelberg (2013)

[8] Skov, M., Ingwersen, P.: Exploring information seeking behaviour in a digital museum context. In: Proceedings of the Second International Symposium on Information Interaction in Context, pp. 110–115. ACM (2008)

[9] Toms, E.G., Hall, M.M.: The CHiC interactive task (CHiCi) at CLEF2013. In: CLEF 2013 Evaluation Labs and Workshop, Online Working Notes (2013)

# LifeCLEF 2014: Multimedia Life Species Identification Challenges

Alexis Joly[1], Hervé Goëau[2], Hervé Glotin[3], Concetto Spampinato[4],
Pierre Bonnet[5], Willem-Pier Vellinga[6], Robert Planque[6],
Andreas Rauber[7], Robert Fisher[8], and Henning Müller[9]

[1] Inria, LIRMM, Montpellier, France
[2] Inria, Saclay, France
[3] IUF & Univ. de Toulon, France
[4] University of Catania, Italy
[5] CIRAD, France
[6] Xeno-canto foundation, The Netherlands
[7] Vienna Univ. of Tech., Austria
[8] Edinburgh Univ., UK
[9] HES-SO, Switzerland

**Abstract.** Using multimedia identification tools is considered as one of the most promising solutions to help bridging the taxonomic gap and build accurate knowledge of the identity, the geographic distribution and the evolution of living species. Large and structured communities of nature observers (e.g. eBird, Xeno-canto, Tela Botanica, etc.) as well as big monitoring equipments have actually started to produce outstanding collections of multimedia records. Unfortunately, the performance of the state-of-the-art analysis techniques on such data is still not well understood and is far from reaching the real world's requirements. The LifeCLEF lab proposes to evaluate these challenges around three tasks related to multimedia information retrieval and fine-grained classification problems in three living worlds. Each task is based on large and real-world data and the measured challenges are defined in collaboration with biologists and environmental stakeholders in order to reflect realistic usage scenarios. This paper presents more particularly the 2014 edition of LifeCLEF, i.e. the pilot one. For each of the three tasks, we report the methodology and the datasets as well as the official results and the main outcomes.

## 1 LifeCLEF Lab Overview

### 1.1 Motivations

Building accurate knowledge of the identity, the geographic distribution and the evolution of living species is essential for a sustainable development of humanity as well as for biodiversity conservation. Unfortunately, such basic information is often only partially available for professional stakeholders, teachers, scientists and citizens, and more often incomplete for ecosystems that possess the highest

E. Kanoulas et al. (Eds.): CLEF 2014, LNCS 8685, pp. 229–249, 2014.
© Springer International Publishing Switzerland 2014

diversity, such as tropical regions. A noticeable cause and consequence of this sparse knowledge is that identifying living plants or animals is usually impossible for the general public, and often a difficult task for professionals, such as farmers, fish farmers or foresters, and even also for the naturalists and specialists themselves. This taxonomic gap [58] was actually identified as one of the main ecological challenges to be solved during the Rio United Nations Conference in 1992.

In this context, using multimedia identification tools is considered as one of the most promising solution to help bridging the taxonomic gap [39,19,11,55,49,1,54,32]. With the recent advances in digital devices, network bandwidth and information storage capacities, the production of multimedia data has indeed become an easy task. In parallel, the emergence of citizen sciences and social networking tools has fostered the creation of large and structured communities of nature observers (e.g. eBird[1], Xeno-canto[2], Tela Botanica[3], etc.) that have started to produce outstanding collections of multimedia records. Unfortunately, the performance of the state-of-the-art multimedia analysis techniques on such data is still not well understood and are far from reaching the real world's requirements in terms of identification tools [32]. Most existing studies or available tools typically identify a few tens or hundreds of species with moderate accuracy whereas they should be scaled-up to take one, two or three orders of magnitude more, in terms of number of species (the total number of living species on earth is estimated to be around 10K for birds, 30K for fishes, 300K for plants and more than 1.2M for invertebrates [7]).

## 1.2  Evaluated Tasks

The LifeCLEF lab proposes to evaluate these challenges in the continuity of the image-based plant identification task [33] that was run within ImageCLEF lab during the last three years with an increasing number of participants. It however radically enlarges the evaluated challenge towards multimodal data by (i) considering birds and fish in addition to plants (ii) considering audio and video contents in addition to images (iii) scaling-up the evaluation data to hundreds of thousands of life media records and thousands of living species. More concretely, the lab is organized around three tasks:

📷 **PlantCLEF**: an image-based plant identification task

🎵 **BirdCLEF**: an audio-based bird identification task

🎥 **FishCLEF**: a video-based fish identification task

As described in more detail in the following sections, each task is based on big and real-world data and the measured challenges are defined in collaboration

---

[1] http://ebird.org/

[2] http://www.xeno-canto.org/

[3] http://www.tela-botanica.org/

with biologists and environmental stakeholders so as to reflect realistic usage scenarios. For this pilot year, the three tasks are mainly concerned with species identification, i.e., helping users to retrieve the taxonomic name of an observed living plant or animal. Taxonomic names are actually the primary key to organize life species and to access all available information about them either on the web, or in herbariums, in scientific literature, books or magazines, etc. Identifying the taxon observed in a given multimedia record and aligning its name with a taxonomic reference is therefore a key step before any other indexing or information retrieval task. More focused or complex challenges (such as detecting species duplicates or ambiguous species) could be evaluated in coming years.

The three tasks are primarily focused on content-based approaches (i.e. on the automatic analyses of the audio and visual signals) rather than on interactive information retrieval approaches involving textual or graphical morphological attributes. The content-based approach to life species identification has several advantages. It is first intrinsically language-independent and solves many of the multi-lingual issues related to the use of classical text-based morphological keys that are strongly language dependent and understandable only by few experts in the world. Furthermore, an expert of one region or a specific taxonomic group does not necessarily know the vocabulary dedicated to another group of living organisms. A content-based approach can then be much more easily generalizable to new floras or faunas contrary to knowledge-based approaches that require building complex models manually (ontologies with rich descriptions, graphical illustrations of morphological attributes, etc.). On the other hand, LifeCLEF lab is inherently cross-modal through the presence of contextual and social data associated to the visual and audio contents. This includes geo-tags or location names, time information, author names, collaborative ratings or comments, vernacular names (common names of plants or animals), organ or picture type tags, etc. The rules regarding the use of these meta-data in the evaluated identification methods will be specified in the description of each task. Overall, these rules are always designed so as to reflect real possible usage scenarios while offering the largest diversity in the affordable approaches.

## 1.3   Main Contributions

The main outcomes of LifeCLEF evaluation campaign are the following:

- give a snapshot of the performances of state-of-the-art multimedia techniques towards building real-world life species identification systems
- provide large and original data sets of biological records, and then allow comparison of multimedia-based identification techniques
- boost research and innovation on this topic in the next few years and encourage multimedia researchers to work on trans-disciplinary challenges involving ecological and environmental data
- foster technological ports from one domain to another and exchanges between the different communities (information retrieval, computer vision, bioaccoustic, machine learning, etc.)

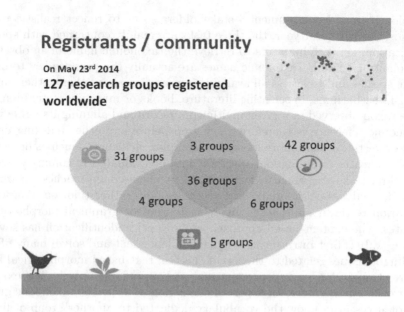

**Fig. 1.** Thematic map of the 127 registrants to LifeCLEF 2014

- promote citizen science and nature observation as a way to describe, analyse and preserve biodiversity

In 2014, 127 research groups worldwide registered to at least one task of the lab. Figure 1 displays the distribution of the registrants per task showing that some of them were interested specifically in one task whereas some others were interested in several or all of them. Of course, as in any evaluation campaign, only a small fraction of this raw audience did cross the finish line by submitting runs (actually 22 of them). But still, this shows the high attractiveness of the proposed datasets and challenges as well as the potential emergence of a wide community interested in life media analysis.

## 2    Task1: PlantCLEF

### 2.1    Context

Content-based image retrieval approaches are nowadays considered to be one of the most promising solution to help bridge the botanical taxonomic gap, as discussed in [22] or [37] for instance. We therefore see an increasing interest in this trans-disciplinary challenge in the multimedia community (e.g. in [26,12,36,41,28,5]). Beyond the raw identification performances achievable by state-of-the-art computer vision algorithms, the visual search approach offers much more efficient and interactive ways of browsing large floras than standard field guides or online web catalogs. Smartphone applications relying on such image-based identification services are particularly promising for setting-up massive ecological monitoring systems, involving hundreds of thousands of contributors at a very low cost.

The first noticeable progress in this way was achieved by the US consortium at the origin of LeafSnap[4]. This popular iPhone application allows a fair identification of 185 common American plant species by simply shooting a cut leaf on a uniform background (see [37] for more details). A step beyond was achieved recently by the Pl@ntNet project [32] which released a cross-platform application (iPhone [21], android[5] and web [6]) allowing (i) to query the system with pictures of plants in their natural environment and (ii) to contribute to the dataset thanks to a collaborative data validation workflow involving Tela Botanica[7] (i.e. the largest botanical social network in Europe).

As promising as these applications are, their performances are however still far from the requirements of a real-world social-based ecological surveillance scenario. Allowing the mass of citizens to produce accurate plant observations requires to equip them with much more accurate identification tools. Measuring and boosting the performances of content-based identification tools is therefore crucial. This was precisely the goal of the ImageCLEF[8] plant identification task organized since 2011 in the context of the worldwide evaluation forum CLEF[9]. In 2011, 2012 and 2013 respectively 8, 10 and 12 international research groups did cross the finish line of this large collaborative evaluation by benchmarking their images-based plant identification systems (see [22], [23] and [33] for more details). Data mobilised during these 3 first years can be consulted at the following url[10], geographic distribution of theses botanical records can be seen on Figure 2.

Contrary to previous evaluations reported in the literature, the key objective was to build a realistic task closer to real-world conditions (different users, cameras, areas, periods of the year, individual plants, etc.). This was initially achieved through a citizen science initiative initiated 4 years ago in the context of the Pl@ntNet project [32] in order to boost the image production of Tela Botanica social network. The evaluation data was enriched each year with the new contributions and progressively diversified with other input feeds (Annotation and cleaning of older data, contributions made through Pl@ntNet mobile applications). The plant task of LifeCLEF 2014 is directly in the continuity of this effort. Main novelties compared to the last years are the following: (i) an explicit multi-image query scenario (ii) the supply of user ratings on image quality in the meta-data (iii) a new type of view called "Branch" additionally to the 6 previous ones (iv) basically more species (about 500 which is an important step towards covering the entire flora of a given region).

---

[4] http://leafsnap.com/
[5] https://play.google.com/store/apps/details?id=org.plantnet
[6] http://identify.plantnet-project.org/
[7] http://www.tela-botanica.org/
[8] http://www.imageclef.org/
[9] http://www.clef-initiative.eu/
[10] http://publish.plantnet-project.org/project/plantclef

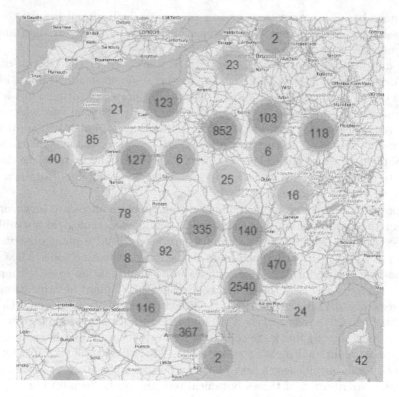

**Fig. 2.** Distribution map of botanical records of the Plant task 2013

## 2.2  Dataset

More precisely, PlantCLEF 2014 dataset is composed of 60,962 pictures belonging to 19,504 observations of 500 species of trees, herbs and ferns living in a European region centered around France. This data was collected by 1608 distinct contributors. Each picture belongs to one and only one of the 7 types of view reported in the meta-data (entire plant, fruit, leaf, flower, stem, branch, leaf scan) and is associated with a single plant observation identifier allowing to link it with the other pictures of the same individual plant (observed the same day by the same person). It is noticeable that most image-based identification methods and evaluation data proposed in the past were so far based on leaf images (e.g. in [37,6,12] or in the more recent methods evaluated in [23]). Only few of them were focused on flower's images as in [42] or [4]. Leaves are far from being the only discriminant visual key between species but, due to their shape and size, they have the advantage to be easily observed, captured and described. More diverse parts of the plants however have to be considered for accurate identification. As an example, the 6 species depicted in Figure 3 share the same French common name of *"laurier"* even though they belong to different taxonomic groups (4 families, 6 genera).

**Fig. 3.** 6 plant species sharing the same common name for laurel in French, belonging to distinct species

The main reason is that these shrubs, often used in hedges, share leaves with more or less the same-sized elliptic shape. Identifying a *laurel* can be very difficult for a novice by just observing leaves, while it is undisputably easier with flowers. Beyond identification performances, the use of leaves alone has also some practical and botanical limitations. Leaves are not visible all over the year for a large fraction of plant species. Deciduous species, distributed from temperate to tropical regions, can't be identified by the use of their leaves over different periods of the year. Leaves can be absent (ie. leafless species), too young or too much degraded (by pathogen or insect attacks), to be exploited efficiently. Moreover, leaves of many species are intrinsically not informative enough or very difficult to capture (needles of pines, thin leaves of grasses, huge leaves of palms, ...).

Another originality of PlantCLEF dataset is that its social nature makes it closer to the conditions of a real-world identification scenario: (i) images of the same species are coming from distinct plants living in distinct areas (ii) pictures are taken by different users that might not used the same protocol to acquire the images (iii) pictures are taken at different periods in the year. Each image of the dataset is associated with contextual meta-data (author, date, locality name, plant id) and social data (user ratings on image quality, collaboratively validated taxon names, vernacular names) provided in a structured xml file. The gps geo-localization and the device settings are available only for some of the images.

Table 4 gives some examples of pictures with decreasing averaged users ratings for the different types of views. Note that the users of the specialized social network creating these ratings (Tela Botanica) are explicitely asked to rate the images according to their plant identification ability and their accordance to the pre-defined acquisition protocol for each view type. This is not an aesthetic or general interest judgement as in most social image sharing sites.

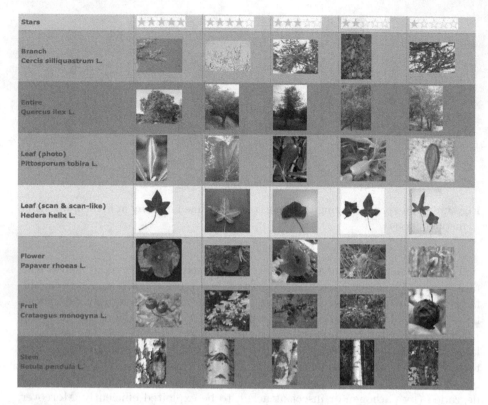

**Fig. 4.** Examples of PlantCLEF pictures with decreasing averaged users ratings for the different types of views

## 2.3  Task Description

The task was evaluated as a plant species retrieval task based on multi-image plant observations queries. The goal is to retrieve the correct plant species among the top results of a ranked list of species returned by the evaluated system. Contrary to previous plant identification benchmarks, queries are not defined as single images but as *plant observations*, meaning a set of one to several images depicting the same individual plant, observed by the same person, the same day. Each image of a query observation is associated with a single view type (entire plant, branch, leaf, fruit, flower, stem or leaf scan) and with contextual metadata (data, location, author). Semi-supervised and interactive approaches were allowed but as a variant of the task and therefore evaluated independently from the fully automatic methods. None of the participants, however, did use such approaches in the 2014 campaign.

In practice, the whole PlantCLEF dataset was split in two parts, one for training (and/or indexing) and one for testing. The training set was delivered to the participants in January 2014 and the test set two months later so that participants had some times to become familiar with the data and train their systems. After the delivery of the test set, participants had two additional months to run their system on the undetermined plant observations and finally send their resuls files. Participants were allowed to submit up to 4 distinct runs. More concretely, the test set was built by randomly choosing 1/3 of the observations of each species whereas the remaining observations were kept in the reference training set. The xml files containing the meta-data of the *query* images were purged so as to erase the taxon name (the ground truth), the vernacular name (common name of the plant) and the image quality ratings (that would not be available at query stage in a real-world mobile application). Meta-data of the observations in the training set were kept unaltered.

The metric used to evaluate the submitted runs was a score related to the rank of the correct species in the returned list. Each query observation was attributed with a score between 0 and 1 reflecting equal to the inverse of the rank of the correct species (equal to 1 if the correct species is the top-1 decreasing quickly while the rank of the correct species increases). An average score was then computed across all plant observation queries. A simple mean on all plant observation queries would however introduce some bias. Indeed, we remind that the PlantCLEF dataset was built in a collaborative manner. So that few contributors might have provided much more observations and pictures than many other contributors who provided few. Since we want to evaluate the ability of a system to provide the correct answers to all users, we rather measure the mean of the average classification rate per author. Finally, our primary metric was defined as the following average classification score $S$:

$$S = \frac{1}{U} \sum_{u=1}^{U} \frac{1}{P_u} \sum_{p=1}^{P_u} \frac{1}{N_{u,p}} s_{u,p} \tag{1}$$

where $U$ is the number of users, $P_u$ the number of individual plants observed by the $u$-th user, $N_{u,p}$ the number of pictures of the $p$-th plant observation of the $u$-th user, $s_{u,p}$ is the score between 1 and 0 equals to the inverse of the rank of the correct species.

## 2.4 Participants and Results

74 research groups worldwide registered to the plant task (31 of them being exclusively registered to the bird task). Among this large raw audience, 10 research groups did cross the finish line by submitting runs (from 1 to 4 depending on the teams). Details on the participants and the methods used in the runs are synthesised in the overview working note of the task [25] and further developed in the individual working notes of the participants who submitted one (BME TMIT [53], FINKI [15], I3S [29], IBM AU [13], IV-Processing [18], MIRACL [34], PlantNet [27], QUT [52], Sabanki-Okan [59], SZTE [44]). We here only report the official scores of the 27 collected runs and discuss the main outcomes of the task.

Figure 5 shows the main official score obtained by each run of the task.

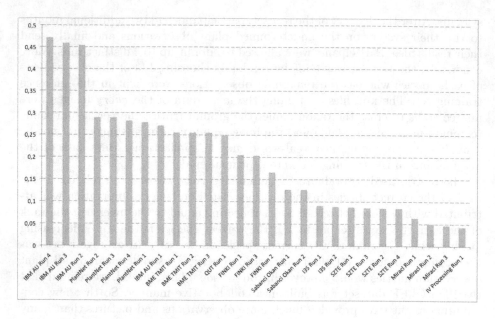

**Fig. 5.** Official results of the LifeCLEF 2014 Plant Identification Task

The best results are indisputably obtained by the three last runs of the IBM AU team (*IBM AU run 2-4*). This confirms that using Fisher Vector encoding and linear support vector machines still provides the best state-of-the-art performances as in many other fine-grained image classification benchmarks. On the other side, the convolutional neural network used in the first run of the same team (*IBM AU run 1*) didn't succeed in outperforming the handcratfed visual features used in the 4 runs of the Pl@ntNet team (whereas they are known to perform very well in generalist benchmarks such as ImageNET). The main reason, as discussed in the working note of IBM AU team [13], is that deep models usually require much training data to learn their millions of parameters and avoid overfitting (e.g. up to 1000 images per class within ImagNet). To solve this issue, deep neural networks are usually pre-trained on generalist classification tasks before being fine-tuned on the targeted task. But as using external training data was not authorized in PlantCLEF 2014, this approach could not be evaluated by the participants. Allowing such approaches in next campaigns might be possible but is a tricky problem as we need to garanty that none of the images of test set could be found somewhere on the web (queries of the 2014 campaign are for instance publicaly available on TelaBotanica website).

Despite the supremacy of IBM fisher vectors runs, it is surprising to see that the performances of BME TMIT runs, which are based on a very close training model, reached much lower performances. It demonstrates that different implementations and parameters tuning can bring very different performances (e.g. 512x60 fisher vectors dimensions for IBM AU vs. 258x80 for BME TMIT).

Another outcome of the task was that the second best performing method from PlantNet was already among the best performing methods in previous plant identification challenges [2] although LifeCLEF dataset is much bigger and somehow more complex because of the social dimension of the data. This demonstrates the genericity and stability of the underlying matching method and feautures.

This year, few teams attempted to explore the use of metadata. The date was exploited in the Sabanki-Okan runs, only on flowers or fruits, but we don't have a point of comparison in order to see if the use of this information was useful or not. Miracl team attempted to combine the whole textual and structural informations contained in the xml files, but it has been showed to degrade the performances of their pure visual approach. Note that for the first year, after three years of unsuccessful attempts during the previous ImageCLEF Plant Identification Tasks, none of the teams tried to use the locality and GPS information.

# 3   Task2: BirdCLEF

## 3.1   Context

The bird and the plant identification tasks share similar usage scenarios. The general public as well as professionals like park rangers, ecology consultants, and of course, the ornithologists themselves might actually be users of an automated bird identifying system, typically in the context of wider initiatives related to ecological surveillance or biodiversity conservation. Using audio records rather than bird pictures is justified by current practices [11,55,54,10]. Birds are actually not easy to photograph as they are most of the time hidden, perched high in a tree or frightened by human presence, and they can fly very quickly, whereas audio calls and songs have proved to be easier to collect and very discriminant.

Only three noticeable previous initiatives on bird species identification based on their songs or calls in the context of worldwide evaluation took place, in 2013. The first one was the ICML4B bird challenge joint to the international Conference on Machine Learning in Atlanta, June 2013. It was initiated by the SABIOD MASTODONS CNRS group[11], the university of Toulon and the National Natural History Museum of Paris [20]. It included 35 species, and 76 participants submitted their 400 runs on the Kaggle interface. The second challenge was conducted by F. Brigs at MLSP 2013 workshop, with 15 species, and 79 participants in August 2013. The third challenge, and biggest in 2013, was organised by University of Toulon, SABIOD and Biotope, with 80 species from the Provence, France. More than thirty teams participated, reaching 92% of average AUC. The description of the ICML4B best systems are given into the on-line book [3], including for some of them reference to some useful scripts.

In collaboration with the organizers of these previous challenges, BirdCLEF 2014 goes one step further by (i) significantly increasing the species number by almost an order of magnitude (ii) working on real-world social data built

---

[11] http://sabiod.org

from hundreds of recordists (iii) moving to a more usage-driven and system-oriented benchmark by allowing the use of meta-data and defining information retrieval oriented metrics. Overall, the task is expected to be much more difficult than previous benchmarks because of the higher confusion risk between the classes, the higher background noise and the higher diversity in the acquisition conditions (devices, recordists uses, contexts diversity, etc.). It will therefore probably produce substantially lower scores and offer a better progression margin towards building real-world generalist identification tools.

## 3.2 Dataset

The training and test data of the bird task is composed by audio recordings collected by Xeno-canto (XC)[12]. Xeno-canto is a web-based community of bird sound recordists worldwide with about 1500 active contributors that have already collected more than 150,000 recordings of about 9000 species. Nearly 500 species from Brazilian forests are used in the BirdCLEF dataset, representing the 500 species of that region with the highest number of recordings, totalling about 14,000 recordings produced by hundreds of users. Figure 6 illustrates the geographical distribution of the dataset samples.

To avoid any bias in the evaluation related to the used audio devices, each audio file has been normalized to a constant bandwidth of 44.1 kHz and coded over 16 bits in wav mono format (the right channel is selected by default). The conversion from the original Xeno-canto data set was done using ffmpeg, sox and matlab scripts. The optimized 16 Mel Filter Cepstrum Coefficients for bird identification (according to an extended benchmark [16]) have been computed with their first and second temporal derivatives on the whole set. They were used in the best systems run in ICML4B and NIPS4B challenges.

Audio records are associated with various meta-data including the species of the most active singing bird, the species of the other birds audible in the background, the type of sound (call, song, alarm, flight, etc.), the date and location of the observations (from which rich statistics on species distribution can be derived), some textual comments of the authors, multilingual common names and collaborative quality ratings. All of them were produced collaboratively by Xeno-canto community.

## 3.3 Task Description

Participants are asked to determine the species of the most active singing birds in each query file. The background noise can be used as any other meta-data, but it is forbidden to correlate the test set of the challenge with the original annotated Xeno-canto data base (or with any external content as many of them are circulating on the web). More precisely and similarly to the plant task, the whole BirdCLEF dataset has been split in two parts, one for training (and/or indexing) and one for testing. The test set was built by randomly choosing 1/3

---

[12] http://www.xeno-canto.org/

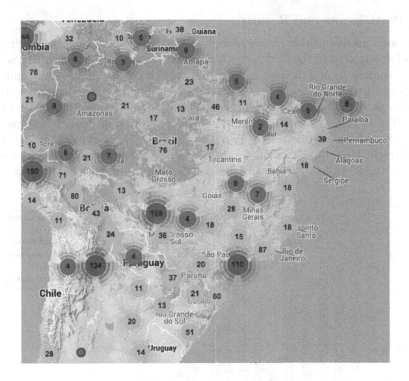

**Fig. 6.** Xeno-canto audio recordings distribution centered around Brazil area

of the observations of each species whereas the remaining observations were kept in the reference training set. Recordings of the same species done by the same person the same day are considered as being part of the same observation and cannot be split across the test and training set. The xml files containing the meta-data of the *query* recordings were purged so as to erase the taxon name (the ground truth), the vernacular name (common name of the bird) and the collaborative quality ratings (that would not be available at query stage in a real-world mobile application). Meta-data of the recordings in the training set are kept unaltered.

The groups participating to the task will be asked to produce up to 4 runs containing a ranked list of the most probable species for each query records of the test set. Each species will have to be associated with a normalized score in the range [0; 1] reflecting the likelihood that this species is singing in the sample. The primary metric used to compare the runs will be the Mean Average Precision averaged across all queries. Additionally, to allow easy comparisons with the previous Kaggle ICML4B and NIPS4B benchmarks, the AUC under the ROC curve will be computed for each species, and averaged over all species.

## 3.4   Participants and Results

87 research groups worldwide registered to the bird task (42 of them being exclusively registered to the bird task). Among this large raw audience, 10 research groups, coming from 9 distinct countries, did cross the finish line by submitting runs (from 1 to 4 depending on the teams). Details on the participants and the methods used in the runs are synthesised in the overview working note of the task [24] and further developed in the individual working notes of the participants who submitted one (MNB TSA [38], QMUL [51], Inria Zenith [31], HTL [46], Utrecht Univ. [57], Golem [40], SCS [43]). We here only report the official scores of the 29 collected runs and discuss the main outcomes of the task.

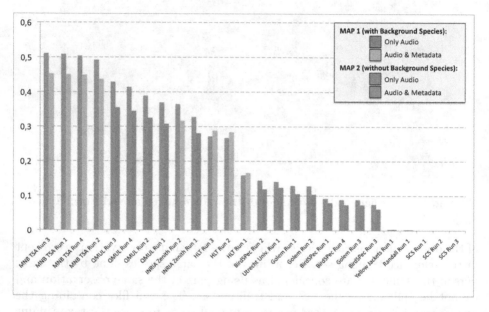

**Fig. 7.** Official scores of the LifeCLEF Bird Identification Task. mAP 1 is the Mean Average Precision averaged across all queries taking int account the Background species (while mAP2 is considering only the foreground species.

Figure 7 displays the two distinct measured mean Average Precision (mAP) for each run, the first one (mAP1) considering only the foreground specie of each test recording and the other (mAP2) considering additionally the species listed in the *Background species* field of the metadata. Note that different colors have been used to easily differentiate the methods making use of the metadata from the purely audio-based methods.

The first main outcome is that the two best performing methods were already among the best performing methods in previous bird identification challenges [3,20] although LifeCLEF dataset is much bigger and somhow more complex because of the social dimension of the data. This clearly demonstrates the genericity and stability of the underlying methods. The best performing runs of MNB

TSA group notably confirmed that using matching probabilities of segments as features was once again a good choice. In their working note [38], Lassek et al. actually show that the use of such Segment-Probabilities clearly outperforms the other feature sets they used (0.49 mAP compared to 0.30 for the OpenSmile features [17] and 0.12 for the metadata features). The approach however remains very time consuming as several days on 4 computers were required to process the whole LifeCLEF dataset.

Then, the best performing (purely) audio-based runs of QMUL confirmed that unsupervised feature learning is a simple and effective method to boost classification performance by learning spectro-temporal regularities in the data. They actually show in their working note that their pooling method based on spherical k-means actually produces much more effective features than the raw initial low level features (MFCC based features). The principal practical issue with such unsupervised feature learning is that it requires large data volumes to be effective. However, this exhibits a synergy with the large data volumes used within LifeCLEF. This might also explain the rather good performances obtained by the runs of Inria ZENITH group who used hash-based indexing techniques of MFCC features and approximate nearest neigbours classifiers. The underlying hash-based partition and embedding method actually works as an unsupervised feature learning method.

## 4   Task3: FishCLEF

### 4.1   Context

Underwater video monitoring has been widely used in recent years for marine video surveillance, as opposed to human manned photography or net-casting methods, since it does not influence fish behavior and provides a large amount of material at the same time. However, it is impractical for humans to manually analyze the massive quantity of video data daily generated, because it requires much time and concentration and it is also error prone. Automatic fish identification in videos is therefore of crucial importance, in order to estimate fish existence and quantity [50,49,47]. Moreover, it would help supporting marine biologists to understand the natural underwater environment, promote its preservation, and study behaviors and interactions between marine animals that are part of it. Beyond this, video-based fish species identification finds applications in many other contexts: from education (e.g. primary/high schools) to the entertainment industry (e.g. in aquarium).

To the best of our knowledge, this is the first worldwide initiative on automatic image and video based fish species identification.

### 4.2   Dataset

The underwater video dataset used for FishCLEF is derived from the Fish4 Knowledge[13] video repository, which contains about 700k 10-minute video clips

---

[13] http://www.fish4knowledge.eu

**Fig. 8.** 4 snapshots of 4 cameras monitoring the Taiwan's Kenting site

that were taken in the past five years to monitor Taiwan coral reefs. The Taiwan area is particularly interesting for studying the marine ecosystem, as it holds one of the largest fish biodiversities of the world with more than 3000 different fish species whose taxonomy is available at [14]. The dataset contains videos recorded from sunrise to sunset showing several phenomena, e.g. murky water, algae on camera lens, etc., which makes the fish identification task more complex. Each video has a resolution of 320x240 with 8 fps and comes with some additional metadata including date and localization of the recordings. Figure 8 shows 4 snapshots of 4 cameras monitoring the coral reef by Taiwan's Kenting site and it illustrates the complexity of automatic fish detection and recognition in real-life settings.

More specifically, the FishCLEF dataset consists of about 3000 videos with several thousands of detected fish. The fish detections were obtained by processing such underwater videos with video analysis tools [48] and then manually labeled using the system in [35].

### 4.3   Task Description

The dataset for the video-based fish identification task will be released in two times: the participants will first have access to the training set and a few months later, they will be provided with the testing set. The goal is to automatically detect fish and its species. The task comprises three sub-tasks: 1) identifying moving objects in videos by either background modeling or object detection

---

[14] http://fishdb.sinica.edu.tw/

methods, 2) detecting fish instances in video frames and then 3) identifying species (taken from a subset of the most seen fish species) of fish detected in video frames.

Participants could decide to compete for only one subtask or all subtasks. Although tasks 2 and 3 are based on still images, participants are invited to exploit motion information extracted from videos to support their strategies.

As scoring functions, the authors are asked to produce:

- ROC curves for sub-task one. In particular, precision, recall and F-measures measured when comparing, on a pixel basis, the ground truth binary masks and the output masks of the object detection methods are required;
- Recall for fish detection in still images as a function of bounding box overlap percentage: a detection is considered true positive if the PASCAL score between it and the corresponding object in the ground truth is over 0.7;
- Average recall and recall per fish species for the fish recognition subtask.

The participants to the above tasks will be asked to produce several runs containing a list of detected fish together with their species (only for subtask 3). When dealing fish species identification, a ranked list of the most probable species (and the related likelihood values) for each detected fish must be provided.

## 4.4  Participants and Results

About 50 teams registered to the fish task, but only two of them finally submitted runs: one, the I3S team, for subtask 3 and one, the LSIS/DYNI team, for subtask 4.

The strategy employed by the I3S team [9] for fish identification and recognition (subtask 3) consisted of, first, applying a background modeling approach based on Mixture of Gaussian for moving object segmentation. SVM learning using keyframes of species as positive entries and background of current video as negative entries was used for fish species classification. The results achieved by the I3S team were compared to the baseline provided by the organizers (ViBe [8] background modeling approach for fish detection combined to VLFeat BoW [56] for fish species recognition). While the average recall obtained by the I3S team was lower than the baseline's recall, the precision was improved, thus implying that their fish species classification approach was reliable more than the fish detection approach. On average More detailed results can be found in the working note of the task [14].

The LSIS/DYNI team submitted three runs for subtask 4 [30]. Each run followed the strategy proposed in [45] which, basically, consisted of extracting low level features, patch encoding, pooling with spatial pyramid for local analysis and a linear large-scale supervised classication by averaging posterior probabilities estimated through linear regression of linear SVM's outputs. No image specific pre-processing regarding illumination correction or background subtraction was performed. Results show that the method of LSIS/DYNI team clearly outperforms the baseline (VLFeat BoW [56]) and achieves near-perfect classification on several species. It is however important to note that the image-based recognition task (subtask 4) was easier than subtask 3 since (i) it didn't need any fish detection module (which is the most complex part in video-based fish identification) and (ii) only ten fish species were included in the ground truth.

## 5     Conclusions and Perspectives

With more than 120 research groups who downloaded LifeCLEF datasets and 22 of them who submitted runs, the pilot edition of LifeCLEF was a success showing a high interest of the proposed challenges in several communities (computer vision, multimedia, bio-accoustic, machine learning). The results of the plant and the bird tasks did show that very promising identification performances can be reached even with such an unprecedent number of species in the repsective training sets (i.e. 500 species for each task). This is clearly good news with regard to the ecological urgency in building effective identification tools. However, we believe that some consistent progress is still needed if we would like to use such tools for automatically monitoring real-world ecosystems. One of the key challenge is notably to deal with the long tail of species that are represented with much fewer images than the top-500 most common species that we targeted within BirdCLEF and PlantCLEF 2014. For the next campaigns, we will notably discuss the possibility of using the whole Pl@ntNet dataset that covers more than 5000 species but in which many species are represented with very few samples. Concerning the fish task, we believe that the main reason for the lower participation is its high complexity. Video contents are actually much harder to manage and implies several difficult subtasks before being able to apply classical image classification techniques. Also, the cost of annotating the raw video contents makes it difficult to produce large-scale ground-truth and training data. But on the other side, this shows the importance of building automatic methods for processing such huge data.

## References

1. MAED 2012: Proceedings of the 1st ACM International Workshop on Multimedia Analysis for Ecological Data. ACM, New York (2012) 433127
2. Inria's participation at ImageCLEF 2013 Plant Identification Task. In: CLEF (Online Working Notes/Labs/Workshop) 2013, Valencia, Espagne (2013)
3. Proc. of the first workshop on Machine Learning for Bioacoustics (2013)
4. Angelova, A., Zhu, S., Lin, Y., Wong, J., Shpecht, C.: Development and deployment of a large-scale flower recognition mobile app. Technical report (December 2012)
5. Aptoula, E., Yanikoglu, B.: Morphological features for leaf based plant recognition. In: Proc. IEEE Int. Conf. Image Process., Melbourne, Australia, p. 7 (2013)
6. Backes, A.R., Casanova, D., Bruno, O.M.: Plant leaf identification based on volumetric fractal dimension. International Journal of Pattern Recognition and Artificial Intelligence 23(6), 1145–1160 (2009)
7. Baillie, J., Hilton-Taylor, C., Stuart, S.: 2004 iucn red list of threatened species. a global species assessment. IUCN, Gland, Switzerland and Cambridge, UK (2004)

8. Barnich, O., Van Droogenbroeck, M.: Vibe: A universal background subtraction algorithm for video sequences. IEEE Transactions on Image Processing 20(6), 1709–1724 (2011)

9. Blanc, K., Lingrand, D., Precioso, F.: Fish species recognition from video using svm classifier. In: Working Notes of CLEF 2014 Conference (2014)

10. Briggs, F., Lakshminarayanan, B., Neal, L., Fern, X.Z., Raich, R., Hadley, S.J., Hadley, A.S., Betts, M.G.: Acoustic classification of multiple simultaneous bird species: A multi-instance multi-label approach. The Journal of the Acoustical Society of America 131, 4640 (2012)

11. Cai, J., Ee, D., Pham, B., Roe, P., Zhang, J.: Sensor network for the monitoring of ecosystem: Bird species recognition. In: 3rd International Conference on Intelligent Sensors, Sensor Networks and Information, ISSNIP 2007, pp. 293–298 (December 2007)

12. Cerutti, G., Tougne, L., Vacavant, A., Coquin, D.: A parametric active polygon for leaf segmentation and shape estimation. In: Bebis, G. (ed.) ISVC 2011, Part I. LNCS, vol. 6938, pp. 202–213. Springer, Heidelberg (2011)

13. Chen, Q., Abedini, M., Garnavi, R., Liang, X.: Ibm research australia at lifeclef2014: Plant identification task. In: Working notes of CLEF 2014 Conference (2014)

14. Concetto, S., Fisher, B., Boom, B.: Lifeclef fish identification task 2014. In: CLEF Working Notes (2014)

15. Dimitrovski, I., Madjarov, G., Lameski, P., Kocev, D.: Maestra at lifeclef 2014 plant task: Plant identification using visual data. In: Working Notes of CLEF 2014 Conference (2014)

16. Dufour, O., Artieres, T., Glotin, H., Giraudet, P.: Clusterized mel filter cepstral coefficients and support vector machines for bird song idenfication (2013)

17. Eyben, F., Wöllmer, M., Schuller, B.: Opensmile: the munich versatile and fast open-source audio feature extractor. In: Proceedings of the International Conference on Multimedia, pp. 1459–1462. ACM (2010)

18. Fakhfakh, S., Akrout, B., Tmar, M., Mahdi, W.: A visual search of multimedia documents in lifeclef 2014. In: Working Notes of CLEF 2014 Conference (2014)

19. Gaston, K.J., O'Neill, M.A.: Automated species identification: why not? 359(1444), 655–667 (2004)

20. Glotin, H., Sueur, J.: Overview of the first international challenge on bird classification (2013)

21. Goëau, H., Bonnet, P., Joly, A., Bakić, V., Barbe, J., Yahiaoui, I., Selmi, S., Carré, J., Barthélémy, D., Boujemaa, N.: et al. Pl@ntnet mobile app. In: Proceedings of the 21st ACM International Conference on Multimedia, pp. 423–424. ACM (2013)

22. Goëau, H., Bonnet, P., Joly, A., Boujemaa, N., Barthélémy, D., Molino, J.-F., Birnbaum, P., Mouysset, E., Picard, M.: The ImageCLEF 2011 plant images classification task. In: CLEF Working Notes (2011)

23. Goëau, H., Bonnet, P., Joly, A., Yahiaoui, I., Barthelemy, D., Boujemaa, N., Molino, J.-F.: The imageclef 2012 plant identification task. In: CLEF Working Notes (2012)

24. Goëau, H., Glotin, H., Vellinga, W.-P., Rauber, A.: Lifeclef bird identification task (2014)

25. Goëau, H., Joly, A., Bonnet, P., Molino, J.-F., Barthélémy, D., Boujemaa, N.: Lifeclef plant identification task 2014. In: CLEF Working Notes 2014 (2014)

26. Goëau, H., Joly, A., Selmi, S., Bonnet, P., Mouysset, E., Joyeux, L., Molino, J.-F., Birnbaum, P., Bathelemy, D., Boujemaa, N.: Visual-based plant species identification from crowdsourced data. In: ACM Conference on Multimedia, pp. 813–814 (2011)

27. Goëau, H., Joly, A., Yahiaoui, I., Bakić, V., Anne, V.-B.: Pl@ntnet's participation at lifeclef 2014 plant identification task. In: Working notes of CLEF 2014 Conference (2014)

28. Hazra, A., Deb, K., Kundu, S., Hazra, P., et al.: Shape oriented feature selection for tomato plant identification. International Journal of Computer Applications Technology and Research 2(4), 449–meta (2013)

29. Issolah, M., Lingrand, D., Precioso, F.: Plant species recognition using bag-of-word with svm classifier in the context of the lifeclef challenge. In: Working notes of CLEF 2014 Conference (2014)

30. Joalland, P.-H., Paris, S., Glotin, H.: Efficient instance-based fish species visual identification by global representation. In: Working Notes of CLEF 2014 Conference (2014)

31. Joly, A., Champ, J., Buisson, O.: Instance-based bird species identification with undiscriminant features pruning - lifeclef2014. In: Working Notes of CLEF 2014 Conference (2014)

32. Joly, A., Goeau, H., Bonnet, P., Bakić, V., Barbe, J., Selmi, S., Yahiaoui, I., Carré, J., Mouysset, E., Molino, J.-F., Boujemaa, N., Barthélémy, D.: Interactive plant identification based on social image data. Ecological Informatics (2013)

33. Joly, A., Goëau, H., Bonnet, P., Bakic, V., Molino, J.-F., Barthélémy, D., Boujemaa, N.: The Imageclef Plant Identification Task 2013. In: International Workshop on Multimedia Analysis for Ecological Data, Barcelone, Espagne (October 2013)

34. Karamti, H., Fakhfakh, S., Tmar, M., Gargouri, F.: Miracl at lifeclef 2014: Multi-organ observation for plant identification. In: Working notes of CLEF 2014 Conference (2014)

35. Kavasidis, I., Palazzo, S., Salvo, R., Giordano, D., Spampinato, C.: An innovative web-based collaborative platform for video annotation. In: Multimedia Tools and Applications, pp. 1–20 (2013)

36. Kebapci, H., Yanikoglu, B., Unal, G.: Plant image retrieval using color, shape and texture features. The Computer Journal 54(9), 1475–1490 (2011)

37. Kumar, N., Belhumeur, P.N., Biswas, A., Jacobs, D.W., Kress, W.J., Lopez, I.C., Soares, J.V.B.: Leafsnap: A computer vision system for automatic plant species identification. In: Fitzgibbon, A., Lazebnik, S., Perona, P., Sato, Y., Schmid, C. (eds.) ECCV 2012, Part II. LNCS, vol. 7573, pp. 502–516. Springer, Heidelberg (2012)

38. Lasseck, M.: Large-scale identification of birds in audio recordings. In: Working notes of CLEF 2014 Conference (2014)

39. Lee, D.-J., Schoenberger, R.B., Shiozawa, D., Xu, X., Zhan, P.: Contour matching for a fish recognition and migration-monitoring system. In: Optics East, pp. 37–48. International Society for Optics and Photonics (2004)

40. Martinez, R., Silvan, L., Villarreal, E.V., Fuentes, G., Meza, I.: Svm candidates and sparse representation for bird identification. In: Working notes of CLEF 2014 Conference (2014)

41. Mouine, S., Yahiaoui, I., Verroust-Blondet, A.: Advanced shape context for plant species identification using leaf image retrieval. In: ACM International Conference on Multimedia Retrieval, pp. 49:1–49:8 (2012)

42. Nilsback, M.-E., Zisserman, A.: Automated flower classification over a large number of classes. In: Indian Conference on Computer Vision, Graphics and Image Processing, pp. 722–729 (2008)
43. Northcott, J.: Overview of the lifeclef 2014 bird task. In: Working Notes of CLEF 2014 Conference (2014)
44. Paczolay, D., Bánhalmi, A., Nyúl, L., Bilicki, V., Sárosi, Á.: Wlab of university of szeged at lifeclef 2014 plant identification task. In: Working notes of CLEF 2014 Conference (2014)
45. Paris, S., Halkias, X., Glotin, H.: Sparse coding for histograms of local binary patterns applied for image categorization: toward a bag-of-scenes analysis. In: 2012 21st International Conference on Pattern Recognition (ICPR), pp. 2817–2820. IEEE (2012)
46. Ren, L.Y., William Dennis, J., Huy Dat, T.: Bird classification using ensemble classifiers. In: Working notes of CLEF 2014 Conference (2014)
47. Shortis, M.R., Ravanbakskh, M., Shaifat, F., Harvey, E.S., Mian, A., Seager, J.W., Culverhouse, P.F., Cline, D.E., Edgington, D.R.: A review of techniques for the identification and measurement of fish in underwater stereo-video image sequences. In: SPIE Optical Metrology 2013, pp. 87910G–87910G. International Society for Optics and Photonics (2013)
48. Spampinato, C., Beauxis-Aussalet, E., Palazzo, S., Beyan, C., Ossenbruggen, J., He, J., Boom, B., Huang, X.: A rule-based event detection system for real-life underwater domain. Machine Vision and Applications 25(1), 99–117 (2014)
49. Spampinato, C., Chen-Burger, Y.-H., Nadarajan, G., Fisher, R.B.: Detecting, tracking and counting fish in low quality unconstrained underwater videos. In: VISAPP (2), pp. 514–519. Citeseer (2008)
50. Spampinato, C., Giordano, D., Di Salvo, R., Chen-Burger, Y.-H.J., Fisher, R.B., Nadarajan, G.: Automatic fish classification for underwater species behavior understanding. In: Proceedings of ACM ARTEMIS 2010, pp. 45–50. ACM (2010)
51. Stowell, D., Plumbley, M.D.: Audio-only bird classification using unsupervised feature learning. In: Working notes of CLEF 2014 Conference (2014)
52. Sunderhauf, N., McCool, C., Upcroft, B., Tristan, P.: Fine-grained plant classification using convolutional neural networks for feature extraction. In: Working Notes of CLEF 2014 Conference (2014)
53. Szúcs, G., Dávid, P., Lovas, D.: Viewpoints combined classification method in image-based plant identification task. In: Working Notes of CLEF 2014 Conference (2014)
54. Towsey, M., Planitz, B., Nantes, A., Wimmer, J., Roe, P.: A toolbox for animal call recognition. Bioacoustics 21(2), 107–125 (2012)
55. Trifa, V.M., Kirschel, A.N., Taylor, C.E., Vallejo, E.E.: Automated species recognition of antbirds in a mexican rainforest using hidden markov models. The Journal of the Acoustical Society of America 123, 2424 (2008)
56. Vedaldi, A., Fulkerson, B.: Vlfeat: An open and portable library of computer vision algorithms. In: Proceedings of the International Conference on Multimedia, pp. 1469–1472. ACM (2010)
57. Vincent Koops, H., van Balen, J., Wiering, F.: A deep neural network approach to the lifeclef 2014 bird task. In: Working notes of CLEF 2014 Conference (2014)
58. Wheeler, Q.D., Raven, P.H., Wilson, E.O.: Taxonomy: Impediment or expedient? Science, 303(5656), 285 (2004)
59. Yanikoglu, B., Tolga, Y.S., Tirkaz, C., FuenCaglartes, E.: Sabanci-okan system at lifeclef 2014 plant identification competition. In: Working notes of CLEF 2014 Conference (2014)

# Benchmarking News Recommendations in a Living Lab

Frank Hopfgartner[1], Benjamin Kille[1], Andreas Lommatzsch[1], Till Plumbaum[1], Torben Brodt[2], and Tobias Heintz[2]

[1] Technische Universität Berlin, Ernst-Reuter-Platz 7, 10587 Berlin, Germany
[2] plista GmbH, Torstraße 33–35, 10119 Berlin, Germany

**Abstract.** Most user-centric studies of information access systems in literature suffer from unrealistic settings or limited numbers of users who participate in the study. In order to address this issue, the idea of a living lab has been promoted. Living labs allow us to evaluate research hypotheses using a large number of users who satisfy their information need in a real context. In this paper, we introduce a living lab on news recommendation in real time. The living lab has first been organized as News Recommendation Challenge at ACM RecSys'13 and then as campaign-style evaluation lab NEWSREEL at CLEF'14. Within this lab, researchers were asked to provide news article recommendations to millions of users in real time. Different from user studies which have been performed in a laboratory, these users are following their own agenda. Consequently, laboratory bias on their behavior can be neglected. We outline the living lab scenario and the experimental setup of the two benchmarking events. We argue that the living lab can serve as reference point for the implementation of living labs for the evaluation of information access systems.

## 1   Introduction

Over the years, significant effort has been done to establish appropriate measures, frameworks, and datasets that allow for a fair and unbiased evaluation of novel approaches for information retrieval and recommender systems, also referred to as information access systems. In the field of information retrieval, consortia such as TREC, CLEF and FIRE provided the ground for focused research on various aspects of information retrieval. In the field of recommender systems, the release of the Netflix dataset and the associated challenge was a key event that led to an advance of research on recommender systems. Although the release of common datasets was of great benefit for the research community, focusing on them does not come without drawbacks [34]. While datasets can be used to fine-tune models and algorithms to increase precision and recall even further, the user is often kept out of the loop [20,6]. However, the user plays an essential role in the evaluation of information access systems. It is the user's information need that needs to be satisfied and it is the user's personal interests that need to be considered when adapting retrieval results when providing good recommendations.

E. Kanoulas et al. (Eds.): CLEF 2014, LNCS 8685, pp. 250–267, 2014.

Consequently, user-centric evaluation of information access systems is essential to evaluate the full performance of such systems. Unfortunately though, most researchers often have limited access to real user interactions that would allow testing research hypotheses in a large scale. In order to address this issue, the application of a living lab has been proposed (e.g., [19,20]) that grant researchers access to real users who follow their own information seeking tasks in a natural and thus realistic contextual setting. For user-centric research on information access systems, realistic context is essential since it is a requirement for a fair and unbiased evaluation.

In this paper, we introduce a living lab for the real-time evaluation of news recommendation algorithms. The lab infrastructure was used during the News Recommender Systems (NRS) challenge which was held in conjunction with ACM RecSys 2013 and during the campaign-style lab NEWSREEL of CLEF 2014. By participating in this living lab, participants were given the opportunity to develop news recommendation algorithms and have them tested by potentially millions of users over a longer period of time. The task which is addressed within this living lab is to provide recommendations under the typical restrictions (e.g., time constraints) of real-world recommender systems. Such restrictions pose requirements regarding scalability as well as complexity for the recommendation algorithms. We introduce this living lab scenario and describe two benchmarking events that show how the living lab can be used to promote research in the news recommendation domain.

This paper is organized as follows. In Section 2, we provide an overview of related work on the evaluation of information access systems. Section 3 introduces the specific domain of providing recommendations on news portals. Section 4 introduces the setup and infrastructure of the living lab for the evaluation of such algorithms. Two benchmarking events where the living lab has been applied are outlined in Section 5. Section 6 concludes this paper.

## 2   Evaluation of Information Access Systems

One of the main prerequisites of modern research is the design and implementation of appropriate evaluation protocols which allow us to compare novel techniques with existing state-of-the-art approaches. In the information retrieval domain, the origin of such protocol is based on the early work of Cleverdon et al. [9] who introduced the idea of evaluating algorithms in a controlled setting using a test dataset. Thanks to the implementation of the Text REtrieval Conference (TREC) initiative [34], the use of test datasets, consisting of document collections, pre-defined search tasks and relevance assessments has become the de-facto evaluation protocol for IR research. Over the years, various datasets from different domains have been published that promoted research on information access systems significantly. In the context of recommender systems evaluation, these domains include books, music, jokes, movies and many others [7,11,14,35].

Although this evaluation paradigm helped us to study multiple research challenges in the field, it did not come without drawbacks. Clough and Sanderson

[10] point out that the main limitations include the artificial nature of the setting that is defined within this batch evaluation and the negligence of the user and their role in the information gathering task. Similar issues have been observed in the evaluation of recommender systems. Konstan and Riedl [22] argue that recommender systems' evaluation should consider the user experience rather than rating prediction accuracy. Additionally, they note that other factors such as scalability, diversity, and novelty play an important role. They propose to define more sophisticated quality measures to capture user experience. Shani and Gunawardana [30] discuss recommender systems evaluation in three settings: (i) experiments on data sets, (ii) user studies, and (iii) online evaluation interacting with actual users. Herein, they state that online evaluation provides the strongest evidence on how well a recommender systems performs. Neither user studies nor experiments on data sets achieve similar expressiveness.

In order to address these limitations, two approaches have been proposed: (1) The extension of test collections by adding user interaction records (e.g., within the TREC Interactive track [12] and the HARD track [2]) and (2) the simulation of user interaction [17,18] that allow to run batch evaluation without the constant requirement of user input.

Both methods come with their own limitations: While bringing the user into the loop can be considered to be a step in the right direction, large user bases are required to confirm research hypotheses [6]. However, this often is not an issue for commercial providers of information access systems. Therefore, having large user bases, user-centric online evaluation is the first choice for the evaluation of such systems. A guideline for large-scale online testing of recommender systems, also referred to as A/B testing, is provided by Amatriain [3]. In order to test improvements or variants of information access systems, new instances of these systems are released that often differ in one key aspect from the original system only. These instances are referred to as System A and System B. Users of the system are then split into different groups: Group A and Group B. When users of Group A want to access the system, they are forwarded to System A. Users of Group B, on the other hand, are forwarded to System B. Observing the users' interactions and their behavior over time, conclusions can be drawn on which of these systems is better.

Although the protocol is rather simple, it comes with a major drawback. In order to get meaningful results, a large user base is required. While this is no problem for commercial providers, the lack of access to actual users hinders non-commercial research significantly. At the SIGIR 2009 workshop on Future Information Retrieval Evaluation [19], participants promoted the application of a living lab to address this issue. Pirolli [27] argues that such living labs could attract researchers from many different domains. Kelly et al. [20] promotes the role of a living lab and its advantages as follows:

*A living laboratory on the Web that brings researchers and searchers together is needed to facilitate ISSS [Information-Seeking Support System] evaluation. Such a lab might contain resources and tools for evaluation as well as infrastructure for collaborative studies. It might also function as a point of contact with those interested in participating in ISSS studies.*

A first proposal for a living lab for information retrieval research is outlined by Azzopardi and Balog [4]. They propose a generic infrastructure for such lab which allows different parties (i.e., researchers, commercial organizations, evaluation forums, and users) to communicate with each other. Moreover, they illustrate how this infrastructure can be used in a specific use case. Although their work can be considered to be a key contribution for the definition of living labs, their work remains theoretical. In this paper, we introduce the application of a living lab for the benchmarking of news recommendation algorithms in real time. Within this living lab, different parties interact with each other using a shared infrastructure: Users visit news portals of commercial providers, these visits are reported to researchers whose task is to identify other news articles of this provider which are then recommended to the user for further reading. To the best of our knowledge, it is the first living lab for the evaluation of information access systems. In the next sections, we first introduce the use case of news article recommendation, followed by an overview of the living lab setup.

## 3   Real-Time News Recommendation

Real-time news recommendation differs from the most *traditional* recommender scenarios which have been studied in literature. Instead of computing recommendations based on a static set of users and items, the challenge here is to provide recommendations for a news article stream characterized by a continuously changing set of users and items. The short lifecycle of items and the strict time-constraints for recommending news articles make great demands on the recommender strategies. In a stream-based scenario the recommender algorithms must be able to cope with lot of newly created articles and should be able to discard old articles, since recommended news articles should be "new". Thus, the recommender algorithms must be steadily adapted to meet the special requirements of the news recommendation scenario. Moreover, the recommendations have to be provided fast since most users are not willing to wait for recommendations that they did not even request in the first place. In order to clarify the types of recommendations which are possible, we outline in this section typical recommendation methods that are able to provide recommendations within a very short period of time, namely: (1) Most recently read articles, (2) Most popular articles, (3) User-based collaborative filtering (CF), (4) Item-based collaborative filtering, and (5) textual similarity of the news article descriptions.

The basic idea of a recommender of most recently read articles is that those articles which are currently read by the community are the most relevant articles for a potential visitor of a news portal. A similar idea is presented by Phelan et al. [26] who use most recent tweets to recommend real-time topical news. The strength of this recommender is that it has a low computational complexity. It provides recommendations very fast and scales well with the number of requests.

Since this algorithm considers neither any contextual feature nor individual user preferences, the recommendation precision is limited. In other words, the recommendations do not reflect the user's profile and are not optimized to the service context.

News articles most frequently requested by the community are typically interesting for most of the users (e.g., [33]). A most popular recommender counts the number of requests per article and suggests the most popular articles still unknown to the user. The strengths of the approach are that the algorithm is simple and provides results having a high probability to be relevant. A weakness of the most popular recommender is that it does not consider individual user preferences and it does not recommend breaking news articles (due to the fact that it takes time for an article to get a large number of impression events). The recommendations are neither personalized nor context-aware.

User-based collaborative filtering (e.g., [15,1]) is the most popular approach in the recommender domain. In order to compute suggestions, this recommender determines similar users based on the accessed items (e.g., news articles). News portals are typically dynamic systems characterized by a large number of article creates and user-article interactions. The advantages of this recommendation approach are that it considers the user preferences and provides personalized results. Disadvantages are that storing the user-item interaction is resource demanding and computing similar users is computational expensive. In addition, collaborative filtering approaches suffer from the "cold-start" problem, making it challenging to compute high-quality recommendations for new users.

Similar to user-based collaborative filtering, item-based collaborative filtering techniques (e.g., [29]) can suggest news articles read by the same users that also read the current news article. In contrast to user-based CF, item-based CF recommenders are robust against noisy user IDs. Additionally, item-based recommendations are often also related on a content-level, due to the observation that users are interested in content-based categories (e.g., basketball). The strength of an item-based collaborative filtering recommender is that this algorithm provides highly relevant suggestions for the documents the user read in the past. The algorithm is robust against noisy user IDs and computes recommendations based on the wisdom of the crowd. Weaknesses are that the algorithm does not consider the context. Additionally, an item-based collaborative filtering approach cannot provide good recommendations for new items having only a small number of ratings ("cold-start problem").

Another approach to provide recommendations is to determine content-based similarity (e.g., [25]) between news articles. The strength of a content-based recommender is that it does not require user feedback and can recommend completely new articles. The disadvantage is that the content does neither say much about the article's quality nor whether the article matches the individual user preferences. The processing of natural language texts and the extraction of the most relevant terms is computational expensive and requires robust linguistic tools. As discussed by several researchers (e.g., [24]), content-based features have a much lower impact on the items' relevance than collaborative features.

Each of the presented methods has its specific strength and weaknesses. The most recently read recommender and the most popular recommender tend to suggest news articles which are of interest for most of the users, but do not consider the individual user preferences. Since both algorithms have a low resource demand, these algorithms can efficiently handle a large number of requests. User-based collaborative filtering provides personalized suggestions based on the preferences of similar users. In contrast to a most popular recommender this algorithm has a higher computational complexity since the preferences of all users must be managed in order to determine the most similar users. Item-based collaborative filtering algorithms as well as algorithms suggesting news articles based on the textual similarity of news articles recommend items related to the currently viewed news article. Both algorithms suggests news articles related to the currently requested article helping the user to track the development of a story and to discover news articles similar with regards to contents.

One approach to overcome the disadvantages of all approaches is to combine the algorithms in a recommender ensemble that can automatically identify the best performing algorithms for a specific domain and adapt its recommendation technique accordingly over time. Lommatzsch [23] analyzes news recommender quality dependent of the domain and the context to find out what approach works best for which type of request. Benchmarking different news recommendation algorithms, he observes that there is not *one* optimal algorithm that outperforms all other recommendation strategies. Therefore, he concludes that the recommendation performance depends on context and domain.

## 4   Living Lab Scenario

As argued above, the aim of a living lab is to bring together users and researchers, e.g., by providing an infrastructure that allows researchers to test algorithms and systems under real-life conditions. In this living lab, researchers can benchmark news recommendation techniques in real-time by recommending news articles to actual users that visit commercial news portals to satisfy their individual information needs, i.e., participants are facing real users in a living lab environment. In Section 4.1, we first introduce the domain of online news recommendation in detail. Section 4.2 provides an overview of the publishers and the user base, i.e., the content and the target group that is relevant for this scenario. The infrastructure is introduced in Section 4.3.

### 4.1   Online News Recommendation: The Plista Use Case

Many online news portals display on the bottom of their articles a small widget box labelled "You might also be interested in", "Recommended articles", or similar where users can find a list of recommended news articles. Dependent on the actual content provider, these recommendations often consist of a small picture and accompanying text snippets. Figure 1 illustrates the typical position of the recommendations on a typical news portal page.

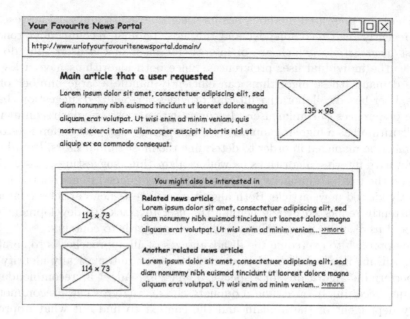

**Fig. 1.** Common position of the recommended news articles on a news portal

While some publishers provide their own recommendations, more and more providers rely on the expertise of external companies such as plista[3], a data-driven media company which provides content and advertising recommendations for thousands of premium websites (e.g., news portals, entertainment portals). Whenever a user reads an article on one of their customers' web portals, the plista service provides a list of related articles. In order to outsource this recommendation task to plista, the publishers firstly have to inform them about newly created articles and updates on already existing articles on their news portal. In addition, whenever a user visits one of these online articles, the content provider forwards this request to plista. These clicks on articles are also referred to as impressions. Plista determines related articles which are then forwarded to the user and displayed in above mentioned widget box as recommendations. Having a large customer base, plista processes millions of user visits in real time on a daily basis. By setting up this living lab, plista grants research teams access to a certain amount of these requests in order to promote research on real-time news article recommendation. An overview of the publishers and users that are relevant for this scenario is provided in the next section.

### 4.2   Publishers and Users

Due to plista's business focus on the German-speaking market in Central Europe, the main target group for their recommendations are German-speaking people.

---

[3] http://www.plista.com/

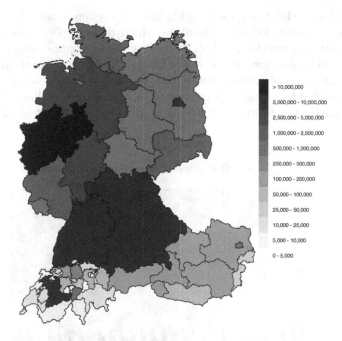

**Fig. 2.** First-level and second-level NUTS in Germany, Austria, and Switzerland from where requests for articles were triggered. The scale indicates the number of requests.

German is the most widely spoken mother tongue in the European Union and understood by 30% of all EU citizens [32]. As of June 2014, it is the second most used language in the internet[4], indicating the strong role that the internet plays as information source for the target group. A shared language, historical ties and geographic proximity provide the ground for an intensive cultural exchange between the largest German-speaking countries Germany, Austria and Switzerland. This is also reflected in the digital media landscape. With all three countries ranked amongst the Top 15 countries on the 2014 World Press Freedom index, publishers of these countries are able to publish articles on their portals without larger fear of political consequences. A multitude of online publishers exist in these countries that focus on daily news on a regional, national or international level, or on specific domains such as sports, business or technology. Thousands of them rely on plista to provide recommendations for their visitors. In the context of this living lab, plista forwards the requests of a diverse selection of these clients, including regional and local news publishers, as well as domain-centric portals. An analysis of a four-week log file dump of activity records for selected domains (see Section 5.1 for further details) reveals that 81.8% of all requests for websites were requested from visitors from Germany,

---

[4] According to http://w3techs.com/technologies/overview/content_language/all, accessed on 19 June 2014.

Austria, or Switzerland. Figure 2 highlights the regions from where these requests were triggered. Figure 3 visualizes which devices (i.e., tablets, phones, desktop computers, crawlers, or bots) were used to access the news portals. We interpret the changing proportions over time as an indication that both time of access and the choice of device is decided by the users. In other words, users were accessing the sites following their own personal agendas. A preliminary analysis of users' behavior is performed by Esiyok et al. [13] and Said et al. [28].

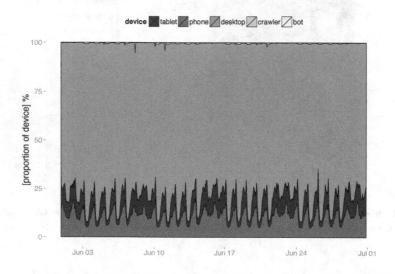

**Fig. 3.** Distribution of devices used to access news portals

Concluding, we argue that the average users of this living lab are German-speaking Europeans who follow their own information need on a diverse set of news portals. How researchers can evaluate their algorithms for these news portals and their visitors is outlined in the next section.

## 4.3  Infrastructure

As described above, access to the publishers and users is provided by plista, who created an API for researchers that allows them to benchmark news recommendation algorithms and have them tested by a subset of their customers' visitors. The infrastructure that is required for this living lab has been developed in the context of the research project EPEN[5]. Figure 4 visualizes the data flow between the different players of this living lab, namely the visitors of news portals, the news portals, the Open Recommendation Platform (ORP) [8], and the servers of the individual participants who benchmark their algorithms.

---

[5] http://www.dai-labor.de/en/irml/epen/

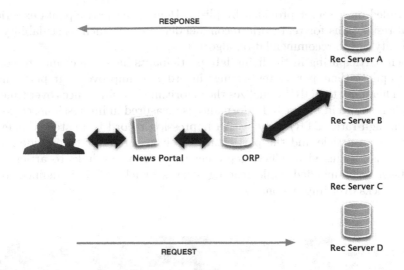

RESPONSE

Rec Server A

Rec Server B

News Portal          ORP

Rec Server C

Rec Server D

REQUEST

**Fig. 4.** Data flow within the living lab

The Open Recommendation Platform (ORP) [8] is the core platform of the living lab since it handles the communication between the participants and plista. ORP receives recommendation requests from visitors from various websites offering news articles and forwards the incoming requests to registered researchers. The platform is capable of delivering different recommendation implementations and of tracking the recommender results.

After registering using the graphical user interface of the platform, researchers first need to provide a server address on which their implementation of a news recommender is running. Moreover, they can register different algorithms that can simultaneously be run. Once registered, ORP will send HTTP POST requests, including item updates, event notifications and recommendation requests to this server. Event notifications are the actual user interactions, i.e., users' visits, referred to as impressions, to one of the news portals that rely on the plista service, or clicks to one of the recommended articles. The item updates include information about the creation of new pages on the content providers server and it allows participants to provide content-based recommendations. Recommender algorithms and evaluation models can also be build on top of the context, which includes the user id provided by a cookie, publisher id, browser, device, operating system and more, either from the http context or additionally being enhanced by plista using categorization heuristics and classifiers. Expected responses to the recommendation requests are related news articles from the same content provider, which are then provided as recommendations to the visitors of the page. Since recommendations need to be provided in real-time, the expected response has to be send within 100ms, i.e., recommenders have to be quick. If too much time is lost due to network latency (e.g., when the participant has a slow internet connection or is physically remote from the ORP server), the algorithms can also be installed on a server provided by plista. Hence, the participants experience typical restrictions for real-world recommender systems such as scalability and complexity of the recommendation algorithms.

When participating in the living lab, participants have the chance to continuously update their parameter settings in order to improve their performance levels. Therefore, the ORP visualizes the algorithms' performances over time. An example is shown in Figure 5. Performance is measured in impressions, clicks and click-through rate (CTR) per day. An impression record is created whenever a user reads an article and the participant received a request to provide recommendations for this visit. Clicks represent users following links to articles that have been recommended while reading a news article. CTR is defined as the ratio of clicks over impressions.

**Fig. 5.** Screenshot of the ORP

## 5    Evaluation Scenarios

So far, the living lab infrastructure and related datasets have been used in two evaluation and benchmarking campaigns, namely in the News Recommendation Challenge (NRS'13), held in conjunction with ACM RecSys 2013 and in NEWS-REEL, a campaign-style evaluation lab of CLEF 2014. In the remainder of this section, we outline the experimental setup of these two events.

## 5.1    The News Recommendation Challenge 2013

The living lab was first introduced to the research community in 2013, when we organized a workshop and challenge on news recommendation systems (NRS) [31] in conjunction with ACM RecSys 2013. The aim of this workshop was to bring together researchers and practitioners around the topics of designing and evaluating novel news recommender systems. Additionally, the aim of the challenge was to allow participants to evaluate their method by directly interacting with real-world news recommender systems. The challenge featured a data set designed to bootstrap a news recommender system and access to the living lab for a few weeks. During the last two weeks leading up to the conference, each participant's system performance was measused with respect to the ratio of clicks per recommendation request. The two phases of the challenge are outlined in the remainder of this section.

*Phase 1: Training.* In the first stage, a log file dump of the activity records that plista processed in June 2013 for recommending news articles in real-time was provided. While plista provides this service for thousands of online portals, this dataset contains records for a limited number of news portals, covering different spectra of the news world such as general, sports-related, or information technology related news. As mentioned above, plista's domestic market is Central Europe. Therefore, all news providers publish articles in German.

The corpus consists of four types of activities that have been performed by two types of actors on selected online domains: Adding and updating articles (done by the online editors of the respective news portal) as well as reading an article and clicking on a recommendation (the latter two activities being performed by the online customer, i.e., the readers of the online portals). Figure 6 visualizes the number of impressions over time for an exemplary news domain. The dataset allowed participants to tune their recommendation algorithms before the actual real-time challenge commenced. For a more detailed description of the dataset, the reader is referred to [21].

*Phase 2: Benchmarking in Living Lab.* In the second stage, participants were asked to provide recommendations in real-time for actual users. After registering with the Open Recommendation Platform, the participants received updates for ten publishers and requests for recommendations triggered by the visitors of these news portals. For a period of two weeks, we recorded the number of clicks, the number of requests and the click-through rate of all participating recommenders.

Eight teams participated in the challenge who could submit a multitude of recommenders. Overall, we counted 23 algorithms that competed against each other and against four baseline runs. For further details about the baseline algorithms, the reader is referred to [23]. Since the main focus of this paper is to outline the living lab scenario, we will only *briefly* discuss the results of the challenge. We could observe a much larger number of requests in the challenge's early stages. This resulted from more and more teams joining the challenge reducing the traffic routed to individual algorithms. Moreover, we noticed that the

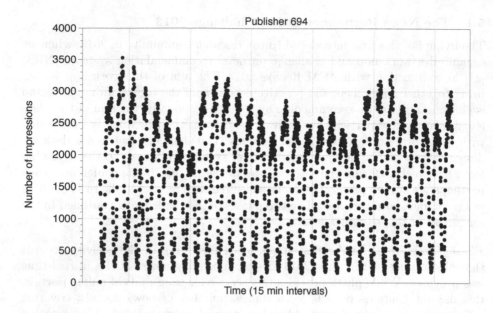

**Fig. 6.** Recorded impressions over time for an exemplary news domain. Each dot corresponds to the number of interactions within a 15 minute time interval. The whole time frame corresponds to a full month of interactions.

click-through rates started relatively low and increased with ≈ factor 2 after 3 days. We also observed that the performance of the recommenders share similarities. On Day 4, for example, all baseline recommenders reported a local high, followed by a local low on Day 6. Similar patterns could be observed on Days 11, 12, and 13. Several tens of thousands recommendations had been submitted until the organizers announced the winners thus concluding the challenge. Since the main focus of this paper is to introduce the evaluation setting of this living lab, a detailed discussion on these effects is out of scope.

## 5.2    CLEF NEWSREEL 2014

Building on the experiences we gained when organizing the NRS challenge, we revised the experimental setup to promote further research on the offline and online evaluation of news recommendation algorithms. In 2014, the introduced infrastructure and dataset was used to organize NEWSREEL[6], a campaign-style evaluation lab of CLEF 2014. NEWSREEL consisted of two tasks that are outlined in the remainder of this section. Note that this section provides an overview of the tasks only. For an overview of the participating teams and their performances, the reader is referred to the lab overview paper in the working notes proceedings of CLEF'14.

---

[6] http://www.clef-newsreel.org/

*Task 1: Predict interactions in an offline dataset.* Due to the organization of the Netflix challenge, evaluation of recommendation algorithms is dominated by offline evaluation scenarios. Addressing this evaluation scenario, we re-used a subset of the above mentioned dataset [21] to allow for an offline evaluation. The subset consisted of all updates and interactions of ten domains, focusing on local news, sports, business, technology, and national news, respectively. Before releasing the dataset, we identified fifteen time slots of 2–6 hours of length for each of the ten domains and removed all (user, item)-pairs within these slots. The task was to predict the interactions that occurred during these time periods. Note that the complete dataset had already been released during the NRS challenge. Participants were therefore advised that they must not use this dataset for this prediction task. Predictions were considered successful if the predicted (user, item)-pair actually occurred in the data set. In the evaluation, all partitions were treated separately, the winning contribution was determined by aggregating the results from the individual partitions. Participants were not asked to provide running code, but instead had to provide files with their predictions.

*Task 2: Recommend news articles in real-time.* In the second task, participants got the chance to benchmark recommendation algorithms in the living lab. Lab registration started in November 2013 and closed in May 2014. Once registered for CLEF, participating teams received an account on the Open Recommendation Platform. After providing a server address and after registering an algorithm in the dashboard, they were constantly receiving requests for recommendations. The platform was constantly online, thus leaving the participants various months time to fine-tune their algorithms. In order to compare the different participating teams, we defined three evaluation periods of two weeks duration each during which we recorded the numbers of clicks, numbers of requests and the click-through rate (CTR). The evaluation periods were scheduled in early February 2014, early April 2014 and late May 2014.

## 5.3   Discussion

The two benchmarking events that we presented allowed researchers to run news recommendation algorithms under real conditions and have them tested by a large number of users. As common in living labs, the users were not controlled, i.e., they were following their own agenda while browsing the different news portals. When setting up a living lab, various issues need to be considered, including legal and ethical issues (e.g., protection of users' privacy and intellectual property and handling of sensitive user interaction streams), but also technical and practical challenges (e.g., setting up and maintaining the lab infrastructure and the definition of evaluation scenarios). In the remainder of this section, we outline how we addressed these issues.

Data protection is a key requirement for running the living lab. The lab infrastructure is provided by plista, a company based in Berlin, Germany. Therefore, they are subject to German data privacy regulations which are considered to be amongst the strictest in the world. Consequently, a special emphasis has to be put on guaranteeing data protection. Little is known about the users themselves, apart from basic things such as their browser type, operation system and similar details that the users' browser reveals. Prior to forwarding requests to the living lab, plista filters out sensitive information (e.g., IP addresses), hence anonymizing the data stream.

In order to join the living lab, participants have to provide a server address and port number. Requests will then be forwarded to these servers. While this guarantees that participants keep complete control over their own code, this setting also comes with the drawback that time is spend for sending and receiving these requests. Keeping in mind that a key requirement for participating in this living lab is that recommendations have to provided within < 100ms, this network latency can be a serious factor. As we observed in the course of the benchmarking events, this is in particular relevant for teams that are physically remote from the servers in Berlin. In order to address this issue, plista provides virtual machines on their server, i.e., participants can participate without the disadvantage of their own network connectivity.

Another challenge when setting up a living lab for the evaluation of information access systems is to thoroughly define the benchmarking metrics and to define the evaluation scenario. Evaluating recommender systems' performance is subject to intense debates. A variety of evaluation criteria has been defined including rating prediction accuracy, classification, and ranking metrics [16,30]. The choice of evaluation criteria not only depends on the items but also on the feedback users provide. For instance, rating prediction accuracy metrics such as root mean squared error (RMSE) require users to express their preferences numerically. In the underlying setting, we only observe users interacting with items or disregarding them. We decided to consider the amount of clicks each algorithm obtains as decisive criteria. During the first benchmarking event, some participants joined the evaluation midway through the challenge, i.e., they processed far smaller requests. Consequently, these teams had no chance to win the actual competition. Nevertheless, we consider this criteria fair as long as all participants receive a comparable number of requests. In order to address this time factor, we defined three separate evaluation periods within NEWSREEL which were all evaluated individually.

In the living lab scenario, participants can run their algorithms over a longer period of time. This gives them the opportunity to try out different recommendation techniques and observe the effect of various parameters on their recommendation performance. An important aspect of a benchmarking campaign, however, is also that participants can compare their own performance with state-of-the-art techniques. In order to provide such reference point, we implemented various baseline recommenders [23] which were constantly running during the competitions. Interestingly enough, the baseline algorithms that have been implemented for the NRS challenge turned out to be the most successful recommenders of the challenge, i.e., no participating team was able to beat their performance with respect to the users' click-through rate. Therefore, we consider them to be the state-of-the-art algorithms of such real-life recommendation scenario.

# 6    Conclusion

In this paper, we introduced a living lab for the evaluation of news recommendations in real-time and described its application during two benchmarking events. The main purpose of living labs is to evaluate user-centric technologies under realistic conditions and context. In the living lab scenario, we interpret this purpose as the provision of news article recommendations for real users who visit news portals to satisfy their personal information needs. The users' context, i.e., the time, interest and the used device is not defined in a laboratory-style evaluation setting but is provided by the actual users themselves. In other words, users follow their own agenda and face no artificial created limitations and conditions. We argue that this challenge can serve as a guideline for the implementation of living labs for the evaluation of information access systems. In fact, first steps towards the creation of a living lab for the evaluation of information retrieval systems are currently discussed [5].

**Acknowledgement.** The work leading to these results has received funding (or partial funding) from the Central Innovation Programme for SMEs of the German Federal Ministry for Economic Affairs and Energy, as well as from the European Union's Seventh Framework Programme (FP7/2007-2013) under grant agreement number 610594.

# References

1. Adomavicius, G., Kwon, Y.O.: Improving aggregate recommendation diversity using ranking-based techniques. Knowledge and Data Engineering 24(5), 896–911 (2012)
2. Allan, J.: Hard track overview in trec 2003: High accuracy retrieval from documents. In: TREC, pp. 24–37 (2003)
3. Amatriain, X.: Mining large streams of user data for personalized recommendations. ACM SIGKDD Explorations Newsletter 14(2), 37 (2013)
4. Azzopardi, L., Balog, K.: Towards a living lab for information retrieval research and development. In: Forner, P., Gonzalo, J., Kekäläinen, J., Lalmas, M., de Rijke, M. (eds.) CLEF 2011. LNCS, vol. 6941, pp. 26–37. Springer, Heidelberg (2011)
5. Balog, K., Elsweiler, D., Kanoulas, E., Kelly, L., Smucker, M.: Report on the cikm workshop on living labs for information retrieval evaluation. SIGIR Forum 48(1) (2014)
6. Belkin, N.J.: Some(what) grand challenges for information retrieval. In: ECIR, p. 1 (2008)
7. Bennett, J., Lanning, S.: The netflix prize. In: KDDCup (2007)
8. Brodt, T., Hopfgartner, F.: Shedding Light on a Living Lab: The CLEF NEWS-REEL Open Recommendation Platform. In: Proceedings of the Information Interaction in Context Conference, IIiX 2014. Springer (to appear, 2014)
9. Cleverdon, C., Mills, J., Keen, M.: Factors determining the performance of indexing systems. Technical report, ASLIB Cranfield project, Cranfield (1966)
10. Clough, P., Sanderson, M.: Evaluating the performance of information retrieval systems using test collections. Information Research 18(2) (2013)

11. Dror, G., Koenigstein, N., Koren, Y., Weimer, M.: The Yahoo! Music Dataset and KDD-Cup. In: JMLR: Workshop and Conference Proceedings, pp. 3–18 (2012)

12. Dumais, S., Belkin, N.: The trec interactive tracks: Putting the user into search. In: TREC (2005)

13. Esiyok, C., Kille, B., Jain, B.J., Hopfgartner, F., Albayrak, S.: Users' reading habits in online news portals. In: IIiX 2014: Proceedings of Information Interaction in Context Conference. ACM (to appear, August 2014)

14. Goldberg, K., Roeder, T., Gupta, D., Perkins, C.: Eigentaste: A constant time collaborative filtering algorithm. Information Retrieval 4(2), 133–151 (2001)

15. Herlocker, J.L., Konstan, J.A., Borchers, A., Riedl, J.: An algorithmic framework for performing collaborative filtering. In: Proceedings of the 22nd Annual International ACM SIGIR Conference on Research and Development in Information Retrieval, SIGIR 1999, pp. 230–237. ACM (1999)

16. Herlocker, J.L., Konstan, J.A., Terveen, L.G., Riedl, J.T.: Evaluating collaborative filtering recommender systems. ACM Transactions on Information Systems 22(1), 5–53 (2004)

17. Hopfgartner, F., Jose, J.M.: Semantic user profiling techniques for personalised multimedia recommendation. Multimedia Syst. 16(4-5), 255–274 (2010)

18. Ivory, M.Y., Hearst, M.A.: The state of the art in automating usability evaluation of user interfaces. ACM Comput. Surv. 33(4), 470–516 (2001)

19. Kamps, J., Geva, S., Peters, C., Sakai, T., Trotman, A., Voorhees, E.M.: Report on the sigir 2009 workshop on the future of ir evaluation. SIGIR Forum 43(2), 13–23 (2009)

20. Kelly, D., Dumais, S.T., Pedersen, J.O.: Evaluation challenges and directions for information-seeking support systems. IEEE Computer 42(3), 60–66 (2009)

21. Kille, B., Hopfgartner, F., Brodt, T., Heintz, T.: The plista dataset. In: NRS 2013: Proceedings of the International Workshop and Challenge on News Recommender Systems, pp. 14–21. ACM (2013)

22. Konstan, J., Riedl, J.: Recommender systems: from algorithms to user experience. User Modeling and User-Adapted Interaction 22(1-2), 101–123 (2012)

23. Lommatzsch, A.: Real-time news recommendation using context-aware ensembles. In: de Rijke, M., Kenter, T., de Vries, A.P., Zhai, C., de Jong, F., Radinsky, K., Hofmann, K. (eds.) ECIR 2014. LNCS, vol. 8416, pp. 51–62. Springer, Heidelberg (2014)

24. Lommatzsch, A., Plumbaum, T., Albayrak, S.: A linked dataverse knows better: Boosting recommendation quality using semantic knowledge. In: Proc. of the 5th Intl. Conf. on Advances in Semantic Processing, Wilmington, DE, USA, pp. 97–103. IARIA (2011)

25. Pazzani, M.J., Billsus, D.: Content-based recommendation systems. In: Brusilovsky, P., Kobsa, A., Nejdl, W. (eds.) Adaptive Web 2007. LNCS, vol. 4321, pp. 325–341. Springer, Heidelberg (2007)

26. Phelan, O., McCarthy, K., Smyth, B.: Using twitter to recommend real-time topical news. In: Proceedings of the Third ACM Conference on Recommender Systems, RecSys 2009, pp. 385–388. ACM, New York (2009)

27. Pirolli, P.: Powers of 10: Modeling complex information-seeking systems at multiple scales. IEEE Computer 42(3), 33–40 (2009)

28. Said, A., Lin, J., Bellogín, A., de Vries, A.: A month in the life of a production news recommender system. In: Proceedings of the 2013 Workshop on Living Labs for Information Retrieval Evaluation, LivingLab 2013, pp. 7–10. ACM (2013)

29. Sarwar, B.M., Karypis, G., Konstan, J.A., Riedl, J.: Item-based collaborative filtering recommendation algorithms. In: WWW, pp. 285–295 (2001)

30. Shani, G., Gunawardana, A.: Evaluating recommendation systems. In: Recommender Systems Handbook, pp. 257–297. Springer (2011)
31. Tavakolifard, M., Gulla, J.A., Almeroth, K.C., Hopfgartner, F., Kille, B., Plumbaum, T., Lommatzsch, A., Brodt, T., Bucko, A., Heintz, T.: Workshop and challenge on news recommender systems. In: RecSys 2013: Proceedings of the International ACM Conference on Recommender Systems. ACM (October 2013)
32. TNS Opinion & Social. Special Eurobarometer 386 – Europeans and their Languages. Technical report, European Commission (2012)
33. Vallet, D., Hopfgartner, F., Jose, J.: Use of implicit graph for recommending relevant videos: a simulated evaluation. In: Macdonald, C., Ounis, I., Plachouras, V., Ruthven, I., White, R.W. (eds.) ECIR 2008. LNCS, vol. 4956, pp. 199–210. Springer, Heidelberg (2008)
34. Voorhees, E.M., Harman, D.K.: TREC: Experiment and Evaluation in Information Retrieval, 1st edn. MIT Press, Cambridge (2005)
35. Ziegler, C.-N., McNee, S.M., Konstan, J.A., Lausen, G.: Improving recommendation lists through topic diversification. In: WWW 2005, pp. 22–32. ACM (2005)

# Improving the Reproducibility of PAN's Shared Tasks:
## Plagiarism Detection, Author Identification, and Author Profiling

Martin Potthast[1], Tim Gollub[1], Francisco Rangel[2,3], Paolo Rosso[3],
Efstathios Stamatatos[4], and Benno Stein[1]

[1] Web Technology & Information Systems, Bauhaus-Universität Weimar, Germany
[2] Autoritas Consulting, S.A., Spain
[3] Natural Language Engineering Lab, Universitat Politècnica de València, Spain
[4] Dept. of Information & Communication Systems Engineering, University of the Aegean, Greece
pan@webis.de
http://pan.webis.de

**Abstract.** This paper reports on the PAN 2014 evaluation lab which hosts three shared tasks on plagiarism detection, author identification, and author profiling. To improve the reproducibility of shared tasks in general, and PAN's tasks in particular, the Webis group developed a new web service called TIRA, which facilitates software submissions. Unlike many other labs, PAN asks participants to submit running softwares instead of their run output. To deal with the organizational overhead involved in handling software submissions, the TIRA experimentation platform helps to significantly reduce the workload for both participants and organizers, whereas the submitted softwares are kept in a running state. This year, we addressed the matter of responsibility of successful execution of submitted softwares in order to put participants back in charge of executing their software at our site. In sum, 57 softwares have been submitted to our lab; together with the 58 software submissions of last year, this forms the largest collection of softwares for our three tasks to date, all of which are readily available for further analysis. The report concludes with a brief summary of each task.

## 1 Introduction

The term "shared task" refers to computer science events that invite researchers and practitioners to work on a specific problem of interest, *the task*.[1] The goals of a shared task may be threefold: (1) to foster the development of new theories and approaches at solving the task, (2) to implement a suited software, and (3) to evaluate the currently achievable performance. A shared task gives rise to a controlled laboratory experiment where contesting softwares are the test subjects. Within the experiment a possibly large number of problem instances of the task have to be solved, whereas the solutions of the competing softwares are compared to the true solutions. If the problem instances are representative of the population of (real-world) problem instances, the achieved performance of a software allows for judging its merits with regard to being applied in practice, as well as the validity of its underlying approach.

---

[1] Typical terms used in this regard are: campaign, challenge, competition, contest, or cup.

E. Kanoulas et al. (Eds.): CLEF 2014, LNCS 8685, pp. 268–299, 2014.

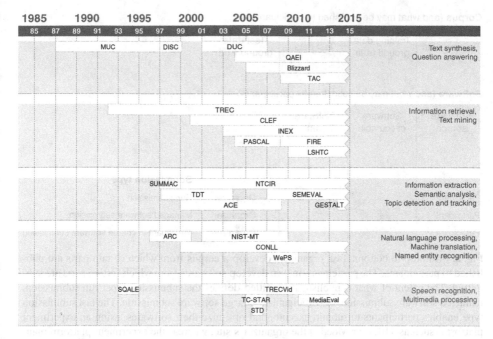

**Fig. 1.** The last thirty years of shared tasks in the human language technologies

Though shared tasks have a long tradition in computer science, only little is written about them. Open questions include: What are best practices to set-up a shared task? How to measure its success? What determines its success? As a step towards answering these and related questions, we have compiled an overview of well-known shared tasks in the Human Language Technologies, which is depicted in Figure 1.

## 1.1   Contrasting Shared Tasks by Submission Type

Our review of shared tasks in the human language technologies reveals that such tasks have been unanimously organized in the same way. Task organizers prepare a corpus comprising problem instances, where parts of the corpus are published as training data (including the ground truth) and test data (without the ground truth) respectively. Task participants develop software that solves the task based on the training data and finally run their software on the test data. Within most shared tasks, the output of this final software run (usually called a *run*, for short) is submitted to the organizers. The organizers, in turn, evaluate the submitted runs using previously announced performance measures against the ground truth of the problem instances in the test data set.

To reach higher levels of automation and reproducibility, participants may submit their executable software, this way enabling the organizers to generate runs by themselves. This approach, which we call "managed software submission," entails a lot of communication overhead and other problems, caused by the fact that now the organizing site becomes part of the software test cycle. These disadvantages are addressed by a third kind of submission type, here called "participant-in-charge software submission,"

**Corpus** (and what may be published to participants)

| Training data | Training data ground truth | Test data | Test data ground truth |
|---|---|---|---|
|  |  |  |  |

**Software** (and what may be submitted by participants)

| Software source | Software executable | Software run |
|---|---|---|
|  |  |  |

| Software source | Software executable | Software run | Submission type |
|---|---|---|---|
| Participant |  | Organizer | Run submission |
| Participant |  | Organizer | Managed software submission |
| Participant | ///////// | Organizer | Participant-in-charge software submission |

**Fig. 2.** From top to bottom: Task organizers develop a corpus from which certain parts are published to participants. The participants in turn develop softwares from which certain parts are submitted. The extent of what is published/submitted defines the submission type: run submission, managed software submission, or participant-in-charge software submission. The last submission type enables participants to submit, execute, and optimize their softwares, using an experiment platform (such as TIRA) provided at the organizer's site, whereas the experiment platform manages a software's access to the test data set.

where a fully-fledged experiment platform is provided at the organizer's site for each participant. Though this approach is technically the most advanced, it comes along with appealing advantages: the softwares can be tested and optimized by the participants, as well as accessed, run, and archived for documentation and re-run purposes by the organizers. See Figure 2 for an illustration of the three submission types.

## 1.2  Related Work

The human language technologies were at the forefront of organizing shared tasks, with early initiatives dating back to the 1980's. Figure 1 places each initiative on a time line according to its primary research focus. Note that today's most established evaluation campaigns, CLEF, CONLL, INEX, NTCIR, TREC, and TRECVid, run successfully for over ten years now, each of them hosting up to dozens of specific shared tasks. The value that shared tasks provide for their respective research fields has been pointed out by Chapman et al. [7]. Most notably, shared tasks push the standardization of evaluation metrics and data formats, provide annotated data sets and benchmarks, foster the cooperation between academia and industry, and constitute a well defined entry point and forum for getting involved in a particular research field. The scientific impact of shared tasks has been attested by Tsikrika et al. [63], who analyzed the citation graph of CLEF publications. Despite their general acceptance, there are also critical voices concerning shared tasks [4,56,57]. The general argument brought forward is that shared tasks turn research fields with a great diversity of streams and ideas into a single, oversimplified task, with fixed inputs and gold-standard outputs, and a single automatic performance metric. In addition, repeated shared tasks bear the risk that the developed approaches converge on the approach that showed most success in previous evaluations. Moreover, Potthast *et al.* [44] observe that participant do not necessary improve upon the performance of their first approach when they participate repeatedly. Given these concerns, the question is which factors influence the success or failure of shared tasks in pushing forward a research field. To the best of our knowledge, this question has not been answered, yet, within a rigorous scientific evaluation.

### 1.3  Contributions

This paper reports on the latest results of our efforts to improve the reproducibility of shared tasks in general, and that of PAN's three shared tasks in particular, namely plagiarism detection, author identification, and author profiling. We introduce the TIRA experimentation platform as a web service for shared tasks: it implements a participant-in-charge software submission platform that hands the responsibility of successful software execution back to participants. This way, inviting software submissions for a shared task becomes significantly less cumbersome, and, given further development, it may reduce the work overhead to a point at which inviting software submission may become as straightforward as inviting run submissions has been previously.

All of the above has not been developed haphazardly, but the development process was tightly integrated with PAN over the past years, using our lab as a beta testing platform for our developments. While first plans for TIRA have been discussed long ago, at PAN 2012 we first invited managed software submissions for one of PAN's shared tasks. Based on this experience, developments commenced which allowed us to scale managed software submissions to all three of PAN's recurring shared tasks in 2013, whereas this year marks the introduction of participant-in-charge software submissions based on the TIRA web service. This way, we can not only claim to have developed the first participant-in-charge software submission platform, but also that this platform is battle-tested based on handling three demanding shared tasks with more than 100 software submissions in total since 2012.

## 2  TIRA: A Web Service for Shared Tasks

This section reports on our efforts to minimize the organizational overhead of software submissions and the ongoing development of the TIRA experimentation platform [14,15]. For three years in a row, our lab has invited software submissions, and for the second time, this was done for all shared tasks. This year, 57 softwares have been submitted to our three tasks all of which were handled using TIRA. In previous work we identified challenges that handling software submissions at scale entail [13]: (1) development environment diversity, (2) untrusted software execution, (3) data leakage, (4) error handling, (5) execution responsibility, and (6) execution cost. Until last year, the first three challenges have been our primary concern, while the focus of this year is on the two challenges of error handling and execution responsibility. Our long-term goal is to make inviting software submissions for shared tasks as simple as inviting run submissions, avoiding the deficiencies of the latter while adding the benefits of the former. All of these efforts are consolidated by developing TIRA's evaluation tools that facilitate software submissions and shared tasks in general. For the first time, we provide public access to these tools via a new web front end.[2]

### 2.1  Software Submissions: Who is Responsible for their Successful Execution?

A major obstacle to a widespread adoption of managed software submissions in shared tasks is the shift of responsibility for a successful software execution. Submitted software is not necessarily free of errors—even more, experience shows that the majority of the participants submit their software prematurely, yet, being convinced from its flawlessness. This fact lets organizers unwillingly become part of the debugging process of each participant's software, whereas the turnaround time to find and fix errors increases severely, especially when both parties are not working simultaneously (i.e., reside in different time zones). Failure on the part of organizers to run a submitted software, to check its output for errors of any kind (e.g., not every execution error results in a crash), and to give participants feedback in a timely manner may cause participants to miss submission deadlines. The risk of this happening is increased by the fact that many participants start working only just in time before a deadline, so that organizers have to handle all submissions at the same time. Besides, prolonged back-and-forth between participants and organizers cause by software errors bears a high potential for friction. As a result, organizers may come to the conclusion they have little to gain but trouble, whereas the benefits of software submissions, such as reproducibility, may be considered insufficient payback.

In previous years, we experienced the following with managed software submissions [13]: to get the 58 softwares submitted in 2013 running for evaluation, 1493 mails had to be exchanged in order to fix runtime errors. It must be noted, though, that we were working hand-in-hand with participants, and that, surprisingly, most participants were not at all disgruntled by having to revisit their software over and over again to fix errors. While our previous versions of TIRA have helped us to manage software submissions in an organized manner, our goal now is to put participants back in charge of their own software (see Figure 2). Therefore, we develop user interfaces for TIRA, which allow participants to remotely control software execution and to collect runtime feedback, thus eliminating the need for organizers to intervene in fixing software execution errors. Figure 3 illustrates the interfaces provided to both parties.

In what follows, both the user interfaces and the workflow of participants and organizers to complete a shared task are described in detail.

### 2.2  Life of a Participant

From the perspective of a participant (Alice, in the following), a software submission via TIRA happens within three basic steps: first, deployment of the software to a given virtual machine, second, configuration of the software for remote execution, and third, remote execution of the software on the available training and test data. The interfaces on the left side of Figure 3 are used for this purpose, whereas the latter two steps are

---

[2] http://www.tira.io

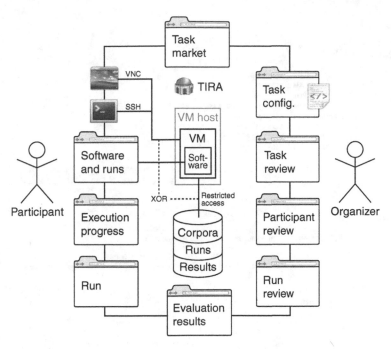

**Fig. 3.** TIRA's interfaces for participants (left), organizers (right), and the public (top, bottom)

accomplished via TIRA's new web interface. The web interface marks an important step forward in terms of putting Alice in charge of deploying her software: it ensures that Alice neither gains direct access to the test data nor to the ground truth of a shared task, but it still allows her to evaluate her software and to obtain filtered runtime feedback. In this regard, TIRA serves as a remote control for evaluation.

TIRA encapsulates Alice's software in a virtual machine that is set up once she registers for a shared task. As depicted in Figure 3, Alice has two ways to access her virtual machine, namely a remote desktop connection and an SSH connection. Alice retains full administrative rights inside her virtual machine, so that she can set up her preferred development environment and deploy her software. To prevent misuse, virtual machines are not allowed to communicate with each other, and, their outgoing bandwidth is limited. By default, virtual machines have only restricted access to TIRA's database, so that only the training data of each task can be read. Once a software has been successfully deployed and tested manually, participants use TIRA's web interface to complete the second and third step outlined above.

For each participant of a shared task, TIRA serves a remote control page for the respective virtual machine, the deployed software, and the software runs. After signing in with her account for the first time, Alice can configure the execution details of her software. Figure 4 shows Alice's software control page in a state after completed configuration and a few successfully executed runs. The software control page is divided into four panels:

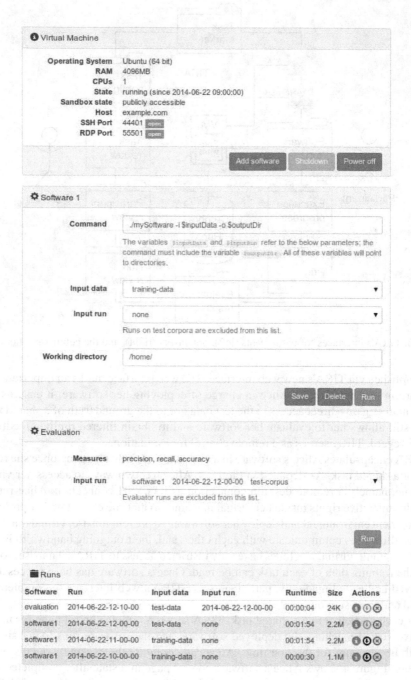

**Fig. 4.** TIRA's web interface for participants to remote control the execution of their software and to review their runs for a given shared task

**Virtual Machine.** Overview of the virtual machine, including information about the operating system, RAM, CPUs, its running state, VM host, and connectivity. The virtual machine can be turned off at the click of a button either by sending a shutdown signal to the operating system, or by powering it off. Clicking "Add Software" creates a new software panel. Alice may deploy an arbitrary number of softwares for the shared task onto her virtual machine, e.g., to compare different paradigms or variants of an approach at solving the task. Each software can be configured individually on the software control page.

**Software 1.** Configuration of a software that has been previously deployed on the virtual machine. The software must be executable as a POSIX-conform command line. Mandatory parameters can be defined by organizers of the shared task. In this case, they include variables for input data and the output directory, and optionally for an input run (i.e., a previous run of one of Alice's softwares). If necessary, the working directory in which the program shall be executed can be specified. Alice may adjust an existing software configuration and save its state, she may delete it, or she may proceed to execute the software. Note that if Alice deletes a software it is not actually deleted on the server, but only hidden from view; rationale for this is to allow organizers to reconstruct Alice's actions for reasons of cheating prevention. The runs obtained from running a software are listed in the "Runs" panel.

**Evaluation.** Run an evaluation software on a given run. This is a special type of software provided by task organizers which processes an input run and outputs the results of the task's performance measures. Once Alice has finished her first successful run on a given input data, she uses this panel to evaluate it. The runs obtained from an evaluation software are also listed in the "Runs" panel.

**Runs.** List of runs that have been obtained either from running a software or from running an evaluation. The table lists run details including software, timestamp (which also serves as run ID), input data, input run, runtime, size on disk, and further actions that can be taken. The colorization indicates a run's status with regard to being successful, where red indicates severe errors, yellow indicates warnings, green indicates complete success, and white indicates that the run has not yet been reviewed. Runs are checked automatically for validity with the shared task's expected output format, and they may be reviewed manually by organizers. Actions that can be taken on each run include viewing more details (the blue *i*-icon), downloading it (the black arrow down), and deleting it (the red x). It is here where Alice first encounters the limitations that TIRA imposes for runs on test data sets: all test data sets are by default hidden from participants, which is why all possible communication channels about test data must be filtered or closed as well. Therefore, TIRA prevents Alice from downloading runs on test data sets (the download action shown grayed is inactive) to foreclose that a malicious software outputs the data itself instead of output that is valid for a given shared task.

The software control page does not display all of the aforementioned panels immediately, but only after Alice has completed the necessary steps. At first, it only shows the virtual machine panel; then, once Alice clicks on "Add Software", a software panel appears; and finally, once Alice runs her software for the first time, the evaluation panel and the runs panel are added after the run is completed. While a software is running, the

**Fig. 5.** TIRA's web interface to monitor the progress of a running software

software control page is replaced with the software progress monitoring page which is divided into two panels, as exemplified in Figure 5:

**Virtual Machine.** Just as on the software control page, the virtual machine panel shows the current state of Alice's virtual machine while the software is running. Before a software is started, the virtual machine is moved into a so-called sandbox: the machine is disconnected from the Internet so that no outside connections are possible, a snapshot is taken to save the machine's state before the software is executed, and, the input data is mounted read-only into the virtual machine as a shared folder. This sandbox state is indicated to Alice in the corresponding list entry as well as by the connectivity flags. Only if a machine has been successfully moved into the sandbox, the software is executed. While a software is running, the buttons to add a software configuration panel as well as those to shutdown or power off the virtual machine are deactivated so that the running software is not interrupted accidentally. After the software terminates, the output is stored in TIRA's database as a run, and the virtual machine is automatically moved out of the sandbox: the input data is unmounted, the virtual machine is restored to the state of the snapshot that was taken just before it was moved into the sandbox, and then it is reconnected to the Internet. Restoring the virtual machine to the snapshot taken ensures that no information about the input data remains in the virtual machine, be it in cache, in temporary files, or in purposefully hidden files. Disconnecting the virtual machine from the Internet while a software is executed ensures that no data can be sent to an unauthorized third party.

**Software Running.** Overview of a running software, including the software's ID, the executed command, the parameters, the run ID, and the running state. Moreover, the current runtime, the time of the last write access to the output directory, the currently used RAM, and the CPU load are displayed and updated periodically. This way, Alice has a way of making sure her software is still working. If, for any reason, Alice wishes to kill her software before it terminates by itself, she may click on the "Kill" button. Before the software is killed, its output up to this point is stored in TIRA's data base as an incomplete run for later inspection.

After her run has completed and the virtual machine has been moved out of the sandbox, Alice's browser shows the software control page again as in Figure 4. The new run appears in the runs table. To make sure the run was successful, Alice clicks on the *i*-icon which redirects her to a run details page for the run in question, as shown in Figure 6a. The details shown about a run are as follows:

**Overview.** Details about the run, including the software that was used, the run ID, parameters, whether the run can be downloaded, runtime details, its size, and the numbers of lines, files, and directories found. Whether the run can be downloaded depends on whether the input data was a test data set or not. As outlined above, runs on test data sets, by default, cannot be downloaded to foreclose data leakage. Besides the runtime, more in-depth runtime details are given, so that Alice can judge whether her software made good use of the hardware available to the virtual machine. For example, if she finds there are many page faults or even swaps, this indicates the software uses too much memory. The size and numbers of lines, files, and directories provide quantitative feedback to quickly verify output sanity, whereas it depends on the task which of these values is most illuminating.

**Review.** Review of this run provided by both automatic validation and organizers. In Alice's case, an organizer reviewed the displayed run and found that it does not contain any obvious errors. In case of errors, explanations are displayed here that give insight into their nature and severity.

**Stdout.** Standard output stream (stdout) which was recorded when executing the software. If Alice's software outputs information to stdout, it will be displayed here. However, in the case of runs on test data sets, the amount of information that is displayed can be limited. In the example, the limit is the 100 last chars of the stdout text. This limitation shall prevent Alice from outputting problem instances to stdout in order to inspect them. This communication channel can be closed entirely on a per-data set basis, for example, if confidential data has to be handled.

**Stderr.** Standard error output stream (stderr) which was recorded when executing the software. While nothing was recorded in the example, the same filtering is applied as for the stdout stream.

**File List.** Directory tree which displays file names and their sizes found in the run. Alice may use this information to determine whether her run has output all the files and directories that are expected, and whether their names and organization are correct.

(a) Details page of a software run

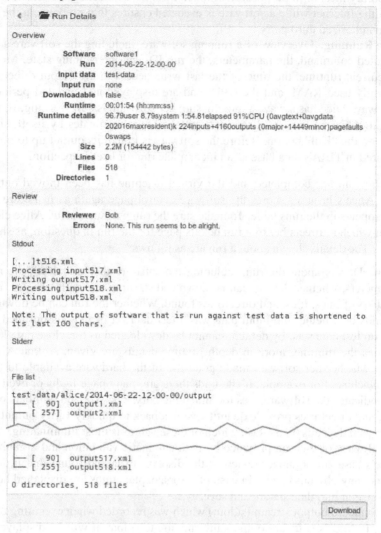

(b) Excerpt of the details page of an evaluation run

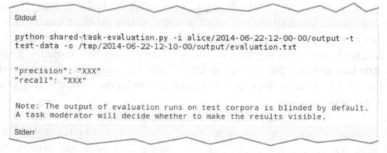

**Fig. 6.** TIRA's web interfaces for participants to review runs

The run details page shall provide Alice with the information necessary to determine whether her remote software execution was successful. Unless the software has been executed on a test data set, Alice may also download the run for local inspection. If she is satisfied with the run, she may proceed to evaluate it using the evaluation software. The resulting evaluation can again be inspected just like before, whereas the corresponding run details page lists the information pertaining to the evaluation software's run when receiving Alice's software run as input. Figure 6b shows an excerpt of an evaluation run details page that Alice will see. The evaluation software typically prints the evaluation results directly to stdout, however, in case the evaluated software run was on a test data set, the results are blinded by default (i.e., the performance values are replaced by "XXX"). Our rationale for blinding the evaluation results is twofold: (1) participants of shared tasks are not supposed to see their software's performances before the task organizers decide to publish them, and, (2) participants are not supposed to optimize their software against the test data, for example, by means of trial and error. This way, the decision of when, if, and how the evaluation results of a given shared task are released is at the full discretion of its organizers. Moreover, just as with filtering stdout and stderr output, the organizers may adjust blinding on a per-data set basis.

After completing her evaluation run, Alice is done; she has submitted her software to the virtual machine, made sure it works to the specifications of the shared task by running it on the available data sets and inspecting the runs for errors, and finally executed the evaluation software on her previous software runs. While Alice can now relax, it is time for the organizers of the shared task to get busy.

## 2.3 Life of an Organizer

From the perspective of an organizer (Bob, for example), using TIRA to manage software submissions for a shared task can be done in three simple steps: first, configuration of the shared task in TIRA; second, supervision of participant progress; and third, compilation and publication of the task's evaluation results. The interfaces on the right side of Figure 3 are used for this purpose. The configuration of a shared task in TIRA is done in a text-based configuration file. Configurable aspects include the data sets and their privacy settings as outlined in the previous section, the evaluation softwares, the command line parameters required for submitted softwares, and various messages displayed on task-specific web pages. The web interface for task configuration basically displays the configuration file as is and allows for editing it; we omit a screenshot for brevity.

In terms of supervising his shared task while it is underway, Bob has three interfaces at his disposal, an overview of participants who have started to work on the shared task, an overview of runs of each participant, and the run details of each participant's runs:

**Task Participants (Figure 7a).** Overview of participants who have configured at least one software for Bob's shared task on their software control page, including their user name, signed in status, numbers of softwares that are configured, deleted, and running, and, numbers of runs that are finished, reviewed, and unreviewed. These figures give Bob an idea of whether the participants of his task are actively engaged, but it also hints problems that may require Bob's attention. The number of deleted

(a) Overview of a task's participants

| User | Signed in | Softwares | Deleted | Now Running | Runs | Reviewed | Unreviewed | Actions |
|------|-----------|-----------|---------|-------------|------|----------|------------|---------|
| Alice | yes | 7 | 6 | none | 63 | 62 | 1 | 👁 |
| Carol | no | 1 | 0 | 6 days, 8:37:25 | 4 | 3 | 1 | 👁 |
| Dan | no | 1 | 0 | none | 5 | 0 | 5 | 👁 |
| Eve | no | 3 | 1 | none | 16 | 16 | 0 | 👁 |
| Frank | no | 3 | 0 | none | 56 | 56 | 0 | 👁 |
| Mallory | no | 1 | 0 | none | 4 | 0 | 4 | 👁 |
| Oscar | no | 1 | 0 | none | 4 | 0 | 4 | 👁 |
| Peggy | no | 1 | 0 | none | 4 | 0 | 4 | 👁 |
| Sybil | no | 3 | 2 | none | 5 | 5 | 0 | 👁 |
| Trent | no | 1 | 0 | none | 4 | 0 | 4 | 👁 |

Participants in *Shared Task*

(b) Overview of a participant's runs

Runs of *Alice* on *test-corpus*

| Software | Run | Input run | Size | Lines | Files | Dirs | Review | Actions |
|----------|-----|-----------|------|-------|-------|------|--------|---------|
| evaluation | 2014-06-22-12-10-00 | 2014-06-22-12-00-00 | 24K | 36 | 1 | 0 | todo | 👁 ⓘ |
| software1 | 2014-06-22-12-00-00 | none | 2.2M | 5180 | 518 | 0 | done | 👁 ⓘ |
| software1 | 2014-06-22-11-00-00 | none | 2.2M | 5180 | 518 | 0 | done | 👁 ⓘ |
| software1 | 2014-06-22-10-00-00 | none | 1.1M | 2590 | 259 | 0 | done | 👁 ⓘ |
| software1 | 2014-06-22-09-00-00ᴰᴱᴸ | none | 0.55M | 1290 | 129 | 0 | done | 👁 ⓘ |
| software1 | 2014-06-22-08-00-00ᴰᴱᴸ | none | 1K | 20 | 2 | 0 | done | 👁 ⓘ |

**Fig. 7.** TIRA's web interfaces for organizers to review a task's participants

softwares may indicate that a participant has trouble setting herself up. In the case of Alice, six of seven softwares have been deleted, so that it may be the case that Alice had some trouble getting the software configuration right. In the case of Carol, Bob observes that her software has been running for more than six days straight, which may be an indication that the software is not working as anticipated, given that the expected runtime of a software for Bob's shared task is a lot lower. Bob may contact the respective participants and offer his help. Moreover, the number of unreviewed runs indicates that some runs have not yet been checked for errors by an organizer. To do so, Bob clicks on the review action (the blue eye-icon in the Actions column) to review all of Alice's runs; he is redirected to the participant runs page described next.

**Participant Runs (Figure 7b).** Overview of a participant's runs on a per-data set basis, including the software that was used, run ID, input run, size, numbers of lines, files, and directories, and whether a run has been reviewed. The colorization indicates a run's status with regard to being successful, where red indicates severe errors, yellow indicates warnings, green indicates complete success, and white indicates that the run has not yet been reviewed. Unlike in the runs table on Alice's software control page, this table shows figures which relate to judging a run's success by

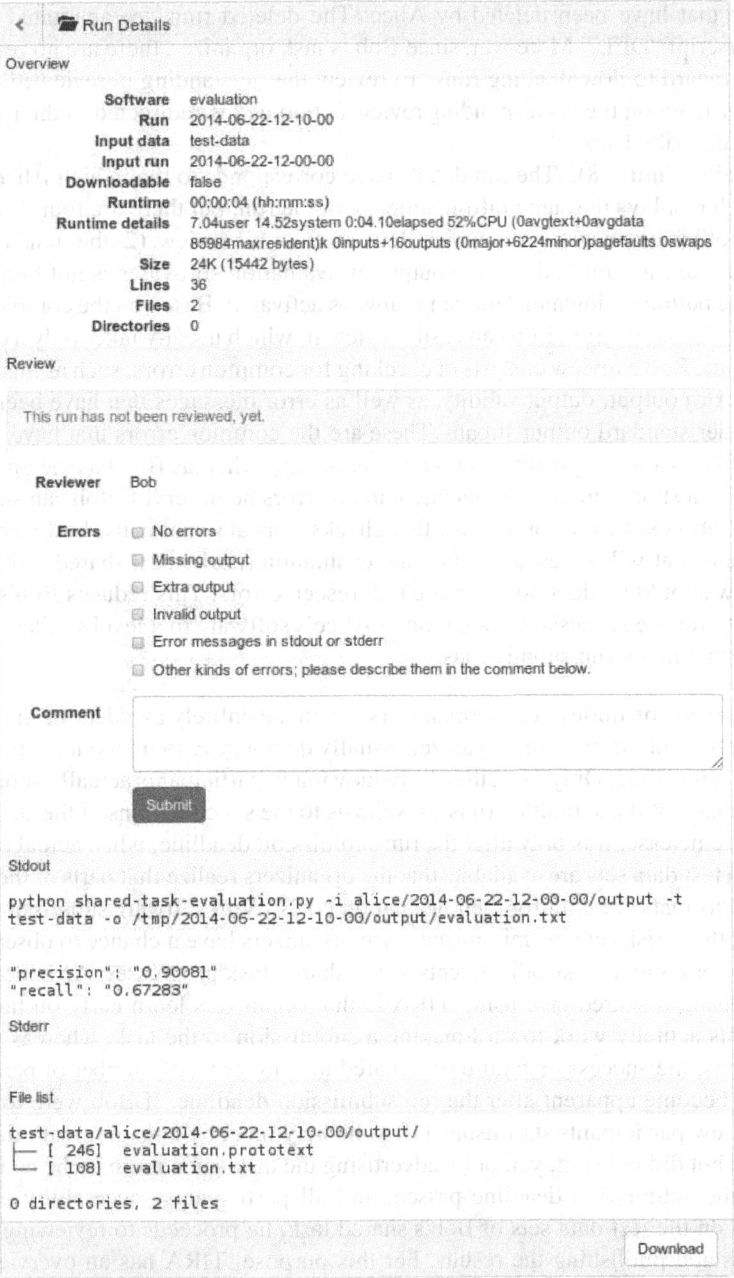

**Fig. 8.** TIRA's web interfaces for organizers to review runs

checking its size or the numbers of lines, files, or directories against the expectation for a given data set. Unlike Alice, Bob has access to all of Alice's runs including those that have been deleted by Alice. The deleted runs are annotated with the superscript "DEL." Moreover, since Bob is task organizer, there are no restrictions with regard to downloading runs. To review the outstanding unreviewed run, Bob clicks again on the corresponding review action and is redirected to the run details page described next.

**Run Details (Figure 8).** The run details page corresponds to that which Alice can access. It displays the same information about the run, but there are four differences. (1) it offers a review form in which Bob can enter his review, (2) the standard output streams are not filtered, (3) the output of evaluation softwares is not blinded, and (4) the button to download the run is always activated. Based on the complete information about the run, Bob can easily review it, which usually takes only a couple of seconds. Bob's review consists of checking for common errors, such as missing output, extra output, output validity, as well as error messages that have been printed to either standard output stream. These are the common errors that have been observed to occur frequently in previous years [13], whereas Bob has the opportunity to write a short comment about uncommon errors he observes. Bob can supply run verification software for his task that checks runs automatically, however, at least for runs that will be used for the final evaluation results of a shared task, a quick review should be done to foreclose unforeseen errors. This reduces Bob's responsibility for the successful evaluation of Alice's software to a level similar to shared tasks that invite run submissions.

The supervision duties of task organizers cannot be entirely avoided. In shared tasks that invite run submission, the organizers usually do not have to intervene until after the submission deadline. Only then, they learn how many participants actually submit a run and how many of the submitted runs are valid as to the specifications of the shared task. In the extreme case, it is only after the run submission deadline, when actual examples of runs on test data sets are available, that the organizers realize that parts of the data set or the run formats are unfit for their evaluation goals. With software submissions based on TIRA, these risks can be minimized since organizers have a chance to observe early bird participants and make adjustments as the shared task progresses. An added benefit of supervising a shared task using TIRA is that organizers learn early on how many participants actually work toward making a submission to the task, whereas with run submissions, the success or failure of a shared task in terms of number of participants will only become apparent after the run submission deadline. If Bob were to observe that only few participants start using TIRA, he may react by engaging with those who registered but did not start, yet, or by advertising the task some more in the community.

Once the submission deadline passed, and all participants successfully evaluated their runs on the test data sets of Bob's shared task, he proceeds to reviewing the performances and publishing the results. For this purpose, TIRA has an overview of all evaluation runs on a per-data set basis (see Figure 9a):

**Evaluations Results.** Overview of evaluation runs and the performance results obtained, including user name, software, ID of the evaluation run, ID of the software

(a) Overview of a task's evaluation results for organizers

📋 Evaluations on *test-corpus*

| User | Software | Evaluation | Input run | Precision | Recall | Actions |
|---|---|---|---|---|---|---|
| Alice | software1 | 2014-06-22-12-10-00 | 2014-06-22-12-00-00 | 0.90081 | 0.67283 | ◉ⓢ◕👤 |
| Carol | software3 | 2014-06-15-17-38-08 | 2014-06-15-17-35-38 | 0.85744 | 0.29661 | ◉ⓢ◕👤 |
| Dan | software2ᴰᴱᴸ | 2014-06-16-17-17-21 | 2014-06-16-16-54-38ᴰᴱᴸ | 0.96022 | 0.84248 | ◉ⓢ◕👤 |
| Dan | software3 | 2014-06-23-20-43-59 | 2014-06-23-20-17-48 | 0.96007 | 0.84511 | ◉ⓢ◕👤 |
| Dan | software1 | 2014-06-16-18-03-43 | 2014-06-16-17-21-44 | 0.96243 | 0.83473 | ◉ⓢ◕👤 |
| Eve | software1 | 2014-06-01-12-52-02 | 2014-06-21-05-56-23 | 0.82882 | 0.84156 | ◉ⓢ◕👤 |
| Frank | software10 | 2014-06-23-13-31-42 | 2014-06-23-13-24-21 | 0.92522 | 0.81819 | ◉ⓢ◕👤 |
| Mallory | software1 | 2014-06-20-23-28-21 | 2014-06-17-09-28-40 | 0.87171 | 0.91539 | ◉ⓢ◕👤 |
| Oscar | software1 | 2014-06-19-00-54-42 | 2014-06-18-23-50-04 | 0.92757 | 0.88916 | ◉ⓢ◕👤 |
| Peggy | software3 | 2014-06-22-03-36-34 | 2014-06-22-03-33-32 | 0.90032 | 0.80267 | ◉ⓢ◕👤 |
| Sybil | software2 | 2014-06-22-02-56-09 | 2014-06-22-02-49-41 | 0.90770 | 0.79931 | ◉ⓢ◕👤 |
| Sybil | software4 | 2014-06-22-16-55-56 | 2014-06-22-16-49-05 | 0.89179 | 0.80590 | ◉ⓢ◕👤 |
| Trent | software5 | 2014-06-15-16-24-05 | 2014-06-15-15-53-28 | 0.86606 | 0.91984 | ◉ⓢ◕👤 |

(b) Overview of a task's *published* evaluation results

📋 Evaluations on *test-corpus*

| User | Precision | Recall | Runtime |
|---|---|---|---|
| Alice | 0.90081 | 0.67283 | 00:04:17 |
| Carol | 0.85744 | 0.29661 | 00:00:56 |
| Dan | 0.96007 | 0.84511 | 00:19:32 |
| Eve | 0.82882 | 0.84156 | 00:05:18 |
| Frank | 0.92522 | 0.81819 | 00:02:49 |
| Mallory | 0.87171 | 0.91539 | 00:05:37 |
| Oscar | 0.92757 | 0.88916 | 00:57:15 |
| Peggy | 0.90032 | 0.80267 | 00:00:31 |
| Trent | 0.86606 | 0.91984 | 00:22:10 |

**Fig. 9.** TIRA's web interfaces for a task's evaluation results

run that served as input to the evaluation run, and performance values, dependent on the measures computed by a given evaluation software. The colorization of the table cells for both run IDs corresponds to that of the run reviews mentioned above. This helps Bob to decide which are successful evaluations. All evaluation runs of all participants on a given data set are listed, including deleted runs. For example, there are multiple runs for participant Dan and Sybil. Bob gets to decide which of their runs are going to be published; there are a number of reasonable decision rules in this situation: (1) all of them (2) the chronologically first or last successful run, (3) the run chosen by the respective participant, or (4) the best performing run according to a given performance measure. While the decision rule that is applied can be chosen by Bob, it is currently not enforced automatically. In the Actions column, there are two publishing options, namely publication of evaluation results to the public evaluation results page (the globe icon), and publication of evaluation results to the respective participant (the person icon). As can be seen in the example, Bob has already globally published evaluations runs for all but one participant. Two of Dan's runs are published only to him, and for Sybil's two runs Bob still needs to make a decision.

The published runs appear on a public evaluation results page that can be found on TIRA alongside each shared task. Figure 9b shows the performance values of the evaluations that Bob decided to publish for his shared task. While he proceeds to announce the results to participants as well as to the scientific community, this is not necessarily the end of the story.

Shared tasks are organized for a reason, and that reason is not to host an individual run-once competition, but to foster research around a problem of interest. While shared tasks are sometimes organized repeatedly, at some point, they are discontinued, whereas later on there are still researchers who want to compare their approach to those of the task's participants. Based on TIRA, this will be easily possible long after a shared task is over, since all the evaluation resources required to run an evaluation are hosted and kept in running state. Moreover, if new evaluation corpora appear, all previously developed approaches can be re-evaluated on the new corpora, since they are also kept in running state inside their virtual machines. This way, TIRA paves the way for ongoing, "asynchronous" evaluations around a shared task while ensuring that everyone is evaluated using the exact same environment. That is, of course, as long as TIRA prevails.

In what follows, we report on the results of three shared tasks which have been organized using TIRA, and for which a total of 57 softwares have been submitted this year. The tasks are plagiarism detection, author identification, and author profiling.

## 3   Plagiarism Detection

This section summarizes the evaluation of 17 plagiarism detectors that have been submitted to our corresponding shared tasks. A complete version of our report can be found in [45], where a more in-depth analysis of the obtained results as well as a survey of detection approaches is given. We evaluate different aspects of plagiarism and text reuse detectors within the two tasks source retrieval and text alignment. Both have been identified as integral parts of plagiarism detection [61]. Since we have organized plagiarism detection-related tasks for six years in a row, we observe a recurrent multi-year life cycle, which can be divided into three phases, namely an innovation phase, a consolidation phase, and a production phase. In the innovation phase, new evaluation resources are being developed; in the consolidation phase, based on the feedback and results obtained from the innovation phase, the new evaluation resources are developed to maturity; and in the production phase, the task is repeated with little changes to allow participants to build upon what has been accomplished, and, to make the most of the prior investment in developing the new evaluation resources. Meanwhile, new ideas are being developed to introduce further innovation. Both, the source retrieval task and the text alignment task are now in production. In what follows, we briefly overview related work as well as the evaluation setup and the results obtained for both tasks.

## 3.1  Related Work

In recent years, the evaluation of plagiarism and text reuse detectors has been studied in the context of the PAN evaluation labs that have been organized annually since 2009. For the purpose of these labs, we developed the first standardized evaluation framework which comprises a series of corpora of (semi-)automatically generated plagiarism as well as detection performance measures [49].[3] During the first three labs, a total of 43 plagiarism detectors have been evaluated using this framework [50,41,42]. The two recent editions refocused on specific sub-problems of plagiarism detection, namely source retrieval and text alignment. This also included the development of new corpora for these problems. Instead of again applying a semiautomatic approach to corpus construction, a large corpus of manually generated plagiarism has been crowdsourced in order to increase the level of realism [12]. This corpus comprises 297 essays of about 5000 words length, written by professional writers. In this regard the writers were given a set of topics to choose from along with two more technical rules: (1) to use the ChatNoir search engine [46] to research their topic of choice, and (2) to reuse text passages from retrieved web pages in order to compose their essay. The resulting essays represent the to-date largest corpus of realistic text reuse cases available, and they have been employed to evaluate another 33 plagiarism detectors in the past three labs [43,44,45]. Besides the mentioned corpora, there are two other ones that comprise text reuse, namely the Meter corpus [8] and the Clough09 corpus [9]. The former contains 445 cases of text reuse among 1716 news articles, whereas the latter contains 57 short cases of manually generated plagiarism. To the best of our knowledge, these corpora have not yet been used in a large-scale evaluation of text reuse or plagiarism detectors.

## 3.2  Source Retrieval

In source retrieval, given a suspicious document and a web search engine, the task is to retrieve all source documents from which text has been reused whilst minimizing retrieval costs. The cost-effectiveness of plagiarism detectors in this task is important since using existing search engines is perhaps the only feasible way for researchers as well as small and medium-sized businesses to implement plagiarism detection against the web, whereas search companies charge considerable fees for automatic usage. To study this task, we employ a controlled, static web environment, which consists of a large web crawl and search engines indexing it. Using this setup, we built a large corpus of manually generated text reuse in the form of essays, which serve as suspicious documents and which are fed into a plagiarism detector. The detection results returned are evaluated using tailored performance measures derived from precision and recall as well as cost-effectiveness statistics. Before discussing the actual performances obtained, we describe each of these resources in some detail.

**Evaluation Setup.**  For the evaluation of source retrieval from the web, we consider the real-world scenario of an author who uses a web search engine to retrieve documents in order to reuse text from them. A plagiarism detector typically uses a search engine,

---

[3] The corpora PAN-PC-2009/2010/2011 are available at
  http://www.webis.de/research/corpora

**Table 1.** Source retrieval results with respect to retrieval performance and cost-effectiveness

| Team (alphabetical order) | Downloaded Sources | | | Total Workload | | Workload to 1st Detection | | No Detect. | Runtime |
|---|---|---|---|---|---|---|---|---|---|
| | $F_1$ | prec | rec | Queries | Dwlds | Queries | Dwlds | | |
| Elizalde | 0.34 | 0.40 | 0.39 | 54.5 | 33.2 | 16.4 | 3.9 | 7 | **04:02:00** |
| Kong | 0.12 | 0.08 | 0.48 | 83.5 | 207.1 | 85.7 | 24.9 | 6 | 24:03:31 |
| Prakash | 0.39 | 0.38 | **0.51** | 60.0 | 38.8 | 8.1 | 3.8 | 7 | 19:47:45 |
| Suchomel | 0.11 | 0.08 | 0.40 | **19.5** | 237.3 | **3.1** | 38.6 | 2 | 45:42:06 |
| Williams | **0.47** | **0.57** | 0.48 | 117.1 | **14.4** | 18.8 | **2.3** | 4 | 39:44:11 |
| Zubarev | 0.45 | 0.54 | 0.45 | 37.0 | 18.6 | 5.4 | **2.3** | 3 | 40:42:18 |

too, to find reused sources of a given document. Over the past years, we assembled the necessary building blocks to allow for a meaningful evaluation of source retrieval algorithms. The setup was described in much more detail in last year's task overview [44]. The main components are two associated search engines for the ClueWeb corpus 2009 (ClueWeb09).[4] This corpus represents one of the most widely adopted web crawls and it is regularly used for large-scale web search-related evaluations. It consists of about one billion web pages, half of which are English ones. Indri[5] and ChatNoir [46] are currently the only publicly available search engines that index the ClueWeb09 corpus. For developer convenience, we also provide a proxy server which unifies the APIs of the search engines. At the same time, the proxy server logs all accesses to the search engines for later analysis.

**Evaluation Corpus.**    The evaluation corpus employed for source retrieval is based on the Webis text reuse corpus 2012 (Webis-TRC-2012) [48,47]. The corpus consists of 297 documents that have been written by 27 writers who worked with our setup: given a topic, a writer used ChatNoir to search for source material on that topic while preparing a document of 5700 words length on average, reusing text from the found sources. In the last years, we sampled 98 documents from the Webis-TRC-2012 as training and test documents. This year, these documents were provided for training, and another 99 documents were sampled as test documents. The remainder of the corpus will be used within future instances of this task.

**Evaluation Results.**    Table 1 shows the performances of the six plagiarism detectors that implemented source retrieval. Their cost-effectiveness is measured as average workload per suspicious document, and as average numbers of queries and downloads until the first true positive detection has been made. These statistics reveal if a source retrieval algorithm finds sources quickly, thus reducing its usage costs. Moreover, we measure precision and recall of downloaded documents with regard to the true source documents and compute $F_1$. For lack of a formula to organize retrieval performance and cost-effectiveness into an absolute order, the detectors are ordered alphabetically, whereas the best performance value for each metric is highlighted.

None of the detectors dominates the others in terms of all of the employed measures, whereas three detectors share the top scores among them. The detector of

---

[4] http://lemurproject.org/clueweb09
[5] http://lemurproject.org/clueweb09/index.php#Services

**Table 2.** Text alignment performances of the 2014 participants on the 2013 test data

| Team | PlagDet | Recall | Precision | Granularity | Runtime |
|------|---------|--------|-----------|-------------|---------|
| Sanchez-Perez | **0.87818** | **0.87904** | 0.88168 | 1.00344 | 00:25:35 |
| Oberreuter | 0.86933 | 0.85779 | 0.88595 | 1.00369 | 00:05:31 |
| Palkovskii | 0.86806 | 0.82637 | 0.92227 | 1.00580 | 01:10:04 |
| Glinos | 0.85930 | 0.79331 | **0.96253** | 1.01695 | 00:23:13 |
| Shrestha | 0.84404 | 0.83782 | 0.85906 | 1.00701 | 69:51:15 |
| R. Torrejón | 0.82952 | 0.76903 | 0.90427 | 1.00278 | **00:00:42** |
| Gross | 0.82642 | 0.76622 | 0.93272 | 1.02514 | 00:03:00 |
| Kong | 0.82161 | 0.80746 | 0.84006 | 1.00309 | 00:05:26 |
| Abnar | 0.67220 | 0.61163 | 0.77330 | 1.02245 | 01:27:00 |
| Alvi | 0.65954 | 0.55068 | 0.93375 | 1.07111 | 00:04:57 |
| Baseline | 0.42191 | 0.34223 | 0.92939 | 1.27473 | 00:30:30 |
| Gillam | 0.28302 | 0.16840 | 0.88630 | **1.00000** | 00:00:55 |

Williams *et al.* [68] achieves the best trade-off between precision and recall in terms of $F_1$ as well as best precision, whereas the detector of Prakash and Saha [51] achieves best recall. Suchomel and Brandejs [62]'s detector requires least query workload, least queries until first detection, and detects source documents for almost all of the test documents. The detector of Williams *et al.* [68], however, performs worst in terms of total querying workload, since it requires 117 queries on average. Posing a query to a search engine may entail significant costs, whereas downloading a document is considered much less costly. By comparison, the detector of Zubarev and Sochenkov [70] achieves a similarly good trade-off between precision and recall with much less querying costs and comparable downloading costs. This detector also competes in terms of workload until first true positive detection with less than 6 queries and about 2 downloads on average.

### 3.3  Text Alignment

In text alignment, given a pair of documents, the task is to identify all contiguous passages of reused text between them. This task has a long tradition at PAN, yet, every year new ideas emerge at solving this task. Since this task is in its production phase, we have made little changes compared to last year in order to allow participants to optimize against the existing evaluation resources.

**Evaluation Corpus.**  As an evaluation corpus we reused both the training and test data from last year [44]. Reusing existing evaluation resources bears the risk that participants may overfit their approaches against them, thereby diminishing the generalizability of their respective approaches. This is why we opted not to tell participants the fact that we reuse last years training and test data, and, we generated a small supplemental evaluation corpus to which participants had no prior access. The supplemental evaluation corpus has been constructed in the same way as last years test corpus to allow for comparability of results. However, only a subset of last year's strategies to obfuscate the reused text passages of a plagiarism cases have been employed. Therefore, last years test data serve as reference for evaluation. Last years corpus consists of 5185 pairs of documents, which contain reused passages of text of varying lengths and obfuscation, such as paraphrasing, random text modification, cyclic translation, and summarization. Moreover, there is verbatim reuse to simulate naive plagiarist behavior. The supplemental test corpus contains 4800 pairs of documents with a limited set of obfuscations, namely verbatim copies and random text modifications.

**Evaluation Results.** Table 2 shows the overall performance of eleven plagiarism detectors that implemented text alignment. The detailed performances of each detector with regard to different kinds of obfuscation can be found in [45]. Performances are measured using precision and recall at character level as well as granularity (i.e., how often the same plagiarism case is detected). Based on these values we compute the PlagDet score by dividing $F_1$ by the granularity's logarithm. The detectors are ranked by PlagDet.

The best performing detector is that of Sanchez-Perez *et al.* [54]; a new contender in this task, closely followed by the detectors of Oberreuter and Eiselt [36] and Palkovsii and Belov [37]. The latter have also been evaluated in previous years, whereas the detector of Palkovskii and Belov [37] has significantly improved. Over the years, it can be observed that the differences in performance between detectors are getting smaller and smaller, which may indicate that improving the algorithms that solve this task becomes more difficult.

# 4   Author Identification

This section summarizes the evaluation of 13 author identifiers that have been submitted to our corresponding shared task. A complete version of our report can be found in [59], where a more in-depth analysis of the obtained results as well as a survey of detection approaches is given. Author identification is the most prevalent field of authorship analysis in terms of published studies [21,58]. The problem variant "authorship attribution" can be viewed as a closed-set classification task where all possible candidate authors (the classes) are known. This is typical for forensic applications, where, based on certain restrictions such as access to specific material or knowledge of specific facts, the investigators of a case can provide a set of suspects. A more general definition of the authorship attribution problem leads to an open-set classification task, where the true author of a disputed text is not necessarily among the set of candidate authors. Compared to the closed-set attribution scenario, this setting is much more difficult, especially if the size of the candidate author set is small [24]. Finally, if the set of candidate authors is singleton, we get the author *verification* problem, which is a fundamental problem in authorship attribution since any problem setting can be decomposed into a series of verification problems [26].

## 4.1   Related Work

Previous work on author verification has been evaluated using sample texts in one language only (Greek [60], Dutch [17,30], English [25,26]) and a specific genre (newspaper articles [60], student essays [30], fiction [25], newswire stories [19], poems [19], blogs [26]). Author verification was also included in previous editions of PAN: the author identification task at PAN-2011 included three author verification problems [1], PAN-2013 focused on author verification and provided corpora in English, Greek, and Spanish [22]. However, the size of the corpora was small and covered only one genre per language.

A variety of performance measures have been used in previous work on this task including false acceptance and false rejection rates [60,17], accuracy [25,26], recall, precision, $F_1$ [30], balanced error rate [19], recall-precision graphs [26] macro-average precision and recall [1], and ROC graphs [22]. Unfortunately, these measures are not able to explicitly estimate the ability of an approach to leave problems unanswered—a fact which is crucial in a cost-sensitive task like this.

The author identification task at PAN-2013 successfully introduced software submissions, this way enabling reproducibility of the results and future evaluation on different corpora. A meta-model combining all the submitted methods achieved the best overall performance, showing the potential of heterogeneous models in this task [22].

## 4.2  Evaluation Setup

Similar to PAN-2013 [22], PAN-2014 focuses on author verification. Given both a set of known documents written by the same author and a single questioned document, the task is to determine whether or not the questioned document was written by the author of the other documents. Each verification problem has been carefully configured to ensure that all known and the questioned documents are matched for genre, register, theme, and the date of writing. The number of known documents has been limited to be at most five, while a variety of languages and genres is covered. The document lengths vary from a few hundred to a few thousand words, depending on the genre.

The participants were asked to submit a software that takes the document language and genre as input parameters. For each verification problem they had to provide a score from the interval [0,1], corresponding to the probability of a positive answer (i.e., the known and the questioned documents are by the same author). To label a verification problem as unanswered, a probability score of 0.5 could be assigned.

## 4.3  Evaluation Corpus

The PAN-2014 corpus comprises author verification problems in the four languages Dutch, English, Greek, and Spanish. For Dutch and English there are two genres in separate parts of the corpus. Beyond language and genre there is a variety of known texts per problem and text length. The training and evaluation sets are balanced in the number of positive and negative examples. The corpus size is significantly larger than the corresponding corpus of PAN-2013.

The Dutch corpus part is a transformed version of the CLiPS Stylometry Investigation (CSI) corpus [64]. This recently released corpus contains documents of the two genres essay and review. All documents are written by language students, native Dutch speakers, at the University of Antwerp between 2012 and 2014.

The English essays are derived from a corpus of English-as-second-language students, the Uppsala Student English (USE) corpus [3], which was originally intended to become a tool for research on foreign language learning. It consists of university-level full-time students' essays. Taking advantage of the USE corpus meta-information, we defined two main constraints: (1) each document in the collection, known or questioned, must contain at least 500 words, and, (2) the number of known documents in a case must range between one and five. We took also advantage of meta information to define case-generation rules that deal with matching terms and student age. The outlined measures allowed us for creating cases where the authors share a similar background. Finally, a source USE document could be considered at most twice: once in a positive case and once in a negative case.

The set of English novels are our attempt to provide a narrower focus in terms of both content and writing style than existing collections. Instead of simply focusing on a single genre or time period, the texts focus on a very small subgenre of speculative and horror fiction, known as the "Cthulhu Mythos." It is based on the writings of the American H. P. Lovecraft ("Lovecraftian horror"), a shared universe with a theme of human ineffectiveness when facing powerful "cosmic horrors." It is characterized by extremely florid prose and an unusual vocabulary. Perhaps most significantly, many of the elements of this genre are unusual terms, thus creating a shared element that is unusual in normal English prose. Similarly, the overall theme and tone of these stories is strongly negative. The documents cover an extended length of time, from Lovecraft's original work to modern fan-fiction. The documents were collected from a variety of on-line sources including the Project Gutenberg[6] and FanFiction.[7]

The Greek part of the corpus comprises newspaper opinion articles published in the Greek weekly newspaper TO BHMA between 1996 and 2012.[8] The length of each article is at least 1,000 words, while the number of known texts per problem varies between one and five. For each verification problem, we ensured strong thematic similarity, indicated by the occurrence of certain keywords. In contrast to PAN-2013, there was no stylistic analysis of the texts to identify authors with similar styles or texts of the same author. The Spanish part of the corpus refers to the same genre and is built from opinion articles of the Spanish newspaper El-Pais.[9] Again, the formed author verification problems ensure thematic similarities between the articles.

### 4.4    Performance Measures

The probability scores provided by the participants are used to built ROC curves, whereas the area under curve, AUC, is used as a scalar evaluation measure [10]. In addition, the performance measures for this task are able to account for unanswered problems: if there is much uncertainty about a decision, it is possible to leave the problem unanswered. We adopted the c@1 measure, originally proposed for question answering tasks, which extends the accuracy based on the number of unanswered problems [38]. The measure rewards participants who maintain a large number of correct answers of high confidence. To rank the participants, a final score is defined as the product of AUC

---

[6] http://www.gutenberg.org
[7] http://www.fanfiction.net
[8] http://www.tovima.gr
[9] http://www.elpais.com

**Table 3.** Author identification results in terms of final score (AUC*c@1) and runtime

| Team | Overall | Essays | | Articles | | Novels | Reviews | Runtime |
|---|---|---|---|---|---|---|---|---|
| | | en | nl | es | gr | en | nl | (hh:mm:ss) |
| Meta classifier | 0.566 | 0.531 | 0.867 | 0.709 | 0.635 | 0.472 | 0.428 | |
| Khonji | **0.490** | 0.349 | 0.770 | **0.698** | **0.720** | 0.458 | 0.479 | 20:59:40 |
| Frery | 0.484 | **0.513** | 0.821 | 0.581 | 0.436 | 0.360 | 0.347 | 00:06:42 |
| Castillo | 0.461 | 0.318 | 0.741 | 0.558 | 0.501 | 0.386 | 0.247 | 03:59:04 |
| Moreau | 0.451 | 0.372 | 0.755 | 0.634 | 0.565 | 0.313 | 0.375 | 01:07:34 |
| Mayor | 0.450 | 0.318 | **0.823** | 0.539 | 0.621 | 0.407 | 0.299 | 05:26:17 |
| Zamani | 0.426 | 0.322 | 0.525 | 0.468 | 0.470 | 0.476 | 0.362 | 02:37:25 |
| Satyam | 0.400 | 0.459 | 0.489 | 0.248 | 0.356 | 0.380 | **0.525** | 02:52:37 |
| Modaresi | 0.375 | 0.350 | 0.378 | 0.416 | 0.294 | **0.508** | 0.247 | **00:00:38** |
| Jankowska | 0.367 | 0.284 | 0.732 | 0.586 | 0.497 | 0.225 | 0.357 | 07:38:18 |
| Halvani | 0.335 | 0.338 | 0.399 | 0.423 | 0.367 | 0.293 | 0.316 | 00:00:54 |
| Baseline | 0.325 | 0.288 | 0.685 | 0.378 | 0.452 | 0.202 | 0.322 | 00:21:10 |
| Vartapetiance | 0.308 | 0.270 | 0.517 | 0.436 | 0.281 | 0.245 | 0.260 | 01:07:39 |
| Layton | 0.306 | 0.363 | 0.307 | 0.299 | 0.403 | 0.260 | 0.261 | 27:00:01 |
| Harvey | 0.304 | 0.312 | 0.396 | 0.514 | 0.000 | 0.283 | 0.170 | 01:06:19 |

and c@1. In addition, the efficiency of the submitted methods is measured in terms of the elapsed runtime.

## 4.5  Evaluation Results

We received 13 submissions of research teams from Australia, Canada (2), France, Germany (2), India, Iran, Ireland, Mexico (2), United Arab Emirates, and United Kingdom. The participants submitted and evaluated their author verification software within the TIRA framework [13]. A separate run for each corpus part (combination of language and genre) was performed.

As a challenging baseline for the submitted approaches a language-independent author verification method from PAN-2013 [20] was employed: the winner of the competition in terms of AUC; note that the respective approach has not been trained on the PAN-2014 corpus. Moreover, following the practice of PAN-2013 [22], we examined the performance of a meta-model that averages the answers of all submitted systems.

The evaluation results in terms of the final score (AUC · c@1), the baseline method, and the meta-classifier are shown in Table 3. The overall (micro-averaged) performances along with the total runtime are also given. In terms of the average performance of all submitted approaches, the Dutch essays are the easiest problems, while the Dutch reviews are the hardest. The latter can be partially explained by the fact that only one known document per problem is used and the review texts are very short. Note that there is a different winner for each corpus part, with the exception of the overall winner approach by Khonji and Iraqi, who won on both the Greek and Spanish corpus subsets. In general, the majority of the submitted methods outperformed the baseline, while the performance of the meta-classifier is significantly better than any individual method.

Similar to PAN-2013, the overall winner was a modification of the *Impostors* method [26]. The performance of this approach was notably stable on all six corpus subsets. This demonstrates the potential of extrinsic verification methods, which transform author verification from a one-class classification task towards a binary classification task, using additional texts from other authors as negative examples. In addition, the significantly larger training set allowed participants to explore, for the first time, the use of eager learning methods. Such an approach, followed by the second overall winner, can be effective as well as efficient.

## 5   Author Profiling

This section summarizes the evaluation of 10 author profilers that have been submitted to our corresponding shared task. A complete version of our report can be found in [52], where a more in-depth analysis of the obtained results as well as a survey of detection approaches is given. Author profiling tries to determine an author's gender, age, native language, personality type, etc. solely by analyzing an author's texts.

### 5.1   Related Work

The study of how certain linguistic features vary according to the profile of their authors is a subject of interest for several different areas such as psychology, linguistics and, more recently, computational linguistics. Pennebaker et al. [40] connected language use with personality traits, studying how the variation of linguistic characteristics in a text can provide information regarding gender and age of its author. Argamon et al. [2] analyzed formal written texts extracted from the British National Corpus, combining function words with part-of-speech features, and achieved approximately 80% accuracy in gender prediction. Other research investigated how to obtain age and gender information from formal texts [18,5]. With the rise of the social media, Koppel et al. [23] built a dataset of blog posts and studied the problem of automatically determining an author's gender based on proposing combinations of simple lexical and syntactic features, also achieving approximately 80% accuracy. Schler et al. [55] collected more than 71 000 blog posts and used a set of stylistic features such as non-dictionary words, parts-of-speech, function words and hyperlinks, combined with content features, such as word unigrams with the highest information gain. They also obtained an accuracy of about 80% for gender identification, and about 75% for age identification. Goswami et al. [16] added some new features to Schler's work, such as slang words and the average length of sentences, improving accuracy to 80.3% in age group detection and to 89.2% in gender detection. Peersman et al. [39] compiled a dataset for the purpose of gender and age prediction from Netlog.[10] Studying short texts, Zhang and Zhang [69] experimented with segments of blog posts and obtained 72.1% accuracy for gender prediction. Similarly, Nguyen et al. [34] studied the use of language and age among Dutch Twitter users. They modeled age as a continuous variable (as they had previously done in [35]), and used a prediction approach based on logistic regression. They also measured the effect of gender in the performance of age detection, considering both variables as interdependent, and achieved correlations of up to 0.74 and mean absolute errors between 4.1 and 6.8 years. Our lab was the first to offer author profiling as a shared task. At

---

[10] http://www.netlog.com

PAN 2013 [53] we aimed at identifying age and gender from a large corpus collected from social media. Most of the participants used combinations of style-based features such as frequency of punctuation marks, capital letters, quotations, and so on, together with POS tags and content-based features such as Latent Semantic Analysis, bag-of-words, $tf \cdot idf$, dictionary-based words, topic-based words, and so on. Notably, the winner of the PAN 2013 task [29] used second order representations based on relationships between documents and profiles, whereas another well-performing approach is the use of collocations of the winner of the English task [33].

## 5.2   Evaluation Corpora

In the Author Profiling task at PAN 2013 [53] participants approached the task of identifying age and gender in a large corpus collected from social media. At PAN 2014, we continue to study the gender and age aspects of the author profiling problem, however, four data sets of different genres were considered—social media, blogs, Twitter, and hotel reviews—both in English and Spanish. We annotated age with the following classes: 18-24; 25-34; 35-49; 50-64; and 65+.

The social media data set was built by sampling parts of the PAN 2013 evaluation corpus. We selected only authors with an average number of words greater than 100 in their posts. We also reviewed manually the data in order to remove authors who appear to be fake profiles such as bots. The blogs and Twitter data sets were manually collected and annotated by three annotators. The Twitter data set was built in collaboration with RepLab,[11] where the main goal of author profiling in the context of reputation management on Twitter is to decide how influential a given user is in a domain of interest. For each blog, we provided up to 25 posts and for each twitter profile, we provided up to 1000 tweets. The hotel review data set is derived from another corpus that was originally used for aspect-level rating prediction [66].[12] The original corpus was crawled from the hotel review site TripAdvisor[13] and manually checked for quality and compliance with the format requirements of PAN 2014.

## 5.3   Evaluation Results

In Table 4 joint identification accuracies for both gender and age prediction are shown per data set and averaged over all data sets, which also serves as ranking criterion. The approach of López-Monroy et al. [28] performs best overall. Moreover, it can be seen that (1) the highest joint accuracies were achieved on Twitter data, and, (2) the smallest joint accuracies were achieved in English social media and hotel reviews. It is an open question why these differences can be observed, whereas possible explanations may be that people express themselves more spontaneously on Twitter compared to the other genres, whereas the low scores are due to the approaches' difficulty of predicting gender in social media and age in hotel reviews.

---

[11] http://nlp.uned.es/replab2014
[12] http://times.cs.uiuc.edu/~{}wang296/data
[13] http://www.tripadvisor.com

**Table 4.** Joint identification results in terms of accuracy for Author Profiling

| Team | Overall | Social Media | | Blogs | | Twitter | | Reviews |
|------|---------|------|------|------|------|------|------|---------|
| | | en | es | en | es | en | es | en |
| López-Monroy | **0.2895** | 0.1902 | 0.2809 | **0.3077** | **0.3214** | **0.3571** | 0.3444 | 0.2247 |
| Liau | 0.2802 | 0.1952 | **0.3357** | 0.2692 | 0.2321 | 0.3506 | 0.3222 | **0.2564** |
| Shrestha | 0.2760 | **0.2062** | 0.2845 | 0.2308 | 0.2500 | 0.3052 | **0.4333** | 0.2223 |
| Weren | 0.2349 | 0.1914 | 0.2792 | 0.2949 | 0.1786 | 0.2013 | 0.2778 | 0.2211 |
| Villena-Román | 0.2315 | 0.1905 | 0.1961 | **0.3077** | 0.2321 | 0.2078 | 0.2667 | 0.2199 |
| Marquardt | 0.1998 | 0.1428 | 0.2102 | 0.1282 | 0.2679 | 0.1948 | 0.3111 | 0.1437 |
| Baker | 0.1677 | 0.1277 | 0.1678 | 0.1282 | 0.2321 | 0.1688 | 0.2111 | 0.1382 |
| Baseline | 0.1404 | 0.0930 | 0.1820 | 0.0897 | 0.0536 | 0.1494 | 0.2333 | 0.1821 |
| Mechti | 0.1067 | 0.1244 | 0.1060 | 0.0897 | 0.1786 | 0.0584 | 0.1444 | 0.0451 |
| Castillo Juarez | 0.0946 | 0.1445 | 0.1254 | 0.1795 | 0.0893 | – | – | 0.1236 |
| Ashok | 0.0834 | 0.1318 | – | 0.1282 | – | 0.1948 | – | 0.1291 |

In summary, simple content features, such as bag-of-words or word n-grams achieve best accuracies. Bag-of-words features are used by Liau and Vrizlynn [27], word n-grams are used by Maharjan *et al.* [31], and term vector models are used by Villena-Román and González-Cristóbal [65]. They achieved competitive performances on almost all data sets. Notably, Weren *et al.* [67] employ information retrieval features and Marquardt *et al.* [32] mix content and style features.

# 6    Conclusion and Outlook

In conclusion, the creation of the TIRA evaluation platform has fundamentally changed the way we organize shared tasks at PAN. While our initial goal was to improve the reproducibility of our shared tasks, the technology that was developed as a result of this endeavor is applicable for more than just software submissions. For example, an initial analysis of the access logs that we recorded allows for a heretofore unknown, exciting insight into the research in progress of participants of a shared tasks. Specific usage patterns can be discerned in real-time which allow organizers of a shared task to engage with participants who exert usage patterns related to software execution errors. Moreover, the overall participation in a shared task can be monitored as it happens, whereas today, most organizers will only learn if their task was successful right after the run submission deadline, when it becomes clear how many of the registered participants actually submit a run.

Besides the exciting opportunities that arise from TIRA, all of these benefits are now readily available to PAN's three tasks plagiarism detection, author identification, and author profiling. For these tasks, we have already assembled an archive of more than 100 virtual machines on which the state of the art approaches are deployed in a manner that makes them immediately executable. It is still unforeseeable how this will impact future research in these tasks.

**Acknowledgements.** We thank the organizing committees of PAN's shared tasks Walter Daelemans, Patrick Juola, Miguel Angel Sánchez Pérez, Ben Verhoeven, Alberto Barrón-Cedeño, and Irina Chugur. Moreover, we thank our student assistants Anna

Beyer and Matthias Busse for helping with maintaining TIRA. Our special thanks go to all of PAN's participants. This work was partially supported by the WIQ-EI IRSES project (Grant No. 269180) within the FP7 Marie Curie action.

# References

1. Argamon, S., Juola, P.: Overview of the International Authorship Identification Competition at PAN-2011. In: Petras, V., Forner, P., Clough, P. (eds.) Working Notes Papers of the CLEF 2011 Evaluation Labs (September 2011),
   http://www.clef-initiative.eu/publication/working-notes
2. Argamon, S., Koppel, M., Fine, J., Shimoni, A.R.: Gender, Genre, and Writing Style in Formal Written Texts. TEXT 23, 321–346 (2003)
3. Axelsson, M.: USE–The Uppsala Student English Corpus: An Instrument for Needs Analysis. ICAME Journal 24, 155–157 (2000), http://nora.hd.uib.no/icame/ij24/
4. Belz, A.: Shared-task Evaluations in HLT: Lessons for NLG. In: Proceedings of INLG 2006 (2006)
5. Burger, J.D., Henderson, J., Kim, G., Zarrella, G.: Discriminating Gender On Twitter. In: Proceedings of the Conference on Empirical Methods in Natural Language Processing, EMNLP 2011, pp. 1301–1309. Association for Computational Linguistics, Stroudsburg (2011)
6. Cappellato, L., Ferro, N., Halvey, M., Kraaij, W. (eds.): CLEF 2014 Evaluation Labs and Workshop – Working Notes Papers, Sheffield, UK, September 15-18. CEUR Workshop Proceedings. CEUR-WS.org (2014),
   http://www.clef-initiative.eu/publication/working-notes
7. Chapman, W.W., Nadkarni, P.M., Hirschman, L., D'Avolio, L.W., Savova, G.K., Uzuner, O.: Overcoming Barriers To NLP For Clinical Text: The Role Of Shared Tasks And The Need For Additional Creative Solutions. Journal of the American Medical Informatics Association: JAMIA 18(5), 540–543 (2011),
   http://dx.doi.org/10.1136/amiajnl-2011-000465
8. Clough, P., Gaizauskas, R., Piao, S., Wilks, Y.: METER: MEasuring TExt Reuse. In: Proceedings of the 40th Annual Meeting on Association for Computational Linguistics, ACL 2002, pp. 152–159. Association for Computational Linguistics, Stroudsburg (2002)
9. Clough, P., Stevenson, M.: Developing a Corpus of Plagiarised Short Answers. Lang. Resour. Eval. 45, 5–24 (2011)
10. Fawcett, T.: An Introduction to ROC Analysis. Pattern Recognition Letters 27(8), 861–874 (2006)
11. Forner, P., Navigli, R., Tufis, D. (eds.): CLEF 2013 Evaluation Labs and Workshop – Working Notes Papers, Valencia, Spain, September 23-26 (2013),
    http://www.clef-initiative.eu/publication/working-notes
12. Gollub, T., Hagen, M., Michel, M., Stein, B.: From Keywords to Keyqueries: Content Descriptors for the Web. In: Gurrin, C., Jones, G., Kelly, D., Kruschwitz, U., de Rijke, M., Sakai, T., Sheridan, P. (eds.) 36th International ACM Conference on Research and Development in Information Retrieval (SIGIR 2013), pp. 981–984. ACM, New York (2013),
    http://dl.acm.org/citation.cfm?id=2484181
13. Gollub, T., Potthast, M., Beyer, A., Busse, M., Rangel, F., Rosso, P., Stamatatos, E., Stein, B.: Recent Trends in Digital Text Forensics and Its Evaluation. In: Forner, P., Müller, H., Paredes, R., Rosso, P., Stein, B. (eds.) CLEF 2013. LNCS, vol. 8138, pp. 282–302. Springer, Heidelberg (2013)

14. Gollub, T., Stein, B., Burrows, S.: Ousting Ivory Tower Research: Towards a Web Framework for Providing Experiments as a Service. In: Hersh, B., Callan, J., Maarek, Y., Sanderson, M. (eds.) 35th International ACM Conference on Research and Development in Information Retrieval (SIGIR 2012), pp. 1125–1126. ACM (August 2012)

15. Gollub, T., Stein, B., Burrows, S., Hoppe, D.: TIRA: Configuring, Executing, and Disseminating Information Retrieval Experiments. In: Tjoa, A.M., Liddle, S., Schewe, K.D., Zhou, X. (eds.) 9th International Workshop on Text-based Information Retrieval (TIR 12) at DEXA, pp. 151–155. IEEE, Los Alamitos (2012)

16. Goswami, S., Sarkar, S., Rustagi, M.: Stylometric Analysis of Bloggers' Age and Gender. In: Adar, E., Hurst, M., Finin, T., Glance, N.S., Nicolov, N., Tseng, B.L. (eds.) ICWSM. The AAAI Press (2009)

17. van Halteren, H.: Linguistic Profiling for Author Recognition and Verification. In: Proceedings of the 42nd Annual Meeting on Association for Computational Linguistics, ACL 2004. Association for Computational Linguistics, Stroudsburg (2004), http://dx.doi.org/10.3115/1218955.1218981

18. Holmes, J., Meyerhoff, M.: The Handbook of Language and Gender. Blackwell Handbooks in Linguistics. Wiley (2003)

19. Escalante, H.J., Montes, M., Villaseñor, L.: Particle swarm model selection for authorship verification. In: Bayro-Corrochano, E., Eklundh, J.-O. (eds.) CIARP 2009. LNCS, vol. 5856, pp. 563–570. Springer, Heidelberg (2009)

20. Jankowska, M., Keselj, V., Milios, E.: CNG Text Classification for Authorship Profiling Task—Notebook for PAN at CLEF 2013. In: Forner et al, [11]

21. Juola, P.: Authorship Attribution. Foundations and Trends in Information Retrieval 1, 234–334 (2008)

22. Juola, P., Stamatatos, E.: Overview of the Author Identification Task at PAN-2013. In: P., T.D.E.F. (ed.) Notebook Papers of CLEF 2013 LABs and Workshops (CLEF-2013) (2013)

23. Koppel, M., Argamon, S., Shimoni, A.R.: Automatically Categorizing Written Texts by Author Gender (2003)

24. Koppel, M., Schler, J., Argamon, S.: Authorship Attribution in the Wild. Language Resources and Evaluation 45, 83–94 (2011)

25. Koppel, M., Schler, J., Bonchek-Dokow, E.: Measuring Differentiability: Unmasking Pseudonymous Authors. J. Mach. Learn. Res. 8, 1261–1276 (2007), http://dl.acm.org/citation.cfm?id=1314498.1314541

26. Koppel, M., Winter, Y.: Determining if Two Documents are Written by the Same Author. Journal of the American Society for Information Science and Technology 65(1), 178–187 (2014)

27. Liau, Y., Vrizlynn, L.: Submission to the Author Profiling Competition at PAN-2014. From the Institute for Infocomm Research, Singapore (2014), http://www.webis.de/research/events/pan-14

28. López-Monroy, A.P., Montes-y Gómez, M., Jair-Escalante, H., Villasenor-Pineda, L.: Using Intra-Profile Information for Author Profiling—Notebook for PAN at CLEF 2014. In: Cappellato et al. [6]

29. López-Monroy, A.P., Montes-y-Gómez, M., Jair-Escalante, H., Villasenor-Pineda, L., Villatoro-Tello, E.: INAOE's Participation at PAN'13: Author Profiling task—Notebook for PAN at CLEF 2013. In: Forner et al. [11]

30. Luyckx, K., Daelemans, W.: Authorship Attribution and Verification with many Authors and Limited Data. In: Proceedings of the Twenty-Second International Conference on Computational Linguistics (COLING 2008), pp. 513–520. Organizing Committee, Manchester (2008)

31. Maharjan, S., Shrestha, P., Solorio, T.: A Simple Approach to Author Profiling in MapReduce—Notebook for PAN at CLEF 2014. In: Cappellato et al. [6]

32. Marquardt, J., Fanardi, G., Vasudevan, G., Moens, M.F., Davalos, S., Teredesai, A., Cock, M.D.: Age and Gender Identification in Social Media—Notebook for PAN at CLEF 2014. In: Cappellato et al. [6]
33. Meina, M., Brodzinska, K., Celmer, B., Czokow, M., Patera, M., Pezacki, J., Wilk, M.: Ensemble-based Classification for Author Profiling Using Various Features—Notebook for PAN at CLEF 2013. In: Forner et al. [11]
34. Nguyen, D., Gravel, R., Trieschnigg, D., Meder, T.: How old do you think I am? A study of Language and Age in Twitter. In: Proceedings of the Seventh International AAAI Conference on Weblogs and Social Media (2013)
35. Nguyen, D., Smith, N.A., Rosé, C.P.: Author Age Prediction from Text Using Linear Regression. In: Proceedings of the 5th ACL-HLT Workshop on Language Technology for Cultural Heritage, Social Sciences, and Humanities, LaTeCH 2011, pp. 115–123. Association for Computational Linguistics, Stroudsburg (2011)
36. Oberreuter, G., Eiselt, A.: Submission to the 6th International Competition on Plagiarism Detection. From Innovand.io, Chile (2014),
    http://www.webis.de/research/events/pan-14
37. Palkovskii, Y., Belov, A.: Developing High-Resolution Universal Multi-Type N-Gram Plagiarism Detector—Notebook for PAN at CLEF 2014. In: Cappellato et al. [6]
38. Peñas, A., Rodrigo, A.: A Simple Measure to Assess Non-Response. In: Proceedings of the 49th Annual Meeting of the Association for Computational Linguistics: Human Language Technologies, HLT 2011, vol. 1, pp. 1415–1424. Association for Computational Linguistics, Stroudsburg (2011),
    http://dl.acm.org/citation.cfm?id=2002472.2002646
39. Peersman, C., Daelemans, W., Vaerenbergh, L.V.: Predicting Age and Gender in Online Social Networks. In: Proceedings of the 3rd International Workshop on Search and Mining User-generated Contents, SMUC 2011, pp. 37–44. ACM, New York (2011)
40. Pennebaker, J.W., Mehl, M.R., Niederhoffer, K.G.: Psychological Aspects of Natural Language Use: Our Words, Our Selves. Annual Review of Psychology 54(1), 547–577 (2003)
41. Potthast, M., Barrón-Cedeño, A., Eiselt, A., Stein, B., Rosso, P.: Overview of the 2nd International Competition on Plagiarism Detection. In: Braschler, M., Harman, D., Pianta, E. (eds.) Working Notes Papers of the CLEF 2010 Evaluation Labs (September 2010),
    http://www.clef-initiative.eu/publication/working-notes
42. Potthast, M., Eiselt, A., Barrón-Cedeño, A., Stein, B., Rosso, P.: Overview of the 3rd International Competition on Plagiarism Detection. In: Petras, V., Forner, P., Clough, P. (eds.) Working Notes Papers of the CLEF 2011 Evaluation Labs (September 2011),
    http://www.clef-initiative.eu/publication/working-notes
43. Potthast, M., Gollub, T., Hagen, M., Graßegger, J., Kiesel, J., Michel, M., Oberländer, A., Tippmann, M., Barrón-Cedeño, A., Gupta, P., Rosso, P., Stein, B.: Overview of the 4th International Competition on Plagiarism Detection. In: Forner, P., Karlgren, J., Womser-Hacker, C. (eds.) Working Notes Papers of the CLEF 2012 Evaluation Labs (September 2012), http://www.clef-initiative.eu/publication/working-notes
44. Potthast, M., Gollub, T., Hagen, M., Tippmann, M., Kiesel, J., Rosso, P., Stamatatos, E., Stein, B.: Overview of the 5th International Competition on Plagiarism Detection. In: Forner, P., Navigli, R., Tufis, D. (eds.) Working Notes Papers of the CLEF 2013 Evaluation Labs (September 2013),
    http://www.clef-initiative.eu/publication/working-notes
45. Potthast, M., Hagen, M., Beyer, A., Busse, M., Tippmann, M., Rosso, P., Stein, B.: Overview of the 6th International Competition on Plagiarism Detection. In: Cappellato, L., Ferro, N., Halvey, M., Kraaij, W. (eds.) CLEF 2014 Evaluation Labs and Workshop – Working Notes Papers. CEUR Workshop Proceedings. CLEF and CEUR-WS.org (September 2014),
    http://www.clef-initiative.eu/publication/working-notes

46. Potthast, M., Hagen, M., Stein, B., Graßegger, J., Michel, M., Tippmann, M., Welsch, C.: ChatNoir: A Search Engine for the ClueWeb09 Corpus. In: Hersh, B., Callan, J., Maarek, Y., Sanderson, M. (eds.) 35th International ACM Conference on Research and Development in Information Retrieval (SIGIR 2012). p. 1004. ACM (August 2012)

47. Potthast, M., Hagen, M., Völske, M., Stein, B.: Crowdsourcing Interaction Logs to Understand Text Reuse from the Web. In: Fung, P., Poesio, M. (eds.) Proceedings of the 51st Annual Meeting of the Association for Computational Linguistics (ACL 2013), pp. 1212–1221. ACL (August 2013), http://www.aclweb.org/anthology/P13-1119

48. Potthast, M., Hagen, M., Völske, M., Stein, B.: Exploratory Search Missions for TREC Topics. In: Wilson, M.L., Russell-Rose, T., Larsen, B., Hansen, P., Norling, K. (eds.) 3rd European Workshop on Human-Computer Interaction and Information Retrieval (EuroHCIR 2013), August 2013, pp. 11–14. CEUR-WS.org (2013), http://www.cs.nott.ac.uk/~mlw/euroHCIR2013/proceedings/paper3.pdf

49. Potthast, M., Stein, B., Barrón-Cedeño, A., Rosso, P.: An Evaluation Framework for Plagiarism Detection. In: Huang, C.R., Jurafsky, D. (eds.) 23rd International Conference on Computational Linguistics (COLING 2010), pp. 997–1005. Association for Computational Linguistics, Stroudsburg, Pennsylvania (2010)

50. Potthast, M., Stein, B., Eiselt, A., Barrón-Cedeño, A., Rosso, P.: Overview of the 1st International Competition on Plagiarism Detection. In: Stein, B., Rosso, P., Stamatatos, E., Koppel, M., Agirre, E. (eds.) SEPLN 09 Workshop on Uncovering Plagiarism, Authorship, and Social Software Misuse (PAN 2009), pp. 1–9. CEUR-WS.org (September 2009), http://ceur-ws.org/Vol-502

51. Prakash, A., Saha, S.: Experiments on Document Chunking and Query Formation for Plagiarism Source Retrieval—Notebook for PAN at CLEF 2014. In: Cappellato et al. [6]

52. Rangel, F., Rosso, P., Chugur, I., Potthast, M., Trenkmann, M., Stein, B., Verhoeven, B., Daelemans, W.: Overview of the Author Profiling Task at PAN 2014. In: Cappellato, L., Ferro, N., Halvey, M., Kraaij, W. (eds.) CLEF 2014 Evaluation Labs and Workshop – Working Notes Papers. CEUR Workshop Proceedings. CLEF and CEUR-WS.org (September 2014), http://www.clef-initiative.eu/publication/working-notes

53. Rangel, F., Rosso, P., Koppel, M., Stamatatos, E., Inches, G.: Overview of the Author Profiling Task at PAN 2013—Notebook for PAN at CLEF 2013. In: Forner et al. [6]

54. Sanchez-Perez, M., Sidorov, G., Gelbukh, A.: A Winning Approach to Text Alignment for Text Reuse Detection at PAN 2014—Notebook for PAN at CLEF 2014. In: Cappellato et al. [6]

55. Schler, J., Koppel, M., Argamon, S., Pennebaker, J.W.: Effects of Age and Gender on Blogging. In: AAAI Spring Symposium: Computational Approaches to Analyzing Weblogs, pp. 199–205. AAAI Press (2006)

56. Scott, D., Moore, J.: An NLG Evaluation Competition? Eight reasons to be Cautious. In: Proceedings of the Workshop on Shared Tasks and Comparative Evaluation in Natural Language Generation, pp. 22–23 (2007)

57. Smeaton, A.F., Over, P., Kraaij, W.: Evaluation Campaigns and TRECvid. In: Proceedings of the 8th ACM International Workshop on Multimedia Information Retrieval, MIR 2006, pp. 321–330. ACM, New York (2006), http://doi.acm.org/10.1145/1178677.1178722

58. Stamatatos, E.: A Survey of Modern Authorship Attribution Methods. Journal of the American Society for Information Science and Technology 60, 538–556 (2009)

59. Stamatatos, E., Daelemans, W., Verhoeven, B., Potthast, M., Stein, B., Juola, P., Sanchez-Perez, M., Barrón-Cedeño, A.: Overview of the Author Identification Task at PAN 2014. In: Cappellato, L., Ferro, N., Halvey, M., Kraaij, W. (eds.) CLEF 2014 Evaluation Labs and Workshop – Working Notes Papers. CEUR Workshop Proceedings. CLEF and CEUR-WS.org (to appear, September 2014), http://www.clef-initiative.eu/publication/working-notes
60. Stamatatos, E., Fakotakis, N., Kokkinakis, G.: Automatic Text Categorization in Terms of Genre and Author. Comput. Linguist. 26(4), 471–495 (2000), http://dx.doi.org/10.1162/089120100750105920
61. Stein, B.: Meyer zu Eißen, S., Potthast, M.: Strategies for Retrieving Plagiarized Documents. In: Clarke, C., Fuhr, N., Kando, N., Kraaij, W., de Vries, A. (eds.) 30th International ACM Conference on Research and Development in Information Retrieval (SIGIR 2007), pp. 825–826. ACM, New York (2007)
62. Suchomel, Šimon., Brandejs, M.: Heterogeneous Queries for Synoptic and Phrasal Search—Notebook for PAN at CLEF 2014. In: Cappellato et al. [6]
63. Tsikrika, T., de Herrera, A.G.S., Müller, H.: Assessing the Scholarly Impact of ImageCLEF. In: Forner, P., Gonzalo, J., Kekäläinen, J., Lalmas, M., de Rijke, M. (eds.) CLEF 2011. LNCS, vol. 6941, pp. 95–106. Springer, Heidelberg (2011), http://dl.acm.org/citation.cfm?id=2045274.2045290
64. Verhoeven, B., Daelemans, W.: Clips Stylometry Investigation (CSI) Corpus: A Dutch Corpus for the Detection of Age, Gender, Personality, Sentiment and Deception in Text. In: Proceedings of the 9th International Conference on Language Resources and Evaluation (LREC 2014), Reykjavik, Iceland (2014)
65. Villena-Román, J., González-Cristóbal, J.C.: DAEDALUS at PAN 2014: Guessing Tweet Author's Gender and Age—Notebook for PAN at CLEF 2014. In: Cappellato et al. [6]
66. Wang, H., Lu, Y., Zhai, C.: Latent Aspect Rating Analysis on Review Text Data: A Rating Regression Approach. In: Proceedings of the 16th ACM SIGKDD International Conference on Knowledge Discovery and Data Mining, pp. 783–792 (2010)
67. Weren, E.R., Moreira, V.P., de Oliveira, J.P.: Exploring Information Retrieval Features for Author Profiling—Notebook for PAN at CLEF 2014. In: Cappellato et al. [6]
68. Williams, K., Chen, H.H., Giles, C.: Supervised Ranking for Plagiarism Source Retrieval—Notebook for PAN at CLEF 2014. In: Cappellato et al. [6]
69. Zhang, C., Zhang, P.: Predicting Gender from Blog Posts. Technical Report. University of Massachusetts Amherst, USA (2010)
70. Zubarev, D., Sochenkov, I.: Using Sentence Similarity Measure for Plagiarism Source Retrieval—Notebook for PAN at CLEF 2014. In: Cappellato et al. [6]

# Overview of CLEF Question Answering Track 2014

Anselmo Peñas[1], Christina Unger[2], and Axel-Cyrille Ngonga Ngomo[3]

[1] NLP&IR group, UNED, Spain
anselmo@lsi.uned.es
[2] CITEC, Bielefeld University, Germany
cunger@cit-ec.uni-bielefeld.de
[3] University of Leipzig, Germany
ngonga@informatik.uni-leipzig.de

**Abstract.** This paper describes the CLEF QA Track 2014. In the current general scenario for the CLEF QA Track, the starting point is always a natural language question. However, answering some questions may need to query Linked Data (especially if aggregations or logical inferences are required), some questions may need textual inferences and querying free text, and finally, answering some queries may require both sources of information. The track was divided into three tasks: QALD focused on translating natural language questions into SPARQL queries; BioASQ focused on the biomedical domain, and Entrance Exams focused on answering questions to assess machine reading capabilities.

## 1 Introduction

In the current general scenario for the CLEF QA Track, the starting point is always a natural language question. However, answering some questions may need to query Linked Data (especially if aggregations or logical inferences are required), some questions may need textual inferences and querying free text, and finally, answering some queries may require both sources of information.

As a matter of example related to CLEF eHealth, consider the use case where patients receive medical reports that they don't understand. Given that report, patients have lots of questions. Some of them will need general definitions as one can find in Wikipedia. Some might need more complex answers about the relations between symptoms, treatments, etc. The final goal, then, is to help users understand the given document by answering their questions.

So, given this general scenario, CLEF QA Track will work on two instances of it: one targeted to (bio)medical experts (the BioASQ task) and a second instance targeted to open domains (the QALD and Entrance Exams tasks). In the first one, medical knowledge bases (KBs), ontologies and articles must be taken into account. In the second one, general resources such as Wikipedia articles and DBpedia are considered.

E. Kanoulas et al. (Eds.): CLEF 2014, LNCS 8685, pp. 300–306, 2014.
© Springer International Publishing Switzerland 2014

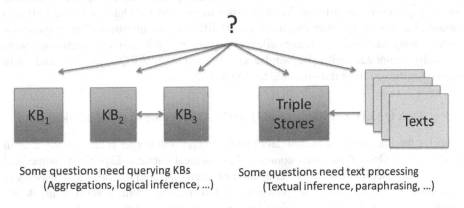

Fig. 1. General scenario of CLEF QA Track

## 2     Tasks

The CLEF QA Track was divided into the following tasks and subtasks:

### 2.1     QALD: Question Answering over Linked Data

QALD-4 is the fourth in a series of evaluation campaigns on multilingual question answering over linked data[1] [1], this time with a strong emphasis on interlinked datasets and hybrid approaches using information from both structured and unstructured data.

The key challenge lies in translating the users' information needs into a form such that they can be evaluated using standard Semantic Web query processing and inference techniques.

QALD-4 proposed the following tasks to participants:

### 2.2     Task QALD-4.1: Multilingual Question Answering

Task QALD-4.1 is the core task of QALD and aims at all question answering systems that mediate between a user, expressing his or her information need in natural language, and semantic data. Given the English DBpedia 3.9 dataset and a natural language question or set of keywords in one of seven languages (English, Spanish, German, Italian, French, Dutch, Romanian), the participating systems had to return either the correct answers, or a SPARQL query that retrieves these answers.

---

[1] http://www.sc.cit-ec.uni-bielefeld.de/qald

To get acquainted with the dataset and possible questions, a set of 200 training questions was provided. These questions were compiled from the QALD-3 training and test questions, slightly modified in order to account for changes in the DBpedia dataset. Later, systems were evaluated on 50 different test questions. These questions were mainly devised by the challenge organizers. All training questions were manually annotated with keywords, corresponding SPARQL queries and with answers retrieved from the provided SPARQL endpoint.

## 2.3     Task QALD-4.2: Biomedical Question Answering over Interlinked Data

Also for the life sciences, linked data plays a bigger and bigger role. Already a tenth of the Linked Open Data cloud consists of biomedical datasets. Especially biomedical data is distributed among a large collection of interconnected datasets, and answers to questions can often only be provided if information from several sources are combined. Task QALD-4.2 therefore focuses on interlinked data.

Given the following three biomedical datasets and a natural language question or set of keywords in English, the participating systems had to return either the correct answers or a SPARQL query that retrieves the answers:

- SIDER[2], describing drugs and their side effects
- Diseasome[3], encompassing description of diseases and genetic disorders
- Drugbank[4], describing FDA-approved active compounds of medication

The training question set comprised 25 questions over those datasets. Later, participating systems were evaluated on 25 similar test questions. Since the focus of the task is on interlinked data, most of the questions require the integration of information from at least two of those datasets.

## 2.4     Task QALD-4.3: Hybrid Question Answering

A lot of information is still available only in textual form, both on the web and in the form of labels and abstracts in linked data sources. Task QALD-4.3 therefore focuses on the integration of both structured and unstructured information in order to gather answers. Given English DBpedia 3.9, containing both RDF data and free text available in the DBpedia abstracts, and a natural language question or keywords, participating systems had to retrieve the correct answer(s). A set of 25 training questions was provided.

## 2.5     BioASQ: Biomedical Semantic Indexing and Question Answering

Bio ASQ[5] [2] aims at assessing:

---

[2] http://sideeffects.embl.de
[3] http://wifo5-03.informatik.uni-mannheim.de/diseasome/
[4] http://www.drugbank.ca
[5] http://www.bioasq.org/participate/challenges

- large-scale classification of biomedical documents onto ontology concepts (semantic indexing),
- classification of biomedical questions onto relevant concepts,
- retrieval of relevant document snippets, concepts and knowledge base triples,
- delivery of the retrieved information in a concise and user-understandable form.

The challenge comprised two tasks: (1) a large-scale semantic indexing task and (2) a question answering task.

## 2.6    Task BioASQ 1: Large-Scale Semantic Indexing

The goal is to classify documents from the PubMed digital library unto concepts of the MeSH2 hierarchy. Here, new PubMed articles that are not yet annotated are collected on a weekly basis.

These articles are used as test sets for the evaluation of the participating systems. As soon as the annotations are available from the PubMed curators, the performance of each system is calculated by using standard information retrieval measures as well as hierarchical ones.

In order to provide an on-line and large-scale scenario, the task was divided into three independent batches. In each batch 5 test sets of biomedical articles were released consecutively. Each of these test sets were released in a weekly basis and the participants had 21 hours to provide their answers.

## 2.7    Task BioASQ 2: Biomedical Semantic Question Answering

The goal of this task was to provide a large-scale question answering challenge where the systems should be able to cope with all the stages of a question answering task, including the retrieval of relevant concepts and articles, as well as the provision of natural language answers.

It comprised two phases: In phase A, BioASQ released questions in English from benchmark datasets created by a group of biomedical experts. There were four types of questions:   yes/no questions, factoid questions, list questions and summary questions. Participants had to respond with relevant concepts (from specific terminologies and ontologies), relevant articles (PubMed and PubMedCentral articles), relevant snippets extracted from the relevant articles and relevant RDF triples (from specific ontologies).

In phase B, the released questions contained the correct answers for the required elements (concepts, articles, snippets and RDF triples) of the first phase. The participants had to answer with exact answers as well as with paragraph-sized summaries in natural language (dubbed ideal answers).

The task was split into five independent batches. The two phases for each batch were run with a time gap of 24 hours. For each phase, the participants had 24 hours to submit their answers. The evaluation in phase B was carried out manually by biomedical experts on the ideal answers provided by the systems.

## 2.8    Entrance Exams Task

The challenge of Entrance Exams[6] [3] aims at evaluating systems reading capabilities under the same conditions humans are evaluated to enter the University.

Participant systems are asked to read a given document and answer a set of questions. Questions are given in multiple-choice format, with several options from which a single answer must be selected. Systems have to answer questions by referring to "common sense knowledge" that high school students who aim to enter the university are expected to have. The exercise do not intend to restrict question types, and the level of inference required to respond is very high.

Exams were created by the Japanese National Center for University Admissions Tests, and the "Entrance Exams" corpus is provided by NII's Todai Robot Project and NTCIR RITE.

For each examination, one text is given, and five questions on the given text are asked. Each question has four choices. For this year campaign, we reused as development data the 12 examinations from last year's campaign. For testing, we provided 12 new documents where a total of 60 questions and 240 candidate answers had to be validated.

As a novelty this year, data sets for development and testing originally in English were manually translated into Russian, French, Spanish and Italian. They are parallel translations of texts, questions and candidate answers.

In addition to the official data, we collected four more unoffcial translations into French. Despite they preserve original meaning, each translation has its particularities that produce different effects on systems performance: text simplification, lexical variation, different uses of anaphora, overall quality, etc. This data is extremely useful to get insights about systems and their level of inference.

Systems received evaluation scores from two different perspectives: at the question answering level and at the test reading level.

## 3    Participation

Table 1 shows the distribution of the 30 participants among the exercises proposed by the QA Track.

**Table 1.** Number of participants in CLEF QA Track 2014

| Task | # Registered | Sub-task | # Participants |
|---|---|---|---|
| QALD-4 | 22 | QALD -4.1 | 6 (English) |
| | | QALD-4,2 | 3 (English) |
| | | QALD-4.3 | (1) (English) |
| BioASQ | 25 | BioASQ 1 | 8 (English) |
| | | BioASQ 2 | 7 (English) |
| Entrance Exams | 20 | Entrance Exams | 5 (English) 1 (French) |
| Total | 67 | - | 30 |

---

[6] http://nlp.uned.es/entrance-exams

QALD-4, the fourth edition of the QALD challenge, has attracted a higher number of participants than previous editions, showing that there is a growing interest among researchers to provide end users with an intuitive and easy-to-use access to the huge amount of data present on the Semantic Web. Although one of the aspects of Task QALD-4.1 was multilinguality, all participating systems worked on English data only. This shows that the multilingual scenario is not yet broadly addressed, although it is starting to attract attention. Similarly, research teams start to look at hybrid question answering, although Task QALD-4.3 did not have participating systems yet.

The participation to the second BioASQ challenge signalizes an uptake of the significance of biomedical question answering in the research community, monitoring an increased participation in both Tasks.

With respect to Entrance Exams, 39 systems were presented by the 5 participating teams. This is a similar level of participation than in the previous edition. However, only one team has participated in the two editions. Despite the benchmarks were provided also in Russian, Spanish, Italian and French, all systems run for English and only one for French.

## 4    Main Conclusions

Readers are referred to the overview papers where a more detailed description of each task is given, together with their evaluation methodology and a general description of the participating systems. Here we draw the main general conclusions derived from 2014 campaign.

Systems performance seems to be improved in all tasks. In the case of BioASQ, the baselines used this year incorporated techniques from last year's winning systems. Best systems outperformed these baselines suggesting an improvement of both large-scale classification systems and question answering.

The results in Entrance Exams were also better than in last edition. At the reading perspective evaluation, we have already three systems (two teams) able to pass at least half of the reading tests.

With respect to earlier challenges of QALD, question answering systems have become more versatile: There is no particular type of questions that systems struggle with, rather most of them can handle all answer types as well as aggregation. The biggest problem, however, remains the matching of natural language questions to correct vocabulary elements.

Something similar was also noticed in Entrance Exams. In this task, there is a big lexical gap between the supporting text, the question and the candidate answer. The level of textual inferences that current systems perform is not enough yet to solve the majority of questions. Therefore, one of the main conclusions of the track is that more resources have to be developed to assess inference in the framework of question answering.

The results show that real question answering is a task far from being solved. However, the CLEF QA Track is providing the benchmarks able to assess real progress in the field along future years.

**Acknowledgements.** Anselmo Peñas was supported by CHIST-ERA READERS project (MINECO PCIN-2013-002-C02-01). Christina Unger was funded by the EU project PortDial (FP7-296170).

# References

1. Unger, C., Forascu, C., Lopez, V., Ngomo, A.-C.N., Cabrio, E., Cimiano, P., Walter, S.: Question Answering over Linked Data (QALD-4). In: CLEF 2014 Working Notes, Sheffield (2014)
2. Balikas, G., Partalas, I., Ngomo, A.-C.N., Krithara, A., Gaussier, E., Paliouras, G.: Results of the BioASQ Track of the Question Answering Lab at CLEF 2014. In: CLEF 2014 Working Notes, Sheffield (2014)
3. Peñas, A., Miyao, Y., Rodrigo, Á., Hovy, E., Kando, N.: Overview of CLEF QA Entrance Exams Task 2014. In: CLEF 2014 Working Notes, Sheffield (2014)

# Overview of RepLab 2014: Author Profiling and Reputation Dimensions for Online Reputation Management

Enrique Amigó[1], Jorge Carrillo-de-Albornoz[1], Irina Chugur[1], Adolfo Corujo[2],
Julio Gonzalo[1], Edgar Meij[3], Maarten de Rijke[4], and Damiano Spina[1]

[1] UNED NLP & IR Group
Juan del Rosal, 16. 28040 Madrid, Spain
nlp.uned.es
[2] Llorente & Cuenca
Lagasca, 88. 28001 Madrid, Spain, www.llorenteycuenca.com
[3] Yahoo Labs
Avinguda Diagonal 177, 08018 Barcelona, Spain
labs.yahoo.com
[4] University of Amsterdam
Science Park 904, 1098 XH Amsterdam, The Netherlands
ilps.science.uva.nl

**Abstract.** This paper describes the organisation and results of RepLab 2014, the third competitive evaluation campaign for Online Reputation Management systems. This year the focus lied on two new tasks: reputation dimensions classification and author profiling, which complement the aspects of reputation analysis studied in the previous campaigns. The participants were asked (1) to classify tweets applying a standard typology of reputation dimensions and (2) categorise Twitter profiles by type of author as well as rank them according to their influence. New data collections were provided for the development and evaluation of systems that participated in this benchmarking activity.

**Keywords:** RepLab, Reputation Management, Evaluation Methodologies and Metrics, Test Collections, Reputation Dimensions, Author Profiling, Twitter.

## 1 Introduction

RepLab is a competitive evaluation exercise supported by the EU project LiMoSINe.[1] It aims at encouraging research on Online Reputation Management and providing a framework for collaboration between academia and practitioners in the form of a "living lab": a series of evaluation campaigns in which task design and evaluation are jointly carried out by researchers and the target user community (in our case, reputation management experts). Similar to the previous campaigns [1,2], RepLab 2014 was organized as a CLEF lab.[2]

---

[1] http://www.limosine-project.eu
[2] http://clef2014.clef-initiative.eu/

E. Kanoulas et al. (Eds.): CLEF 2014, LNCS 8685, pp. 307–322, 2014.
© Springer International Publishing Switzerland 2014

Previous RepLab editions focused on problems such as entity resolution (resolving name ambiguity), topic detection (what are the issues discussed about the entity?), polarity for reputation (which statements and opinions have negative/positive implications for the reputation of the entity?) and alert detection (which are the issues that might harm the reputation of the entity?). Although online monitoring pervades all online media (news, social media, blogosphere, etc.), RepLab has always been focused on Twitter content, as it is the key media for early detection of potential reputational issues.

In 2014, RepLab focused on two additional aspects of reputation analysis – reputation dimensions classification and author profiling – that complement the tasks tackled in the previous campaigns. As we will see below, reputation dimensions contribute to a better understanding of the topic of a tweet or group of tweets, whilst author profiling provides important information for priority ranking of tweets, as certain characteristics of the author can make a tweet (or a group of tweets) an alert, requiring special attention of reputation experts. Section 2 explains the tasks in more detail. A description of the data collections created for RepLab 2014 and chosen evaluation methodology can be found in Sections 3 and 4, respectively. In Section 5, we briefly review the list of participants and employed approaches. Section 6 is dedicated to the display and analysis of the results, based on which we, finally, draw conclusions in Section 7.

# 2    Tasks Definition

In 2014, RepLab proposed to its participants the following tasks: (1) classification of Twitter posts by reputation dimension and (2) classification and ranking of Twitter profiles.

## 2.1    Reputation Dimensions Classification

The aim of this task is to assign tweets to one of the seven standard reputation dimensions of the RepTrak Framework[3] developed by the Reputation Institute. These dimensions reflect the affective and cognitive perceptions of a company by different stakeholder groups. The task can be viewed as a complement to topic detection, as it provides a broad classification of the aspects of the company under public scrutiny. Table 1 shows the definition of each reputation dimension, supported by an example of a labelled tweet:

## 2.2    Author Profiling

This task is composed of two subtasks that were evaluated separately.

---

[3] http://www.reputationinstitute.com/about-reputation-institute/
the-reptrak-framework

**Table 1.** RepTrak dimensions. Definitions and examples of tweets.

| Dimension | Definition and Example |
|---|---|
| Performance | Reflects long term business success and financial soundness of the company.<br>`Goldman Profit Rises but Revenue Falls: Goldman Sachs reported a`<br>`second-quarter profit of $1.05 billion,... http://dlvr.it/bmVY4` |
| Products & Services | Information about the company's products and services, as well as about consumer satisfaction.<br>`BMW To Launch M3 and M5 In Matte Colors: Red, Blue, White but no`<br>`black...` |
| Leadership | Related to the leading position of the company.<br>`Goldman Sachs estimates the gross margin on ACI software to be 95% O_o` |
| Citizenship | The company's acknowledgement of the social and environmental responsibility, including ethical aspects of business: integrity, transparency and accountability.<br>`Find out more about Santander Universities scholarships, grants,`<br>`awards and SME Internship Programme bit.ly/1mMl20X` |
| Governance | Related to the relationship between the company and the public authorities.<br>`Judge orders Barclays to reveal names of 208 staff linked to Libor`<br>`probe via @Telegraph soc.li/mJVPh1R` |
| Workplace | Related to the working environment and the company's ability to attract, form and keep talented and highly qualified people.<br>`Goldman Sachs exec quits via open letter in The New York Times, brands`<br>`bank working environment ''toxic and destructive'' ow.ly/9EaLc` |
| Innovation | The innovativeness shown by the company, nurturing novel ideas and incorporating them into products.<br>`Eddy Merckx Cycles announced a partnership with Lexus to develop their`<br>`ETT Hme trial bike. More info at...http://fb.me/1VAeS3zJP` |

*Author Categorisation.* The task was to classify Twitter profiles by type of author: Company (i.e., corporate accounts of the company itself), Professional (in the economic domain of the company), Celebrity, Employee, Stockholder, Investor, Journalist, Sportsman, Public Institution, and Non-Governmental Organisation (NGO). The systems' output was expected to be a list of profile identifiers with the assigned categories, one per profile.

*Author Ranking.* Using as input the same set of Twitter profiles as in the task above, systems had to find out which authors had more reputational influence (who the influencers or opinion makers are) and which profiles are less influential or have no influence at all. For a given domain (e.g., automotive or banking), the systems' output was a ranking of profiles according to their probability of being an opinion maker with respect to the concrete domain, optionally including the corresponding weights. Note that, because the number of opinion makers is expected to be low, we modelled the task as a search problem (hence the system output is a ranked list) rather than as a classification problem.

Some aspects that determine the influence of an author in Twitter (from a reputation analysis perspective) can be the number of followers, number of comments on a domain or type of author. As an example, below is the profile description of an influential financial journalist:

---

**Description:** New York Times Columnist & CNBC Squawk Box (@SquawkCNBC) Co-Anchor. Author, Too Big To Fail. Founder, @Deal-Book. Proud father. RTs endorsements
**Location:** New York, New York  nytimes.com/dealbook
**Tweets:** 1,423
**Tweet examples:**
"Whitney Tilson: Evaluating the Dearth of Female Hedge Fund Managers http://nyti.ms/1gpClRq @dealbook"
"Dina Powell, Goldman's Charitable Foundation Chief to Lead the Firm's Urban Investment Group http://nyti.ms/1fpdTxn @dealbook"

---

***Shared PAN-RepLab Author Profiling:*** Participants were also offered the opportunity to attempt the shared author profiling task RepLab@PAN.[4] In order to do so, systems had to classify Twitter profiles by gender and age. Two categories, female and male, were used for gender. Regarding age, the following classes were considered: 18-24, 25-34, 35-49, 50-64, and 65+.

## 3  Data Sets

This section briefly describes the data collections used in each task. Note that the current amount of available tweets may be lower, as some posts may have been deleted or made private by the authors: in order to respect the Twitter's terms of service (TOS), we did not provide the contents of the tweets, but only tweet ids and screen names. Tweet texts can be downloaded using any of the following tools:

1. TREC Microblog Track[5]
2. SemEval-2013 Task 2 Download script[6]
3. A Java tool provided by the RepLab organisers[7]

---

[4] http://pan.webis.de/
[5] https://github.com/lintool/twitter-tools
[6] http://www.cs.york.ac.uk/semeval-2013/task2/index.php?id=data
[7] http://nlp.uned.es/replab2013/replab2013_twitter_texts_downloader_latest.tar.gz

### 3.1   Reputation Dimensions Classification Data Set

This data collection is based on the RepLab 2013 corpus[8] and contains over 48,000 manually labelled English and Spanish tweets related to 31 entities from the automotive and banking domains. The tweets were crawled from the 1st June 2012 to the 31st Dec 2012 using the entity's canonical name as query. The balance between languages depends on the availability of data for each entity. The distribution between the training and test sets was established as follows. The training set was composed of 15,562 Twitter posts and 32,446 tweets were reserved for the test set. Both data sets were manually labelled by annotators trained and supervised by experts in Online Reputation Management from the online division of a leading Public Relations consultancy Llorente & Cuenca.[9]

The tweets were classified according to the RepTrak dimensions[10] listed in Section 2. In case a tweet could not be categorised into any of these dimensions, it was labelled as "Undefined".

The reputation dimensions corpus also comprises additional background tweets for each entity (up to 50,000, with a large variability across entities). These are the remaining tweets temporally situated between the training (earlier tweets) and test material (the latest tweets) in the timeline.

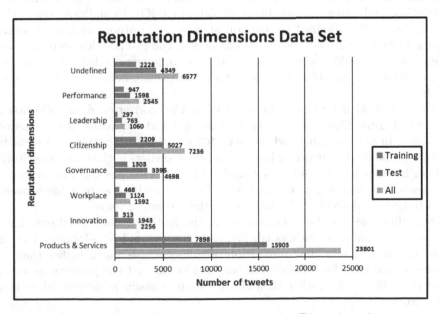

**Fig. 1.** Distribution of classes in the Reputation Dimensions data set

---

[8] http://nlp.uned.es/replab2013
[9] http://www.llorenteycuenca.com/
[10] http://www.reputationinstitute.com/about-reputation-institute/
the-reptrak-framework

Figure 1 shows the distribution of the reputation dimensions in the training and test sets, and in the whole collection. As can be seen, the Products & Services dimension is the majority class in both data sets, followed by the Citizenship and Governance. The large number of tweets associated with the Undefined dimension in both sets is noteworthy, which suggests the complexity of the task, as even human annotators could not specify the category of 6,577 tweets.

## 3.2 Author Profiling Data Set

This data collection contains over 7,000 Twitter profiles (all with at least 1,000 followers) that represent the automotive, banking and miscellaneous domains. The latter includes profiles from different domains. The idea of this extra set is to evaluate if approaches designed for a specific domain are suitable for a broader multi-domain scenario. Each profile contains (i) screen name; (ii) profile URL, and (iii) the last 600 tweets published by the author at crawling time.

The collection was split into training and test sets: 2,500 profiles in the training set and 4,991 profiles in the test set. Reputation experts performed manual annotations for two subtasks: *Author Categorisation* and *Author Ranking*. First, they categorised profiles as company (i.e., corporate accounts of companies), professional, celebrity, employee, stockholder, journalist, investor, sportsman, public institution, and non-governmental organisation (NGO). In addition, reputation experts manually identified the opinion makers (i.e., authors with reputational influence) and annotated them as "Influencer". The profiles that were not considered opinion makers were assigned the "Non-Influencer" label. Those profiles that could not be classified into one of these categories, were labelled as "Undecidable".

The distribution by classes in the Author Categorisation data collection is shown in Figure 2. As can be seen, Professional and Journalist are the majority classes in both training and test sets, followed by the Sportsman, Celebrity, Company and NGO. Surprisingly, the number of authors in the categories Stockholder, Investor and Employee is considerably low. One possible explanation is that such authors are not very active on Twitter, and more specialized forums need to be considered in order to monitor these types of users.

Regarding the distribution of classes in the Author Ranking dataset, Table 2 shows the number of authors labelled as Influencer and Non-Influencer in the training and test sets. The proportion of influencers is much higher than we expected, and calls for a revision of our decision to cast the problem as search (find the influentials) rather than classification (classify as influential or non-influential).

## 3.3 Shared PAN-RepLab Author Profiling Data Set

For the shared PAN-RepLab author profiling task, 159 Twitter profiles from several domains were annotated with gender (female and male) and age (18-24, 25-34, 35-49, 50-64, and 65+). The profiles were selected from the RepLab

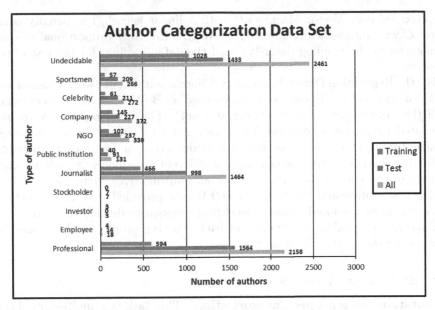

**Fig. 2.** Distribution of classes in the Author Categorisation data set

**Table 2.** Distribution of classes in the Author Ranking data set

|          | Influencer | Non-Influencer |
|----------|-----------|----------------|
| Training | 796       | 1704           |
| Test     | 1563      | 3428           |
| All      | 2359      | 5132           |

2013 test collection and from a list of influential authors provided by Llorente & Cuenca.

131 profiles were included into the miscellaneous data set of the RepLab author profiling data collection accompanied by the last 600 tweets published by the authors at crawling time. 28 users had to be discarded because more than 50% of their tweets were written in languages other than English or Spanish. The selected 131 profiles, in addition to age and gender, were manually tagged by reputation experts as explained in Section 3.2: with (1) type of author and (2) opinion-maker labels.

## 4  Evaluation Methodology

### 4.1  Baselines

For both classification tasks — Reputation Dimensions and Author Categorisation — a simple Bag-of-Words (BoW) classifier was proposed as official baseline.

We used Support Vector Machines,[11] with a linear kernel. The penalty para-meter $C$ was automatically adjusted by weights inversely proportional to class frequencies in the training data. We used the default values for the rest of pa-rameters.

For the Reputation Dimensions task, a different multi-class tweet classifier was built for each entity. Tweets were represented as BoW with binary occurrence (1 if the word is present in the tweet, 0 if not). The BoW representation was generated by removing punctuation, lowercasing, tokenizing by white spaces, reducing multiple repetitions of characters (from $n$ to 2) and removing stopwords.

For the Author Categorisation task, a different classifier was built for each domain in the training set (i.e., banking and automotive). Here, each Twitter profile was represented by the latest 600 tweets provided with the collection. Then, the built pseudo-documents were preprocessed as described before.

Finally, the number of followers of each Twitter profile has been used as baseline for the Author Ranking task.

## 4.2   Evaluation Measures

**Reputation Dimensions Categorisation.** This task is a multi-class classi-fication problem and its evaluation is an open issue. The traditional *Accuracy* measure presents drawbacks for unbalanced data. On the other hand, the com-monly used *F-measure* over each of the classes does not allow to produce a global system ranking. In this evaluation campaign we chose *Accuracy* as the official measure for the sake of interpretability. It is worth mentioning that, in the Rep-utation Dimensions task, systems outperformed a most-frequent baseline which always selects the majority class labels (see Section 6.1).

**Author Categorisation.** Similar to the Reputation Dimensions, the first sub-task of Author Profiling is a categorization task. We also used *Accuracy* as the official evaluation measure. However, the obtained empirical results suggest that *Accuracy* is not able to discriminate system outputs from the majority class baseline. For this reason, the results were complemented with *Macro Average Accuracy* (*MAAC*), which penalizes non-informative runs.

**Author Ranking.** The second subtask of Author Profiling is a ranking prob-lem. Influential authors must be located at the top of the system output ranking. This is actually a traditional information retrieval problem, where relevant and irrelevant classes are not balanced. Studies on information retrieval measures can be applied in this context, although author profiling differs from information re-trieval in a number of aspects. The main difference (which is a post-annotation finding) is that the ratio of relevant authors is much higher than the typical ratio of relevant documents in a traditional information retrieval scenario.

Another differentiating characteristic is that the set of potentially influential authors is rather small, while information retrieval test sets usually consist of

---

[11] http://scikit-learn.org/stable/modules/svm.html

millions of documents. This has an important implication for the evaluation methodology. All information retrieval measures state a weighting scheme which reflects the probability of users to explore a deepness level in the system's output ranking. In the Online Reputation Management scenario, this deepness level is still not known. We decided to use *MAP* (*Mean Average Precision*) for two reasons. First, because it is a well-known measure in information retrieval. Second, because it is recall-oriented and also considers the relevance of authors at lower ranks.

## 5   Participation

49 groups signed in for RepLab 2014, although only 11 of them (from 9 different countries) finally submitted results in time for the official evaluation. Overall, 8 groups participated in the Reputation Dimensions task, and 5 groups submitted their results to Author Profiling (all of them submitted to the author ranking subtask, and all but one to the author categorization subtask).

Table 3 shows the acronyms and affiliations of the research groups that participated in RepLab 2014. In what follows, we list the participants and briefly describe the approaches they used.

**Table 3.** List of participants: acronyms and affiliations

| Acronym | Affiliation | Country |
|---------|-------------|---------|
| CIRGIRDISCO | National University of Ireland, Galway | Ireland |
| DAE | Daedalus, S.A. | Spain |
| LIA | University of Avignon | France |
| LyS | Departamento de Computación, Universidade da Coruña | Spain |
| ORM_UNED | Universidad Nacional de Educación a Distancia | Spain |
| STAVICTA | Linnaeus University,Växjö and Lund University | Sweden |
| UAMCLYR | Universidad Autónoma Metropolitana Cuajimalpa | Mexico |
| uogTr | School of Computing Science, University of Glasgow | United Kingdom |
| UTDBRG | University of Tehran | Iran |
| UvA | ISLA, University of Amsterdam | The Netherlands |
| SIBtex | SIB Swiss Institute of Bioinformatics, Genève University of Applied Sciences, Carouge | Switzerland |

***CIRGIRDISCO*** participated in the Reputation Dimensions task. They used dominant Wikipedia categories related to a reputation dimension in a Random Forest classifier. Additionally, they also applied tweet-specific, language-specific and similarity-based features. The best run significantly improved over the baseline accuracy.

*DAE* attempted the Reputation Dimensions Classification. Their initial idea was to evaluate the best combination strategy of a machine learning classifier with a rule-based algorithm that uses logical expressions of terms. However, the baseline experiment employing just Naive Bayes Multinomial with a term vector model representation of the tweet text was ranked second among runs from all participants in terms of *Accuracy*.

*LIA* carried out a considerable number of experiments for each task. The proposed approaches rely on a large variety of machine learning methods. The main accent was put on exploiting tweet contents. Several methods also included selected metadata. Marginally, external information was considered by using provided background messages.

*LyS* attempted all the tasks. For Dimensions Classification and Author Categorisation a supervised classifier was employed with different models for each task and each language. A NLP perspective was adopted, including preprocessing, PoS tagging and dependency parsing, relying on them to extract features for the classifier. For author ranking, their best performance was obtained by training a bag-of-words classifier fed with features based on the Twitter profile description of the users.

*ORM_UNED* proposed a learning system based on voting model for the Author Profiling task. They used a small set of features based on the information that can be found in the text of tweets: POS tags, number of hashtags or number of links.

*SIBtex* integrated several tools into a complete system for tweet monitoring and categorisation which uses instance-based learning (K-Nearest Neighbours). Dealing with the domain (automotive or banking) and the language (English or Spanish), their experiments showed that even with all data merged into one single Knowledge Base (KB), the observed performances were close to those with dedicated KBs. Furthermore, English training data in addition to the sparse Spanish data were useful for Spanish categorisation.

*STAVICTA* devised an approach based on the textual content of tweets without considering metadata and the content of URLs for the reputation dimensions classification. They experimented with different feature sets including bag of n-grams, distributional semantics features, and deep neural network representations. The best results were obtained with bag of bi-gram features with minimum frequency thresholding. Their experiments also show that semi-supervised recursive auto-encoders outperform other feature sets used in the experiments.

*UAMCLYR* participated in the Author Profiling task. For Author Categorisation they used a supervised approach based on the information found in Twitter users' profiles. Employing attribute selection techniques, the most representative attributes from each user's activity domain were extracted. For Author Ranking they developed a two-step chained method based on stylistics attributes (e.g. lexical richness, language complexity) and behavioural attributes (e.g. posts' frequency, directed tweets) obtained from the users' profiles and posts. These attributes were used in conjunction with a Markov Random Fields to improve an initial ranking given by the confidence of Support Vector Machine classification algorithm.

*uogTr* investigated two approaches to the Reputation Dimensions classification. Firstly, they used a term's Gini-index score to quantify the term's representativeness of a specific class and constructed class profiles for tweet classification. Secondly, they performed tweet enrichment using a web scale corpus to derive terms representative of a tweet's class, before training a classifier with the enriched tweets. The tweet enrichment approach proved to be effective for this classification task.

*UTDBRG* participated in the Author Ranking subtask. The presented system utilizes a Time-sensitive Voting algorithm. The underlying hypothesis is that influential authors tweet actively about hot topics. A set of topics was extracted for each domain of tweets and a time-sensitive voting algorithm was used to rank authors in each domain based on the topics.

*UvA* addressed the Reputation Dimensions task by using corpus-based methods to extract textual features from the labelled training data to train two classifiers in a supervised way. Three sampling strategies were explored for selecting training examples. All submitted runs outperformed the baseline, proving that elaborate feature selection methods combined with balanced datasets help improve classification performance.

## 6    Evaluation Results

### 6.1    Reputation Dimensions Classification

Eight groups participated in the Reputation Dimensions task. 31 runs were submitted. Most approaches employed different machine learning algorithms such as Support Vector Machine (UvA, uogTr), Random Forest (CIRGIRDISCO,uogTr), Naive Bayes (DAE, UvA, STAVICTA), distance to class vectors (uogTr), Lib-Linear (LyS). SIBtex focussed on instance based learning techniques.

Regarding the employed features, some approaches considered information beyond the tweets' textual content. For instance, uogTr expanded tweets with pseudo-relevant document sets and Wikipedia entries, CIRGIRDISCO employed Wikipedia categories, LyS considered psychometric dimensions and linguistic information such as dependency trees and part of speech. STAVICTA expanded tweets by means of Distributional Semantic Models.

Table 4 shows the final ranking for the Reputation Dimensions task in terms of *Accuracy*. The table contains only the best run for each participant. The last column represents the ratio of classified tweets from the set of tweets that were available at the time of evaluation. Note that tweets manually tagged as "Undefined" were excluded from the evaluation and tweets tagged by systems as "Undefined" were considered as non-processed.

**Table 4.** Official ranking for the Reputation Dimensions task

| Run | Accuracy | Ratio of processed tweets |
|---|---|---|
| uogTr_RD_4 | 0.73 | 0.99 |
| DAE_RD_1 | 0.72 | 0.96 |
| LyS_RD_1 | 0.72 | 0.91 |
| SIBtex_RD_1 | 0.70 | 0.95 |
| CIRGIRDISCO_RD_3 | 0.71 | 0.95 |
| STAVICTA_RD_4 | 0.70 | 0.89 |
| UvA_RD_4 | 0.67 | 0.95 |
| Baseline-SVM | 0.62 | 0.86 |
| LIA_DIM_2 | 0.618 | 0.96 |
| Majority class baseline | 0.56 | 1 |

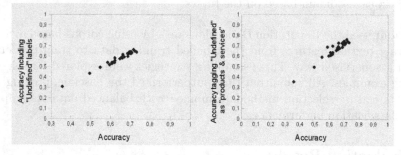

**Fig. 3.** Correspondence between the Accuracy results including "Undefined" or assigning them to the majority class. Each dot represents a run.

Besides participant systems, we included a baseline based on Machine Learning (SVM) using words as features. Note that classifying every tweet as the most frequent class (majority class baseline) would get an accuracy of 56%. Most runs are above this threshold and provide, therefore, some useful information beyond a non-informative run.

There is no clear correspondence between performance and algorithms. For instance, the top systems included a basic Naive Bayes approach (DAE_RD_1), enrichment with pseudo-relevant documents (uogTR_RD_4), or multiple features such as dependency relationships, POS tags, and psycometric dimensions (Lys_RD_1).

Given that tweets tagged as "Undefined" in the gold standard were not considered for evaluation purposes, systems that tagged tweets as "Undefined" had a negative impact on their performance. In order to check to what extent this affects the evaluation results, we computed accuracy without considering this label. The leftmost graph in Figure 3 shows that there is a high correlation between both evaluation results across single runs. In addition, replacing the "Undecidable" labels by "Product & Services" (majority class) also produces similar results (see rightmost graph in Figure 3).

## 6.2  Author Categorisation

Four groups participated in this task providing 10 official runs. Most runs are based on some kind of machine learning mechanism over Twitter profiles. For instance, LIA employed Hiden Markov Models, Cosine distances with TF-IDF and Gini purity criteria and Poisson modelling. UAMCLYR and LyS applied Support Vector Machine, and LyS used a combination of four algorithms: ZeroR, Random Tree, Random Forest and Naive Bayes.

As for features, the proposal of LyS includes term expansion with WordNet, ORM_UNED considered different metadata (profile domain, number of mentions, tags, etc), and LyS included psychometric properties.

**Table 5.** Accuracy of systems for the Author Categorisation task, per domain

| Run | Automotive | Banking | Miscellaneous | Average (Aut.&Bank.) |
|---|---|---|---|---|
| LIA_AC_1 | 0.45 | 0.5 | 0.46 | 0.47 |
| Baseline-SVM | 0.43 | 0.49 | - | 0.46 |
| Most frequent | 0.45 | 0.42 | 0.51 | 0.44 |
| UAM-CALYR_AC_2 | 0.38 | 0.45 | 0.39 | 0.41 |
| UAM-CALYR_AC_1 | 0.39 | 0.42 | 0.42 | 0.4 |
| ORM_UNED_AC_1 | 0.37 | 0.41 | 0.39 | 0.39 |
| UAM-CALYR_AC_3* | 0.37 | 0.41 | 0.22 | 0.39 |
| ORM_UNED_AC_3 | 0.39 | 0.39 | 0.18 | 0.39 |
| UAM-CALYR_AC_4* | 0.36 | 0.41 | 0.19 | 0.39 |
| LIA_AC_2 | 0.36 | 0.4 | 0.38 | 0.38 |
| ORM_UNED_AC_2 | 0.35 | 0.39 | 0.3 | 0.37 |
| LIA_AC_3 | 0.29 | 0.31 | 0.37 | 0.3 |
| LyS_AC_1 | 0.14 | 0.15 | 0.25 | 0.15 |
| LyS_AC_2 | 0.13 | 0.14 | 0.22 | 0.13 |

Table 5 shows the ranking for the Author Categorisation task. Two unofficial runs (submitted shortly after the deadline) are marked with an asterisk (*). The *Accuracy* values were computed separately for each domain (automotive, banking and miscellaneous). We included two baselines: Machine Learning (SVM) using words as features, and a baseline that assigns the most frequent class (in the training set) to all authors. This table includes also five unofficial runs which were sent after the official deadline. *Average Accuracy* of the banking and automotive domains was used to rank systems.

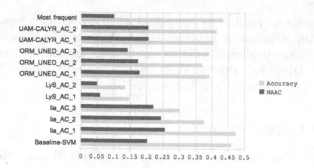

**Fig. 4.** Accuracy and MAAC for author categorization task

Interestingly, there is a high correlation between system scores in automotive vs. banking domains (0.97 Pearson coefficient). The low *Accuracy* values in the case of LyS is due to the fact that more than half of the authors were not included in the output file.

The most relevant aspect of these results is that, in terms of *Accuracy*, assigning the majority class outperforms most runs. However, of course, this output is not informative. The question is then how much information the systems are able to produce. In order to answer this question we have computed the *Macro Average Accuracy* (*MAAC*), which has the characteristic of assigning the same low score to any non informative classifier (e.g., random classification or one label for all instances). Figure 4 shows that most systems are able to improve the majority class baseline according to *MAAC*. The conclusion is that systems are able to produce information about classes, although they reduce the amount of accurate decisions with respect to the majority class baseline.

**Table 6.** Mean Average Precision of systems in the Author Ranking task

| Run | Automotive | Banking | Miscellaneous | Average (Banking and Automotive) |
|---|---|---|---|---|
| UTDBRG_AR_4 | 0.72 | 0.41 | 0.00 | 0.57 |
| LyS_AR_1.txt | 0.60 | 0.52 | 0.68 | 0.56 |
| UTDBRG_AR_1 | 0.70 | 0.40 | 0.00 | 0.55 |
| UTDBRG_AR_5 | 0.69 | 0.32 | 0.00 | 0.50 |
| UTDBRG_AR_3 | 0.68 | 0.32 | 0.00 | 0.50 |
| LIA | 0.50 | 0.45 | 0.65 | 0.48 |
| UAMCLYR_AR_5 | 0.44 | 0.49 | 0.77 | 0.47 |
| UAMCLYR_AR_1 | 0.45 | 0.42 | 0.77 | 0.44 |
| UAMCLYR_AR_2 | 0.45 | 0.42 | 0.77 | 0.44 |
| UTDBRG_AR_2 | 0.46 | 0.37 | 0.00 | 0.41 |
| LyS_AR_2 | 0.36 | 0.45 | 0.80 | 0.40 |
| UAMCLYR_AR_3 | 0.39 | 0.38 | 0.78 | 0.38 |
| UAMCLYR_AR_4 | 0.39 | 0.38 | 0.78 | 0.38 |
| Followers | 0.37 | 0.39 | 0.90 | 0.38 |
| ORM_UNED_AR_3 | 0.38 | 0.32 | 0.65 | 0.35 |

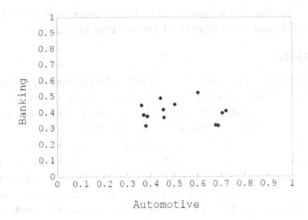

**Fig. 5.** Correlation of MAP values: Automotive vs. Banking

## 6.3   Author Ranking

Five groups participated in this task, for a total of 14 runs. The author influence estimation is grounded on different hypotheses. The approach proposed by LIA assumes that influencers tend to produce more opinionated terms in tweets. UTDBRG assumed that influential authors tweet more about hot topics. This requires a topic retrieval step and a time sensitive voting algorithm to rank authors. Some participants trained their systems over the biography text (LyS, UAMCLYR), binary profile metadata such as the appearance of URL, verified account, user image (LyS), quantitative profile metadata such as the number of followers (LyS, UAMCLYR), style-behaviour features such as the number of URLs, hashtags, favourites, retweets etc. (UAMCLYR).

Table 6 shows the results for the Author Ranking task according to the TREC_EVAL tool. In the table, systems are ordered according to the average *MAP* between the automotive and banking domains. Unfortunately, some participants returned their results in the gold standard format (binary classification as influencers or non influencers) instead of using the prescribed ranking format. Instead of discarding those submissions, we decided to turn those results into the official format by locating profiles marked as influencers at the top, respecting otherwise the original list order.

The baseline "Followers" simply ranks the authors by descending number of followers. It is clearly outperformed by most runs, indicating that additional signals provide useful information. The exception is the miscellaneous domain, where probably additional requirements over the number of followers, such as expertise in a given area, do not clearly apply.

On the other hand, runs from three participants exceeded 0.5 *MAP*, using very different approaches. Therefore, current results do not clearly point towards a certain technique.

Figure 5 shows the correlation between the *MAP* values achieved by the systems in the automotive vs. banking domains. There seems to be little correspondence between results in both domains, suggesting that the performance of systems is highly biased by the domain. For future work, it is probably necessary to consider multiple domains to extract robust conclusions.

## 7   Conclusions

After two evaluation campaigns on core Online Reputation Management tasks (name ambiguity resolution, reputation polarity, topic and alert detection), RepLab 2014 developed an evaluation methodology and test collections for two different reputation management problems: (1) classification of tweets according to the reputation dimensions, and (2) identification and categorisation of opinion makers. Once more, the manual annotations were provided by reputation experts from Llorente & Cuenca (48,000 tweets and 7,000 author profiles annotated).

Being the first shared evaluation on these tasks, participants explored a wide range of approaches in each of them. The classification of tweets according to their reputation dimensions seems to be feasible, although it is not yet clear which are the best signals and techniques to optimally solve it. Author categorisation, on the other hand, proved to be challenging in this initial approximation.

Current results represent simply a first attempt to understand and solve the tasks. Nevertheless, we expect that the data set we are releasing will allow for further experimentation and for a substantial improvement of the state of the art in the near future, as has been the case with the RepLab 2012 and RepLab 2013 data sets.

**Acknowledgements.** This research was partially supported by the European Community's Seventh Framework Programme (FP7/2007-2013) under grant agreements nr 288024 (LiMoSINe) and nr 312827 (VOX-Pol), ESF grant ELIAS, the Spanish Ministry of Education (FPU grant AP2009-0507), the Spanish Ministry of Science and Innovation (Holopedia Project, TIN2010-21128-C02), the Regional Government of Madrid under MA2VICMR (S2009/TIC-1542), Google Award (Axiometrics), the Netherlands Organisation for Scientific Research (NWO) under project nrs 727.011.005, 612.001.116, HOR-11-10, 640.006.013, the Center for Creation, Content and Technology (CCCT), the QuaMerdes project funded by the CLARIN-nl program, the TROVe project funded by the CLARIAH program, the Dutch national program COMMIT, the ESF Research Network Program ELIAS, the Elite Network Shifts project funded by the Royal Dutch Academy of Sciences (KNAW), the Netherlands eScience Center under project number 027.012.105, the Yahoo! Faculty Research and Engagement Program, the Microsoft Research PhD program, and the HPC Fund.

## References

1. Amigó, E., Carrillo de Albornoz, J., Chugur, I., Corujo, A., Gonzalo, J., Martín, T., Meij, E., de Rijke, M., Spina, D.: Overview of RepLab 2013: Evaluating Online Reputation Monitoring Systems. In: Forner, P., Müller, H., Paredes, R., Rosso, P., Stein, B. (eds.) CLEF 2013. LNCS, vol. 8138, pp. 333–352. Springer, Heidelberg (2013)
2. Amigó, E., Corujo, A., Gonzalo, J., Meij, E., de Rijke, M.: Overview of RepLab 2012: Evaluating Online Reputation Management Systems. In: CLEF 2012 Labs and Workshop Notebook Papers (2012)

# Author Index